T0314213

HANDBOOK OF RESEARCH ON NEW VENTURE CREATION

Handbook of Research on New Venture Creation

Edited by

Kevin Hindle

Chair of Entrepreneurship Research and Director, Centre for Entrepreneurship Innovation and Community, Deakin University, Australia

Kim Klyver

Professor of Entrepreneurship, University of Southern Denmark

Edward Elgar
Cheltenham, UK • Northampton, MA, USA

Published by
Edward Elgar Publishing Limited
The Lypiatts
15 Lansdown Road
Cheltenham
Glos GL50 2JA
UK

Edward Elgar Publishing, Inc.
William Pratt House
9 Dewey Court
Northampton
Massachusetts 01060
USA

A catalogue record for this book
is available from the British Library

Library of Congress Control Number: 2010929025

ISBN 978 1 84720 095 2 (cased)

Typeset by Servis Filmsetting Ltd, Stockport, Cheshire
Printed and bound by MPG Books Group, UK

Contents

PART III   DATA AND MEASUREMENT

PART IV   NVC THROUGH CONTEXTUAL LENSES

Contributors

Howard E. Aldrich is Kenan Professor of Sociology at the University of North Carolina, Chapel Hill, where he won the Carlyle Sitterson Award for Outstanding Teaching in 2002. He is Chair of the Department of Sociology and Adjunct Professor of Strategy and Entrepreneurship in the Kenan Flagler Business School. In 2000, he received two honours: the Swedish Foundation of Small Business Research named him the Entrepreneurship Researcher of the Year, and the Organization and Management Division of the Academy of Management presented him with an award for a Distinguished Career of Scholarly Achievement. His book *Organizations Evolving* won the Academy of Management George Terry Award as the best management book published in 1998–99 and was co-winner of the Max Weber Award from the American Sociological Association's Section on Organizations, Occupations, and Work. His 1979 book *Organizations and Environments* was reprinted in 2007 as a 'classic' by Stanford University Press.

Fredrik Åström attained his Ph.D. in library and information science (LIS) in 2006 at Umeå University, Sweden. Since then, he has been employed as Assistant Professor at the LIS Master's programme at Lund University, Sweden. Currently, he is active as Research Assistant at Lund University Libraries, where he is pursuing his postdoctoral project on visualizations of research fields. He spent the academic year 2008–09 as a visiting scholar at the University of Technology, Sydney, Australia. His research interest lies in the fields of science studies, scholarly communication and informetrics/bibliometrics, where he has been publishing internationally since 2002 in journals such as the *Journal of the American Society for Information Science and Technology* and the *Journal of Documentation*, as well as both presenting at, and being a member of the programme committee for, international conferences such as the biannual International Society for Scientometrics and Informetrics (ISSI) conference.

Torben Bager is Professor at the University of Southern Denmark, Department of Entrepreneurship and Relationship Management, and Director of IDEA Entrepreneurship Centre. From 2005 to 2009 he was Managing Director for the International Danish Entrepreneurship Academy, a nationwide network of universities and colleges aiming to strengthen entrepreneurship teaching and training at higher educational institutions as well as enhancement of student-based entrepreneurial activities. From 2006 to 2008 he was a member of the EU Expert Group on Entrepreneurship Education, especially within non-business studies. His research interests fall into four areas: organization theory and management; economic sociology, immigrant business and globalization; entrepreneurship and firm growth; and entrepreneurship teaching and training.

Olivier Basso is currently devoting his time to teaching international executives and researching in the field of management studies at Singleton Institute (Belgium). His primary research interest is corporate entrepreneurship with particular emphasis in the areas of organizational behaviours and firm-level parameters fostering an entrepreneurial spirit.

Deborah Blackman obtained her Ph.D. for work entitled 'How learning organisation practices close knowledge creation' from Nottingham Trent University. This was a combination of philosophy and organizational learning research which considered why currently accepted theory was not effective; this is a common theme in her work, where she uses epistemological theory to reconsider management concepts. She currently works as an Associate Professor in the Faculty of Business and Government at the University of Canberra, where she is a member of the Australia and New Zealand Institute of Governance. She entered academia after working in the hospitality industry in the UK, Belgium and France. Her other research interests include knowledge management, innovation, public sector governance and change management.

Malin Brännback is Vice Rector of Åbo Akademi University and Chair of International Business at Åbo Akademi University, where she received her doctoral degree in management science in 1996. She also holds a B.Sc. in pharmacy. She has served as Associate Professor in Information Systems at the University of Turku, and Professor of Marketing at Turku School of Economics, Finland. She has co-authored, with Alan L. Carsrud, two books: *Entrepreneurship* and *Understanding the Entrepreneurial Mind: Inside the Black Box*. She has published widely on entrepreneurship, biotechnology business, and knowledge management. Her current research interests are in entrepreneurial cognition, intentionality, and firm growth and performance in high-technology entrepreneurship. Her research appears in the *Journal of Small Business Management*, the *Journal of Enterprising Culture*, *New Biotechnology, Screenings, VINE: Journal of Information and Knowledge Management Systems*, *Knowledge Management Research and Practice*, *Knowledge and Process Management*, *Human Systems Management*, the *Journal of Decision Systems*, the *Journal of Market-Focused Management*, and the *European Management Journal*.

Candida G. Brush is Professor of Entrepreneurship, holder of the Paul T. Babson Chair in Entrepreneurship, and Chair of the Entrepreneurship Division at Babson College. She is a Visiting Adjunct Professor to the Norwegian School of Engineering and Technology in Trondheim, Norway. She is a founding member of the Diana Project International, and received the 2007 FSF-NUTEK Award for outstanding contributions to entrepreneurship research. Her research investigates women's growth businesses and resource acquisition strategies in emerging ventures. She is the author of 100 refereed journal articles, books and other publications. She is an Editor for *Entrepreneurship Theory and Practice*, and serves on several editorial boards. She is an active angel investor and board member of several emerging ventures and non-profit organizations.

Alan L. Carsrud, Ph.D. holds the Loretta Rogers Chair in Entrepreneurship in the Ted Rogers School of Management at Ryerson University in Canada. He is Docent at Åbo Akademi University in Finland. He has co-authored, with Malin Brännback, *Entrepreneurship* and *Understanding the Entrepreneurial Mind: Inside the Black Box*. He is Associate Editor of the *Journal of Small Business Management* and was founding Associate Editor of *Entrepreneurship and Regional Development*. His over 170 articles, books and chapters are in technology, entrepreneurship, innovation systems, entrepreneurial cognitions, family business, and clinical and social psychology. His research appears in the *Journal of Business Venturing, Entrepreneurship: Theory and Practice, Entrepreneurship and Regional Development, Family Business Review*, the *Journal of Small Business Management*, the *Journal of Enterprising Culture, New Biotechnology, Screenings, VINE: Journal of Information and Knowledge Management Systems*, the *Journal of Applied Psychology*, the *American Journal on Mental Deficiency* and the *Journal of Consulting and Clinical Psychology*.

Per Davidsson is Professor in Entrepreneurship and Director for the Australian Centre for Entrepreneurship Research (ACE) at the Queensland University of Technology, Australia. He has additional affiliations with the Jönköping International Business School, Sweden, Zhejiang University, China, and University of Louisville, US, and is the 2011/12 Chair of the Entrepreneurship Division of the Academy of Management. He has led and/or participated in multiple international-collaborative research projects addressing a broad array of entrepreneurship issues on the individual, team, organizational, regional and national levels. His primary areas of expertise are new venture creation, small firm growth and research methods, and he has authored more than 100 published works on entrepreneurship topics, including some of the best cited works in the leading journals in this field. He is associate editor of *Small Business Economics*, is former manuscript editor of *Entrepreneurship Theory and Practice*, and serves on the editorial boards for several other leading journals.

Gavin Don is an expert in the field of entrepreneurial finance. Trained in corporate finance in the City of London, he established his own corporate finance practice (Equitas) in 1994, sourcing capital and debt finance for young Scottish high-growth companies. Since then he has arranged some £40 million of finance for dozens of companies, and has also started other businesses, including Newsbase, a global energy news publishing company. In 1998 he founded the first commercial news service aimed at informing the marketplace (Young Company Finance), and has been a leading thinker and innovator in the Scottish market for nearly 20 years. He is an Honorary Senior Lecturer at the Hunter Centre, Strathclyde University, and is also Visiting Professor of Entrepreneurial Finance at the Edinburgh University Management School. He regularly teaches entrepreneurial finance to undergraduate and postgraduate students, including MBAs, and is Edinburgh University's first Entrepreneur in Residence.

Amanda Elam is President of Galaxy Diagnostics, Inc., a diagnostics company spun out from North Carolina State University. She holds a Ph.D. in sociology from the University of North Carolina at Chapel Hill. Her research to date has involved the application of sociological theories of social structure and societal change to multilevel, cross-national analyses of patterns of gender and entrepreneurship and to gendered patterns of work and social networks. Prior to her current engagement, she spent two years researching gender and entrepreneurship at two leading management schools in the field of entrepreneurship research at Education, the Queensland University of Technology in Brisbane, Australia and Babson College in Wellesley, Massachusetts. She recently published her dissertation research – a cross-national study of gender and entrepreneurship – with Edward Elgar Publishing. This research was recognized by the Academy of Management's Entrepreneurship Division as one of the top dissertation projects completed in 2006.

Majbritt Rostgaard Evald received her Ph.D. from the Faculty of Social Sciences, University of Southern Denmark in 2005. Since 2006, she has been Assistant Professor at the Department of Entrepreneurship and Relationship Management, University of Southern Denmark. Her research is mainly focused on corporate entrepreneurship with particular interest in intrapreneurs' networks, private incubator systems and various types of growth ventures located within or outside the incumbent firm. She has published articles in the field of entrepreneurship in journals such as the *Journal of Enterprising Culture* and the *International Entrepreneurship and Management Journal*. She has also written and edited books.

Alain Fayolle is Professor and Director of the Entrepreneurship Research Centre at EMLYON Business School (France). He is also Visiting Professor at Solvay Brussels School of Economics and Management (Belgium). His current research works focus on the dynamics of entrepreneurial processes, the influences of cultural factors on organizations' entrepreneurial orientation and the evaluation of entrepreneurship education. His books include *Entrepreneurship and New Value Creation: The Dynamic of the Entrepreneurial Process* (Cambridge University Press, 2007) and *The Dynamics between Entrepreneurship, Environment and Education* (Edward Elgar, 2008). His published research from 2009 appeared in *Academy of Management Learning & Education, Entrepreneurship and Regional Development, International Journal of Entrepreneurship and Innovation* and *Frontiers of Entrepreneurship Research*.

William B. Gartner holds the position of Arthur M. Spiro Professor of Entrepreneurship at Clemson University. Prior to Clemson he was at the University of Virginia, Georgetown University, San Francisco State University and the University of Southern California. He is the 2005 winner of the FSF-NUTEK Award for outstanding contributions to entrepreneurship and small business research. Besides his scholarship on entrepreneurial behaviour using the Panel Study of Entrepreneurial Dynamics (PSED), his research on entrepreneurial narrative explores: (a) the kinds of stories that entrepreneurs tell about their business development efforts, (b) the ways that stories are used to raise financing and generate support to transform ideas into ongoing businesses, and (c) insights that can be ascertained through new methods in evaluating entrepreneurial narrative. In January 2009, his entrepreneurship and small business management textbook *Enterprise* was published by Cengage.

Scott Gordon is a doctoral researcher with the Australian Centre for Entrepreneurship Research (ACE), at the Queensland University of Technology, Australia. His research examines the processes that enable entrepreneurial emergence. To this end he is currently applying socio-cognitive and behavioural approaches to understanding nascent entrepreneurial action, with a particular focus on the influence of prior experience. Entrepreneurship research is his second career. Originally trained as an electronics engineer, he spent a decade in scientific research with CSIRO.

Patricia G. Greene is the F.W. Olin Distinguished Chair in Entrepreneurship at Babson College, where she formerly served as Provost (2006–08) and Dean of the Undergraduate School (2003–06). Prior to joining Babson she held the Ewing Marion Kauffman/Missouri Chair in Entrepreneurial Leadership at the University of Missouri-Kansas City (1998–2003) and the New Jersey Chair of Small Business and Entrepreneurship at Rutgers University (1996–98). Her research focuses on the identification, acquisition and combination of entrepreneurial resources, particularly by women and minority entrepreneurs. She is a founding member of the Diana Project, a research group focusing on women and the venture capital industry. In 2007 the Diana Project was awarded the SFS-NUTEK Award, given to recognize those who produce scientific work of outstanding quality and importance related to entrepreneurship.

Gary Hancock is Lecturer and Undergraduate Programme Coordinator for the Entrepreneurship, Commercialisation and Innovation Centre at the University of Adelaide. He has taught and developed courses in the areas of small business management, business start-up, consulting and entrepreneurship. His experience includes working in a large organization in both technical and senior management roles. He has spent over 16 years starting, operating and harvesting growth-oriented ventures in franchise and non-franchise environments. He provides volunteer mentor support and advice to young entrepreneurs via the South Australian Young Entrepreneur Scheme (SAYES). He is the President of a local not-for-profit education organization (WEA-SA). He is carrying out Ph.D. research in the field of early-stage business financing, investigating behaviour and motivation of investors and entrepreneurs who are friends or family.

Kevin Hindle is the foundation Research Director of the Centre for Entrepreneurship, Innovation and Community at Deakin University, Australia. His credentials include winning the highest award for entrepreneurial education in both Australia (Entrepreneurship Educator of the Year) and the United States (the Academy of Management Award for Innovative Pedagogy). He has over 80 peer-reviewed publications and global experience in teaching, research, management consulting and private equity investment. His research agenda focuses on understanding the role that contextual and community factors play in the entrepreneurial process. His mission is to apply the knowledge gained from rigorous research to the enhancement of entrepreneurial capacity: the ability to turn new knowledge into new value, for defined stakeholders. His scholarship and consulting embrace theory development, venture evaluation, entrepreneurial business planning, change management, organizational design, corporate strategy and management training. He is a pioneer in the field of Indigenous entrepreneurship. On an international scale, he has initiated and developed a wide range of new ventures, innovative teaching programmes and insightful, applied research. The unifying theme of all his work is to develop and execute constructive, internationally relevant research whose findings can be used to enhance the teaching and development of ethical entrepreneurs in Australia and the world.

Miguel Imas obtained his Ph.D. in social psychology at the London School of Economics and Political Science and is a Senior Lecturer at the Faculty of Business and Law, Kingston University. His research interest focuses on art, social creativity and innovation in alternative communities and organizations primarily located in the developing world.

Jerome A. Katz (Ph.D. Michigan) is the Coleman Chair in Entrepreneurship at Saint Louis University, and founding Director of the University's Billiken Angel Network. He has been involved in entrepreneurial development efforts in Sweden, Italy, the West Bank, Croatia and Israel, as well as the USA. He publishes in the areas of organizational emergence, career models of entrepreneurship, and infrastructural analyses of the discipline of entrepreneurship. He is founding Editor of the Emerald series *Advances in Entrepreneurship, Firm Emergence and Growth* and co-author of the text *Entrepreneurial Small Business* (McGraw-Hill).

Phillip H. Kim is an Assistant Professor of Management and Human Resources at the University of Wisconsin-Madison's School of Business. He earned his MA and Ph.D. in Sociology at the University of North Carolina at Chapel Hill and his BS (Economics) and BAS (Materials Sciences) at the University of Pennsylvania. His research bridges macro- and micro-level explanations of entrepreneurship along societal, institutional and political dimensions. Specifically, his research examines entrepreneurial team and social network configurations, entrepreneurship in highly regulated industries, and the political economy of entrepreneurship. He also investigates how occupational mobility shapes founders' work experiences. His research has been published in the *Strategic Entrepreneurship Journal, Small Business Economics* and *American Behavioral Scientist*.

Kim Klyver received his Ph.D. in 2005. Subsequently he worked as a post-doctoral fellow at the Australian Graduate School of Entrepreneurship at Swinburne University of Technology from 2006 to 2007 and as a post-doctoral fellow at Stanford University in 2009 after being awarded the Scancor Postdoctoral Fellowship Award 2009. Currently, he works as a Professor at the University of Southern Denmark. He has been a member of the Global Entrepreneurship Monitor (GEM) project since 2000 and has been part of both the Australian national team and the Danish national team. He has more than 80 publications and has published intensively in international peer-reviewed journals. He has won several awards for his research. His main interests are entrepreneurial networks, nascent entrepreneurship, women's entrepreneurship, entrepreneurship policy, and consultancy of entrepreneurs.

Fredric Kropp is a Professor of Entrepreneurship, Creativity and Innovation at the Monterey Institute of International Studies, and an Adjunct Professor at the University of Adelaide. He received his doctorate in marketing from the University of Oregon. He also taught at Bond University, Australia, and the University of Oregon and in South Africa, Canada and Austria. He has conducted workshops and seminars in creativity and innovation in several countries. He has published over 100 articles, book chapters and conference proceedings in outlets such as the *Journal of Advertising*, the *Journal of Business Research*, the *Journal of Consumer Psychology*, *International Marketing Review*, *Advances in Consumer Research* and *Advances in Entrepreneurship Research*. He worked as a management consultant conducting futures-oriented and marketing studies for clients including Hewlett-Packard, Timex, General Electric, Dow Corning, the US Departments of Energy and Transportation, and the Federal Aviation Administration. He is currently a consultant for nascent entrepreneurs, established firms and non-profit organizations.

Hans Landström attained his Ph.D. in industrial management at Lund Institute of Technology, Sweden, at the end of the 1980s. Since 2001 he has held a Chair in Entrepreneurship at Lund University School of Economics and Management, Sweden. He is a founding member and member of the executive group of the Centre for Innovation, Research and Competence in the Learning Economy (CIRCLE), and also responsible for programmes and courses in entrepreneurship at Lund University. His research interest includes entrepreneurial finance, informal and institutional venture capital, entrepreneurial learning and teaching, and the doctrine history of entrepreneurship research. He has published in journals including the *Journal of Business Venturing*, *Entrepreneurship and Regional Development*, *Venture Capital*, *Entrepreneurship Theory and Practice*, *Small Business Economics* and the *Journal of Small Business Management*.

John Legge started tertiary-level teaching after 28 years' experience in technology-oriented business, including four years as a corporate business strategist for a multinational computer firm. His business career included extensive periods in the UK and Australia, and involved technical and marketing assignments in nine other countries. Since 1988 he has concentrated on consulting, research, writing and teaching. Nine of his books have been published, and he has completed a number of significant research papers.

He was Lecturer in Innovation and Entrepreneurship at Swinburne University between 1991 and 1996 and taught at the Royal Melbourne Institute of Technology Graduate School of Engineering in 1997 and in the Graduate School of Management, La Trobe University, from 1999 to 2002. He is currently a Senior Teaching Fellow, Ballarat University, a Fellow of the Chifley Business School, and a Teaching Fellow, Swinburne University of Technology, where he convenes the subject 'Growth Venture Evaluation' in the Australian Graduate School of Entrepreneurship. He is the principal consultant in his family consulting business.

Benoît Leleux is the Stephan Schmidheiny Professor of Entrepreneurship and Finance at IMD in Lausanne (Switzerland). He was previously Visiting Professor of Entrepreneurship at INSEAD and Director of the 3i VentureLab and Associate Professor and Zubillaga Chair in Finance and Entrepreneurship at Babson College, Wellesley, MA (USA) from 1994 to 1999. He obtained his Ph.D. at INSEAD, specializing in corporate finance and venture capital. He is the author of *Investing Private Capital in Emerging and Frontier Market SMEs* (IFC, 2009), *Nurturing Science-Based Startups: An International Case Perspective* (Springer Verlag, 2008), *From Microfinance to Small Business Finance* (Palgrave Macmillan, 2007), and *A European Casebook on Entrepreneurship and New Ventures* (Prentice Hall, 1996). He earned an M.Sc. in agricultural engineering, an M.Ed. in natural sciences from the Catholic University of Louvain (Belgium) and an MBA from Virginia Tech (USA).

Jonathan Levie is a Reader in the Hunter Centre for Entrepreneurship at the University of Strathclyde, Glasgow, UK, where he was Director from 2000 to 2005. He has held research and teaching posts at the London Business School, Babson College, INSEAD, and University College, Cork, Ireland. He is a visiting member of the teaching faculty of Audencia School of Management, Nantes, France. He has been researching and teaching entrepreneurship for over 25 years and has managed both new and growing firms. His current research interests include entrepreneurship and institutions, entrepreneurial management and performance, and strategic value creation and exit. He is an elected board member of the Global Entrepreneurship Research Association, and he leads the Global Entrepreneurship Monitor UK team with Professor Mark Hart. He holds a Ph.D. from London Business School and a B.Sc. and M.Sc. from the National University of Ireland.

Noel J. Lindsay dropped out of school at 16 to start his first business, which initially succeeded but then failed. Learning from this failure prompted him to complete his high school education and enter university.

After completing his Ph.D. in commerce at the University of Queensland, he co-founded and developed successful businesses in Australia, South Africa and Malaysia. He also worked in corporate insolvency and then private equity as a director of a successful venture capital firm that invested $1 million to $3 million in growth-oriented entrepreneurial ventures. As Professor of Entrepreneurship and Commercialisation and Director of the Entrepreneurship, Commercialisation and Innovation Centre at the University of Adelaide, he leads a team that undertakes research and teaches in the areas of entrepreneurship, innovation, technology commercialization and project management. He is a Fellow of, and holds a practising certificate with, CPA Australia and is an Affiliate of the Institute of Chartered Accountants in Australia.

Matjaž Mulej retired from the University of Maribor, Faculty of Economics and Business, as Professor Emeritus of Systems and Innovation Theory. He has over 1400 publications in over 40 countries. He was a visiting professor abroad for 15 semesters. He is the author of the Dialectical Systems Theory and Innovative Business Paradigm for catching-up countries. He is a member of the New York Academy of Sciences (1996), the European Academy of Sciences and Arts, Salzburg, and the European Academy of Sciences and Humanities, Paris, and president of the International Federation for Systems Research (IFSR). He has an MA in development economics and doctorates in systems theory and management.

Miroslav Rebernik, Ph.D. is Professor of Business Economics and Entrepreneurship, Head of the Department for Entrepreneurship and Business Economics, and Director of the Institute for Entrepreneurship and Small Business Management at the Faculty of Economics and Business, University of Maribor, Slovenia. His bibliography contains over 600 bibliographic units. Currently he leads the Global Entrepreneurship Monitor research for Slovenia. Since 1999 he has run the research project Slovenian Entrepreneurship Observatory and since 2004 the research programme Entrepreneurship for Innovative Society. He chairs the International Conference on Innovation and Entrepreneurship PODIM, co-chairs the International Conference STIQE, and runs and/or cooperates in national and international projects. He is country vice-president of the European Council for Small Business and Entrepreneurship, a member of the ECSB Board of Directors, and a member of the Working Group on Policy-Relevant Research on Entrepreneurship and SMEs organized by the European Commission. He is engaged in the editorial and reviewers' boards of the refereed journals *Naše gospodarstvo*, *Business & Economics Review*, *Journal of Small Business Management* and *International Journal of Entrepreneurial Venturing*.

Dhafar Al-Shanfari is a Lecturer in the College of Commerce and Economics at Sultan Qaboos University, Sultanate of Oman and is the first Omani academic to specialize in entrepreneurship. In Oman, he is engaged in a range of academic and commercial projects. Beyond academia, he is a practising entrepreneur and an equity investor in local ventures. He is currently completing a doctoral candidature in the Centre for Entrepreneurship, Innovation and Community at Deakin University, Australia. His dissertation involves development of a framework for understanding the influence of the national environment pertaining in developing countries upon the successful generation of high-potential entrepreneurial ventures and the design of policies to enhance that environment. His wider research agenda embraces high-potential new venture creation, the entrepreneurial process in developing country environments and entrepreneurship policy. His principal goal as scholar and educator is to establish programmes of rigorous entrepreneurship research in his country, Oman.

David Smallbone is Professor of Small Business and Entrepreneurship and Associate Director of the Small Business Research Centre at Kingston University in the UK and Visiting Professor in Entrepreneurship at the China University of Geosciences in Wuhan, China. David is a Past President of the European Council for Small Business and Entrepreneurship (ECSB) and President Elect of the International Council for Small Business and Entrepreneurship (ICSB). He has published widely on topics that include high-growth SMEs, enterprise development in rural areas, innovation and innovation policy, internationalization and SME development, entrepreneurship and SME policy, immigrant and ethnic minority enterprise, and entrepreneurship and SME development in transition economies. David has recent experience of empirically based entrepreneurship projects in China, as well as in a variety of former Soviet republics and post-socialist economies in Central and Eastern Europe.

Paul Steffens is Associate Professor and Deputy Director of the Australian Centre for Entrepreneurship Research (ACE), Faculty of Business at Queensland University of Technology (QUT), Australia. He has also held positions at the University of Queensland, Monash University, Penn State University and the University of Kiel. Based on his research he has published over 50 works on various entrepreneurship- and innovation-related topics, including articles in leading entrepreneurship journals. He serves on the editorial board for the *Journal of Business Venturing*. He has been a chief investigator for several major research programmes, including the current Comprehensive Australian Study on Entrepreneurial Emergence (CAUSEE).

Jon Sundbo is a Professor in Business Administration and Innovation at Roskilde University, Denmark. He has throughout his whole career been doing research in innovation and entrepreneurship and has published articles and books (including *The Theory of Innovation* and *The Strategic Management of Innovation*) about these topics. He has particularly studied innovation and entrepreneurship in services and the experience economy. He is Director of the Innovation Research Group at the Department of Communication, Business and Information Technologies, Centre of Service Studies and Centre of Experience Research at Roskilde University. He is co-director of the university's unit for practical entrepreneurship and relations between firms and the university (RUCinnovation). He has developed courses and taught innovation and entrepreneurship at Roskilde University and other universities. He has been director of the Roskilde Ph.D. programme in business and innovation and a member of the board of the Danish Doctoral Programme in Organization and Management.

Siri Terjesen is an Assistant Professor of Management and Entrepreneurship in the Kelley School of Business at Indiana University, USA and a visiting research scholar at the Max Planck Institute of Economics Group for Entrepreneurship, Growth and Public Policy in Jena, Germany. Her main research interests include international entrepreneurship, strategy and female entrepreneurship. She is a member of the Global Entrepreneurship Monitor team and co-leads the Social Entrepreneurship Study. She is the co-author of *Strategic Management: Logic and Action* (Wiley, 2008) and has also published numerous articles in leading journals. She holds a Ph.D. from Cranfield University, a Master's degree from the Norwegian School of Economics and Business Administration and a Bachelor's degree from the University of Richmond.

Erno T. Tornikoski has been Dean of the Faculty at the Saint-Etienne School of Management (SESOM) since September 2009. Before joining SESOM, he was an Associate Professor in Entrepreneurship at EMLYON Business School, Principal Lecturer in Entrepreneurship at Seinäjoki University of Applied Sciences, and Research Fellow at ESSEC New Business Centre. He was one of the founders of the entrepreneurship research team in Seinäjoki, and the Centre for Research in New Venture Creation and Growth at EMLYON Business School. His research interests are related to the role of personal networks and legitimacy in organizational emergence, the development of entrepreneurial intentions among the general population, and new venture growth. His published research has appeared in the *Journal of Business Venturing*, the *International Journal of Entrepreneurship and Small Business* and the *International Entrepreneurship and Management Journal*.

Friederike Welter is Professor at Jönköping International Business School (JIBS) in Sweden and Visiting Professor at the Small Business Research Centre at Kingston University in the UK. In 2005, she was awarded the TeliaSonera Professorship of Entrepreneurship at the Stockholm School of Economics in Riga, Latvia for her research on entrepreneurship in a transition context. She is also Past President of the European Council for Small Business and Entrepreneurship (ECSB). Her main research interests are related to entrepreneurship and small business development and entrepreneurial behaviour in different regional contexts, women's entrepreneurship and support policies, on which topics she has published widely. She is on the review board of several international academic journals and is Associate Editor of *Entrepreneurship Theory and Practice*.

PART I

SETTING THE AGENDA

1 New venture creation research: from established perspectives to new horizons
Kevin Hindle and Kim Klyver

THE PHILOSOPHY AND DESIGN OF THE COLLECTION

It is the principal aim of this handbook on new venture creation (NVC) research to contribute to the greater unification of our knowledge through presentation of a diverse range of scholarship on various aspects of the topic. This is not a paradox. Greater unity can only be achieved by canvassing a broad range of perspectives and interests within the field and searching for the common ground. The chapters in this collection are, principally, forward-looking works of critique. In soliciting contributions for this volume we did not seek papers that fitted the traditional moulds of either empirically or conceptually oriented studies. Instead, when we issued our call for papers, we stressed that the mission of the book was that of critical commentary. We sought work that would focus on important aspects of new venture creation research and critically discuss, explore, criticize and suggest improvements to the field in that focal area. A reader of this book and any individual chapter within it should obtain a strong sense of both the 'state of the art' (what has and has not been done in the field of new venture creation research) and the 'state of what could and should be' (future directions the field should take to improve knowledge and address urgent issues). We provided an opportunity for experienced new venture researchers to tell the world not only where the field has been, but where it should be going. Their responses have provided an insightful and stimulating collection of essays which will, we hope, be of great practical value to researchers working in this vital and rapidly expanding field.

It is important to point out that, as editors, we do not equate the term 'new venture creation' with the whole field of entrepreneurship. We regard it as a distinct subcategory of the wider entrepreneurship literature. We have not forced this view on any of the contributors to this volume but we did ask every author or authorial team, should they so wish, to provide a short explanation, for the benefit of readers of the handbook, of the distinction (if any) which they believe exists between entrepreneurship and new venture creation. These authorial views are provided as the

Appendix, where it can be seen that most authors share our perspective. Without restricting diverse views or putting words in our authors' mouths, this handbook, in common with Hindle and Al-Shanfari in Chapter 2, is happy to adopt the Carter *et al.* (1996, p. 52) definition of new venture creation, which is: 'organization creation involves those events before an organization becomes an organization, that is, organization creation involves those factors that lead to and influence the process of starting a business'. The word 'creation' is important. The focus in this handbook is relentlessly upon new business creation rather than existing ventures. This is the case even, for chapters that may seem to depart from this emphasis. For instance, Jonathan Levie, Gavin Don and Benoît Leleux's chapter on exploding business failure myths would seem, superficially, to be about businesses at the end of their life-cycle rather than the beginning. However, in the seed lies the tree. Fear of failure is a major deterrent to the birth of new ventures. So the dispelling of false myths about failure rates is of fundamental importance to understanding the rationale behind business births and the confidence of their creators.

We have organized the collection under four main headings:

- setting the agenda;
- theoretical perspectives;
- data and measurement;
- NVC through contextual lenses.

SETTING THE AGENDA

To open the collection, Kevin Hindle and Dhafar Al-Shanfari offer an analytical investigation of the new venture creation literature with the aim of providing a comprehensive and parsimonious picture of the themes that literature contains. They attempt to 'map the landscape' of new venture creation research beginning with a succinct visit to the wider literature to try to tease out some key issues and themes in the 'parent' field of entrepreneurship and its 'child', new venture creation. They summarize some key definitional issues, clarify what is meant by and covered by the term 'new venture creation' and highlight some of the controversies, perspectives and problems associated with the conceptualization and classification of new ventures before exploring and evaluating several extant approaches to the conduct of entrepreneurship research as they affect new venture creation. They conclude by articulating the landscape of new venture creation research as it stands prior to the publication of the essays presented in this book. They produce a 'new venture creation research theme map' which encapsulates an overview of the NVC literature that may be helpful to researchers who wish to position specific future work in the context of the general development of the field to date.

Complementing the analytical approach of Hindle and Al-Shanfari is the historical emphasis presented in Hans Landström and Fredrik Åström's 'Who's asking the right question? Patterns and diversity in the literature of new venture creation'. Highlighting the pioneering works of William B. Gartner, Landström and Åström place the research on new venture creation into the historical context of entrepreneurship research in general. Analysis and discussion are based principally on a set of bibliometric analyses using the Social Sciences Citation Index (SSCI) for refereed publications on entrepreneurship and new venture creation published between 1956 and 2007. Surprisingly, the results indicate that venture creation can be characterized as a rather small area within the field of entrepreneurship research. At the same time, many different conversations are going on within the area, using different concepts in order to understand the various phenomena associated with venture creation. Over time, the research has been changeable and dynamic in terms of focal research topics. Despite this variety, however, the research on new venture creation appears to demonstrate a relatively clear distinction into two broad knowledge bases distinguished by whether the focus is on the micro or macro level of analysis.

We are always at risk of thinking that new scholarship replaces old rather than builds upon it. In his 'Re-imagining *The Achieving Society*' William B. Gartner demonstrates why it is that he will always hold the prominent and honoured place accorded to him not only by Landström and Åström but by everyone who cares and thinks deeply about entrepreneurship research and respects its heritage. Gartner is the scholar who was and remains at the forefront of the challenge to what many regard as the old and discredited approach of seeking understanding about entrepreneurship and new venture creation in the traits and characteristics of the individual entrepreneur. Didn't we throw that 'wrong' idea out long ago? Well, no. Gartner's (1988) ground-breaking article entitled 'Who is an entrepreneur? is the wrong question' was a direct challenge by a young scholar to the overly dominant and under-challenged preeminence of a renowned sage: David McClelland. Yet here, in his chapter for this handbook, Gartner demonstrates his breadth and openness of mind and generosity of spirit by revisiting and exploring McClelland's 1961 book *The Achieving Society* in search of wisdom he may have missed in his earlier critique. His exploration reveals that McClelland's 'need for achievement' might be seen as an act of the imagination. In his insightful re-reading of McClelland's classic work, Gartner discovers that 'need for achievement' is less a characteristic or trait of individuals and more of a 'sensibility' about one's future. Gartner focuses on portions of *The Achieving Society* to develop the intriguing perspective that 'need for achievement' is an attribution that individuals make about how they might imagine themselves. 'Need for achievement' is, therefore, seen as a prospective (and, more specifically, an 'apperceptive') characteristic of an individual's view of themself. The chapter ends with some suggestions for how a reading of 'need for achievement' as an act of the imagination might impact both theory and practice in entrepreneurship.

Readers are bound to leave this chapter with a greater sensitivity to the fact that outstanding works of scholarship are historical as well as scientific artefacts. They always repay revisiting. Our understanding of new venture creation should be both cumulative and fluid. The first task of the *Handbook of Research on New Venture Creation* is to say 'Handle with care.' The best challenges to established ideas come from those with the deepest respect for the thinking that created them.

THEORETICAL PERSPECTIVES

In 'Gender and new venture creation', Siri Terjesen, Amanda Elam and Candida G. Brush provide an overview of the state of the field with respect to female entrepreneurship research, including extant literature reviews on female entrepreneurship and an assessment of progress. They replicate Brush's (1992) review of entrepreneurship research, using an updated set of articles published from 1993 to 2008. They examine classification type, stated theory base, methodology, and statistical analysis techniques and conclude with suggestions for promising directions for the future, including new theories, new data, new methodologies and a focus on pragmatic issues.

In 'Transgressive knowledge creation in entrepreneurship', Deborah Blackman and Miguel Imas suggest alternative ways of addressing questions which can engender more imaginative interpretations about researching new venture creation. Discussion focuses not upon what entrepreneurship and new venture creation are or are not but upon how knowledge is created. They show how dialogue utilized to generate interpretations of actions and behaviours may limit the potential for alternative explanations. The authors posit that the concept of *transgression* could be adopted to break many currently accepted boundaries and mental models found within venture creation research. Different epistemological foundations are considered to explore how they might lead to changed outcomes in research and how different methodologies will favour some venture creation forms and not others. The authors challenge NVC researchers to construct new venture creation research under a dynamic dialogical understanding of knowledge creation. This approach, they argue, will allow for 'unique' configurations that cannot be explained in terms of predictable, replicable, mechanical, a-contextual processes. New venture creation can only be understood as a process of creation within the context of encompassing events. The authors conclude by proposing an increased focus upon social constructivism, postmodernism and complexity theory, combined with a greater awareness of scepticism and pragmatism and the importance of 'wholes'. These are themes that resonate strongly with subsequent authors – particularly Mulej and Rebernik. Many entrepreneurship scholars and new venture creation researchers are massively overconditioned and have become creatures of research habit. Whether we agree with some of their more radical prescriptions or not, Blackman and Imas alert us to the dangers of treading only where we have gone before and the exciting potentials of paths not yet explored.

In his chapter, John Legge asks the question 'What does the economic literature contribute to understanding new venture creation?' He concludes that the mainstream economics literature has relatively little to say about new venture formation, and what it does say has little resonance with reality as experienced by entrepreneurs and those who study the entrepreneurial process. While some economics writing touches on isolated aspects of the new venture creation process, none that he has discovered attempts comprehensive coverage of all the critical aspects. He goes on to show that it is possible to construct an economically stylized new venture creation process.

Matjaž Mulej and Miroslav Rebernik offer a refreshing and challenging approach to the way we might think about new venture creation, 'Modelling the innovative new venturing process in terms of dialectical systemic thinking'. They argue that creating a new venture can be considered a type of the invention–innovation–diffusion process resulting in innovation, if it transforms an invention into a new benefit for its users, authors and owners. New ventures succeed in a similarly small percentage as other innovative attempts do. Mulej and Rebernik explain the challenging concept of 'requisite holism'. Derived from systems thinking, it is the idea that a holistic approach to new venturing (or, indeed, any activity) need not be so overwhelming a task as to become impossible for all practical purposes. It is possible to embrace the spirit of realistic holism rather than debilitating reductionism through the notion of what is 'requisite' for a given problem. One does not and could never consider everything that acts on a situation, but one can and ought to address a wide range of issues that are demonstrably germane – and not just assume away complexity by considering only an artificially reduced set of variables. Mulej and Rebernik argue that requisitely holistic behaviour can provide a better basis for new venture success than the one-sidedness of specialists, who are inflexible and too narrow to succeed without interdisciplinary creative cooperation. Of course, this capability is difficult for many specialists to attain. While other variants of systems theory are helpful about other problems, Mulej and Rebernik argue that Mulej's Dialectical Systems Theory has, in 35 years of development and application, proved to offer a helpful conceptual and practical approach to modelling the innovative new venturing process and a potent antidote to the poison of taking too narrow an approach to such a complex activity.

In their chapter 'Social networks and new venture creation: the dark side of networks', Kim Klyver, Majbritt Rostgaard Evald and Kevin Hindle are trying to re-direct future research on entrepreneurial networks to include not only the positive and optimistic perspective on how social networks enhance new venture creation but also the constraining mechanisms that social networks may impose. Based on a critical review of prior studies on entrepreneurial networks, they attack many assumptions previously taken for granted and develop four new propositions that they argue should be the baseline for future research on entrepreneurial networks: 1) individuals are not only purposeful actors; 2) part of the network is derived from the past; 3) relationships are diffuse; and 4) different spheres in life are mixed together.

Alain Fayolle, Olivier Basso and Erno T. Tornikoski's 'Entrepreneurial commitment and new venture creation: a conceptual exploration' constitutes a significant introduction to better understanding of the phenomenon of *commitment* to the new venture creation process. They review the principal psycho-social theories of commitment, starting with an analysis of the concepts and theories developed in the fields of both social and cognitive psychology. They then examine the notion of commitment within the field of entrepreneurship by analysing the most prominent works devoted to the subject and scrutinizing two empirical cases. They employ psycho-social approaches to analyse the cases and, through the light of their findings, propose two perspectives to better understand the formation and persistence of entrepreneurial commitment before presenting the initial elements of a potential model of the phenomenon.

DATA AND MEASUREMENT

Phillip H. Kim and Howard E. Aldrich's chapter, 'Are we there yet? Measurement challenges in studying new ventures', directly confronts the difficulties scholars face when they attempt to accurately explain and measure new venture outcomes. Given the non-linear and multi-dimensional aspects of organizing new ventures, this is not surprising. And yet new venture research often uses single indicators or relies on founders' perceptions regarding their status. Because theoretical explanations suggest that venture creation is a process, Kim and Aldrich propose that future research should strive to integrate multi-dimensional measurement models that reflect the complexity of the founding process. They show that such models would enable scholars to move beyond linear-based founding explanations and accommodate learning and other feedback mechanisms.

In an important challenge to broadly and wrongly held received wisdom, Jonathan Levie, Gavin Don and Benoît Leleux review the literature on perceptions and measures of new business mortality, and note wide and persistent gaps between perceptions and measures. Official statistics suggest that survival rates of new businesses in advanced economies tend to be around 80 per cent after one year and around 50 per cent after five years. Failure rates appear to be around half to a third of the inverse of the survival rate, depending on how failure is defined. A survey of estimates on the world wide web found the most quoted failure rate was 50 per cent after one year. Explanations for this gap between perception and official statistics include the way firm births are measured, vested interests, and misleading referencing. Using the UK as an example, Levie, Don and Leleux estimate that nascent entrepreneurship rates could be increased by a third if people knew the true failure rate for new businesses.

Per Davidsson, Paul Steffens and Scott Gordon's chapter 'Comprehensive Australian Study of Entrepreneurial Emergence (CAUSEE): design, data collection and descriptive results' is a detailed description of an ongoing research programme aiming to uncover factors that initiate, hinder and facilitate the process of emergence of new economic activities and organizations. CAUSEE is a longitudinal panel study of new economic activities that follows the design logic developed in the programme Panel Studies of Entrepreneurial Dynamics (PSED). In this chapter, the authors explain carefully how CAUSEE distinguishes itself from forerunners such as the PSED, before they elaborate on the research design and the data collection regime and present some interesting descriptive results.

NVC THROUGH CONTEXTUAL LENSES

Addressing the importance of context to entrepreneurial process stressed in previous chapters by Blackman and Imas and by Mulej and Rebernik, the concluding group of chapters explores aspects of the contextual dependency of new venture creation. Our authors demonstrate that new venture creation involves different meanings and values to people embedded in different contexts and plays different roles dependent upon these contexts.

In 'Cultural context as a moderator of private entrepreneurship investment behavior' Fredric Kropp, Noel J. Lindsay and Gary Hancock examine the effects of national culture on the investment decisions of three different groups of private equity investors: venture capitalists (VCs), business angels (BAs) and relation-based investors (friends and families). They argue that national culture will influence the decision to invest in entrepreneurial business ventures in different ways for each of the three private equity investor groups. VCs are professional investors and have a professional culture that transcends and minimizes some of the differences in national culture. In contrast, relation-based investors, many of whom invest altruistically on an ad hoc basis in family or friends' businesses, are most affected by national culture. The investment decision for friends and family is a function of the strength and distance of the relationship, perceived needs and alternatives for the entrepreneur, and a sense of obligation. The authors propose that the effects of national culture on business advisers' investor decision making will lie somewhere between VC and relation-based investor decision making depending on the business advisers' investment experience levels.

Malin Brännback, Alan L. Carsrud and Jerome A. Katz investigate 'Perceptual differences and perceptual problems in providing government support for new venture creation'. Government economic development programmes making investments in existing or potential businesses face several problems. This chapter addresses the perceptions of entrepreneurship by various players in society and discusses a particular problem – when public policies are based on bureaucratic perceptions very different from and in potential conflict with those of the entrepreneur. The problem is explained using three factors: prospect theory driven political needs, investment timing decisions, and perceptual differences between entrepreneurs and policy makers. Examples are drawn from several famous instances of economic development decision making in Finland and the United States. Based on this analysis, the authors provide suggestions on how to improve future economic decision-making efforts that affect entrepreneurs.

In 'Entrepreneurship education and new venture creation: a comprehensive approach', Torben Bager elaborates on the role of university education for new venture creation. University education in entrepreneurship and new venture creation is increasingly seen as a foundation for more knowledge-intensive start-ups and more high-end innovation in existing firms. Although this is a dominant line of thinking among policy makers, it is generally not embraced by educators and educational institutions and often meets substantial resistance. Some of the resistance arises from difficulties in aligning these practical teaching approaches promoted by policy makers with fundamental university principles and the way academia understands itself. Bager elaborates on the components of comprehensive entrepreneurship education at university level as a means of paving the way toward 'the entrepreneurial university'.

Adopting an administrator's perspective, Patricia G. Greene provides deep-seated insight into 'Managing NVC research in institutional context: an academic administrator's perspective'. She uses the context of Babson College to explore institutional connections between new venture creation research and teaching by providing a review of Babson's history and programmes, a short consideration of the growth and scope of the field of entrepreneurship and the context of the educational system. She applies Béchard and Grégoire's pedagogical innovation framework to explore the teaching model, considering both the ontological assumptions supporting Babson's work in entrepreneurship and the operational elements which characterize the school. Research is explored from the perspective of both relevance and rigour, and the blend of teaching and research is presented as a pedagogical innovation. The chapter concludes with a summary of lessons learned relating to research on new venture creation, specifically those concerning faculty recruitment and the balance between theory and practice.

In 'Creative artists and entrepreneurship' Jon Sundbo poses two principal questions: What is artistic entrepreneurship? Which specific problems are associated with artistic entrepreneurship? He concludes that artistic creativity is a good precondition for entrepreneurship understood as new venture creation; however, it is not sufficient. Artistic creativity and entrepreneurship are not the same phenomenon. Exploiting the entrepreneurship potential latent in artistic endeavour may require an effort in which the often solitary artist has to engage in plural activities, with a wide range of other people offering a wide variety of supporting roles. In particular, an artist of today could benefit from association with a 'modern Maecenas' capable of providing patronage or from 'arts incubators'. Many artists demonstrate a range of entrepreneurial potentials, particularly marketing possibilities that may arise via exposure of interesting aspects of their personality. Artistic entrepreneurs face some highly particular problems centred on the difficulty of procuring the finances for business projects and severe impediments to the growth of their enterprise. So they can definitely benefit professionally from courses aimed at teaching them 'artistic entrepreneurship'.

In the book's concluding chapter Friederike Welter and David Smallbone explore the distinctive features of post-Soviet entrepreneurship, associated with the historical legacy inherited by entrepreneurs in the post-socialist period and the transformation path followed by countries which until less than 20 years ago were operating under socialism and the rules of central planning. While sharing many common features with venture creation imperatives in other environments, post-socialist countries exhibit some key differences. These arise from the precise nature and impact of the historical legacy, as well as the economic and institutional development path followed during the transformation period. Such differences give rise to many implications concerning the nature of entrepreneurship in a post-socialist context. A key theme emerging from Welter and Smallbone's examination concerns the institutional embeddedness of post-socialist entrepreneurship. This refers to the embeddedness of entrepreneurship in legal and regulatory contexts as well as in society and is reflected by the impact of socialist legacy and societal attitudes toward entrepreneurship on entrepreneurial behaviour during transition.

IS THERE A SYNTHESIS? DO WE NEED ONE?

The chapters in this book demonstrate that new venture creation research currently embraces a wide range of disciplines, perspectives and methodological approaches. This handbook leaves open the question of whether the field could benefit by a refined synthesis of approaches and methods or would be better left as an area characterized more by variety than conformity.

It was not our ambition as editors to promote any commonly agreed synthesis. We opened a forum where a wide diversity of approaches and opinions were encouraged to engage in a vigorously eclectic debate. This is very much in line with Gartner's (2001) comparison of entrepreneurship research with the 'blind man and the elephant' story.

This handbook presents no solutions but it could well be a catalyst. We hope the challenging contributions presented between these covers will enhance readers' interest in conducting original new venture creation research, in a manner that is fully alert to the stimulating possibilities of performing collaborative work with scholars who possess different theoretical perspectives, come from different disciplines and apply different methods. The horizon for future work is both wide and alluring.

REFERENCES

Brush, C.G. (1992), 'Research on women business owners: Past trends, a new perspective and future directions', *Entrepreneurship Theory and Practice*, **16**(4), 5 30.

Carter, N.M., W.B. Gartner and P.D. Reynolds (1996), 'Exploring start-up event sequences', *Journal of Business Venturing*, **11**(3), 151–66.

Gartner, W.B. (1988), 'Who is an entrepreneur? is the wrong question', *American Journal of Small Business*, **12**(4), 11–32.

Gartner, W.B. (2001), 'Is there an elephant in entrepreneurship? Blind assumptions in theory development', *Entrepreneurship Theory and Practice*, **25** (4), 27–39.

2 Mapping the landscape of new venture creation research
Kevin Hindle and Dhafar Al-Shanfari

INTRODUCTION

In this chapter we will attempt an analytical investigation of the new venture creation literature with the aim of providing a comprehensive and parsimonious picture of the themes that literature contains. We want to map the landscape of new venture creation research. However, every journey of exploration demands thorough preparation, and in our case this leads to a necessary consideration of some of the thorniest controversies in the larger domain of entrepreneurship. Though some researchers and practitioners still maintain that entrepreneurship and new venture creation are synonymous, there is a broader agreement that new venture creation is a specific subset of entrepreneurship: just one manifestation that an entrepreneurial process might take (Shane and Venkataraman 2000). Unfortunately, there is very little agreement about what the larger phenomenon, entrepreneurship, actually *is* beyond recognizing that the unresolved entrepreneurship definitional debate is a hurdle to developing any solid framework, model or theory as the basis of a recognizably consistent body of research in any area of entrepreneurship. There simply is still no concise universally accepted definition of what 'entrepreneurship' stands for (Hisrich *et al.* 2005). The exact definition of entrepreneurship and the issue of how far that definition extends constitute a major question that continues to exercise academics (Birley and Muzyka 2000) because of the need to have clear boundaries of what constitutes a study that qualifies as 'entrepreneurship research' (Busenitz *et al.* 2003). Those interested in new venture creation research cannot avoid some attempt to address the issues and controversies of the larger field in which it is situated.

We do not need or intend to try readers' patience with yet another long-winded list, litany and evaluation of the various contending definitions of entrepreneurship. However, we feel that a chapter in a tome that purports to be a handbook of new venture creation has to enter the definitional minefield (treading as lightly as possible) because such a book has a key responsibility to distinguish new venture creation as a specific entrepreneurial activity from entrepreneurship as a more general phenomenon.

That is what we try to do in this chapter, which takes the following form. First, as an essential predicate to creating the map of the landscape which is our principal objective, we visit the wider literature to try to tease out some key issues and themes in the 'parent' field of entrepreneurship and its 'child', new venture creation. We summarize the key definitional issues, clarify what is meant by and covered by the term 'new venture creation' and highlight some of the controversies, perspectives and problems associated with the conceptualization and classification of new ventures. Second, we explore and evaluate several extant approaches to the conduct of entrepreneurship research as they affect new venture creation. Third, we do our best to articulate the landscape of new venture creation research as it stands prior to the publication of the essays presented in this book. The study culminates in an artefact we call the 'new venture creation research theme map'. Hopefully, our analytical approach can serve as a useful complement to the historical emphasis presented in Chapter 3, Hans Landström and Fredrik Åström's insightful chapter.

PREDICATE ISSUES AND CONTROVERSIES IN NEW VENTURE CREATION

Summarizing Definitional Issues Concerning Entrepreneurship and New Venture Creation

Entrepreneurship is one of the youngest research areas in the management discipline family, with limited numbers of academic scholars focusing solely on it (Wortman Jr 1987; McCarthy and Nicholls-Nixon 2001; Hisrich and Drnovsek 2002). Nevertheless, it is a dynamic, evolving and emerging field (Busenitz *et al.* 2003; Hindle 2004). The increase in endowed chairs, programmes, centres and journals dedicated to the field (Katz 1991, 2003) and the increasing number of entrepreneurship publications in top management journals are good indicators of the field's growing distinction as a domain (Busenitz *et al.* 2003).

Moreover, entrepreneurship is very much an interdisciplinary field which draws from various social and business disciplines. Entrepreneurship research until the middle of the last century was overwhelmingly a subject of maverick interest to scholars trained in economics, though not (as Chapter 7 demonstrates) to the economics discipline's mainstream. Today, as well as developing as a field in its own right, interest in entrepreneurship has matured to encompass an array of disciplines and traditions including economics, strategic management, organizational behaviour, marketing, sociology and psychology to name a few (Hisrich and Drnovsek 2002).

The nature of the field's interconnected and elastic boundaries allows the field to augment other disciplinary perspectives (Busenitz *et al.* 2003). For instance, renowned economist Israel Kirzner (1982) emphasized the importance of considering entrepreneurship by economists when developing economic models. Morris and Lewis (1995) argue that entrepreneurship shares much ground with the marketing field and that they are strongly linked. Nearly every mainstream social science professes an interest in and produces work about entrepreneurship. Although this interdisciplinary input can be very enriching, one negative outcome of its cross-disciplinary nature is a concern that the field has been fragmented across scholars from different disciplines who do not converge and make use of their collective work (Ucbasaran *et al.* 2001).

Accordingly, there is much debate on the legitimacy of entrepreneurship as a separate domain (Busenitz *et al.* 2003). Some argue that since entrepreneurship is multi-disciplinary there is no need for a distinctive entrepreneurship theory (Kuratko and Hodgetts 2001). Instead fields such as management, marketing, finance, psychology and economics each need to have a theory that addresses entrepreneurship within their own domains (Low 2001). In light of this, Shane and Venkataraman (2000) argue that for entrepreneurship to become a legitimate social science it has to create for itself a distinctive domain by having a framework that explores and predicts phenomena not explained by other fields.

So, despite growing contributions through various disciplinary and theoretical perspectives, there is still a lack of agreement about a unifying framework of both entrepreneurship itself and one of its most important subsets: the new venture creation phenomenon (Hisrich 1988; Bygrave and Hofer 1991; Shane and Venkataraman 2000; Hisrich and Drnovsek 2002; Moroz and Hindle forthcoming). One of the main challenges facing entrepreneurship researchers and the field is the challenge to embrace the interdisciplinary, complex phenomena of entrepreneurship, in general, and new venture creation, in particular, within a comprehensive theory and set of models that are able to predict how, when and why it happens. This has caused some drawbacks to the field and generated an increase of 'folklore or myths' tied to entrepreneurship (Kuratko and Hodgetts 2001). The lack of general theory has also resulted in slow progress in the maturing of the literature to the extent that some scholars argue that research has increased in volume but not grown much in quality (Sexton 1988).

Definitional emphases have varied in past literature from the establishment of innovative new organizations independent of where they exist, to general organization renewal, to starting a new business regardless of its innovativeness (McCarthy and Nicholls-Nixon 2001), to not privileging the creation of an organization, business or venture in any way (Shane and Venkataraman 2000). Wennekers (2006) summarizes the bewildering array of competing definitions by suggesting that there are, at bedrock, two perspectives in how the terms *entrepreneur* and *entrepreneurship* have been used and presented as the literature has developed. The first and earliest, which he calls the 'occupational notion of entrepreneurship', is traced to the eighteenth century and ties entrepreneurship to self-employment and starting a business only. The second, more recent, is a 'behavioural notion of entrepreneurship' which does not limit entrepreneurship to new venture creation but encompasses a wider understanding based on a distinctive entrepreneurial behaviour that can extend to corporations and the public sector and to non-business activity.

This distinction was raised separately and earlier using slightly different terms by Davidsson (2004), who distinguished the 'emergence perspective' and 'opportunity perspective'. The latter is exemplified through Shane and Venkataraman's (2000, p. 218) articulation of the scope of the field as 'the scholarly examination of how, by whom and with what effects opportunities to create goods and services are discovered, evaluated and exploited'. Basically their viewpoint is that researchers in the field should focus on the following questions: 1) how, why and when opportunities exist; 2) study of the processes of discovering, evaluating and exploiting opportunities; 3) study of the individual entrepreneur. In this perspective they believe that new venture creation is a subtopic in the larger entrepreneurship field, where the essence of the entrepreneurial process is being innovative and new. They believe that entrepreneurs, to be worthy of the name, create high-growth innovative new businesses, not 'mom and pop' shops. The main fundamental argument in this school is that entrepreneurship involves creating new means–end relationships, not maximizing existing means–end relationships (Blackman and Hindle 2008). On the other hand, optimizing existing relationships *is* accepted as entrepreneurship by the second perspective led by Gartner (Gartner 1985; Katz and Gartner 1988). Scholars in this camp define entrepreneurship as the process of creating a new organization (Gartner, 1988; Low and MacMillan 1988; Krueger and Brazeal 1994). They are willing to apply the term *entrepreneurship* to the act of creating a new organization (predominantly starting a new business) regardless of the degree of innovation inherent in the endeavour (Birley and Muzyka 2000).

Blackman and Hindle (2007), following Klyver (2005), summarize and clarify these two main schools of thought in entrepreneurship definition as a four-quadrant matrix (see Figure 2.1). Columns represent the principal action focus: either creating a new means and ends relationship (innovating) or maximizing an existing means and ends relationship. Rows indicate whether the action takes place through starting a new organization or

		Principal Action Focus	
		Creation of new means–ends relationships	Maximizing existing means–ends relationships
Organizational Context	New organizations	(A) Innovation-oriented venture creation	(B) Non-innovation-oriented venture creation
	Existing settings	(C) Innovation-oriented venturing in existing contexts (e.g. corporate venturing, licensing via markets, etc.)	(D) Traditional management

Sources: Klyver (2005); developed by Blackman and Hindle (2008).

Figure 2.1   Distinguishing the two main perspectives of entrepreneurship research

within the context of existing organizations (this could involve intrapreneurship or market mechanisms such as licensing). The four quadrants in the matrix indicate what constitutes the emergence perspective (quadrants A and B, where organizational creation matters more than deriving value from innovation and novelty), what constitutes the opportunity perspective (quadrants A and C, where deriving value from novelty and innovation matters more than organizational creation) and what is not entrepreneurship in either perspective (quadrant D).

This chapter is not principally concerned with promoting or adding much to this dynamic debate about the exact definition of the field. We accept Arnold Cooper's advice that, regardless of the particular definition a researcher adopts, what is crucially important is that he or she makes clear the definition or perspective that is being adopted for the purposes of the work in hand (McCarthy and Nicholls-Nixon 2001). It is the oldest mandate of research honesty: state your biases. In any case, a great deal of new venturing research is located in 'quadrant A': where the opportunity and emergence perspectives overlap, because the issue is the creation of a new venture based on developing the new value inherent in an opportunity.

What Is Meant by 'New Venture Creation' and How Do You Classify New Ventures?

We are happy to adopt the Carter *et al.* (1996, p. 52) definition of new venture creation, which is: 'organization creation involves those events before an organization becomes an organization, that is, organization creation involves those factors that lead to and influence the process of starting a business'. Although scrutiny of new businesses, post-start-up growth and performance is important in the overall understanding of entrepreneurship, the fundamental necessity is first to understand the antecedents which constitute the pre-start-up stage (Carland and Carland 2000). According to Chrisman (1999, p. 99), 'serious gaps in our knowledge remain about the events that occur before an independent organization is started'. These quotations raise key questions: how do we measure business conception and what is considered to be the birth date of a venture? In Chapter 11, Kim and Aldrich address these issues. In the extant literature, Katz and Gartner (1988) focused on four properties of new organization formation which they believe constitute the minimum necessity in considering an organization as emerging: first, intention to create a new venture; second, acquisition of resources needed; third, working on the boundary (e.g. registration); fourth, exchange process initiated with outsiders (e.g. sales). They suggest that, when studying organization creation, one needs to use at least one of these properties as a sampling frame to examine the issue of when a pre-venture becomes a complete organization.

Past studies use different ways to classify both entrepreneurs and the categories of new venture that they create (Gartner *et al.* 1989; Hisrich *et al.* 2005). For instance, Allen (1999) divides them into micro-businesses (intends to be small, not innovative and fewer than 25 employees) and high-growth ventures (intend to grow in revenue and employees, and innovative). Hisrich *et al.* (2005) classify the *types* of new business start-ups into four main categories based on employee and revenue growth speed (see Table 2.1).

The special case of high-potential new ventures

There is no doubt that individuals or teams of aspiring entrepreneurs will produce different economic effects at a national level depending on their aspirations for growth and innovation (Hessels *et al.* 2008). At one end of the spectrum are those who want to produce something new, compete globally and change industries (gazelles, high growth) and at the other end of the spectrum are those who want to stay small (lifestyle).

An approach for distinguishing 'entrepreneurial' – high-potential – ventures from 'normal' ventures is provided by Schramm (2005, p. 163). He calls them new 'high-impact firms' and describes them as 'the kind that create value and stimulate growth by bringing new ideas to market, be they new technologies, new business methods, or simply new and better ways of performing routine tasks'. Moreover, Carland *et al.* (1984) suggest using four criteria adopted from Vesper (1980) as the basis for

Table 2.1   Types of start-ups

Type	Definition	Expectation
Lifestyle	A small venture that supports the owners and usually does not grow.	Grow to 30–40 employees after several years. Annual revenues $2 million. Limited money to R&D.
Foundation company	A type of company formed from research and development that does not usually go public.	Grow 5–10 years from 40 to 400 employees. From $10 million to $20 million yearly revenue.
High-potential venture	A venture that has high growth potential and therefore receives great investor interest.	Grow 5–10 years to 500 employees. $20 million to $30 million in revenue.
Gazelle	Very high-growth ventures.	More than high growth.

Source: Hisrich *et al.* (2005).

distinguishing an entrepreneurial venture as opposed to a small business. These include: 1) providing a new product or service; 2) practising a new method of production or business conduct; 3) opening a new market; 4) changing an industry's structure. Compliance with any one of these criteria would qualify the new venture as an entrepreneurial one, and the overall key word is 'innovation'. Autio (2003) uses four similar criteria for classifying high-potential new ventures. First, they expect to employ at least 20 people in the next five years. Second, innovativeness is behind the business's aspiration for market expansion. Third, they have some international customers. Fourth, they employ very recent technology (not older than a year).

Despite the clear economic value and importance of high-potential new ventures, very little research has been conducted on distinguishing the characteristics of these new ventures and their founders (Autio 2003) and virtually nothing on the environmental conditions in which they might thrive. Firms in the category of high-potential new ventures possess some very distinct characteristics. They are strong in their innovative capabilities, surpassing large corporations in patent production per sale dollar (Kuratko and Hodgetts 2001). One of the few studies attempting to identify special attributes that characterize these ventures and their founders was conducted by Barringer *et al.* (2005). They performed a comparison of 50 rapid-growth firms and 50 slow-growth firms and discovered a number of special attributes for high-potential firms. First, the founders were better educated, had a higher work experience and were more highly moti-vated. Second, the firm had a stronger longing for growth in its mission statement. Third, their business model was more innovative and aware of the market. Fourth, their internal human resource management (HRM) practice emphasized improving their employees' skills and provided more financial incentives. Autio (2005) found that firms with these characteris-tics were usually founded by men between 25 and 35 years old who were wealthy, better educated, serial entrepreneurs and opportunity driven.

While we recognize the extreme importance of high-potential new ven-tures (those in quadrant A of Figure 2.1), our attempt to provide a map of the field covers the wide spectrum of ventures embraced by both the opportunity and the emergence perspectives concerning the nature of the entrepreneurship and new venturing phenomena.

Since this is a handbook of new venture creation *research*, we turn next to a brief consideration of various approaches that have been taken to researching entrepreneurship and new venture creation.

APPROACHES TO ENTREPRENEURSHIP AND NVC RESEARCH

The complex and interdisciplinary nature of the field has increased the dif-ficulty of executing good entrepreneurship research (Gartner *et al.* 1989). Therefore, the categorization of schools of thought and approaches in researching entrepreneurship is helpful in organizing a researcher's direc-tion and focus. We will briefly articulate some of what the literature dis-cusses and displays as the main research approaches in entrepreneurship.

Deakins and Freel (2006) posit that there have been three approaches to entrepreneurship research. One is an economic approach, where eco-nomic thinkers like Cantillon, Say, Knight, Kirzner, Schumpeter and others wrote on the relationship between an entrepreneur and economic development: basically the *output* of the entrepreneurial process. This is the earliest contribution to the entrepreneurship literature until the 1950s, when researchers outside the economic perspective started contributing (Kuratko and Hodgetts 2001).

The psychological trait approach places the focus more on the indi-vidual entrepreneur. This is one of the earliest approaches in entrepre-neurship research and aimed, initially, to find personal characteristics that distinguished entrepreneurs from the rest. Following McClelland (1961), this school of thought considers personal traits such as need for achieve-ment, internal locus of control and risk-taking ability as main driving factors for entrepreneurial action (Robertson *et al.* 2003). Generally, the attribute approach focused on long lists of entrepreneurial traits that have been identified and examined as potential characteristics associated with entrepreneurial behaviour (Volery *et al.* 1997). Followers of this approach emphasized that entrepreneurs have inherent skills and cannot be 'made'. Fascination with entrepreneurs as individuals is similar to people's fascination with successful people in any other field, such as movie stars, presidents and others. Entrepreneurs attract researchers to study what made them successful in the business world. However, this school was not leading to new answers to why people create businesses, and its popularity was declining (Volery *et al.* 1997) and has – according to some – reached a dead end (Gartner 1985, 1988; Gartner *et al.* 1989; Aldrich 1990). In Chapter 4, William B. Gartner finds a new life for the old wisdom when he revisits David McClelland's (1961) classic work *The Achieving Society*. Later psychologically influenced work has maintained the importance of the psychology of the individual but shifted well away from traits to an interest in cognition (Greenberger and Sexton 1988; Shaver and Scott 1991; Learned 1992; Busenitz and Lau 1996; Carland and Carland 2000; Kolvereid and Isaksen 2006).

There is a social behavioural research cluster that emphasizes the relationship between the external environment and personal characteristics on the entrepreneurship process (Deakins and Freel 2006). As the study of entrepreneurship evolved, many researchers focused on the act rather than the actor (Gartner 1988). 'As intellectually stimulating as it may be to find out what motivates entrepreneurs and how they differ from ordinary mortals, the more critical question is how these individuals manage to create and sustain successful organizations, despite severe obstacles' (Aldrich and Martinez 2001, p. 41). Many of the models used in this approach emphasize the importance of the external environment and its resources for new business start-ups (Mazzarol *et al.* 1999).

Vitally important to entrepreneurship and new venturing research is the influence of the discipline of corporate strategy. Like the field of entrepreneurship, the strategic management paradigm consists of various schools of thought and research approaches (Sandberg 1992). Schendel and Hofer (1979, p. 11) describe strategic management as 'a process that deals with the entrepreneurial work of organizations, with organizational renewal and growth, and, more particularly, with developing and utilizing the strategy which is to guide the organization's operations'. Cooper (1979) and Sandberg (1992) provide important studies on the relationship between the field of strategic management and entrepreneurship. Sandberg (1992) suggests possible avenues for strategic management contribution to future entrepreneurship research in general but more particularly corporate entrepreneurship. Sandberg (1992) suggests drawing from the 'Design

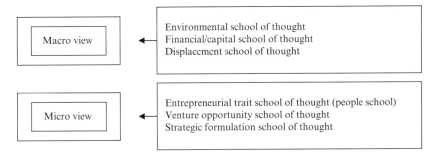

Source: Kuratko and Hodgetts (2001).

Figure 2.2 Main approaches in entrepreneurship research

School' (one of the ten strategic management schools of thought posited by Mintzberg (1990; Mintzberg *et al.* 2005)), which mainly considers the process of matching internal resources to external opportunities. The strategic management process involves six main tasks as described by Schendel and Hofer (1979) that comprise 'goal formulation', 'environmental analysis', 'strategy formulation', 'strategy evaluation', 'strategy implementation' and 'strategic control'. Some of these tasks require the same generic skills needed during the new venture creation process, particularly environmental analysis, formulation and evaluation during business plan development.

A succinct illustration of the main extant approaches to researching entrepreneurship (and the classification applies equally to the subfield of new venture creation) is presented by Kuratko and Hodgetts (2001). They plot six perspectives: three that take a 'macro' view and three a 'micro' view of the phenomenon (Figure 2.2). The macro school includes environment, capital and displacement schools of thought. The micro view includes the entrepreneurial trait, venture opportunity and strategic formulation schools of thought.

Cutting the pie with a different knife, Lee and Peterson (2000) suggest that entrepreneurship research approaches can be classified under three main headings: the individual, the environment/contextual and the firm approaches. Research in the contextual approach heavily focuses on the role of the environment climate in enhancing or hindering entrepreneurial activity. According to Lee and Peterson (2000, p.402) in this approach the 'larger societal factors such as cultural, economic, political, and social forces can combine to create threats or opportunities in the environments where entrepreneurs operate'.

Having briefly considered the definitional controversies, focal study points and research approaches to entrepreneurship and new venture creation we can now attempt to map the landscape.

MAPPING THE NVC RESEARCH LANDSCAPE

Given the complexity, controversy and diversity of approaches taken by researchers to the new venture creation process and the sheer variety of themes and issues covered, it is by no means certain that everyone will accept that the field can be parsimoniously encompassed by an attempt to provide some kind of map of what might be called the landscape of new venture creation research. Despite the difficulties, in what follows we have attempted to do this. After an intensive electronic and manual search and filtration using various key words such as *firm gestation* (Reid and Smith 2000), *organizational emergence* (Gartner 1993), *pre-organization* (Katz and Gartner 1988) and *start-up* (Vesper 1990), 72 papers were scrutinized intensely. More than half of the papers were published in the last ten years, and the publication years ranged from 1980 to 2007. Our study, based on content analysis of the body of extant new venture creation research, resulted in four main themes, which are illustrated in Figure 2.3, a device we call the 'new venture creation theme map'.

We conclude this chapter with a brief summary of the themes detected in our content analysis and represented in our map of the new venture creation landscape.

Determinants of New Venture Creation

The first theme represented in the majority of papers revolves around questions centred on the determinants of new venture creation. The main thematic question in this area of research is centred on 'What factors internal or external, perceived or actual, have an impact on increasing creation of new ventures?' Papers reflecting this theme shared similar broad objectives but their approaches, lenses and scale of focus varied greatly. They are further subdivided into two subthemes based on level of focus: A. micro-level factors influencing an individual's decision to start a new venture; and B. factors influencing new venture creation rates. The first subtheme occurred in papers whose direction was more cognitive and focused on analysis of the individual and looked at what influences a person's decision to start a business. Most of the papers in this subtheme reflect a direction in the new venture creation literature that wants to bring back the individual into entrepreneurship research. Their argument is that the individual entrepreneur cannot be neglected in future research

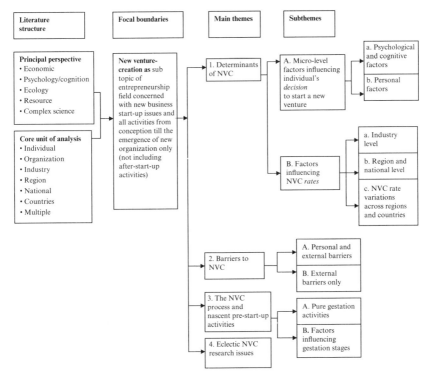

Figure 2.3   New venture creation research theme map

on understanding the entrepreneurial process, since he or she is the soul of entrepreneurial activity (Herron and Sapienza 1992; Carland and Carland 2000). It is possible to claim that this is a refocused and new direction that has sprung away from the old trait school through shifting focus from attempting to distinguish entrepreneurs from managers to asking questions similar to Learned's (1992, p.41) inquiry 'Are there person-level characteristics which, in certain situations, lead to an intention to found, and further, are these characteristics, again in certain situations more likely to lead to a successful attempt to found?'

This subtheme can be further subdivided into two streams: a. psychological cognitive factor focus (Greenberger and Sexton 1988; Shaver and Scott 1991; Learned 1992; Busenitz and Lau 1996; Carland and Carland 2000; Kolvereid and Isaksen 2006) consists of studies that mainly employ a cognitive lens in conceptualizing the process of venture creation, and most of them posit models of organization formation; b. personal traits focus that considers personal factors in new venturing such as personal confidence, risk propensity, alertness to opportunity, etc. (Powell and Bimmerle 1980; Hansen and Allen 1992; Herron and Sapienza 1992). This stream of papers moves from cognitive models to papers that investigate the role of various personal factors such as entrepreneurs' traits and background on the decision to form a venture.

The second subtheme involves factors influencing new venture creation rates. This category contains theoretical and empirical studies that have postulated and examined over the years various personal and contextual factors that are believed to impact on the rate of venture creation at the industry, regional and national level. We further subdivide this subtheme into three categories based on level of analysis: a. industry-level new venture creation rate (Pennings 1982; Aldrich 1990; VanderWerf 1993; Dean and Meyer 1996); for instance, Dean and Meyer (1996) investigate dynamic industries and find that new venture creation is positively related to dynamic industries with high sales growth rate, niche market and dynamic consumer taste and fast technological development; b. within a region or country level (Manning *et al.* 1989; Gatewood 1993; Specht 1993; Gnyawali and Fogel 1994; Capaldo 1997; Mazzarol *et al.* 1999; Lin *et al.* 2000; Feldman 2001; Neck *et al.* 2004; Sternberg and Wennekers 2005; Mueller 2006; Zhang and Yang 2006); these articles consider a mixture of personal and macro external determinates of new venture creation rates at a more macro level in either regions or a specific country; c. new venture rates variation across regions or countries (Malecki 1990; Moyes and Westhead 1990; Davidsson *et al.* 1994; Keeble and Walker 1994; Reynolds *et al.* 1994; Armington and Acs 2002; Wennekers *et al.* 2002; Todtling and Wanzenbock 2003; Lee *et al.* 2004; Wagner and Sternberg 2004; Begley *et al.* 2005; Freytag and Thurik 2007).

Barriers to New Venture Creation

The second category of papers explored and discussed various barriers to new venture creation. It is important to distinguish between the interpretation of 'barriers' in economics which is usually associated with factors like entry cost that restrict market penetration (Bain 1956) and the intended meaning of the term as we employ it here. Barriers in our conception as revealed by the literature we examined refer to a more comprehensive meaning that covers any factor internal or external that hinders the creation of a new venture (Kouriloff 2000). The challenges or barriers faced by those that succeeded or failed seem to be neglected and fragmented (Hatala 2005). According to Kouriloff (2000, p. 63) 'there is a need for systematic research in a priori barriers'. This call is echoed by Sarasvathy (2004), who suggests reshaping research questions instead of examining incentives that increase entrepreneurial activity to focusing on identifying barriers to entrepreneurship. The papers found in this school are subdivided between two subthemes: A. those that involve both personal and external barriers; and B. those that only discuss macro external barriers to new venture creation. In sum, personal or intrinsic barriers include family security, well-being, commitments (Finnerty and Krzystofik 1985), aversion to risk (Choo and Wong 2006), lack of ideas, lack of knowledge, aversion to stress, time for family (Volery *et al.* 1997; Kouriloff 2000; Robertson *et al.* 2003) and uncertainty of the future (Volery *et al.* 1997; Choo and Wong 2006). On the other hand, environmental or extrinsic barriers that a person has no control over include general market environment, high taxes (Finnerty and Krzystofik 1985; Volery *et al.* 1997), lack or scarcity of financial resources (Barth *et al.* 2006; Choo and Wong 2006), government regulation (Volery *et al.* 1997; Lopez 1999; Kouriloff 2000; Barth *et al.* 2006; Klapper *et al.* 2006), bad economic indicators (Choo and Wong 2006), lack of suitable labour (Volery *et al.* 1997; Choo and Wong 2006), rigid labour regulations (Klapper *et al.* 2006), the education and advisory system (Robertson *et al.* 2003), cultural barriers such as fear of failure (Volery *et al.* 1997; Kouriloff 2000; Robertson *et al.* 2003), negative social and cultural attitude (Robertson *et al.* 2003), and racial discrimination (Barth *et al.* 2006).

The New Venture Creation Process and Nascent Pre-Start-Up Activities

The third category focuses on the new venture creation process and nascent pre-start-up activities. These papers look at the earliest possible events and activities that occur before the organization's emergence. There have been limited studies focusing on the new venture creation or gestation process theoretically and even fewer empirical attempts (Reynolds and Miller 1992; Bhave 1994). Overall the main theme in this category is to understand the process events and activities that are involved in creating a new venture by mainly studying nascent entrepreneurs. Moreover, the theme is subdivided into two groups. A. The first group is purely focused on gestation activities. An important stream of work among those we classify as 'gestation researchers' is the body of literature on entrepreneurial intentions most closely associated with Krueger and his colleagues (Krueger 1993, 2000; Krueger and Carsrud 1993; Krueger and Dickson 1993, 1994; Krueger and Brazeal 1994; Krueger *et al.* 2000; Shepherd and Krueger 2002; Krueger Jr 2003). Researchers interested in other aspects of gestation include: Katz and Gartner (1988); Reynolds and Miller (1992); Carter *et al.* (1996); Alsos and Kolvereid (1998); Liao and Welsch (2003); Liao *et al.* (2005); Brush *et al.* (2008). They attempt to understand and posit models of the dynamic, complex, unique, unorganized process of creating a new venture, which involve activities like getting resources, finding employees and financing. B. The second group is factors that influence the gestation stages and process (Bhave 1994; Reynolds 1997; Davidsson and Honig 2003; Jin-ichiro 2004; Gelderen *et al.* 2005; Rotefoss and Kolvereid 2005; Benyamin *et al.* 2006; Parker and Belghitar 2006; Tornikoski and Newbert 2006; Lichtenstein *et al.* 2007). This group of papers mostly study factors influencing nascent entrepreneurs' success or failure in the different venture creation stages. For example, Rotefoss and Kolvereid (2005) investigated empirically the individual and environmental factors that are more likely to predict an individual's success to reach any one of three milestone stages: 'aspiring entrepreneur, nascent entrepreneur and actual business owner'.

Eclectic Research Perspectives in New Venture Creation

Our final category is unashamedly something of a pot-pourri. Honest content analysis can only go so far. It is desirable to distinguish categories where possible but necessary to recognize the absence of structured classification where a binding structure does not exist. So our final category covers a wide array of theoretical and conceptual areas of new venture creation research. Three are theoretical contributions to our understanding of the new venture creation phenomenon (Gartner 1985, 1993; Gartner *et al.* 1989), two provide different literature reviews of some aspect in the area (Forbes 1999; Shook *et al.* 2003), and one discusses how the certain characteristics of a technological opportunity impact chances of its commercialization and hence venture creation (Shane 2001).

Such is our view of the landscape of new venture creation research prior to the stimulating contributions which form this handbook.

REFERENCES

Aldrich, H.E. (1990), 'Using an ecological perspective to study organizational founding rates', *Entrepreneurship Theory and Practice*, **14**(3), 7–24.
Aldrich, H.E. and M.A. Martinez (2001), 'Many are called, but few are chosen: An evolutionary perspective for the study of entrepreneurship', *Entrepreneurship Theory and Practice*, **25**(4), 41.
Allen, K.R. (1999), *Launching New Ventures: An Entrepreneurial Approach*, Boston: Houghton Mifflin.
Alsos, G.A. and L. Kolvereid (1998), 'The business gestation process of novice, serial, and parallel business founders', *Entrepreneurship Theory and Practice*, **22**(4), 101–14.
Armington, C. and Z.J. Acs (2002), 'The determinants of regional variation in new firm formation', *Regional Studies*, **36**(1), 33–45.
Autio, E. (2003), 'High-potential entrepreneurship', *First Annual Global Entrepreneurship Symposium*, New York: United Nations.
Bain, J.S. (1956), *Barriers to New Competition*, Boston: Harvard University Press.

Barringer, B.R., F.F. Jones and D.O. Neubaum (2005), 'A quantitative content analysis of the characteristics of rapid-growth firms and their founders', *Journal of Business Venturing*, **20**(5), 663–87.

Barth, J.R., G. Yago and B. Zeidman (2006), *Barriers to Entrepreneurship in Emerging Domestic Markets: Analysis and Recommendations*, Santa Monica, CA: Milken Institute.

Begley, T.M., W.-L. Tan and H. Schoch (2005), 'Politico-economic factors associated with interest in starting a business: A multicountry study', *Entrepreneurship Theory and Practice*, **29**(1), 35–56.

Benyamin, B.L., J.D. Kevin and G.T. Lumpkin (2006), 'Measuring emergence in the dynamics of new venture creation', *Journal of Business Venturing*, **21**(2), 153.

Bhave, M.P. (1994), 'A process model of entrepreneurial venture creation', *Journal of Business Venturing*, **9**(3), 223.

Birley, S. and D. Muzyka (2000), *Mastering Entrepreneurship*, Edinburgh, UK: Prentice Hall/FT.

Blackman, D. and K. Hindle (2008), 'Would using the psychological contract increase entrepreneurial business development potential?', in R. Barrett and S. Mayson (eds), *International Handbook of Entrepreneurship and HRM*, Cheltenham, UK and Northampton, MA, USA: Edward Elgar Publishing, pp. 382–97.

Brush, C.G., T.S. Manolova and L.F. Edelman (2008), 'Properties of emerging organizations: An empirical test', *Journal of Business Venturing*, **23**(5), 547–66.

Busenitz, L.W. and C.-M. Lau (1996), 'A cross-cultural cognitive model of new venture creation', *Entrepreneurship Theory and Practice*, **20**(4), 25–40.

Busenitz, L.W., G.P. West III, D. Shepherd, T. Nelson, G.N. Chandler and A. Zacharakis (2003), 'Entrepreneurship research in emergence: Past trends and future directions', *Journal of Management*, **29**(3), 285–308.

Bygrave, W.D. and C.W. Hofer (1991), 'Theorizing about entrepreneurship', *Entrepreneurship Theory and Practice*, **16**(2), 13–22.

Capaldo, G. (1997), 'Entrepreneurship in southern Italy: Empirical evidence of business creation by young founders', *Journal of Small Business Management*, **35**(3), 86.

Carland, J.W. and J.A.C. Carland (2000), 'A new venture creation model', *Journal of Business and Entrepreneurship*, **12**(3), 29–48.

Carland, J.W., F. Hoy, W.R. Boulton and J.A.C. Carland (1984), 'Differentiating entrepreneurs from small business owners: A conceptualization', *Academy of Management Review*, **9**(2), 354–9.

Carter, N.M., W.B. Gartner and P.D. Reynolds (1996), 'Exploring start-up event sequences', *Journal of Business Venturing*, **11**(3), 151–66.

Choo, S. and M. Wong (2006), 'Entrepreneurial intention: Triggers and barriers to new venture creations in Singapore', *Singapore Management Review*, **28**(2), 47.

Chrisman, J.J. (1999), 'The influence of outsider-generated knowledge resources on venture creation', *Journal of Small Business Management*, **37**(4), 42–58.

Cooper, A.C. (1979), 'Strategic management: New ventures and small business', in D.E. Schendel and C.W. Hofer (eds), *Strategic Management: A New View of Business Policy and Planning*, Boston: Little, Brown, pp. 316–27.

Davidsson, P. (2004), *Researching Entrepreneurship*, New York: Springer.

Davidsson, P. and B. Honig (2003), 'The role of social and human capital among nascent entrepreneurs', *Journal of Business Venturing*, **18**(3), 301.

Davidsson, P., L. Lindmark and C. Olofsson (1994), 'New firm formation and regional development in Sweden', *Regional Studies*, **28**(4), 395–410.

Deakins, D. and M. Freel (2006), *Entrepreneurship and Small Firms*, Berkshire, UK: McGraw-Hill.

Dean, T.J. and G.D. Meyer (1996), 'Industry environments and new venture formations in U.S. manufacturing: A conceptual and empirical analysis of demand determinants', *Journal of Business Venturing*, **11**(2), 107.

Feldman, M.P. (2001), 'The entrepreneurial event revisited: Firm formation in a regional context', *Industrial and Corporate Change*, **10**(4), 861–91.

Finnerty, J.F. and A.T. Krzystofik (1985), 'Barriers to small business formation', *Journal of Small Business Management*, **23**(3), 50–58.

Forbes, D.P. (1999), 'Cognitive approaches to new venture creation', *International Journal of Management Reviews*, **1**(4), 415.

Freytag, A. and R. Thurik (2007), 'Entrepreneurship and its determinants in a cross-country setting', *Journal of Evolutionary Economics*, **17**(2), 117–31.

Gartner, W.B. (1985), 'A conceptual framework for describing the phenomenon of new venture creation', *Academy of Management Review*, **10**(4), 696.

Gartner, W.B. (1988), '"Who is an entrepreneur?" is the wrong question', *Entrepreneurship Theory and Practice*, **13**(4), 47–68.

Gartner, W.B. (1993), 'Words lead to deeds: Towards an organizational emergence vocabulary', *Journal of Business Venturing*, **8**(3), 231–9.

Gartner, W.B., T.R. Mitchell and K.H. Vesper (1989), 'A taxonomy of new business ventures', *Journal of Business Venturing*, **4**(3), 169–89.

Gatewood, E. (1993), 'The expectancies in public sector venture assistance', *Entrepreneurship Theory and Practice*, **17**(2), 91–5.

Gelderen, M. van, R. Thurik and N. Bosma (2005), 'Success and risk factors in the pre-startup phase', *Small Business Economics*, **24**(4), 365.

Gnyawali, D.R. and D. Fogel (1994), 'Environments for entrepreneurship development: Key dimensions and research implications', *Entrepreneurship Theory and Practice*, **18**(4), 43–62.

Greenberger, D.B. and D.L. Sexton (1988), 'An interactive model of new venture initiation', *Journal of Small Business Management*, **26**(3), 1–7.

Hansen, E.L. and K.R. Allen (1992), 'The creation corridor: Environmental load and pre-organization information-processing ability', *Entrepreneurship Theory and Practice*, **17**(1), 57–65.

Hatala, J.-P. (2005), 'Identifying barriers to self-employment: The development and validation of the barriers to entrepreneurship success tool', *Performance Improvement Quarterly*, **18**(4), 50–70.

Herron, L. and H.J. Sapienza (1992), 'The entrepreneur and the initiation of new venture launch activities', *Entrepreneurship Theory and Practice*, **17**(1), 49–55.

Hessels, J., M. van Gelderen and R. Thurik (2008), 'Entrepreneurial aspirations, motivations, and their drivers', *Small Business Economics*, **31**(3), 323–39.

Hindle, K. (2004), 'A practical strategy for discovering, evaluating and exploiting entrepreneurial opportunities: Research-based action guidelines', *Journal of Small Business and Entrepreneurship*, **17**(4), 267–76.

Hisrich, R. (1988), 'Entrepreneurship: Past, present and future', *Journal of Small Business Management*, **26**(4), 1–4.

Hisrich, R. and M. Drnovsek (2002), 'Entrepreneurship and small business research: A European perspective', *Journal of Small Business and Enterprise Development*, **9**(2), 172–222.

Hisrich, R., M. Peters and D. Shepherd (2005), *Entrepreneurship*, New York: McGraw-Hill Irwin.

Jin-ichiro, Y. (2004), 'A multi-dimensional view of entrepreneurship: Towards a research agenda on organisation emergence', *Journal of Management Development*, **23**(3/4), 289–320.

Katz, J.A. (1991), 'The institution and infrastructure of entrepreneurship', *Entrepreneurship Theory and Practice*, **15**(3), 85–102.

Katz, J.A. (2003), 'The chronology and intellectual trajectory of American entrepreneurship education 1876–1999', *Journal of Business Venturing*, **18**(2), 283–300.

Katz, J. and W.B. Gartner (1988), 'Properties of emerging organizations', *Academy of Management Review*, **13**(3), 429–41.

Keeble, D. and S. Walker (1994), 'New firms, small firms and dead firms: Spatial patterns and determinants in the United Kingdom', *Regional Studies*, **28**(4), 411–17.

Kirzner, I.M. (1982), 'The theory of entrepreneurship in economic growth', in C.A. Kent,

D.L. Sexton and K.H. Vesper (eds), *Encyclopedia of Entrepreneurship*, Englewood Cliffs, NJ: Prentice-Hall, pp. 272–6.

Klapper, L., L. Laeven and R. Rajan (2006), 'Entry regulation as a barrier to entrepreneurship', *Journal of Financial Economics*, **82**(3), 591–629.

Klyver, K. (2005), 'Entrepreneurship and social network development: A lifecycle approach', Ph.D. dissertation, Syddansk Universitet, Department of Entrepreneurship and Relationship Management, Kolding.

Kolvereid, L. and E. Isaksen (2006), 'New business start-up and subsequent entry into self-employment', *Journal of Business Venturing*, **21**(6), 866–85.

Kouriloff, M. (2000), 'Exploring perceptions of a priori barriers to entrepreneurship: A multidisciplinary approach', *Entrepreneurship Theory and Practice*, **25**(2), 59–79.

Krueger, N. (1993), 'The impact of prior entrepreneurial exposure on perceptions of new venture feasibility', *Entrepreneurship Theory and Practice*, **18**(1), 5–21.

Krueger, N.F. (2000), 'The cognitive infrastructure of opportunity emergence', *Entrepreneurship Theory and Practice*, **24**(3), 5–23.

Krueger Jr, N. (2003), 'The cognitive psychology of entrepreneurship', in Z.J. Acs and D.B. Audretsch (eds), *Handbook of Entrepreneurship Research: An Interdisciplinary Survey and Introduction*, Boston: Kluwer Academic, pp. 105–40.

Krueger, N.F. and A.L. Carsrud (1993), 'Entrepreneurial intentions: Applying the theory of planned behavior', *Entrepreneurship and Regional Development*, **5**(4), 315–30.

Krueger, N.F. and P.R. Dickson (1993), 'Self-efficacy and perceptions of opportunities and threats', *Psychological Reports*, **722**(3, pt. 2.), 1235–40.

Krueger, N.F. and D.V. Brazeal (1994), 'Entrepreneurial potential and potential entrepreneurs', *Entrepreneurship Theory and Practice*, **18**(3), 91–104.

Krueger, N. and P.R. Dickson (1994), 'How believing in ourselves increases risk taking: Perceived self-efficacy and opportunity', *Decision Sciences*, **25**(3), 385–400.

Krueger, N.F., M.D. Reilly and A.L. Carsrud (2000), 'Competing models of entrepreneurial intentions', *Journal of Business Venturing*, **15**(5/6), 411–32.

Kuratko, D. and R. Hodgetts (2001), *Entrepreneurship: A Contemporary Approach* (5th edn), Orlando, FL: Harcourt.

Learned, K.E. (1992), 'What happened before the organization? A model of organization formation', *Entrepreneurship Theory and Practice*, **17**(1), 39–48.

Lee, S.M. and S.J. Peterson (2000), 'Culture, entrepreneurial orientation, and global competitiveness', *Journal of World Business*, **35**(4), 401–16.

Lee, S.Y., R. Florida and Z.J. Acs (2004), 'Creativity and entrepreneurship: A regional analysis of new firm formation', *Regional Studies*, **38**(8), 879–91.

Liao, J. and H. Welsch (2003), 'Exploring the venture creation process: Evidences from tech and non-tech nascent entrepreneurs', in *Frontiers of Entrepreneurship Research, 2003: Proceedings of the 2003 Conference on Entrepreneurship at Babson College*, Wellesley, MA: Center for Entrepreneurial Studies, Babson College.

Liao, J., H. Welsch and W.L. Tan (2005), 'Venture gestation paths of nascent entrepreneurs: Exploring the temporal patterns', *Journal of High Technology Management Research*, **16**(1), 1–22.

Lichtenstein, B.B., N.M. Carter, K.J. Dooley and W.B. Gartner (2007), 'Complexity dynamics of nascent entrepreneurship', *Journal of Business Venturing*, **22**(2), 236–61.

Lin, Z., G. Picot and J. Compton (2000), 'The entry and exit dynamics of self-employment in Canada', *Small Business Economics*, **15**(2), 105–25.

Lopez, N. (1999), *Barriers to Entrepreneurship: How Government Undermines Economic Opportunity*, Lewisville, TX: Institute for Policy Innovation.

Low, M. (2001), 'The adolescence of entrepreneurship research: Specification of purpose', *Entrepreneurship Theory and Practice*, **25**(4), 17–26.

Low, M.B. and I.C. MacMillan (1988), 'Entrepreneurship: Past research and future challenges', *Journal of Management*, **14**(2), 139–61.

Malecki, E.J. (1990), 'New firm formation in the USA: Corporate structure, venture capital, and local environment', *Entrepreneurship and Regional Development*, **2**(3), 247–66.

Manning, K., S. Birley and D. Norburn (1989), 'Developing a new ventures strategy', *Entrepreneurship Theory and Practice*, **14**(1), 68–76.

Mazzarol, T., T. Volery, N. Doss and V. Thein (1999), 'Factors influencing small business start-ups: A comparison with previous research', *International Journal of Entrepreneurial Behaviour & Research*, **5**(2), 48–63.

McCarthy, A.M. and C.L. Nicholls-Nixon (2001), 'Fresh starts: Arnold Cooper on entrepreneurship and wealth creation', *Academy of Management Executive*, **15**(1), 27–36.

McClelland, D.C. (1961), *The Achieving Society*, New York: Van Nostrand.

Mintzberg, H. (1990), 'Strategy formation: Schools of thought', in J.W. Fredrickson (ed.), *Perspectives on Strategic Management*, New York: Harper & Row, pp. 105–235.

Mintzberg, H., B.W. Ahlstrand and J. Lampel (2005), *Strategy Safari: A Guided Tour through the Wilds of Strategic Management*, New York: Free Press.

Moroz, P. and K. Hindle (forthcoming), 'Entrepreneurship as a process: Toward harmonizing multiple perspectives', *Entrepreneurship Theory and Practice*.

Morris, M.H. and P.S. Lewis (1995), 'The determinants of entrepreneurial activity: Implications for marketing', *European Journal of Marketing*, **29**(7), 31–49.

Moyes, A. and P. Westhead (1990), 'Environments for new firm formation in Great Britain', *Regional Studies*, **24**(2), 123–36.

Mueller, P. (2006), 'Entrepreneurship in the region: Breeding ground for nascent entrepreneurs?', *Small Business Economics*, **27**(1), 41–58.

Neck, H.M., G.D. Meyer, B. Cohen and A.C. Corbett (2004), 'An entrepreneurial system view of new venture creation', *Journal of Small Business Management*, **42**(2), 190–208.

Parker, S.C. and Y. Belghitar (2006), 'What happens to nascent entrepreneurs? An econometric analysis of the PSED', *Small Business Economics*, **27**(1), 81–101.

Pennings, J.M. (1982), 'Organizational birth frequencies: An empirical investigation', *Administrative Science Quarterly*, **27**(1), 120–44.

Powell, J.D. and C.F. Bimmerle (1980), 'A model of entrepreneurship: Moving toward precision and complexity', *Journal of Small Business Management*, **18**(1), 33–6.

Reid, G.C. and J.A. Smith (2000), 'What makes a new business start-up successful?', *Small Business Economics*, **14**(3), 165–82.

Reynolds, P.D. (1997), 'Who starts new firms? Preliminary explorations of firms-in-gestation', *Small Business Economics*, **9**(5), 449–62.

Reynolds, P. and B. Miller (1992), 'New firm gestation: Conception, birth, and implications for research', *Journal of Business Venturing*, **7**(3), 405–17.

Reynolds, P., D.J. Storey and P. Westhead (1994), 'Cross-national comparisons of the variation in new firm formation rates', *Regional Studies*, **28**(4), 443–56.

Robertson, M., A. Collins, N. Medeira and J. Slater (2003), 'Barriers to start-up and their effect on aspirant entrepreneurs', *Education & Training*, **45**(6), 308–16.

Rotefoss, B. and L. Kolvereid (2005), 'Aspiring, nascent and fledgling entrepreneurs: An investigation of the business start-up process', *Entrepreneurship & Regional Development*, **17**(2), 109–27.

Sandberg, W.R. (1992), 'Strategic management's potential contributions to a theory of entrepreneurship', *Entrepreneurship Theory and Practice*, **16**(3), 73–90.

Sarasvathy, S.D. (2004), 'The questions we ask and the questions we care about: Reformulating some problems in entrepreneurship research', *Journal of Business Venturing*, **19**(5), 707–17.

Schendel, D.E. and C.W. Hofer (1979), *Strategic Management: A New View of Business Policy and Planning*, Boston: Little, Brown.

Schramm, C.J. (2005), 'Building entrepreneurial economies', *Transition Studies Review*, **12**(1), 163–71.

Sexton, D. (1988), 'Field of entrepreneurship: Is it growing or just getting bigger?', *Journal of Small Business Management*, **26**(1), 5–8.

Shane, S. (2001), 'Technological opportunities and new firm creation', *Management Science*, **47**(2), 205–20.

Shane, S. and S. Venkataraman (2000), 'The promise of entrepreneurship as a field of research', *Academy of Management Review*, **25**(1), 217–26.

Shaver, K.G. and L.R. Scott (1991), 'Person, process, choice: The psychology of new venture creation', *Entrepreneurship Theory and Practice*, **16**(2), 23–45.

Shepherd, D.A. and N.F. Krueger (2002), 'An intentions-based model of entrepreneurial teams' social cognition', *Entrepreneurship Theory and Practice*, **27**(2), 167–85.

Shook, C.L., R.L. Priem and J.E. McGee (2003), 'Venture creation and the enterprising individual: A review and synthesis', *Journal of Management*, **29**(3), 379–99.

Specht, P.H. (1993), 'Munificence and carrying capacity of the environment and organization formation', *Entrepreneurship Theory and Practice*, **17**(2), 77–86.

Sternberg, R. and S. Wennekers (2005), 'Determinants and effects of new business creation using global entrepreneurship monitor data', *Small Business Economics*, **24**(3), 193–203.

Todtling, F. and H. Wanzenbock (2003), 'Regional differences in structural characteristics of start-ups', *Entrepreneurship & Regional Development*, **15**(4), 351–70.

Tornikoski, E.T. and S.L. Newbert (2006), 'Exploring the determinants of organizational emergence: A legitimacy perspective', *Journal of Business Venturing*, **22**(2), 311–35.

Ucbasaran, D., P. Westhead and M. Wright (2001), 'The focus of entrepreneurial research: Contextual and process issues', *Entrepreneurship Theory and Practice*, **25**(4), 57–80.

VanderWerf, P.A. (1993), 'A model of venture creation in new industries', *Entrepreneurship Theory and Practice*, **17**(2), 39–47.

Vesper, K. (1980), *New Venture Strategies*, Englewood Cliffs, NJ: Prentice-Hall.

Vesper, K.H. (1990), *New Venture Strategies*, Englewood Cliffs, NJ: Prentice-Hall.

Volery, T., N. Doss and T. Mazzarol (1997), 'Triggers and barriers affecting entrepreneurial intentionality: The case of Western Australian nascent entrepreneurs', *Journal of Enterprising Culture*, **5**(3), 273–91.

Wagner, J. and R. Sternberg (2004), 'Start-up activities, individual characteristics, and the regional milieu: Lessons for entrepreneurship support policies from German micro data', *Annals of Regional Science*, **38**(2), 219–40.

Wennekers, A.R.M. (2006), *Entrepreneurship at Country Level: Economic and Non-Economic Determinants*, Rotterdam: RSM Erasmus University, Erasmus Research Institute of Management (ERIM).

Wennekers, S., L.M. Uhlaner and R. Thurik (2002), 'Entrepreneurship and its conditions: A macro perspective', *International Journal of Entrepreneurship Education*, **1**(1), 25–65.

Wortman Jr, M.S. (1987), 'Entrepreneurship: An integrating typology and evaluation of the empirical research in the field', *Journal of Management*, **13**(2), 259–79.

Zhang, Y. and J. Yang (2006), 'New venture creation: Evidence from an investigation into Chinese entrepreneurship', *Journal of Small Business and Enterprise Development*, **13**(2), 161–73.

3 Who's asking the right question? Patterns and diversity in the literature of new venture creation
Hans Landström and Fredrik Åström

INTRODUCTION

During the last 30 years, entrepreneurship has become one of the most popular fields of research in management studies, having grown more or less exponentially since the early 1990s. Although entrepreneurship research has a very long history – we can find early research with a focus on entrepreneurship as long ago as the eighteenth and nineteenth centuries – more systematic research emerged during the 1980s, not least among management scholars. Initially the research was dominated by an interest in searching for the entrepreneur as an individual and attempting to reveal his/her personality and traits. However, this research was strongly criticized and by the late 1980s there was a systematic shift in entrepreneurship research, from a focus on the entrepreneur as an individual towards the entrepreneurial process and behaviour.

One researcher played a very influential role in the above-mentioned shift. In his seminal article 'Who is the entrepreneur? is the wrong question' in 1988, William Gartner was one of the first to claim that entrepreneurship researchers ought to pay more attention to the behavioural aspects of entrepreneurship and in particular to the creation of new organizations. However, Gartner was not alone in his argumentation for a change of focus in entrepreneurship research. A similar line of reasoning was, for example, pursued by William Bygrave and Charles Hofer (1991), who stated that 'the entrepreneurial process involves all the functions, activities and actions associated with the perceiving of opportunities and the creation of organizations to pursue them' (p. 14). They argued that the entrepreneurial process could be characterized as an act of human volition involving a change of state and as a unique and dynamic process with numerous antecedent variables, where outcomes are extremely sensitive to the initial condition of these variables.

However, over the years, there has been no consensus among entrepreneurship scholars regarding what should form the focus of studies on the entrepreneurial process, and we can identify two different streams of interest in research: the emergence of new opportunities (what the editors of this book call the 'opportunity perspective') and the emergence of new organizations (what Hindle and Klyver term the 'emergence perspective').

- The main exponents of an approach that focuses on the emergence of opportunities are Sankaran Venkataraman and Scott Shane, who, inspired by Austrian economics, argued that entrepreneurship as a scholarly field should 'seek to understand how opportunities to bring into existence "future" goods and services are discovered, created, and exploited, by whom, and with what consequences' (Venkataraman 1997, p. 120; see also Shane and Venkataraman 2000).
- The chief exponent of an approach that focuses on the emergence of new organizations is perhaps William Gartner (1985, 1988, 1990, 1993), who talks about a process of organizational emergence. Gartner uses the 'organizational emergence' concept to illustrate how an organization manifests itself, i.e. the process that pre-dates the existence of the organization.

Since the early works of Gartner (and others), several scholars have focused on the question of how new ventures are created, and the research on new venture creation has become an important theme in entrepreneurship research in the 1990s and 2000s. In the present chapter we will elaborate on this development, with the aim of: 1) placing the research on new venture creation into the historical context of entrepreneurship research in general; 2) highlighting the pioneering studies of William Gartner in 1985 and 1988 and his contribution to the further development of the research area; and 3) describing the development and characteristics of the research on new venture creation as an area within entrepreneurship research.

It is always challenging to write a history of a research area. Many scholars have their own images of history, and history can be depicted from many different perspectives as well as focusing on various aspects of development. Therefore we strongly emphasize that this chapter reflects our view of the development of research on new venture creation – one history among many others.

In our search of a history of new venture creation research we performed a set of bibliometric analyses. We began by searching the Social Sciences Citation Index (SSCI) through the ISI Web of Science (WoS) topic field – covering titles, keywords and abstracts – for refereed academic publications on entrepreneurship[1] and new venture creation,[2] published between 1956 and 2007. The search on entrepreneurship research resulted in 14 901 articles citing 288 670 documents published between 1613 and 2007, of which 90 per cent dated from 1960 or later. The new venture creation search yielded 435 articles citing 14 359 documents from 1755 onwards. Using the SSCI has limitations: many of the journals that published entrepreneurial research in the early stages, as well as entrepreneurial research published in media other than peer-reviewed journals, are not included among the documents indexed in the SSCI. However, the cited reference field does not have such restrictions; thus all documents cited by the articles indexed in the SSCI are included, regardless of age or type of publication.

The result of the SSCI searches was downloaded for processing and analyses using Bibexcel software (Persson *et al.* 2009), which is able to extract data from fields in, for example, SSCI records and perform a wide variety of bibliometric analyses. For the purpose of this chapter, two basic kinds of analysis were performed: frequency analysis, examining the distribution of citations between cited documents; and co-occurrences of characteristics related to the articles, such as documents cited together.

In order to place the development of research on new venture creation in a historical context, the next section of this chapter will provide a brief overview of the emergence of entrepreneurship as a research field and relate the research on new venture creation to this broader development of the field. After this discussion we will focus on the work of William Gartner and his pioneering studies in 1985 and 1988. In addition we will discuss the development and characteristics of research on new venture creation as a sub-domain of entrepreneurship research, based on bibliometric analyses. Finally, some conclusions will be drawn regarding past, present and future research on new venture creation.

THE EMERGENCE OF ENTREPRENEURSHIP AS A RESEARCH FIELD

Emergence of Entrepreneurship Research – Three Eras of Entrepreneurship Thinking

Researchers within different disciplines have for a long time taken an interest in entrepreneurship, not least scholars in political economy and economics in the eighteenth and nineteenth centuries, represented by precursors such as Richard Cantillon, Jean-Baptiste Say and Alfred Marshall (see Figure 3.1).

Since these early contributions, the research field has become highly multi-disciplinary. At the risk of oversimplification we argue that three

Early contributions (France)	Classical economists (Britain)	Political economists (Germany)
Richard Cantillon 'The Physiocrats' (e.g. Quesnay, Baudeau and Turgot) Jean-Baptiste Say	Entrepreneurship was more or less neglected in classical economics, the exceptions being: Jeremy Bentham John Stuart Mill *Neoclassical economists:* Alfred Marshall	J.H. von Thünen Hans von Mangoldt Gottlieb Hufeland Friedrich Hermann Adolph Riedel

Figure 3.1   Early thinking on entrepreneurship

different eras of entrepreneurship research can be identified, during which some specific 'parent' disciplines were dominant.

1850–1940: economics era

At the beginning of the twentieth century there was an extensive discussion among economists concerning the phenomenon of entrepreneurship, even if it is difficult to identify a consensus that would enable us to talk about a 'theory' of entrepreneurship. A major figure in this development was of course Joseph Schumpeter, who recognized the role of innovation in economic growth and he understood that innovation had to be implemented by someone – the entrepreneur. The entrepreneur created imperfections and growth in the market by introducing innovation. However, in the course of the last half-century, it seems that entrepreneurship had been more or less overlooked in economic models. As a scientific discipline, economics seemed to focus mainly on equilibrium models, which constituted the dominant paradigm in the field and did not appear to leave any room for the entrepreneur.

1940–70: social science era

In the 1940s a number of economic historians and sociologists, partly inspired by Schumpeter, began to study entrepreneurship as an empirical historical phenomenon, with particular focus on the process of 'modernization' of societies around the world and the employment of theories of long-term economic development and historical change (Wadhwani and Jones 2007). However, by the 1960s this stream of research had lost momentum. Instead, social scientists became interested in the entrepreneur as an individual, and the works of psychologists started to investigate his/her key traits and personality. Two landmarks in this respect were David McClelland's study *The Achieving Society* (1961), in which he examined the achievement orientation in different societies over historical time, and Everett Hagen's *On the Theory of Social Change* (1962), a study on the historical emergence of innovation and technology in England, Japan, Colombia and Burma.

1970 onwards: management studies era

The 1960s and 1970s were characterized by great economic and political changes in society. It was a period of 'creative destruction' in which new technologies were gaining ground, changes were taking place in the industrial structure, questions were being raised about the efficiency of larger companies, attitudes toward entrepreneurship and small business were evolving ('Small is beautiful' became a catchphrase), and there was an increased political debate, supported by politicians such as Ronald Reagan in the USA and Margaret Thatcher in the UK. Against this background, entrepreneurship and industrial dynamics became a dominant theme in society. Many scholars from different fields of management studies rushed into this promising field of research. The development of entrepreneurship research since the 1980s can be described as three phases: 1) take-off; 2) growth; and 3) a search for maturation.

The take-off phase: pioneering studies on entrepreneurship   At first, the management scholars interested in entrepreneurship picked up where the social scientists had left off – searching for entrepreneurial traits and personalities. Over time, the research on the individual characteristics of the entrepreneur became the subject of criticism and regarded as a 'dead end' in entrepreneurship research. However, owing to the newness of the field and its lack of identity in terms of concepts, theories and methods, it was easy for researchers from different fields of management studies to carry out research on entrepreneurship without experiencing obvious deficits in competence (entrepreneurship was a 'low barriers to entry' field, in which researchers relied on concepts and theories anchored in their home field of research, thus making research on entrepreneurship more diversified); it was a question of discovering this 'new' phenomenon from many different angles. To illustrate the situation during the 1970s and 1980s, Churchill (1992) made an analogy to the story of the blind men and the elephant, where six blind men touched different parts of the elephant and gave quite different descriptions of its characteristics; thus in this relatively unstructured exploration of the 'elephant' the researchers discovered that the animal was different, composed of a number of rather unusual parts and that it was quite large.

It is obvious that this period was highly influenced by the early research on entrepreneurship, which was anchored in economics (e.g. Kirzner, Schumpeter and Knight) as well as the social sciences, i.e. contributions by economic historians, sociologists and social anthropologists (e.g.

Table 3.1   Most cited works in entrepreneurship research 1956 to 1989

Citations anchored in economics		Citations anchored in the social sciences	
No. cit.	Documents	No. cit.	Documents
28	Kirzner (1973)	83	McClelland (1961)
28	Kolakowski (1978)	28	Collins *et al.* (1964)
25	Schumpeter (1934)	27	Hagen (1962)
17	Knight (1921)	26	Chandler (1962)
16	Casson (1982)	17	Hirschmeier (1964)
		15	McClelland and Winter (1969)
		15	Bonacich and Modell (1980)
		15	Carroll (1965)
		14	Long and Roberts (1984)
		14	Smith (1967)
		14	Cochran and Reina (1962)
Citations anchored in management studies		Citations anchored in pioneering studies on entrepreneurship	
No. cit.	Documents	No. cit.	Documents
23	Drucker (1985)	29	Kilby (1971)
22	Burns and Stalker (1961)	20	Hornaday and Aboud (1971)
16	Porter (1980)	16	Storey (1982)
15	Kanter (1983)	14	Birch (1979)
14	Williamson (1975)	14	Miller (1983)
14	Peters and Waterman (1982)		

Source: Web of Science/Social Sciences Citation Index.

Chandler and Cochran) and psychologists studying the individual characteristics of the entrepreneur (e.g. McClelland, Collins *et al.* and Smith). In entrepreneurship research during the period from 1956 to 1989 we can also find citations of management scholars with an interest in entrepreneurship, innovation and corporate entrepreneurship such as Drucker, Burns and Stalker, and Kanter. Finally, some pioneering studies focusing on the specific characteristics of entrepreneurship and small businesses emerged among the most cited works at this point in time, for example by Kilby, Birch and Storey (see Table 3.1).

The growth phase: building an infrastructure and fragmented research   Since the early 1990s there has been an enormous growth in entrepreneurship research; and, when looking at the whole period 1956–2007, the growth is

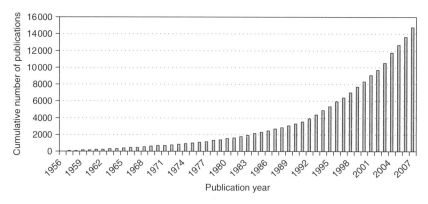

Source: Web of Science/Social Sciences Citation Index.

Figure 3.2   Growth of entrepreneurship research publications 1956–2007 – cumulative number of publications

almost exponential, much like how Price (1963) described the growth of science in general. A tentative comparison with management literature in general reveals a more linear development of management research over the whole period, whereas a comparison of the trends over the last 20 years reveals a similar pattern in both management and entrepreneurial research with a steady growth of the literature. The differences in development over the longer time span can most probably be explained by the earlier establishment of management research. This growth can be measured in various ways – the number of researchers, the number of published articles (see Figure 3.2), or the number of conferences and journals focusing on or opening up for entrepreneurship contributions – and is obvious, irrespective of the measurements employed.

The 1990s was to a very large extent characterized by the building of a strong infrastructure within the field, expressed in terms of an increase in the number of organized forums for communication between researchers (e.g. conferences and scientific journals), and role models (e.g. chairs in entrepreneurship), and an increase in undergraduate, Master's and Ph.D. programmes and courses in entrepreneurship. For example, at the start of the new millennium, Katz (2003) identified more than 2200 courses in entrepreneurship and small business in the USA, 277 endowed positions and 44 English language refereed academic journals.

The research on entrepreneurship was driven by an ambition for a complete understanding of the 'entire' phenomenon – to understand what this complex and heterogeneous phenomenon really looks like

– or what Davidsson (2008) calls 'phenomenon-driven research'. As a consequence, we can find an increased fragmentation of the field, with many parallel 'conversations', and the field was criticized for having little convergence and low knowledge accumulation. For example, Shane and Venkataraman (2000) argued that entrepreneurship research 'has become a broad label under which a "hodgepodge" of research is housed' (p. 217), Low (2001) spoke about a 'potpourri' of entrepreneurship research (pp. 20–21) and Zahra (2005) described entrepreneurship research as loosely connected and with a 'mosaic of issues to be explored' (p. 254).

One very important change that took place during the 1990s, which can more or less be regarded as a systematic shift in entrepreneurship research and of decisive importance for the argumentation in this chapter, was the decline in research on the entrepreneur as an individual, i.e. entrepreneurial traits, in favour of a focus on behavioural and process-related aspects of entrepreneurship. The research on psychological characteristics of the entrepreneur seemed to reach a 'dead end' on both conceptual and methodological grounds. The seminal works of William Gartner deserve to be mentioned in relation to this shift in interest. As early as 1988, Gartner claimed that 'Who is the entrepreneur? is the wrong question', arguing that a more relevant question was: How are new organizations created? (Gartner 1988). In a number of articles, Gartner (1990, 1993) stressed that entrepreneurship is about 'the creation of new organizations' (see similar reasoning by Bygrave and Hofer 1991). Despite the fact that the development towards a process-oriented approach has taken time, Gartner's ideas are now firmly anchored within entrepreneurship research.

A search for maturation: domain discussion and an increased theoretical interest As in many young research fields – in the same way as in many mature disciplines – there has been ongoing uncertainty about and debate on the central concepts used as well as the delimitation of entrepreneurship as a research field. The seminal article by Scott Shane and Sankaran Venkataraman (2000) triggered an intense debate regarding the domain of entrepreneurship research. On the one hand, proponents argue for developing entrepreneurship into a distinctive domain, i.e. a domain that predicts a set of empirical phenomena not explained in other fields of research, for example, newness, novelty and creation (Shane and Venkataraman 2000; Bruyat and Julien 2001; Busenitz *et al.* 2003). In this respect, a narrow domain focus permits scholars to compare and contrast studies but means that the field becomes less inclusive and the breadth of the topics studied more limited.

On the other hand, some researchers are less concerned with the distinctiveness of the domain, pursuing various research interests on innovation, family business, venture capital, etc. For example, Gartner (2001) argues that it is not possible to obtain a comprehensive theory of entrepreneurship – there is no overarching theory that can connect all the phenomena currently studied under the entrepreneurship umbrella or, as Gartner expresses it, 'there is no elephant in entrepreneurship' – as the various topics in entrepreneurship do not constitute a congruous whole. There is simply no theoretical way of connecting all these disparate research interests. As a consequence, scholars should actively divide into more homogeneous communities, and these communities would study more specific topic areas. Gartner *et al.* (2006) reveal that there seem to be a number of such distinct groups of scholars in the entrepreneurship field within topics such as venture capital, corporate entrepreneurship, 'the economists', strategic entrepreneurship and ethnic entrepreneurship (see also Brush *et al.* 2008). This suggests that there is an active dialogue going on around similar research interests, which supports Gartner's (2001) contention that the field of entrepreneurship may be evolving into informal homogeneous communities.

As a consequence, developing a theory of entrepreneurship is not possible. What we must search for is a diverse range of theories applicable to various kinds of phenomena (Gartner 2001) – the development of 'middle-range' theories that fall somewhere between grand theories and empirical findings and which attempt to understand and explain a limited aspect of the entrepreneurship phenomenon (Blackburn and Smallbone 2008). In this respect, we can identify an increased interest in the theoretical development of the field (Brush *et al.* 2008) – entrepreneurship researchers are to a lesser extent starting from what is going on 'out there', instead placing greater emphasis on testing theories that could help us understand the phenomenon of entrepreneurship (Davidsson 2008).

Entrepreneurship is a multi-disciplinary field, and entrepreneurship researchers borrow heavily from other fields of research. The use of various theoretical lenses may allow scholars not only to 'think outside the box' but also to 'create entirely new boxes' (Ireland and Webb 2007). According to Zahra (2005), importation of theories from other fields is a necessary first step towards developing unique theories that help us understand entrepreneurial phenomena. However, we need not only borrow from other fields but should invent our own concepts and theories – entrepreneurship research needs to make use of theories from other research fields as well as developing theories and models of its own that explain distinctive phenomena of entrepreneurship that theories from other disciplines cannot achieve (p. 256).

The Emergence of Entrepreneurship: Conclusions and Reflections

The emergence of entrepreneurship as a research field seems to follow much the same patterns as many other young research fields in the social sciences. This includes the development of the social structure of research expressed in terms of the characteristics of the research community (e.g. organized forums for communication between researchers, role models and ideals). It also includes the cognitive structure, which means a general delimitation of the object of study, and wide-ranging knowledge about the phenomenon as well as accepted methods and ways of reasoning.

In order to describe the cognitive structure of research fields, Hansson (1993) uses the concepts of 'technical' and 'theoretical' approaches to knowledge creation. Young research fields are characterized by a technical approach to knowledge creation. Research is closely linked to the development and problems identified in society, and the aim of the research is primarily to obtain knowledge that can be applied in practical situations. The focus is on the object of study – to gain knowledge about the phenomenon, not the theories and methods used. Because of the lack of any conceptual platform, the knowledge is nevertheless very fragmented and thus not cumulative. As a discipline develops, the research gradually becomes more specialized and assumes more complex nuances, at the same time as clearer definitions are being hammered out to provide building blocks for theory. The volume of research increases rapidly, in terms of, for example, the number of discoveries and publications and the size of the research community (Crane 1972). Moreover, the research becomes increasingly institutionalized, whereby an 'infrastructure' is established in the form of chairs, education programmes, research networks and institutes, etc. According to Hansson (1993), mature scientific research fields exhibit a strongly theoretical approach to knowledge, where immediate applicability is played down. The research is often more speculative, the aim being to move away from simple empirical descriptions. In mature research fields, the core literature is used by different researchers, each from his/her own perspective. The development of knowledge is cumulative in that together with the core literature a relatively limited number of publications constitute a common theoretical platform, which is successively enlarged.

Krohn and Küppers (1989) view the development of a social structure of sciences as a self-organized system. In this development the first phase is described as an increase in the cognitive beliefs among researchers that the phenomenon in focus is something important and interesting. In this phase researchers develop basic assumptions about the need for the research, the importance of the study object and ensuring a certain degree of continuity. These beliefs are then strengthened, i.e. a stabilization of the cognitive

	Take-off	Growth	Search for maturation
	1980s	1990s	2000s
Cognitive structure	Pioneering studies with strong linkages to the changes in society, and with the aim of 'discovering' this 'new' phenomenon.	Phenomenon-driven research with a vision of obtaining a complete understanding of the 'entire' phenomenon => fragmented research. Shift from a focus on the individual to a stronger process/behavioural approach to entrepreneurship research.	Domain discussion and stronger theoretical orientation.
Approaches to knowledge (Hansson 1993)	*Technical approach to knowledge*	⎯⎯⎯⎯⎯⟶	*Search for a theoretical understanding of the phenomena*
Social structure	Inflow of individual researchers from different fields of research.	Strong infrastructure building with an increase in organized forums for communication, education programmes and courses.	Specialization of research and emerging 'tribes' among scholars in entrepreneurship research.
Social dimension of research (Krohn and Küppers 1989)	*Cognitive beliefs*	*Stabilizing the cognitive belief*	*Search for an identity*

Figure 3.3   The development of entrepreneurship as a research field

belief takes place in that researchers start to show a liberalization from mainstream disciplines and an increasing tendency to regard themselves as belonging to the field. Finally, researchers within the field create an identity, i.e. a self-image with a body of consistently formulated values and beliefs as well as the development of an image derived from researchers in other fields.

Using the theoretical lenses of Hansson (1993) and Krohn and Küppers (1989) we can discuss and better understand the emergence of entrepreneurship as a research field (Figure 3.3).

The conclusion that can be drawn is that entrepreneurship has developed from a field with a strong technical approach to knowledge grounded in the changes that occurred in society during the 1970s and 1980s. In this respect there was a strong belief among the scholars who rushed into this new field of research that entrepreneurship was something important and interesting for society. At present, the field of entrepreneurship research seems to be caught between the efforts to overcome the drawbacks of newness and the need to achieve maturity. The research has become more theory-driven – researchers devote more attention to finding theories and models that can help us understand the phenomenon and are less occupied with descriptions of 'what is going on out there'. Entrepreneurship research also struggles to create an identity of its own. The struggle concerns the self-images of entrepreneurship researchers, which to a high extent relate to the cognitive development of the research field. For example, it is important to develop a 'cognitive style' including a professional language and concepts that play a 'boundary-establishing' role. However, it is equally essential to develop a 'social culture' within the field, which requires a regular and intensive forum for discussion. In this respect, the informal communication between researchers becomes of paramount importance, i.e. the creation of smaller 'research circles' in which consensus can be reached regarding the problems of interest, definitions, methodological approaches, etc. (Landström 2005). One such research circle may be associated with the research on new venture creation.

As has been demonstrated above, in the late 1980s and early 1990s we could identify a more or less systematic shift in entrepreneurship research, from a focus on the entrepreneur as an individual towards more process-related aspects of venture creation. In this respect the early works of William Gartner have been highly influential. Gartner has, over time, published an impressive number of articles on new venture creation. In his research, Gartner showed an interest in combining a strongly quantitative US research tradition in entrepreneurship (e.g. he was the co-founder of the Entrepreneurship Research Consortium, which initiated and developed the Panel Study of Entrepreneurial Dynamics) with the more qualitatively oriented research approach that can be found in Europe (e.g. he is currently collecting and analysing entrepreneurs' stories about their entrepreneurial adventures). In the next section we will meet William Gartner and present his pioneering works on new venture creation.

THE PIONEERING STUDY OF WILLIAM GARTNER

One of the first to claim that entrepreneurship researchers should devote more attention to the creation of new organizations was William (Bill)

Gartner. In his seminal article 'Who is the entrepreneur? is the wrong question' (1988), he argued that 'entrepreneurship is the creation of organizations' (p.11). What distinguishes entrepreneurs from non-entrepreneurs is that the former create organizations, while the latter do not. Gartner talks about a 'behavioural approach' in which entrepreneurship is seen as a set of activities involved in the creation of organizations, instead of the 'trait approach', where an entrepreneur is viewed as a set of personality traits and characteristics. The latter approach dominated entrepreneurship research during the 1970s and 1980s, and many different traits were identified, such as the need for achievement, locus of control, risk taking and values which differentiated entrepreneurs from non-entrepreneurs. In the article Gartner makes a strong case that the behavioural approach is a far more productive perspective for future entrepreneurship research, and his article can be considered a starting-point for the shift in entrepreneurship research from a focus on the entrepreneur to an increased interest in behavioural and process-related aspects.

The Article: 'Who Is the Entrepreneur? Is the Wrong Question' (1988)

Pre-history

A couple of years ago, Bill Gartner told the story of his difficulty in getting the article published (Gartner 2004; see also Gartner 2008). He published his thesis *An Empirical Model of the Business Startup, and Eight Entrepreneurial Archetypes* in 1982, the main purpose of which was to explore the effects of entrepreneurship training. As very few entrepreneurs had any entrepreneurship training, the purpose of the study changed somewhat, and Gartner decided to 'figure out' what was going on within the sample of 106 entrepreneurs who had completed an in-depth telephone interview as well as responding to a postal questionnaire. His analysis showed that the stories told by the entrepreneurs were very diverse – they had started ventures from all kinds of backgrounds, with a variety of business ideas, and their ways of starting a venture varied greatly. Using sophisticated statistical analysis, Gartner grouped the cases into eight clusters. However, in Gartner's mind there was always a sense that these 'archetypes' (influenced by Miller and Friesen 1978) were at best a compromise of all variety that could be found in the data – there was great heterogeneity among the entrepreneurs and the ways in which they had started their businesses.

The thesis formed the basis for a well-cited article by Gartner – the theoretical section of the thesis was published in the *Academy of Management Review* in 1985 ('A framework for describing the phenomenon of new venture creation'). The article provided a logical explanation for the way in which start-ups varied, i.e. entrepreneurs and entrepreneurship exhibited far more differences than similarities. Thus the new venture creation process is not a single well-worn route, and entrepreneurs and their ventures vary widely. The article provided a framework to facilitate an understanding of this variation in entrepreneurship – in entrepreneurs, their activities, the kinds of organizations they started and the contexts in which these activities took place – and the framework could thus be seen as a kaleidoscope for viewing the varying patterns of new venture creation.

As the 1985 article was accepted by the *Academy of Management Review*, Gartner had the impression that the journal accepted his perspective that 'entrepreneurship was about variation'. But, before his 1985 article was published, the *Academy of Management Review* published another article, written by Carland *et al.*, 'Differentiating entrepreneurs from small business owners: A conceptualization' (1984), which took a completely opposite view on entrepreneurship. In the article, the authors tried to differentiate between 'entrepreneurs' and 'small business owners' and took a strong trait approach position. Gartner was upset and decided to write a rebuttal, namely the article 'Who is an entrepreneur? is the wrong question', and duly submitted it to the *Academy of Management Review* on 31 July 1984. After the manuscript was 'revised and resubmitted' on five occasions it was finally rejected by the *Academy of Management Review* on 12 December 1986 (almost 2.5 years after its original submission date). The manuscript suffered the same fate with the *California Management Review*, the *Journal of Management* and the *Journal of Business Venturing*. Finally, it was sent to the *American Journal of Small Business* (later renamed *Entrepreneurship Theory and Practice*), where the reviewers rejected it but the editor of the journal took an opposite decision and published the article in 1988 (later the editorial board of the journal awarded the article 'Best Article of the Year').

The article
Gartner was not the first to ask 'How does an organization come into existence?' At the beginning of the nineteenth century, Jean-Baptiste Say viewed the entrepreneur as an economic agent who united all means of production – labour, capital and land – and thus placed the entrepreneur within the process of new venture creation. In modern times the question has been raised by, for example, Shapero and Sokol (1982), who argue that different kinds of entrepreneurial events trigger the creation of new ventures.

In the article, Gartner conducted a comprehensive review of entrepreneurship articles based on a trait approach. In particular, he highlighted the article by Carland *et al.* (1984) as an example of the strong focus in entrepreneurship research on 'if-we-can-just-find-out-who-the-entrepreneur-is-then-we'll-know-what-entrepreneurship-is' (Gartner 1988, p. 23). Gartner demonstrated that this approach was inadequate for explaining the phenomenon of entrepreneurship. He pointed out some critical aspects of this approach, for example the view that 'once an entrepreneur, always an entrepreneur' (since an entrepreneur is a personality type, a state of being that doesn't go away), although empirical evidence indicates that this is not the case. He also revealed that studies based on the trait approach seldom used the same definitions and employed heterogeneous samples. Not least, the results of these studies presented a startling number of often contradictory traits and characteristics attributed to the entrepreneur – indicating that entrepreneurs are some sort of generic 'everyman'. The conclusion was that 'Who is the entrepreneur?' is the wrong question in entrepreneurship research.

In the article, Gartner argued for the 'behavioural approach'; research on entrepreneurship should focus on what the entrepreneur does and not who he/she is. Gartner used a story to illustrate his point:

> What if the United States suddenly found itself unable to field a team of baseball players that could win in world competition? One response to such a problem might be to do research on baseball players to learn 'Who is a baseball player?', so that individuals with baseball playing propensity could be selected from the population. Such studies might determine that, on average, baseball players weigh 185 pounds, are six feet tall, and most of them can bench press over 250 pounds. We could probably develop a very good personality profile of the baseball player. Based on upbringing and experience we could document a baseball player's locus of control, need for achievement, tolerance of ambiguity, and other characteristics that we thought must make for good baseball playing. We could then recruit individuals with this set of characteristics and feel confident once again in our competitive edge. Yet, this type of research simply ignores the obvious – that is, the baseball player, in fact, plays baseball. Baseball involves a set of behaviours – running, pitching, throwing, catching, hitting, sliding, etc. – that baseball players exhibit. To be a baseball player means that an individual is behaving as a baseball player. A baseball player is not something one is, it is something one does. . . . How can we know the baseball player from the game? (Gartner 1988, pp. 22–3)

Entrepreneurs, like baseball players, are identified by a set of behaviours which link them to organization creation. To understand the phenomenon of entrepreneurship we need to focus on the process by which new organizations are created. A reorganization of research towards a behavioural approach begins by asking the question 'How do organizations come into existence?' The research needs to focus on what individuals do to enable organizations to come into existence, rather than on the traits and characteristics of these individuals.

Gartner's conclusion is that the creation of an organization is a complicated and intricate process, influenced by many factors, and the behavioural approach challenges us to develop research questions and methodologies that do justice to the complexity of entrepreneurship.

Gartner continued to argue that entrepreneurship is about the process of creating new ventures and that this process is characterized by a great heterogeneity – there is no one way of starting a business. For example, at the beginning of the 1990s, Gartner wrote an article 'What are we talking about when we talk about entrepreneurship?' (Gartner 1990), in which he argued that academics have a very diffuse view of entrepreneurship and what constitutes entrepreneurship as a phenomenon. Together with Nancy Carter, Kelly Shaver and Paul Reynolds, he has written several articles in order to contribute to the understanding of the diversity of the venture creation process (Gatewood *et al.* 1995; Carter *et al.* 1996, 2003).

Interview with Bill Gartner

How does Bill Gartner himself look upon his seminal studies in the 1980s and the research on new venture creation? In the interview below he elaborates on the development of the research area.

We have tried to present your seminal articles of 1985 and 1988, and interpreted them, but how would you describe the major ideas behind the articles?
The important part of what the 1985 article talks about was the issue of the heterogeneity of entrepreneurship. First of all, the problem with the English language is that we talk about *the* entrepreneur . . . we have a tendency to use the singular and talk about a particular kind of individual, rather than discussing entrepreneurs. Secondly, the phenomenon is much larger than an individual starting a business . . . actually, there are many kinds of people, many kinds of environments, many different ways of doing this and many different kinds of start-up.

I saw the framework as primarily saying that entrepreneurship is a heterogeneous phenomenon and as a reaction against the unidimensional view of entrepreneurship that was prevalent in research in the 1970s and 1980s, talking about *the* entrepreneur, *the* entrepreneurial firm, *the* entrepreneurial environment or *the* entrepreneurial process, and ignoring the heterogeneity and multilevel aspects of the phenomenon. It continuously surprises me that the heterogeneity issue is still ignored in entrepreneurship research.

The 1988 article was also a celebration of the heterogeneity of entrepreneurship, in particular that there are many kinds of entrepreneurs. Since reading the book by Collins, Moore and Unwalla (1964) on *The*

Enterprising Man it always troubled me that we could only find two types of entrepreneur, and my feeling was that this perspective was misguided: as a phenomenon, entrepreneurs as individuals are very heterogeneous. So, an important aspect of the article was to say that entrepreneurs are a very broad set of people – there are many different kinds of entrepreneurs. But the purpose of the article was also to demonstrate that the entrepreneurial process was heterogeneous as well – there are many different ways of starting a business – and my argument was that we might make more progress in research if we focused less on these individuals and who they are and devoted more attention to what they do . . . the behaviour, the process of entrepreneurship.

As I see it, the big contribution of both articles concerns the heterogeneity of the phenomenon, but this is frequently lost in the reading . . . researchers constantly misread my articles and fail to obtain an understanding of the heterogeneity of the phenomenon. In our society we have a tendency to disregard variation as an issue, but to me entrepreneurship is variation and it generates variation, and we need to have models in order to appreciate it.

It took some time for the articles to be acknowledged . . . what was the reaction from other scholars?
Looking back, the reactions from scholars within the field really surprised me. To my mind, the nature of scholarship requires a dialogue and you need to have advocates for certain ideas. I actually thought and expected that, after the 1988 article, there should be stronger argumentation in favour of the benefit of looking at the individual characteristics of the entrepreneur . . . saying here are the arguments for doing it and here is how we should lay out the research programme for the future in order to show its value. But what happened was that researchers read the article, understood it to mean that entrepreneurial traits are of no value and therefore we will only look at entrepreneurial behaviours, thus abandoning the entrepreneur as an individual.

That has now changed. We can see a reorientation, not least due to the opportunity–individual nexus framed by Shane and Venkataraman in their article in 2000. I think that we are reintroducing the value of the individual. The major problem is that scholars in entrepreneurship are not strong psychologists, or strong in the area of social psychology or organizational behaviour . . . we don't have enough entrepreneurship scholars with a strong disciplinary background who understand how we really should study individuals and how the entrepreneur fits into the environment. But the interesting thing is that this was what the 1985 and 1988 articles were really about . . . saying that individuals are important, but we need to account for the fact that there are many different kinds of entrepreneurs . . . there is variation in the phenomenon.

As you indicate, your articles at the end of the 1980s and early 1990s can in many ways be regarded as a starting-point for a stronger focus on the behavioural and process-related aspects of entrepreneurship as well as on the research on 'new venture creation'. In your view, what are the major achievements in the area of new venture creation since your seminal works?
Not many! The entrepreneurship field is primarily firm-level based and mainly studies what can be called 'liabilities of newness issues' rather than emergence and individual behaviour in relation to organizational formation. It has always surprised me that a field that celebrates new venture creation actually has very few scholars within the area . . . it is a small research community and people are interested in many different things – economic development, regional aspects, etc.

However, I would say that the Panel Study of Entrepreneurship Dynamics (PSED) as well as the Global Entrepreneurship Monitor (GEM) are outgrowths of this new venture creation tradition and both projects can be regarded as major achievements within the area . . . there are many interesting things coming from these projects.

If you were to recommend Ph.D. students to read a couple of works on new venture creation, what would your suggestions be?
In my opinion there are a couple of key works that need to be read:

1. The foundation text is Karl Vesper's book *New Venture Strategies* from 1980. I call him the Schumpeter of entrepreneurial behaviour and new venture creation in the sense that he was the one who first started to explore the issue of entrepreneurial behaviour – what people do when starting new businesses.
2. I have always felt that the article I wrote together with Jerome Katz 'Properties of emerging organizations' (1988) is at least a first attempt to really understand the emergence process. And the article by Carter, Reynolds and I in the *Journal of Business Venturing* in 1996 is an attempt to make empirical sense of the start-up event sequences.
3. I like everything from the PSED project related to entrepreneurial behaviour, for example, Paul Reynolds' [2007] exploration of the PSED in *Trends in Entrepreneurship*, which provides an overview of what the phenomenon is, from an empirically grounded perspective. Another behavioural aspect, from the PSED, is the business planning issue, for example the studies by Delmar and Shane (2003) and Davidsson and Honig (2003). Our recent article on complexity

and entrepreneurial behaviour seems to make a great deal of sense (Lichtenstein *et al.* 2007), as well.

So, what have we learned about new venture creation?

Honestly, we have learned very little. One reason is methodological concerns. For example, we have used very broad and crude ways of measuring the entrepreneurial processes, and we do not have a great deal of rich and detailed data on how people go about starting businesses over time – that is really a fundamental flaw in the area. However, there have been some interesting studies, and I will mention Andrew Van de Ven's set of studies on the innovation process (Van de Ven *et al.* 2000). The studies are very rich and contain a lot of venture creation knowledge. But in general we lack detailed longitudinal knowledge of how organization formation occurs over time, and the PSED data did not capture the process in a really fine-tuned way.

What you are saying is that we need other methodological approaches to capture the new venture creation process. In this respect, you are one of the advocates of linking European and American research traditions. Do we have anything to learn from the European research tradition?

Yes, I would say that the European tradition has greater respect for process-oriented research . . . greater respect for the kind of knowledge obtained in rich process studies . . . but also a tradition of what I will call 'multi-disciplinary perspectives' . . . appreciating the fact that even within a discipline there are multiple theoretical perspectives that could be applied to a problem.

In the European debate there is also a much stronger concern about the philosophy of science . . . how and why we know things . . . an appreciation that there are many different research approaches, not only a logical positivistic approach, and that these other approaches are just as valid and important as the positivistic approach to knowledge.

The tradition in the US is based more on a normal logical positivistic approach. I would say that the American tradition has power because there are many researchers playing the same game, and if you follow the rules of the game you can make a good career out of it. But you develop some form of interpretive problems . . . to understand the phenomenon of new venture creation you may need other approaches.

Looking back on my own career, you can say that narrative methodological approaches were emerging during the 1980s, and I had to make a choice between playing the quantitative logical positivistic game and using more narrative approaches in my research. My own fears about my career made me take the safe direction and employ more quantitative approaches. Today, having obtained tenure and some security in my career I can choose other methodological approaches.

On the subject of the career of young researchers in the area of new venture creation, what are the challenges that have to be met within the next five to ten years?

Based on my earlier argumentation, to obtain a more fine-tuned understanding of what is going on in the process of venture creation, we need intensive real-time process studies. This kind of study requires 'time'. In a new venture creation process there is often a long period when nothing really happens, but then some events suddenly occur that get the venture going . . . so the new venture creation process, from the conception of the idea to the reality of actually having an organizational form, may take two years. In the academic world that is a very long time to be involved in a research project, but that is really what is required . . . the phenomenon is actually a two-year phenomenon, at a minimum . . . maybe longer.

So, if you were to give some advice to a Ph.D. student who wanted to study the new venture creation process, what would that advice be?

I have struggled a great deal with this. Of course, the easy way is to continue to do what has been done previously and follow the footsteps of others, based on some of the old ideas and methodologies that we have seen for a long time. Actually, the easiest way is to go to the PSED database, which has a lot of data that have not been analysed, and use it to search for some interesting hypotheses to be tested . . . that would be a safe way and you would probably have a rather secure career.

On the other hand, there are scholars who have their own agenda. In the area of new venture creation I am fascinated by Saras Sarasvathy and her ideas about effectuation thinking. Her writing, not least in her book *Effectuation* (2008), does not have many attachments to the entrepreneurship field, per se, and most of her citations are made to a lot of dead people, Simon, Knight, Schumpeter, etc., rather than making connections through citations to scholars currently working in the entrepreneurship field. So what she is saying to the reader is that 'Either you come along and read my book, or not; it is up to you. If you come along, you have to make your own connections to my ideas about entrepreneurship.' This is very risky, but a brilliant way of moving the field forward.

NEW VENTURE CREATION AS A SUB-DOMAIN OF ENTREPRENEURSHIP RESEARCH

In this section we will discuss the development of new venture creation research during recent decades, using bibliometric analysis. Our discussion will be centred around the questions: is there any growth in the research on new venture creation, what do we mean when we talk about new venture creation, which are the most cited works on new venture creation and can they be said to form an intellectual base for the area?

Is There Any Growth in the Research on New Venture Creation? A Rather Small but Stable Area within Entrepreneurship Research

The influence of the article by Gartner was not instant – it took a while before the process-related aspects of entrepreneurship gained support, although it should be borne in mind that this was a period (the 1990s) during which the number of conversations in entrepreneurship research increased substantially and the research on entrepreneurship became very fragmented – many new conversations struggled for attention. A bibliometric analysis of the number of publications on new venture creation shows that the number of articles included in the WoS/SSCI increased from less than 6 per year between 1978 and 1994, to between 15 and 20 per year between 1995 and 2003 and to around 40 articles per year between 2004 and 2007.

Despite the fact that new venture creation can in many ways be regarded as a core theme of entrepreneurship, since the mid-1980s such research has only attracted a small, but stable, number of researchers (as evidenced in our interview with William Gartner). Moreover, the relative rate of publications on new venture creation within entrepreneurship research in general has been rather constant (see Figure 3.4). There has been a small increase in the relative proportion of publications on new venture creation, from about 2–3 per cent of entrepreneurship publications in general to 3–5 per cent from the mid-1990s. In this respect we need to bear in mind that the number of publications in entrepreneurship research in general has increased substantially over these years, which means that in absolute terms the number of publications on new venture creation has also increased.

What Do We Mean when We Talk about 'New Venture Creation'? Many Different Conversations within New Venture Creation Research

In order to obtain an overview of the concepts used in new venture creation research, we extracted keywords from the descriptor field in the SSCI

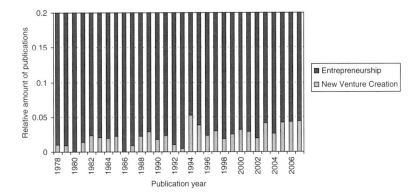

Figure 3.4   *Relative number of new venture creation publications in entrepreneurship documents/year in WoS/SSCI*

records, i.e. author-added keywords for the articles in our source data, and made a co-occurrence of keywords analysis (Whittaker 1989; Law and Whittaker 1992). The aim is to see whether a map based on keywords used in combination to describe the content of the articles reveals any structures in terms of similar concepts and research orientations appearing closely together, thus giving us an idea of the conceptual structure of new venture creation research.

A problem with author-added keywords is the lack of standardization and homogeneity of classification, as opposed to indexing terms from controlled lists. Therefore the list of keywords required processing before the analysis could take place, in order to deal with singular/plural forms of words (e.g. firm/firms) and more or less synonymous concepts such as firm/venture/business and start-up/formation/creation. Out of the standardized list of keywords, we selected the 38 that occur three or more times in the SSCI records. The keywords were organized into a symmetric co-occurrence matrix, showing how many times each of the selected keywords occurred together in the descriptor fields of the article records downloaded from the SSCI (Figure 3.5).

The co-occurrence frequencies are then used as proximity measures for a multi-dimensional scaling (MDS) analysis, transforming the multi-dimensional relations in the matrix to a two-dimensional graphic representation of these relations, where the MDS places those keywords that co-occur more frequently closer together, whereas those that less often occur together in individual SSCI article records are further away from each other (Figure 3.6). Since the MDS reduces the complexities of multi-dimensional relations into fewer dimensions, the two-dimensional representation contains some compromises. The extent to which the integrity of the

	A	B	C	D	E	F	G	H	I
1		biotechnol	business i	business s	capital stru	clusters	decision m	ECONOMI	EDUCATIC
2	biotechnol	0							
3	business i	0	0						
4	business s	0	0	0					
5	capital stru	1	0	0	0				
6	clusters	0	0	0	0	0			
7	decision m	0	0	1	0	0	0		
8	ECONOMI	0	0	0	0	0	0	0	
9	EDUCATIC	0	0	0	0	0	0	0	0
10	emergence	0	0	0	0	0	0	0	0
11	employme	0	0	0	0	0	0	1	1
12	entreprene	0	0	0	0	0	0	0	0
13	firm growth	0	0	0	0	0	0	0	0
14	gender	0	0	0	0	0	0	0	0
15	Global Ent	1	0	0	0	1	0	0	0
16	growth	0	0	0	0	0	0	0	0
17	human cap	1	0	0	0	1	0	0	0
18	innovation	0	0	0	0	0	0	0	0
19	joint ventur	1	0	0	0	0	0	0	0
20	knowledge	0	0	0	0	0	0	0	0

Figure 3.5   Example of the co-occurrence matrix

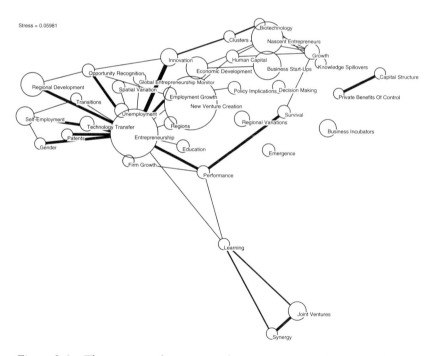

Figure 3.6   The conceptual structure of new venture creation research: co-occurrence map of keywords from SSCI descriptor fields

multi-dimensional data is compromised is measured by the stress value, a statistical value indicating how much the MDS has had to modify the original relations between units in the analysis in order to fit them into the map.

In addition to the links between the keywords, the frequencies of the keywords were used to permit the circle size to indicate how many times a specific keyword was employed to describe an article. At first glance, the map reveals a distinct structure with concepts grouped at the bottom, upper left and upper right; the stress value is low, indicating a close fit between the matrix and its graphic representation. However, when looking at the linked keywords, the topic relatedness is not immediate. As a result, and not least due to the high use of different concepts to describe the same or similar phenomena, there does not seem to be a distinct conceptual formation in the research. This indicates a research area that is fragmented, with many different discussions around new venture creation that employ various kinds of concepts in order to understand different aspects of the phenomena being analysed.

Which Are the Most Cited Works on New Venture Creation? A Changeable Area of Research

Table 3.2 presents the 28 most cited documents. As can be seen, Gartner's seminal article in the *Academy of Management Review* (1985) is top of the list, followed by the article by Shane and Venkataraman on 'The promise of entrepreneurship as a field of research' in the *Academy of Management Review* in 2000 and the special issue of *Regional Studies* on Regional Variations in New Firm Formation edited by Paul Reynolds, David Storey and Paul Westhead (1994).

We argue that many different discussions seem to occur in new venture creation research, and the list of the most cited works seems to verify this argument. Several research themes can be identified. One that has occupied the interest of researchers is the regional aspect of new venture creation, with works by Reynolds *et al.*, Keeble and Walker, Cross, Armington and Acs, Gudgin, and Audretsch and Fritsch. Another interesting theme seems to be what could be described as a small business economics approach, with a focus on the changes in the industrial structure and growth of society (e.g. works by Kihlstrom and Laffont 1979; Storey 1982; Evans and Jovanovic 1989; Evans and Leighton 1989). Thirdly, we can identify a group of researchers who focus on the entrepreneurial process and the behaviour of the entrepreneur such as Gartner, Katz and Gartner, Carter *et al.*, Reynolds and Miller, and Aldrich. Finally, for a long time the individual aspect of venture creation attracted a great deal of attention among researchers. Early works by McClelland (1961) are among the most cited

Table 3.2   The 28 most cited documents in new venture creation research

Citations	Document
58	Gartner (1985)
43	Shane and Venkataraman (2000)
39	Reynolds *et al.* (1994)
37	Schumpeter (1934)
35	Storey (1982)
32	Evans and Jovanovic (1989)
31	Busenitz and Barney (1997)
31	Keeble and Walker (1994)
31	Katz and Gartner (1988)
30	Evans and Leighton (1989)
29	McClelland (1961)
29	Carter *et al.* (1996)
29	Kihlstrom and Laffont (1979)
26	Gartner (1988)
25	Gatewood *et al.* (1995)
24	Baron (1998)
24	Shaver and Scott (1991)
24	Kirzner (1973)
24	Cross (1981)
23	Shane (2000)
23	Low and MacMillan (1988)
22	Armington and Acs (2002)
22	Aldrich (1999)
22	Reynolds and Miller (1992)
21	Simon *et al.* (2000)
20	Lucas (1978)
20	Gudgin (1978)
20	Audretsch and Fritsch (1994)

works with a focus on the entrepreneur as an individual, as are studies with a more modern approach, represented by, for example, Busenitz and Barney, Baron, Shane and Venkataraman, and Simon *et al.*

It is also interesting to note that the focus of research on new venture creation seems to have shifted over time (see Table 3.3) from a strong focus on regional aspects of new venture creation during the first period (1990–93) towards a stronger interest in the change in the industrial structure and the creation of new ventures in the economy (1994–97) and a broadening of the research in the final period (2002–05), including an interest in regional aspects as well as process-related and individual aspects of new venture creation.

Table 3.3   *Most cited documents in articles published in 1990–93,
1994–97, 1998–2001, 2002–05*

Period 1990–93		Period 1994–97	
No. cit.	Documents	No. cit.	Documents
4	Storey (1982)	13	Storey (1982)
4	Cross (1981)	9	Evans and Jovanovic (1989)
3	O'Farrell and Crouchley (1984)	9	Kihlstrom and Laffont (1979)
2	Gudgin and Fothergill (1984)	9	Schumpeter (1934)
2	Storey and Johnson (1987a)	9	Gartner (1985)
2	Moyes and Westhead (1990)	8	Knight (1921)
2	Hamilton (1989)	8	Acs and Audretsch (1989)
2	Beesley and Hamilton (1986)	7	Fritsch (1992)
2	Hofer and Schendel (1978)	7	Storey and Johnson (1987b)
2	Ansoff (1965)	6	Gudgin (1978)
Period 1998–2001		**Period 2002–05**	
No. cit.	Documents	No. cit.	Documents
10	Gartner (1985)	18	Reynolds *et al.* (1994)
9	Reynolds *et al.* (1994)	17	Shane and Venkataraman (2000)
9	Keeble and Walker (1994)	15	Gartner (1985)
7	Brockhaus (1980)	13	Busenitz and Barney (1997)
6	Beamish (1985)	13	Carter *et al.* (1996)
6	McClelland (1961)	12	Aldrich (1999)
6	Audretsch and Fritsch (1994)	12	Baron (1998)
6	Krueger (1993)	11	Katz and Gartner (1988)
5	Davidsson *et al.* (1994)	11	Schumpeter (1934)
5	Gartner (1988)	10	Armington and Acs (2002)

The impression of a changeable research area is further reinforced by the fact that few works appear to maintain their importance over time. Only the article by Gartner (1985) seems to be among the most cited works in three time periods (1994–97, 1998–2001 and 2002–05) and only three works appear in two periods (Schumpeter 1934; Storey 1982; Reynolds *et al.* 1994).

However, having argued that this is a fragmented and dynamic area of research, our analysis reveals an interesting tendency, albeit a very subtle indication of a more established knowledge base within the area, which could be based on the fact that: 1) the number of citations of the top-rated works for each period has increased (in the period 1990–93 it required only four citations for a top ranking whereas in 2002–05 18 citations were needed; and, following the same line of argumentation, 2) the most cited works on new venture creation (Table 3.2) are overrepresented during the period 2002–05.

We will not, at this point of the analysis, overemphasize the argument that supports the idea of a stronger knowledge base (we will elaborate on it in more detail in the next section), whereby 'key works' within the area become the basis for further research. However, the argument seems reasonable, based on the experiences from the development of research fields in general. In earlier periods of the development of a research field, citations are usually focused around the individual researcher's own research agenda – researchers take their starting-point in their own research interest and make citations to works that are close to their own research interests, which means that the citation patterns are very fragmented. In later periods, researchers take their point of departure from the developed knowledge base within the field and search for their own research interests.

Are There Any Intellectual Knowledge Bases within the Area? A Macro and Micro Knowledge Base

As new venture creation starts developing a knowledge base 'of its own', we can also begin to pose questions on the structures that can be found in the relations between the cited documents. One way of identifying research orientation structures is by using co-citation analyses (Marshakova 1973; Small 1973). The basic idea is to study documents occurring in the same reference lists – assuming that, since they are cited together, they have some kind of intellectual similarity in terms of subject matter – and the more often two documents are cited together, the stronger is the intellectual link between them. Thus, when looking at citation links between documents on an aggregated scale, we should be able to identify intellectual structures representing different research orientations within a research field. And, since the cited documents constitute the theoretical, methodological and/or empirical background of the citing articles, the aggregation of cited documents is assumed to form an intellectual knowledge base for the citing articles and the area of new venture creation research.

The co-citation analysis is basically performed in the same way as the keyword co-occurrence analysis in the 'What do we mean when we talk about "new venture creation"?' section of this chapter. However, instead of extracting keywords from the descriptor field, we extracted the cited references from the SSCI records and made the selection of cited documents for further analysis by ranking the references according to the number of times they have been cited and choosing the most frequently cited. Based

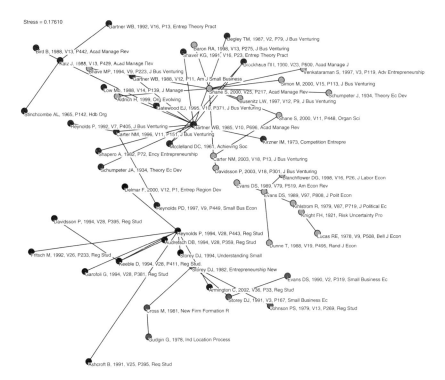

Figure 3.7   The research base of new venture creation research: co-citation analysis of the 52 most cited documents (15 citations or more) in new venture creation articles 1956–2007

on these, we created a symmetric co-citation matrix, which was visualized by the use of **MDS** analysis (Figure 3.7).

In the first results of the analysis, the representation in the map did not yield many clear structures, other than a tendency for micro-level new venture creation research to orient itself towards the upper half of the map, while research focusing on the macro level was found in the lower half, with many links connecting most documents. Furthermore, the stress value was relatively high, 0.176, while the threshold for what is generally accepted as a sound representation of data was 0.2 (McCain 1990), which emphasized the need for some caution when interpreting the relations between the various documents. To strengthen the existing structures and enhance the interpretation of the map, another analysis focusing on the strongest de facto citation relations was performed by means of a clustering routine suggested by Persson (1994). Instead of using co-cited pairs as the basis for the analysis, the clustering routine groups couples of co-cited pairs with at least one common unit. Thus, document pair A–B forms a cluster together with B–C, while the document pairs A–B and C–D do not. The result of the cluster analysis is presented in Table 3.4, and the strongest links forming the lines connecting the documents can be seen in Figure 3.7. The MDS analysis yields results with few clearly distinguishable structures and a high stress value. However, when removing the links formed by the co-cited pairs and retaining only the stronger links from the cluster analysis, we obtain a map with clearer structures and distinguishable groups of documents on both the horizontal and vertical axes which is also more statistically sound and reflects de facto citation relations.

Our co-citation analysis revealed five clusters focusing on various aspects of new venture creation, indicating some form of differentiated research orientation and different knowledge bases within the area.

- *Cluster 1:* This is the largest cluster and reflects new venture creation as a behavioural process and also includes the discussion raised by Gartner on the differences between the behavioural and the trait approach.
- *Cluster 2:* To some extent, Cluster 2 also has a process-related dimension but essentially presents a cognitive dimension of new venture creation with focus on the opportunity approach based on the works by Shane and Venkataraman.
- *Cluster 3:* This cluster could be labelled 'small business economics' and includes the early interest among economists in the entrepreneurs' decision to create new ventures and the entry of new ventures in different industries.
- *Cluster 4:* This cluster focuses on the regional aspects of venture creation, and almost all references are based on articles in the *Regional Studies Journal*, not least the special issue on Regional Variations in New Firm Formation, published in 1994.
- *Cluster 5:* This cluster focuses on new firm formation, employment growth and regional development. Several of the works originate from studies in the UK; thus it could be labelled a UK cluster.

The area of new venture creation research seems to be divided into two major research communities. In the analysis, the distinction between a micro-level approach (represented by the Cluster 1 'behavioural approach' and the Cluster 2 'opportunity approach') and a macro-level approach to new venture creation (Clusters 3, 4 and 5 representing small business economics and regional aspects of venture creation) is pronounced. Thus our interpretation is that there is some intellectual base within the area, focusing on a macro and micro level of analysis.

Table 3.4   Clusters of the research base on new venture creation

Cluster 1	Cluster 2	Cluster 3	Cluster 4	Cluster 5
Gartner (1985)	Shane and Venkataraman (2000)	Evans and Jovanovic (1989)	Reynolds *et al.* (1994)	Storey (1982)
Katz and Gartner (1988)	Shane (2000)	Kihlstrom and Laffont (1979)	Keeble and Walker (1994)	Cross (1981)
Carter *et al.* (1996)	Bhave (1994)	Evans and Leighton (1989)	Audretsch and Fritsch (1994)	Storey (1991)
McClelland (1961)	Busenitz and Barney (1997)	Blanchflower and Oswald (1998)	Davidsson *et al.* (1994)	Johnson and Cathcart (1979)
Brockhaus (1980)	Carter *et al.* (2003)	Dunne *et al.* (1988)	Delmar and Davidsson (2000)	Evans and Leighton (1990)
Begley and Boyd (1987)	Davidsson and Honig (2003)	Knight (1921)	Fritsch (1992)	Gudgin (1978)
Gartner *et al.* (1992)	Schumpeter (1934)	Lucas (1978)	Garofoli (1994)	
Gatewood *et al.* (1995)	Aldrich (1999)		Armington and Acs (2002)	
Gartner (1988)	Baron (1998)		Ashcroft *et al.* (1991)	
Kirzner (1973)	Simon *et al.* (2000)		Storey (1994)	
Low and MacMillan (1988)	Venkataraman (1997)			
Bird (1988)				
Reynolds and Miller (1992)				
Reynolds (1997)				
Schumpeter (1934)				
Shapero and Sokol (1982)				
Shaver and Scott (1991)				
Stinchcombe (1965)				

CONCLUSIONS – PAST, PRESENT AND FUTURE

Entrepreneurship research has a long history. Over time, the research has been grounded in different disciplines, and in this chapter we have divided the development of the field into three eras: economics (1850–1940), social science (1940–70) and management studies (1970 onwards). Research on entrepreneurship really took off in the 1970s and 1980s. It was initially dominated by an interest in tracing the characteristics of the entrepreneur as an individual. We have argued that there was a more or less systematic shift towards a focus on the entrepreneurial process and entrepreneurial behaviour, in which William Gartner played a central role as a pioneer and important advocate of the behavioural approach. In this chapter we have highlighted the contribution made by William Gartner.

Our bibliometric analyses indicate that research on new venture creation can be characterized as follows:

- It is a rather small but stable area within entrepreneurship research.
- Many different conversations are going on within the area of new venture creation research, using different concepts in order to understand the phenomenon.
- The research area seems to be changeable and dynamic in terms of the research topics in focus at different points in time.
- New venture creation appears to be anchored in two different knowledge bases, with a focus on micro and macro levels of analysis respectively.

The results of the bibliometric analyses for this literature are quite typical for many social sciences: the absence of formalized terminology makes it difficult to identify conceptual structures within the field; the citation analyses show a field where the knowledge base extends over a long period of time and is significantly influenced by other research fields. These characteristics can be considered signs of a fragmented and immature research field. Richard Whitley (2000) describes business and management studies as a 'fragmented adhocracy', i.e. a research field where the outcome of research is unpredictable, where the results are open to various interpretations and research is not typically produced to contribute to other scholars' research programmes but to broad and fluid intellectual goals. The heterogeneous nature of the field can to some extent be explained by the large variation in the locations at which the research is performed (from universities to consulting firms) and by whom it is funded, which results in different intellectual goals and performance criteria. These traits are often seen as a weakness; note for instance the critique on entrepreneurship research showing little convergence and low knowledge accumulation. And, pursuing Whitley's line of thought, Fuchs (1993) holds that fragmented adhocracies are, according to the organizational logic of the field, destined for further fragmentation. This is, however, not inevitable; studies of other fields sharing similar characteristics and also quite easily identifiable as fragmented adhocracies exhibit signs of convergence (Åström 2007).

An alternative point of view is to question the normative use of the word *fragmented* and whether the divergence of a field into different research themes and orientations is necessarily a sign of weakness. The idea of the sciences being cumulative is based on a model of research organization and scholarly communication emanating from the hard sciences where, for example, one builds on previous research to identify new strands of DNA, whereas studies of social phenomena are often dependent on contextual aspects and not bound in the same way by laws as, for example, physics. Thus phenomena in the social realm are more open to interpretation and can be understood from various perspectives. Furthermore, the understanding of science as cumulative and research fields as converging into a commonly accepted way of studying certain phenomena is strongly connected to a disciplinary-based organization of the sciences, whereas in many cases research is increasingly performed in an interdisciplinary setting with a strong focus on its applicability and cooperation – in terms of both co-authorship and research funding – with actors outside academia. This change in organization is particularly obvious in research since 1945 and has sometimes been labelled 'mode 2' research (Gibbons *et al.* 1994).

The above-mentioned development is most certainly visible in both entrepreneurship research generally and new venture creation research specifically, where there is a strong tie between research and professional practice and where the impact of various contexts (such as organizational cultures, national differences and types of businesses) is of great importance. Thus research cannot be assessed only by its contribution to the knowledge base of the research field or by scholars in the academic research field. Its contribution to professional practice and evaluation by other interested parties must also be taken into account.

NOTES

1. In the bibliometric analyses, 'entrepreneurship research' is defined in the following way: Web of Science/Social Science Citation Index using entrepreneur* OR 'small business*' OR 'small firm*' OR 'emerging business*' OR 'emerging firm*' OR 'new venture*' OR 'emerging venture*' OR 'founder OR founders'.
2. In the bibliometric analyses, 'new venture creation research' is defined in the following

way: Web of Science/Social Science Citation Index using 'new venture creation*' OR 'new firm formation*' OR 'venture emergence*' OR 'venture creation*' OR 'venture formation*' OR 'firm emergence*' OR 'firm creation*' OR 'firm formation*' OR 'organizational formation*' OR 'organizational creation*' OR 'organizational emergence*' OR 'creation of new enterprise*' OR 'creation of new firm*' OR 'creation of new venture*' OR 'creation of new organization*' OR 'nascent entrepreneur*' OR 'business start-up*'.

REFERENCES

Åström, F. (2007), 'Changes in the LIS research front: Time-sliced co-citation analyses of LIS journal articles, 1990–2004', *Journal of the American Society for Information Science and Technology*, **58**(7), 947–57.

Blackburn, R.A. and D. Smallbone (2008), 'Researching small firms and entrepreneurship in the U.K.: Developments and distinctiveness', *Entrepreneurship Theory and Practice*, **32**(2), 267–88.

Brush, C.G., T.S. Manolova and L.F. Edelman (2008), 'Separated by common language? Entrepreneurship research across the Atlantic', *Entrepreneurship Theory and Practice*, **32**(2), 249–66.

Bruyat, C. and P.A. Julian (2001), 'Defining the field of entrepreneurship', *Journal of Business Venturing*, **16**(2), 165–80.

Busenitz, L.W., G.P. West III, D. Shepherd, T. Nelson, G.N. Chandler and A. Zacharakis (2003), 'Entrepreneurship research in emergence: Past trends and future directions', *Journal of Management*, **29**(3), 285–308.

Bygrave, W.D. and C.W. Hofer (1991), 'Theorizing about entrepreneurship', *Entrepreneurship Theory and Practice*, **16**(2), 13–23.

Carland, J.W., F. Hoy, W.R. Boulton and J.C. Carland (1984), 'Differentiating entrepreneurs from small business owners: A conceptualization', *Academy of Management Review*, **9**(2), 354–9.

Carter, N.M., W.B. Gartner and P.D. Reynolds (1996), 'Exploring start-up event sequences', *Journal of Business Venturing*, **11**(3), 151–66.

Carter, N.M., W.B. Gartner, K.G. Shaver and E.J. Gatewood (2003), 'The career reasons of nascent entrepreneurs', *Journal of Business Venturing*, **18**(1), 13–39.

Churchill, N.C. (1992), 'Research issues in entrepreneurship', in D.L. Sexton and J.D. Kasarda (eds), *The State of the Art of Entrepreneurship*, Boston, MA: PWS-Kent Publishers, pp. 579–96.

Collins, O., D. Moore and D.B. Unwalla (1964), *The Enterprising Man*, East Lansing: Michigan State University.

Crane, D. (1972), *Invisible Colleagues: Diffusion of Knowledge in Scientific Communities*, Chicago: University of Chicago Press.

Davidsson, P. (2008), 'Looking back at 20 years of entrepreneurship research: What did we learn?', in H. Landström, H. Crijns, E. Laveren and D. Smallbone (eds), *Entrepreneurship, Sustainable Growth and Performance*, Cheltenham, UK and Northampton, MA, USA: Edward Elgar Publishing, pp. 13–26.

Davidsson, P. and B. Honig (2003), 'The role of social and human capital among nascent entrepreneurs', *Journal of Business Venturing*, **18**(3), 301–31.

Delmar, F. and S. Shane (2003), 'Does business planning facilitate the development of new ventures?', *Strategic Management Journal*, **24**(12), 1165–85.

Fuchs, S. (1993), 'A sociological theory of scientific change', *Social Forces*, **71**(4), 933–53.

Gartner, W.B. (1982), *An Empirical Model of the Business Startup, and Eight Entrepreneurial Archetypes*, Seattle: University of Washington.

Gartner, W.B. (1985), 'A framework for describing the phenomenon of new venture creation', *Academy of Management Review*, **10**(4), 696–706.

Gartner, W.B. (1988), 'Who is the entrepreneur? is the wrong question', *American Journal of Small Business*, **12**(4), 11–32.

Gartner, W.B. (1990), 'What are we talking about when we talk about entrepreneurship?', *Journal of Business Venturing*, **5**(1), 15–28.

Gartner, W.B. (1993), 'Words lead to deeds: Towards an organizational emergence vocabulary', *Journal of Business Venturing*, **8**(3), 231–9.

Gartner, W.B. (2001), 'Is there an elephant in entrepreneurship? Blind assumptions in theory development', *Entrepreneurship Theory and Practice*, **24**(4), 27–39.

Gartner, W.B. (2004), 'The edge defined the (w)hole: Saying what entrepreneurship is (not)', in D. Hjorth and C. Steyaert (eds), *Narrative and Discursive Approaches in Entrepreneurship*, Cheltenham, UK and Northampton, MA, USA: Edward Elgar Publishing, pp. 245–54.

Gartner, W.B. (2008), 'Variations in entrepreneurship', *Small Business Economics*, **31**, 351–61.

Gartner, W.B., P. Davidsson and S.A. Zahra (2006), 'Are you talking to me? The nature of community in entrepreneurship scholarship', *Entrepreneurship Theory and Practice*, **30**(3), 321–31.

Gatewood, E.J., K.G. Shaver and W.B. Gartner (1995), 'A longitudinal study of cognitive factors influencing start-up behaviors and success at venture creation', *Journal of Business Venturing*, **10**(5), 371–91.

Gibbons, M., C. Limoges, S. Schwartzman, H. Nowotny, M. Trow and P. Scott (1994), *The New Production of Scientific Knowledge: The Dynamics of Science and Research in Contemporary Society*, London: Sage.

Hagen, E. (1962), *On the Theory of Social Change: How Economic Growth Begins*, Homewood, Ill: Dorsey.

Hansson, B. (1993), *Vetenskapsfilosofi*, Lund: Filosofiska institutionen, Lunds Universitet.

Ireland, R.D. and J.W. Webb (2007), 'A cross-disciplinary exploration of entrepreneurship research', *Journal of Management*, **33**(6), 891–927.

Katz, J.A. (2003), 'The chronology and intellectual trajectory of American entrepreneurship education, 1876–1999', *Journal of Business Venturing*, **18**(2), 283–300.

Katz, J.A. and W.B. Gartner (1988), 'Properties of emerging organizations', *Academy of Management Review*, **13**(3), 429–41.

Krohn, W. and G. Küppers (1989), *Die Selbstorganisation der Wissenschaft*, Frankfurt: Suhrkamp.

Landström, H. (2005), *Pioneers in Entrepreneurship and Small Business Research*, New York: Springer.

Law, J. and J. Whittaker (1992), 'Mapping acidification research: A test of the co-word method', *Scientometrics*, **23**(3), 417–61.

Lichtenstein, B.B., N.M. Carter, K.J. Dooley and W.B. Gartner (2007), 'Complexity dynamics of nascent entrepreneurship', *Journal of Business Venturing*, **22**(2), 236–61.

Low, M.B. (2001), 'The adolescence of entrepreneurship research: Specification of purpose', *Entrepreneurship Theory and Practice*, **24**(4), 17–39.

Marshakova, I.V. (1973), 'A system of document connections based on references', *Scientific and Technical Information Serial of VINITI*, **6**, 3–8.

McCain, K.W. (1990), 'Mapping authors in intellectual space: A technical overview', *Journal of the American Society for Information Science*, **41**(6), 433–43.

McClelland, D.C. (1961), *The Achieving Society*, Princeton, NJ: Van Nostrand.

Miller, D. and P. Friesen (1978), 'Archetypes of strategy formulation', *Management Science*, **24**(9), 921–33.

Persson, O. (1994), 'The intellectual base and research fronts of JASIS 1986–1990', *Journal of the American Society for Information Science*, **45**(1), 31–8.

Persson, O., R. Danell and J.W. Schneider (2009), 'How to use Bibexcel for various types of bibliometric analysis', in F. Åström, R. Danell, B. Larsen and L.W. Schneider (eds), *Celebrating Scholarly Communication Studies: A Festschrift for Olle Persson at his 60th Birthday*, ISSI, pp. 9–24, available at http://www.issi-society.info/ollepersson60/ollepersson60.pdf (accessed 8 September 2009).

Price, D.J.D. (1963), *Little Science, Big Science*, New York: Columbia.

Reynolds, P.D. (2007), 'New firm creation in the United States: A PSED I overview', *Foundations and Trends in Entrepreneurship*, **3**(1).

Sarasvathy, S.D. (2008), *Effectuation: Elements of Entrepreneurial Expertise – New Horizons in Entrepreneurship*, Cheltenham, UK and Northampton, MA, USA: Edward Elgar Publishing.

Shane, S.A. and S. Venkataraman (2000), 'The promise of entrepreneurship as a field of research', *Academy of Management Review*, **25**(1), 217–26.

Shapero, A. and L. Sokol (1982), 'The social dimension of entrepreneurship', in C.A. Kent, D.L. Sexton and K.H. Vesper (eds), *The Encyclopedia of Entrepreneurship*, Englewood Cliffs, NJ: Prentice Hall, pp. 72–90.

Small, H. (1973), 'Co-citation in the scientific literature: A new measure of the relationship between two documents', *Journal of the American Society for Information Science and Technology*, **24**(4), 265–9.

Van de Ven, A.H., H.L. Angle and M.S. Poole (eds) (2000), *Research on the Management of Innovation: The Minnesota Studies*, New York: Oxford University Press.

Venkataraman, S. (1997), 'The distinctive domain of entrepreneurship research', in J.A. Katz (ed.), *Advances in Entrepreneurship, Firm Emergence and Growth*, Vol. 3, Oxford: Elsevier/JAI Press, pp. 119–38.

Vesper, K.H. (1980), *New Venture Strategies*, Englewood Cliffs, NJ: Prentice Hall.

Wadhwani, R.D. and G. Jones (2007), 'Schumpeter's plea: Historical methods in the study of entrepreneurship', paper presented at Babson-Kaufmann Entrepreneurship Conference, Madrid, 8–10 June.

Whitley, R. (2000), *The Intellectual and Social Organization of the Sciences*, Oxford: Oxford University Press.

Whittaker, J. (1989), 'Creativity and conformity in science: Titles, keywords, and co-word analysis', *Social Studies of Science*, **19**(3), 473–96.

Zahra, S.A. (2005), 'Entrepreneurship and disciplinary scholarship: Return to the fountainhead', in S.A. Alvarez, R. Agarwal and O. Sorenson (eds), *Handbook of Entrepreneurship Research: Interdisciplinary Perspectives*, New York: Springer, pp. 253–68.

REFERENCES DISPLAYED IN TABLES 3.1 TO 3.4

Acs, Z.J. and D.B. Audretsch (1989), 'Small-firm entry in the United States manufacturing', *Economica*, **56**(222), 255–65.

Aldrich, H.E. (1999), *Organizations Evolving*, Thousand Oaks, CA: Sage.

Ansoff, H.I. (1965), *Corporate Strategy*, New York: McGraw-Hill.

Armington, C. and Z.J. Acs (2002), 'The determinants of regional variation in new firm formation', *Regional Studies*, **36**(1), 33–45.

Ashcroft, B., J.H. Love and E. Malloy (1991), 'New firm formation in the British counties with a special reference to Scotland', *Regional Studies*, **25**(5), 395–409.

Audretsch, D.B. and M. Fritsch (1994), 'The geography of firm births in Germany', *Regional Studies*, **28**(4), 359–65.

Baron, R.A. (1998), 'Cognitive mechanisms in entrepreneurship: Why and when entrepreneurs think differently than other people', *Journal of Business Venturing*, **13**(4), 275–94.

Beamish, P.W. (1985), 'The characteristics of joint-ventures in developing and developed countries', *Columbia Journal of World Business*, **20**(3), 13–29.

Beesley, M.E. and R.T. Hamilton (1986), 'Births and deaths of manufacturing firms in the Scottish regions', *Regional Studies*, **20**(4), 281–8.

Begley, T.M. and D.P. Boyd (1987), 'Psychological characteristics associated with performance in entrepreneurial firms and smaller businesses', *Journal of Business Venturing*, **2**(1), 79–93.

Bhave, M.P. (1994), 'A process model of entrepreneurial venture creation', *Journal of Business Venturing*, **9**(2), 223–42.

Birch, D.L. (1979), *The Job Generation Process*, Cambridge, MA: MIT Program on Neighborhood and Regional Change.

Bird, B. (1988), 'Implementing entrepreneurial ideas: The case for intention', *Academy of Management Review*, **13**(3), 442–53.

Blanchflower, D.G. and A.J. Oswald (1998), 'What makes an entrepreneur?', *Journal of Labor Economics*, **16**(1), 26–60.

Bonacich, E. and J. Modell (1980), *The Ethnic Basis of Economic Solidarity*, Berkeley: California University Press.

Brockhaus, R.H. (1980), 'Risk taking propensity of entrepreneurs', *Academy of Management Journal*, **23**(3), 509–20.

Burns, T. and G.M. Stalker (1961), *The Management of Innovation*, London: Tavistock Publications.

Busenitz, L.W. and J.B. Barney (1997), 'Differences between entrepreneurs and managers in large organizations: Biases and heuristics in strategic decision-making', *Journal of Business Venturing*, **12**(1), 9–30.

Carroll, J.J. (1965), *The Filipino Manufacturing Entrepreneur: Agent and Product of Change*, Ithaca, NY: Cornell University Press.

Carter, N.M., W.B. Gartner and P.D. Reynolds (1996), 'Exploring start-up event sequences', *Journal of Business Venturing*, **11**(3), 151–66.

Carter, N.M., W.B. Gartner, K.G. Shaver and E.J. Gatewood (2003), 'The career reasons of nascent entrepreneurs', *Journal of Business Venturing*, **18**(1), 13–39.

Casson, M. (1982), *The Entrepreneur: An Economic Theory*, Oxford: Martin Robertson.

Chandler, A.D. (1962), *Strategy and Structure*, Cambridge, MA: MIT Press.

Cochran, T.C. and R.E. Reina (1962), *Entrepreneurship in Argentine Culture*, Philadelphia: University of Pennsylvania Press.

Collins, O., D. Moore and D.B. Unwalla (1964), *The Enterprising Man*, East Lansing: Michigan State University.

Cross, M. (1981), *New Firm Formation and Regional Development*, Farnborough: Gower.

Davidsson, P. and B. Honig (2003), 'The role of social and human capital among nascent entrepreneurs', *Journal of Business Venturing*, **18**(3), 301–31.

Davidsson, P., L. Lindmark and C. Olofsson (1994), 'New firm formation and regional development in Sweden', *Regional Studies*, **28**(4), 395–410.

Delmar, F. and P. Davidsson (2000), 'Where do they come from? Prevalence and characteristics of nascent entrepreneurs', *Entrepreneurship and Regional Development*, **12**(1), 1–23.

Drucker, P. (1985), *Innovation and Entrepreneurship*, New York: Harper & Row.

Dunne, T., L. Samuelson and M.J. Roberts (1988), 'Patterns of firm entry and exit in US manufacturing industries', *RAND Journal of Economics*, **19**(4), 495–515.

Evans, D.S. and B. Jovanovic (1989), 'An estimated model of entrepreneurial choice under liquidity constraints', *Journal of Political Economy*, **97**(4), 808–27.

Evans, D.S. and L.S. Leighton (1989), 'Some empirical aspects of entrepreneurship', *American Economic Review*, **79**(3), 519–35.

Evans, D.S. and L.S. Leighton (1990), 'Small business formation by unemployed and employed workers', *Small Business Economics*, **2**(4), 319–30.

Fritsch, M. (1992), 'Regional differences in new firm formation: Evidence from West Germany', *Regional Studies*, **26**(3), 233–41.

Garofoli, G. (1994), 'New firm formation and regional development: The Italian case', *Regional Studies*, **28**(4), 381–93.

Gartner, W.B. (1985), 'A framework for describing the phenomenon of new venture creation', *Academy of Management Review*, **10**(4), 696–706.

Gartner, W.B. (1988), 'Who is the entrepreneur? is the wrong question', *American Journal of Small Business*, **12**(4), 11–32.

Gartner, W.B., B.J. Bird and J.A. Starr (1992), 'Acting as if: Differentiating entrepreneurial from organizational behavior', *Entrepreneurship Theory and Practice*, **16**(3), 13–31.

Gatewood, E.J., K.G. Shaver and W.B. Gartner (1995), 'A longitudinal study of cognitive factors influencing start-up behaviors and success at venture creation', *Journal of Business Venturing*, **10**(5), 371–91.
Gudgin, G. (1978), *Industrial Location Processes and Regional Employment Growth*, London: Saxon House.
Gudgin, G. and S. Fothergill (1984), 'Geographical variation in the rate of formation of new manufacturing firms', *Regional Studies*, **18**(3), 203–206.
Hagen, E. (1962), *On the Theory of Social Change: How Economic Growth Begins*, Homewood, Ill: Dorsey.
Hamilton, R.T. (1989), 'Unemployment and business formation rates: Reconciling time series and cross section evidence', *Environmental Planning A*, **21**, 249–55.
Hirschmeier, J. (1964), *The Origins of Entrepreneurship in Meiji Japan*, Cambridge, MA: Harvard University Press.
Hofer, C.W. and D.E. Schendel (1978), *Strategy Formulation: Analytical Concepts*, St Paul, MN: West Publishing.
Hornaday, J.A. and J. Aboud (1971), 'Characteristics of successful entrepreneurs', *Personnel Psychology*, **24**(2), 141–53.
Johnson, P.S. and D.G. Cathcart (1979), 'New manufacturing firms and regional development: Some evidence from the Northern Regions', *Regional Studies*, **13**(3), 269–80.
Kanter, R.M. (1983), *Change Masters*, New York: Simon & Schuster.
Katz, J.A. and W.B. Gartner (1988), 'Properties of emerging organizations', *Academy of Management Review*, **13**(3), 429–41.
Keeble, D. and S. Walker (1994), 'New firms, small firms and dead firms: Spatial patterns and determinants in the United Kingdom', *Regional Studies*, **28**(4), 411–27.
Kihlstrom, R.E. and J.J. Laffont (1979), 'A general equilibrium entrepreneurial theory of firm formation based on risk aversion', *Journal of Political Economy*, **87**(4), 719–48.
Kilby, P. (ed.) (1971), *Entrepreneurship and Economic Development*, New York: Free Press.
Kirzner, I.M. (1973), *Competition and Entrepreneurship*, Chicago: University of Chicago Press.
Knight, F.H. (1921), *Risk, Uncertainty and Profit*, New York: Houghton Mifflin.
Kolakowski, L. (1978), *Main Currents of Marxism: Its Origins, Growth and Dissolution*, Oxford/New York: Oxford University Press.
Krueger, N. (1993), 'The impact of prior entrepreneurial exposure on perceptions of new venture feasibility and desirability', *Entrepreneurship Theory and Practice*, **18**(1), 5–21.
Long, N. and B. Roberts (1984), *Miners, Peasants and Entrepreneurs: Regional Development in the Central Highlands of Peru*, Cambridge: Cambridge University Press.
Low, M.B. and I.C. MacMillan (1988), 'Entrepreneurship, past research and future challenges', *Journal of Management*, **14**(2), 139–61.
Lucas, R.E. (1978), 'On the size distribution of business firms', *Bell Journal of Economics*, **9**(2), 508–23.
McClelland, D.C. (1961), *The Achieving Society*, Princeton, NJ: Van Nostrand.
McClelland, D.C. and D.G. Winter (1969), *Motivating Economic Achievement*, New York: Free Press.
Miller, D. (1983), 'The correlates of entrepreneurship in three types of firms', *Management Science*, **29**(7), 770–91.
Moyes, A. and P. Westhead (1990), 'Environments for new firm formation in Great Britain', *Regional Studies*, **24**(2), 123–36.
O'Farrell, P.N. and R. Crouchley (1984), 'An industrial and special analysis of new firm formation in Ireland', *Regional Studies*, **18**(3), 221–36.
Peters, T.J. and R.H. Waterman (1982), *In Search of Excellence*, New York: Harper & Row.
Porter, M.E. (1980), *Competitive Strategy*, New York: John Wiley.
Reynolds, P.D. (1997), 'Who starts new firms? Preliminary explorations of firms in gestation', *Small Business Economics*, **9**(5), 449–62.
Reynolds, P.D. and B. Miller (1992), 'New firm gestation: Conception, birth, and implications for research', *Journal of Business Venturing*, **7**(5), 405–17.

Reynolds, P.D., D.J. Storey and P. Westhead (1994), 'Cross-national comparisons of the variation in new firm formation rates', *Regional Studies*, **28**(4), 443–56.

Schumpeter, J.A. (1934), *The Theory of Economic Development*, Cambridge, MA: Harvard University Press.

Shane, S.A. (2000), 'Prior knowledge and the discovery of entrepreneurial opportunities', *Organization Science*, **11**(4), 448–69.

Shane, S.A. and S. Venkataraman (2000), 'The promise of entrepreneurship as a field of research', *Academy of Management Review*, **25**(1), 217–26.

Shapero, A. and L. Sokol (1982), 'The social dimension of entrepreneurship', in C.A. Kent, D.L. Sexton and K.H. Vesper (eds), *The Encyclopedia of Entrepreneurship*, Englewood Cliffs, NJ: Prentice Hall, pp. 72–90.

Shaver, K.G. and L.R. Scott (1991), 'Person, process, and choice: The psychology of new venture creation', *Entrepreneurship Theory and Practice*, **16**(2), 23–46.

Simon, M., S.M. Houghton and K. Aquino (2000), 'Cognitive biases, risk perception and venture formation: How individuals decide to start companies', *Journal of Business Venturing*, **15**(2), 113–34.

Smith, N.R. (1967), *The Entrepreneur and His Firm*, East Lansing: Michigan State University Press.

Stinchcombe, A.L. (1965), 'Organizations and social structure', in J.G. March (ed.), *Handbook of Organizations*, Chicago: Rand McNally, pp. 142–93.

Storey, D.J. (1982), *Entrepreneurship and the New Firm*, London: Routledge.

Storey, D.J. (1991), 'The birth of new firms – does unemployment matter? A review of the evidence', *Small Business Economics*, **3**(3), 167–78.

Storey, D.J. (1994), *Understanding the Small Business Sector*, London: Routledge.

Storey, D.J. and S. Johnson (1987a), *Job Generation and Labour Market Change*, Basingstoke, Hants.: Macmillan.

Storey, D.J. and S. Johnson (1987b), 'Regional variations in entrepreneurship in the UK', *Scottish Journal of Political Economy*, **34**(2), 161–73.

Venkataraman, S. (1997), 'The distinctive domain of entrepreneurship research', in J.A. Katz (ed.), *Advances in Entrepreneurship, Firm Emergence and Growth*, Oxford: Elsevier/ JAI Press, pp. 119–38.

Williamson, O.E. (1975), *Markets and Hierarchies*, New York: Free Press.

4 Re-imagining *The Achieving Society*
William B. Gartner

INTRODUCTION

In earlier work (Gartner 1985, 1988, 1989) I questioned the value of focusing on the traits or characteristics of entrepreneurs, primarily because of my initial empirical exploration of entrepreneurship that suggests that entrepreneurs, themselves, are very different from each other (Gartner *et al.* 1989). There is no one 'type' of entrepreneur, and there is no one particular set of characteristics that differentiate entrepreneurs from other types of individuals.

As I have suggested in previous articles (Gartner 1990, 1993, 2001; Gartner *et al.* 2006), the phenomenon of entrepreneurship covers a broad range of topics, meanings and definitions, so when I use the word 'entrepreneur' I am talking about individuals involved in the process of starting organizations. In this view, then, individuals are 'entrepreneurs' or are acting in an 'entrepreneurial' way when they are engaged in starting organizations. As in Schumpeter's view of these individuals, when people are engaged in entrepreneurial activities they are entrepreneurs, and when they are not engaged in entrepreneurial activities they are not entrepreneurs.

On a more fundamental level, I believe that the primary attributes of entrepreneurship can be acquired by all individuals. That is, these attributes are ways of thinking and behaving that entrepreneurs can learn, rather than characteristics that individuals either have or don't. If one assumes that the critical aspects of entrepreneurship can be acquired, then, testing for whether an individual has, at some point, the requisite skill (which was likely tested for after the experience of the entrepreneurial activity) simply doesn't make much sense (Gartner 1989). The characteristic that is being tested for would have likely been acquired during the experience itself. Since many studies of entrepreneurial characteristics explore correlations among variables rather than explore causality between the independent and dependent variables (which, from my point of view, would require that the independent variable data be collected at one point in time and then the dependent variable data be collected at a later point in time (Gartner 1989)), I find studies that compare and contrast differences between entrepreneurs and others to be of limited value. It should be noted that, while I have been involved in studies that compare entre-preneurs to others, for example Carter *et al.* (2003), these studies, such as this example, offer evidence that entrepreneurs, per se, are more similar to non-entrepreneurs, rather than being significantly different.

Given this point of view regarding the value of traits and character-istics, my interest in David McClelland's work on 'need for achieve-ment' has been ambivalent. While McClelland emphasized that 'need for achievement' can be learned and developed (McClelland 1961, 1965a, 1965b; McClelland and Winter 1969) the majority of research on need for achievement has tended to treat this construct as something that an individual has, rather than something that is acquired (Collins *et al.* 2004; Stewart and Roth 2007). While I cited McClelland's research early in my career, I realize that I have not thought much about his contributions to entrepreneurship scholarship until very recently.

My interest in re-reading McClelland's *The Achieving Society* stems from two concurrent influences. First, my recent 'epiphany' regarding the value of narrative as a way to inform a science of the imagination (Gartner 2007) has generated an interest in looking for prior scholarship that focuses on the imagination as it applies to entrepreneurship. I believe there is some value in viewing an aspect of entrepreneurial activity as that of imagining the future by offering plausible visions for what the future might be like vis-à-vis descriptions of possible business opportunities. As suggested in Gartner *et al.* (2003), the nature of opportunity is as varied as the nature of entrepreneurship itself. Opportunities can be 'objective reali-ties', social constructions, imagined futures, hopes, dreams or a glimmer in the distance (Gartner 1987). However an opportunity might be experi-enced, enacted, discovered or understood, there is still a requirement to engage in the development of that opportunity and, more specifically, to act 'as if' this opportunity will become something viable. Part of acting 'as if' in entrepreneurship (Gartner *et al.* 1992) involves imaging (seeing) what and how a business opportunity will exist in the future. While the study of narratives in entrepreneurship has tended towards retrospective stories (cf. *Journal of Business Venturing*, **22** (5)), there is much to be said for looking at whether stories that entrepreneurs tell about their futures subsequently affect the ability of these visions to become real (Martens *et al.* 2007).

Second, I had recently been asked to appear on a number of panels that focused on the role of entrepreneurship in furthering economic develop-ment. These panels were populated with economists and sociologists who have a significant body of knowledge to draw from regarding what factors tend to encourage entrepreneurship and, one would argue, eco-nomic development as well. Since I am not an economist or sociologist by training, I felt that my value would be in offering some other domain of knowledge that might also shed some light on factors that encourage entrepreneurship and economic development as well. McClelland's *The Achieving Society* called out to me from the bookshelf. My memory suggested that McClelland would have something to say about economic development from the perspective of psychology that would likely not be addressed by either the economists or the sociologists. In re-reading *The Achieving Society*, I found a perspective on entrepreneurship that I hadn't recognized in earlier readings.

THE ACHIEVING SOCIETY

David McClelland's *The Achieving Society* is a bold attempt to use a psychological perspective to understand the forces that drive economic development:

> It is important, therefore, to understand at the outset the simplicity of this book – what it can accomplish and what it cannot. What it does try to do is to isolate certain psychological factors and to demonstrate rigorously by quantitative scientific methods that these factors are *generally* important in economic development. (McClelland 1961, p. ix)

McClelland's fundamental view of economic development assumes that the primary forces that drive this phenomenon are likely to be exogenous to most economic models (McClelland 1961, p. 11). McClelland suggests that psychological and sociological explanations are necessary and that, based on prior theory and thought beginning with Weber, Parsons and others, the primary causal force in economic development is 'need for achievement'.

How McClelland elicits 'need for achievement' as this primary causal force of economic development is not, specifically, the construct that I had originally considered. I had remembered 'need for achievement' through the past 20 years of research on the construct, and had viewed 'need for achievement' as a characteristic that people, or societies, either had or didn't. 'Need for achievement' was, in most of these studies, identified through questionnaires. In *The Achieving Society*, 'need for achievement' is uncovered by having individuals write stories based on pictures they see:

> the stories represented short samples of the things people are most likely to think about or imagine when they are in a state of heightened motivation having to do with achievement. It may be worth considering for a moment why fantasy as a type of behavior has many advantages over any other type of behavior for sensitively reflecting the effect of motivational arousal. In fantasy anything is at least symbolically possible .. . . Overt action, on the other hand,

is much more constrained by limits set by reality or by the person's abilities. Furthermore, fantasy is more easily influenced than other kinds of behavior. (McClelland 1961, p. 40)

McClelland suggests that researchers can count the number of times that individuals offer achievement-related ideas in the stories they write as a way to identify whether these individuals possess high or low 'need for achievement' levels. A coding scheme for how achievement-related ideas are identified will be described later, but, suffice to say, for now the determination of 'need for achievement', in McClelland's work on 'need for achievement', begins with looking at stories.

For example, one of the first major arguments McClelland offers in *The Achieving Society* for the importance of 'need for achievement' in economic development comes from an analysis of children's stories collected in 40 different countries. McClelland and his colleagues collected a random sample of 21 stories from two different time periods (23 countries from the 1920s and 40 countries from the 1950s) and coded these stories for three motives: achievement, affiliation and power. After much discussion of how these stories in various countries are coded for reliability and validity, and with details offered about how economic growth in various countries might be compared, McClelland found that the levels of 'need for achievement' in stories written in the 1920s were significantly correlated to subsequent economic growth decades later (McClelland 1961, pp. 89–106). He offers an insight worth noting about how 'need for achievement' is described in these stories:

> Achievement is not only more frequently present in stories from more rapidly developing countries, but when it is present, it is more apt to be 'means' oriented. The achievement sequence more often dwells on obstacles to success and specific means of overcoming them, rather than on the goal itself, the desire for it, and the emotions surrounding attaining or failing to attain it. The adaptive quality of such concern with means is obvious: a people who *think* in terms of ways of overcoming obstacles would seem more likely to find ways of overcoming them in fact. At any rate that is precisely what happens: the 'means' oriented stories come from countries which have managed to overcome the obstacles to economic achievement more successfully than other countries. . . . These results serve to direct our attention as social scientists away from an exclusive concern with the external events in history to the 'internal' psychological concerns that in the long run determine what happens in history. (McClelland 1961, pp. 104–105)

It is plausible to suggest that McClelland's view of the 'internal' psychological concerns of individuals is based on stories: stories told to people (as in these children's stories) and the stories these people tell about themselves. Indeed, the value of telling stories that have 'need for achievement' characteristics may be the culminating gist of *The Achieving Society*. As McClelland summarizes various methods that might increase levels of 'need for achievement' in individuals, he suggests that 'One study suggests that the most effective way to increase *n* Achievement may be to try simply and directly to alter the nature of an individual's fantasies' (McClelland 1961, p. 417).

What I shall explore in more detail is the primary way that McClelland generated the stories that individuals provided for analyses of 'need for achievement': the Thematic Apperception Test (TAT).

THE THEMATIC APPERCEPTION TEST

The Thematic Apperception Test is a method for generating stories (Morgan and Murray 1935; Murray 1938, 1943). The word 'apperception' is critical to understanding the basis of the TAT. 'Apperception' is defined by James (1925, pp. 121–31) as follows:

> Educated as we already are, we never get an experience that remains for us completely nondescript: it always *reminds* of something similar in quality, or of some context that might have surrounded it before, and which it now in some way suggests. This mental escort which the mind supplies is drawn, of course, from the mind's ready-made stock. We *conceive* the impression in some definite way. We dispose of it according to our acquired possibilities, be they few or many, in the way of 'ideas.' This way of taking in the object is the process of apperception. The conceptions which meet and assimilate it are called by Herbart the 'apperceiving mass.' The apperceived impression is engulfed in this, and the result is a new field of consciousness, of which one part (and often a very small part) comes from the outer world, and another part (sometimes by far the largest) comes from the previous contents of the mind. (James 1925, p. 123)

Apperception, therefore, is 'providing meaning to what is perceived'. It is the 'meaning making' that is inherent to the process of perceiving. So it is assumed that a projective technique, such as the TAT, would generate meanings based on an individual's own beliefs and values when perceiving situations:

> based on the well recognized fact that when someone attempts to interpret a complex social situation he is apt to tell as much about himself as he is about the phenomenon on which his attention is focused. At such times, the person is off his guard, since he believes he is merely explaining objective occurrences. To one with 'double hearing', however, he is exposing certain inner forces and arrangements, wishes, fears and traces of past experiences. (Morgan and Murray 1935, p. 390)

The TAT process seeks to elicit stories from images that individuals are shown. In most uses of the TAT, researchers and clinicians look to see what apperceptions are generated from the stories that individuals create from their perceptions of the images they are shown. The stories, then, should be a reflection (consciously and unconsciously) of each individual's beliefs and values.

The way in which stories are generated is as follows. The TAT consists of 30 cards that depict various situations. Individuals are asked to make up stories for each of the cards they see. These are words that interviewers are asked to use to begin the TAT process:

> This is a test of imagination, one form of intelligence. I am going to show you some pictures, one at a time; and your task will be to make up as dramatic a story as you can for each. Tell what has led up to the event shown in the picture, describe what is happening at the moment, what the characters are feeling and thinking; and then give the outcome. Speak your thoughts as they come to your mind. Do you understand? Since you have fifty minutes for ten pictures, you can devote about five minutes to each story. Here is the first picture. (Murray 1943, p. 3)

The first card (Card 1), described as 'A young boy is contemplating a violin that rests on the table in front of him', is based on a photograph of Yehudi Menuhin taken by Samuel Lumiere at some point in the 1920s. A reproduction of the photograph upon which Card 1 is based is given in Figure 4.1. As part of the process of reading this chapter, please take five minutes to write a story based on the photograph.

Here are examples of five stories that were written by students about Card 1, after being given the instructions quoted above:

- *Story 1:* Tim doesn't know what to do. All of his friends are outside playing and having a good time. They invited him to play, but his mom said 'no'. He played it off to them and acted like it was all her fault he couldn't come outside. He practically convinced himself that she is the one to blame. She is 'mean' and inconsiderate, and it is all her fault. He would never tell his friends that really it is his fault why he can't come out and play. He was the one who asked for a violin for his birthday, and he is the one who promised he would practise every day. It is his fault that he wasted time this morning and didn't practise. He acts like he is mad at his mom and he has everyone, including himself, thinking that it is her fault. But really he is mad at himself. It is such a beautiful day outside.
- *Story 2:* Johnny was a small boy at the age of eight living in St Louis, Missouri. His father was a carpenter and his mother was a

YEHUDI
MENUHIN

A glimpse of the home life and training of the boy who is the foremost child musician in the world today

Figure 4.1   This photograph of Yehudi Menuhin by New York photographer Samuel Lumiere appeared in the January 1930 issue of the Parents' Magazine *to illustrate an article by Block (1930)*

school teacher. Growing up, Johnny's family never had a great deal of money. For Johnny's eighth birthday, his grandmother gave him her violin from her childhood. He was shocked by the gift because he had never expressed interest. She said he would learn and this would make him a better person. Over the next ten years Johnny took lessons and became a great violinist. It was when he got a job making great money to play that he began to appreciate the gift his grandmother gave him. This gift was the gift of persistence. His grandmother had given him persistence, patience and determination.

- *Story 3:* It is an hour after little Johnny comes home from school. His parents had recently enrolled him in an orchestra class and today was the first day of testing to determine what chair of the violin section he would be seated in. Little Johnny is frustrated and anxious about telling his parents he is third from last chair. His father was first chair violinist in the New York Symphony Orchestra and Johnny doesn't know how to fill such large shoes. He can hear the sound of the grandfather clock in the living room tick away every second until 6 o'clock. Every tick increases the anticipation of the disappointed look on his father's face. With the violin, bow and sheet music sitting in front of him at the kitchen table he debates whether to try and practise some before the dreaded moment.

- *Story 4:* There was once a little boy who desperately wanted to play the violin. He had heard a Mr Perlman playing the violin on the radio one evening; and since that night, all the boy wanted to do was play violin. Learning to play violin was no easy task and the boy often became frustrated. When this happened, he would set the violin down on the table. With his head at the violin; seemingly asking the violin why he couldn't play it. Eventually the boy honed his violin skills and is now the top symphony violinist in the world. He often thinks back to those times when he would sit and gaze at his violin.
- *Story 5:* One day a little boy decided he wanted to be like everyone else and play the violin. The boy was so excited about the first day of lessons with a violin instructor. When he went to the lessons that day he couldn't get over the pretty sound the instruments made. When he went into class, he took out his violin. The instructor began to show him how to make sound and played a few notes. The boy tried to repeat but couldn't get the hang of it. After lessons that day his mom picked him up and drove him home. When he got home he took his violin out and placed it on the table. His mom asked him to play what he learned, but all he could do was stare at the violin on the table. He wondered 'How could such a pretty instrument be so difficult to play?'

As an aside to these stories, Yehudi Menuhin was asked by W.G. Morgan about the picture, and Menuhin responded:

> Actually, I was gazing in my usual state of being half absent in my own world and half in the present. I have usually been able to 'retire' in this way. I was also thinking that my life was tied up in the instrument and would I do it justice? (Yehudi Menuhin, personal communication, 31 October 1993)

ACHIEVEMENT THEMES

What would constitute a story that has an achievement-related theme? Cramer (1996, p. 274) summarizes various scoring systems offered by McClelland (McClelland *et al.* 1953) and others (Smith 1992) in terms of the criteria for identifying 'need for achievement' as:

1. Competition with a standard of excellence.
   - Winning, or doing as well as or better than others, is actually stated as a primary concern.
   - If not actually stated, then affective concern over achievement (vis-à-vis others) is evident.

- The competition may be with a self-imposed standard of excellence, rather than with others.
2. Involvement with a unique accomplishment.
3. Involvement in attaining a long-term goal.

In looking at the five stories offered above, and in Menuhin's own TAT remembrance, see whether you can identify 'need for achievement' themes. My evaluation of these stories would suggest that stories 2 and 4 and Menuhin's remembrance have 'need for achievement' themes.

Would individuals who offered such 'need for achievement' themes in their stories be likely to seek to achieve in other aspects of their lives? Certainly the Menuhin remembrance reflects his actual achievements, and McClelland's work would suggest that individuals who do offer achievement-oriented themes in their stories are more likely to strive to achieve. So, by implication, is it possible that one might, as McClelland suggests, increase need for achievement: 'to try simply and directly to alter the nature of an individual's fantasies' (McClelland 1961, p. 417)?

IMPLICATIONS FOR ENTREPRENEURSHIP AND NEW VENTURE CREATION RESEARCH AND PRACTICE

As I indicated at the beginning of the chapter, my intention in re-examining McClelland's *The Achieving Society* was to look for ways to legitimize the value of stories and story telling as avenues to spark the entrepreneurial imagination and entrepreneurial action. I believe that it would be of value to look at the stories that entrepreneurs tell to explore what kinds of themes (i.e. achievement, power, etc.) might be embedded in them. Assuming that entrepreneurs offer apperceptions of their values and beliefs in the stories they offer, analyses of their stories might provide important insights into the meanings that entrepreneurs create during the creation of their businesses. I think that more attention should be given to the 'ways of worldmaking' (Goodman 1978) that entrepreneurs use both to account for their entrepreneurial creations (as retrospective sense making) and when proposing possible entrepreneurial futures (as in prospective sense giving). Ideally, it would be of great value to have longitudinal studies that captured the evolution of the entrepreneur's stories from a venture's initial vision to its fruition. Seeing how these stories change, and why they change, as the process of creation unfolds could offer critical insights into how entrepreneurs both shape and are shaped by their situations.

The exploration of apperceptive story telling in *The Achieving Society* has given me a deeper appreciation of research that has utilized prospective story telling to uncover insights into entrepreneurial thinking. I believe that Sarasvathy's research (Sarasvathy 2008, pp. 309–22) that asked expert entrepreneurs to speculate about how they would solve particular business problems (e.g. identifying and defining markets for a computer game, meeting payroll, financing, growing the company, exit) is as yet underappreciated for uncovering the ways that entrepreneurs engage their imaginations to create new possibilities. I hope that efforts are undertaken to explore differences between expert entrepreneurs and novice entrepreneurs in how they approach entrepreneurial endeavours. Many insights on the theory and empirical evidence of expertise can be gleaned from such sources as Ericsson *et al.* (2006) and applied to studies that might explore the development of entrepreneurial expertise.

CONCLUSIONS

I am not sure, yet, that my suggestion that 'need for achievement' is an act of the imagination relevant to new venture creation (among many other things) is fully developed as a coherent idea. I think a more thorough exploration of McClelland's research activities that utilized the TAT would generate a richer and more comprehensive understanding of the use of stories as a conduit for the 'need for achievement' construct. I hope to provide opportunities, for myself and others, for such an exploration to occur in the near future.

REFERENCES

Block, E.B. (1930), 'Yehudi Menuhin', *Parents' Magazine*, **5**(1), 17–50.
Carter, N.M., W.B. Gartner, K.G. Shaver and E.J. Gatewood (2003), 'The career reasons of nascent entrepreneurs', *Journal of Business Venturing*, **18**(1), 13–39.
Collins, C.J., P.J. Hanges and E.A. Locke (2004), 'The relationship of achievement motivation to entrepreneurial behavior: A meta-analysis', *Human Performance*, **17**(1), 95–117.
Cramer, P. (1996), *Storytelling, Narrative, and the Thematic Apperception Test*, New York: Guilford Press.
Ericsson, K.A., N. Charness, P.J. Feltovich and R.R. Hoffman (2006), *The Cambridge Handbook of Expertise and Expert Performance*, Cambridge: Cambridge University Press.
Gartner, W.B. (1985), 'A framework for describing and classifying the phenomenon of new venture creation', *Academy of Management Review*, **10**(4), 696–706.
Gartner, W.B. (1987), 'A pilgrim's progress', *New Management*, **4**(4), 4–7.
Gartner, W.B. (1988), 'Who is an entrepreneur? is the wrong question', *American Journal of Small Business*, **12**(4), 11–32.

Gartner, W.B. (1989), 'Some suggestions for research on entrepreneurial traits and characteristics', *Entrepreneurship Theory and Practice*, **14**(1), 27–38.

Gartner, W.B. (1990), 'What are we talking about when we talk about entrepreneurship?', *Journal of Business Venturing*, **5**(1), 15–28.

Gartner, W.B. (1993), 'Words lead to deeds: Towards an organizational emergence vocabulary', *Journal of Business Venturing*, **8**(3), 231–40.

Gartner, W.B. (2001), 'Is there an elephant in entrepreneurship? Blind assumptions in theory development', *Entrepreneurship Theory and Practice*, **25**(4), 27–39.

Gartner, W.B. (2007), 'Entrepreneurial narrative and a science of the imagination', *Journal of Business Venturing*, **22**(5), 613–27.

Gartner, W.B., T.R. Mitchell and K.H. Vesper (1989), 'A taxonomy of new business ventures', *Journal of Business Venturing*, **4**(3), 169–86.

Gartner, W.B., B.J. Bird and J. Starr (1992), 'Acting as if: Differentiating entrepreneurial from organizational behavior', *Entrepreneurship Theory and Practice*, **16**(3), 13–32.

Gartner, W.B., N.M. Carter and G.E. Hills (2003), 'The language of opportunity', in C. Steyaert and D. Hjorth (eds), *New Movements in Entrepreneurship*, Cheltenham, UK and Northampton, MA, USA: Edward Elgar Publishing, pp. 103–24.

Gartner, W.B., P. Davidsson and S.A. Zahra (2006), 'Are you talking to me? The nature of community in entrepreneurship scholarship', *Entrepreneurship Theory and Practice*, **30**(3), 321–31.

Goodman, N. (1978), *Ways of Worldmaking*, Indianapolis, IN: Hackett Publishing.

James, W. (1925), *Talks to Teachers: On Psychology and to Students on Some of Life's Ideals*, New York: Henry Holt.

Martens, M.L., J.E. Jennings and P.D. Jennings (2007), 'Do the stories they tell get them the money they need? The role of entrepreneurial narratives in resource acquisition', *Academy of Management Journal*, **50**(5), 1107–32.

McClelland, D.C. (1961), *The Achieving Society*, New York: Free Press.

McClelland, D.C. (1965a), 'Need achievement and entrepreneurship: A longitudinal study', *Journal of Personality and Social Psychology*, **1**(4), 690–702.

McClelland, D.C. (1965b), 'Toward a theory of motive acquisition', *American Psychologist*, **20**(5), 321–33.

McClelland, D.C. and D.G. Winter (1969), *Motivating Economic Achievement*, New York: Free Press.

McClelland, D.C., J.W. Atkinson, R.A. Clark and E.L. Lowell (1953), *The Achievement Motive*, New York: Appleton-Century-Crofts.

Morgan, C.D. and H.A. Murray (1935), 'A method for investigating fantasies: The Thematic Apperception Test', *Archives of Neurology and Psychiatry*, **34**, 289–306.

Murray, H.A. (1938), *Explorations in Personality*, New York: Oxford University Press.

Murray, H.A. (1943), *Thematic Apperception Test Manual*, Cambridge, MA: Harvard University Press.

Sarasvathy, S.D. (2008), *Effectuation: Elements of Entrepreneurial Expertise,* Cheltenham, UK and Northampton, MA, USA: Edward Elgar Publishing.

Smith, C.P. (ed.) (1992), *Motivation and Personality: Handbook of Thematic Content Analysis*, New York: Cambridge University Press.

Stewart, W.H. and P.L. Roth (2007), 'A meta-analysis of achievement motivation differences between entrepreneurs and managers', *Journal of Small Business Management*, **45**(4), 401–21.

PART II

THEORETICAL
PERSPECTIVES

5 Gender and new venture creation

Siri Terjesen, Amanda Elam and Candida G. Brush

INTRODUCTION

Entrepreneurship is recognized as a major driver of economic growth through innovation, industry dynamics, job creation and other effects. This chapter takes a broad approach to the definition of female entrepreneurship, incorporating Global Entrepreneurship Monitor (GEM) guidelines (Reynolds *et al.* 2005) that the individual is actively involved in starting or is currently an owner of a business, as well as definitions from Lavoie (1984–85, p. 34): 'head of a business who has taken the initiative of launching a new venture, who is accepting the associated risks and the financial, administrative, and social responsibilities, and who is effectively in charge of its day-to-day management', and Starr and Yudkin (1996): 'person who has played a significant management role in the start and building of the business and has held equity'.

Women play important roles in this entrepreneurial activity as creators, owners and managers of business ventures. For example, in the United States, women-owned firms with 50 per cent ownership number 10.4 million, employ 12.8 million people and generate $1.9 trillion in sales (Center for Women's Business Research 2008). However, many countries are not realizing their full entrepreneurial potential, owing to the lack of women creating and managing new business activities (Allen *et al.* 2008). A consistent finding in comparative population studies is that entrepreneurship is a predominantly male activity. As depicted in Figure 5.1, GEM's annual survey of start-up activity entrepreneurship reveals that women account for roughly one in three of the world's entrepreneurs, although the number has increased over the ten years of the GEM study (Allen *et al.* 2008).

Despite women's increased participation in entrepreneurial activities and the recognition of their economic contribution, women's entrepreneurship is vastly understudied (Brush 1992; Brush and Edelman 2000; Gatewood *et al.* 2003; Terjesen 2004; de Bruin *et al.* 2007). Taken together, these studies estimate that only 6–7 per cent of research published in the top eight entrepreneurship journals (since 1994) addresses female entrepreneurship topics.[1]

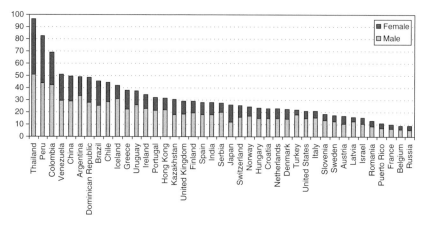

Source: GEM data, 2008.

Figure 5.1   Overall business ownership (nascent, new and established firms) by gender and country

In the entrepreneurship field, scholars have addressed progress and potential new research directions (Low and MacMillan 1988; Aldrich 1992; Aldrich and Baker 1997). Similar reviews occur in subfields, that is, strategy's dynamic capabilities (Zahra *et al.* 2006), international entrepreneurship (Rialp *et al.* 2005) and women's entrepreneurship (Carter *et al.* 2001; Gatewood *et al.* 2003; Terjesen 2004; Brush 2006; Fenwick 2008; Minniti 2009). Literature reviews are important in order to determine progress in the field.

Howard Aldrich (1992) offers three perspectives to assess the progress of entrepreneurship research. The first perspective follows unified or normal science, which views progress as having been achieved once there is a collection of well-grounded generalizations and hypotheses tested with rigorous quantitative data and statistical techniques (Kuhn 1970). Hypotheses help to test theories by replicating and confirming previous findings and working to achieve continuity (Aldrich and Baker 1997). A second important perspective involves a diversity of theories and methods with subgroups of entrepreneurship researchers in communities who employ varying methods and standards (Gartner 2001). A third perspective involves a pragmatic view in which the issues have a greater status than the methods as the researcher's purpose and conditions change. According to this thinking, a pursuit of uniqueness is more valuable than a pursuit of continuity (Mone and McKinley 1993) and might achieve practical relevance if investigations are phenomena driven, seeking to obtain results which have implications for education, practitioners or policy (Hoy 1997).

In keeping with the aims and philosophy of this volume, this chapter provides an overview of the 'state of the field' and the 'state of what could and should be' in research on gender and new ventures. Next, we present a 'state of the field' by topic, theory and statistical analysis, updating Brush's (1992) survey of female entrepreneurship. We comment on the female entrepreneurship field's progress with respect to Aldrich's (1992) three perspectives. The chapter concludes with suggestions for future theoretical, methodological and practical contributions to gender and venture creation research.

WHERE ARE WE NOW? EXTANT RESEARCH ON GENDER AND VENTURE CREATION

There are several recent literature reviews of female entrepreneurship. Table 5.1 provides a summary of eight leading literature reviews on gender and new venture creation. As it is outside the scope of this chapter to review all of the literature, interested readers are directed to these works. Generally, several assessments of women's entrepreneurship research have addressed the question of progress (Brush 1992; Greene *et al.* 2006). Some focused on the context and process of understanding women's entrepreneurship, while others examined different trends in the area, for instance assumptions in theory development (Ahl 2004), new perspectives (de Bruin *et al.* 2006), level of analysis (Brush 1992) and research design and construct measurement (Carter *et al.* 2001).

State of the Field

Candida Brush (1992) mapped the past, present and future of research on women business owners using a population of 57 articles published from 1977 to 1991 in the following categories: Gartner's (1985) new venture creation framework, research design, samples, theory bases and statistical analysis techniques. Based on her analysis, Brush developed an integrated view of women business owners and suggested promising avenues for future research. Brush's (1992) study is the most cited in the field of female entrepreneurship.[2]

This replication uses Brush's (1992) framework and, in so doing, enables an exploration of the purpose of research (Low 2001), assumptions in theory development (Gartner 2001), new perspectives (Aldrich and Martinez 2001), level of analysis (Davidsson and Wiklund 2001) and

Table 5.1   Recent literature reviews on female entrepreneurship

Authors	Topics
Carter *et al.* (2001)	Numbers and trends of women in business; International comparisons; Characteristics and motivations; Start-up patterns, resources and constraints; Management of female-owned firms; Finance and related issues; Gender and business networks; Performance and growth; Women and enterprise: popular literature; Internet sites for women entrepreneurs; Overview of websites for women entrepreneurs; Research and information gaps.
Gatewood *et al.* (2003)	Personal attributes (human capital, motivation); Business unit (founding strategies, initial resources, strategic choice, investment process and growth); Context (social networks, inhibiting factors, international studies, public policy issues); Feminist theory and sex roles (gender-based perceptions and stereotypes, social roles); Public policy (assistance programmes); Special topics; Secondary data analysis; Future research (human capital, strategic choice, structural barriers); Implications for educators.
Terjesen (2004)	Journals publishing research on women business owners; New venture classification; Theory; Methodology; Future directions.
Brush (2006)	Extent of research on women's entrepreneurship; Women's entrepreneurship: the phenomenon; Why are women entrepreneurs under-studied?; What have we learned about women entrepreneurs from academic research?; Conclusions and implications.
Greene *et al.* (2006)	Gender as variable: who is the woman entrepreneur? How do women entrepreneurs compare to men entrepreneurs? Gender as a lens: individual, businesses, growth and performance, financing, country context; Themes in the new millennium; Constructing new approaches: sex, gender and theory.
de Bruin *et al.* (2007)	Themes in women's entrepreneurship research; Approaches used in researching women's entrepreneurship: an overview; Methodological concerns regarding research on women's entrepreneurship; Advancing a theory of women's entrepreneurship; Concluding comments: toward an integrated framework.
Fenwick (2008)	Women business owners' characteristics and development; Women's motives for starting and leading a business; Barriers and conflicts encountered by women business owners; Considerations for future research.
Minniti (2009)	History of the field; Evidence on female entrepreneurship; Determinants of entrepreneurial behaviour at the individual level: objectively measurable variables, perceptions and subjective variables, social environment; Female entrepreneurship and the family; Gender gap in self-employment earnings; Female entrepreneurship and financing constraints; Female-owned businesses, female entrepreneurship and macroeconomic variables: where do we go next?

Table 5.2 Research on gender and new business creation by Gartner
*   (1985) classification type*

Classification	Number (1977–91)	Percentage (1977–91)	Number (1992–2008)	Percentage (1992–2008)
Individual	34	56	53	55
Environment	3	4	15	15
Organization	12	20	16	17
Process	12	20	13	13
Total	61	100	96	100

Sources: Brush (1992); Terjesen (2004); authors' research.

research design and construct measurement (Chandler and Lyon 2001). These criteria are particularly important in the study of women's entrepreneurship. The 1992–2008 replication focus was narrowed to publications in 'high-impact' journals. Furthermore, only those articles which mentioned a focus on female or women entrepreneurs or small business owners in the abstract are included, excluding research studies where gender was included only as a control variable. An initial set of articles (1992–2003) was identified using Proquest, EBSCO and other online article databases (Terjesen 2004). In December 2008, the search was expanded to 2003–08 publications, again using Proquest and EBSCO and also Google Scholar.[3] A total of 97 articles were identified in *American Economic Review, British Journal of Management, Entrepreneurship Theory and Practice, Journal of Business Ethics, Journal of Business Venturing, Journal of Small Business Management, Small Business Economics* and *Venture Capital*.

We follow Brush (1992) in mapping the studies to Gartner's (1985) four venture creation classifications: individual, environment, organization and process. Brush's mapping of 1977–91 research is captured in columns 1 and 2 of Table 5.2; columns 3 and 4 track 1992–2008 research.

As can be seen, recent female entrepreneurship scholarship continues to focus on the 'individual' aspect of entrepreneurship, including the entrepreneur's motivations (Buttner and Moore 1997; Mallon and Cohen 2001), career reasons (Carter *et al.* 2003) and education (Dolinsky *et al.* 1993). This may be partly due to gender being, at its core, an individual characteristic. Also, researchers may have been answering calls for a renewed focus on the individual at the heart of entrepreneurship (Bygrave 1993). Research on the environment explores issues related to the availability of financing in the form of bank loans (Buttner and Rosen 1992; Haynes and Haynes 1999) and venture capital (Greene *et al.* 2001). Organization-oriented research focuses on management and products

Table 5.3   *Research on gender and new business creation by stated theory base*

Stated theory base	Number (1977–91)	Percentage (1977–91)	Number (1992–2008)	Percentage (1992–2008)
None stated	22	39	28	29
Psychology theories (i.e. trait, psychoanalytic)	15	26	21	22
Sociology (i.e. network, social interaction)	10	17	28	29
Exploratory (i.e. grounded theory)	6	11	4	4
Business strategy and policy (i.e. problem solving, decision making)	4	7	16	16
Total	57	100	97	100

Sources: Brush (1992); Terjesen (2004); authors' research.

(Chaganti and Parasuraman 1997) and management practices and age (Fasci and Valdez 1998). Finally, process research examines issues such as the franchising process (Dant *et al.* 1996) and strategy decision making (Sonfield *et al.* 2001).

Stated Theory Base

Brush reported primarily psychology-based theoretical perspectives, particularly trait and psychoanalytic theories, with a recent uptake in sociology theory. Since 1991, researchers have continued to focus on psychology theories (Orser *et al.* 2000), but have also explored other sociology perspectives, such as social learning (Anna *et al.* 1999), relational (Buttner 2001), network (Cromie and Birley 1992) and social capital (Carter *et al.* 2003) theories. Still, many studies had no explicit theory base. The lack of theory may be a primary barrier to publication, as top journals often stipulate an interest in an explicit theoretical orientation and contribution. See Table 5.3.

Methodology

Brush examined statistical analysis techniques, finding that more than half of the articles published from 1977 to 1991 report only frequency distributions, though works in the final years of the review employ more robust methodologies.

Table 5.4   Research on gender and new business creation by statistical analysis techniques

Statistical analysis techniques	Number (1977–91)	Percentage (1977–91)	Number (1992–2008)	Percentage (1992–2008)
Descriptive statistics	25	44	15	17
Descriptive and chi-square, or correlation or t-test	17	30	16	19
Multiple regression, MANOVA, ANOVA, logit	7	12	43	49
Factor, cluster, discriminant analysis	4	7	6	6
Qualitative analysis	4	7	8	9
Total	57	100	88	100

Sources: Brush (1992); Terjesen (2004); authors' research.

An update utilizing Brush's (1992) methodology indicates that many researchers have moved on from the descriptive nature of past studies. While most articles began with descriptive statistics, many include more robust techniques such as analyses of variance and regressions. This trend reflects the general increase in quality of methodology in peer-reviewed journals and in entrepreneurship research. See Table 5.4.

With respect to Aldrich's (1992) three perspectives, what can be said of the progress of the field of entrepreneurship? First, concerning the unified science view of the accumulation of well-grounded generalizations and rigorously tested hypotheses, there appears to be some progress. As highlighted in Table 5.4, statistical techniques have become more sophisticated. While some female entrepreneurship studies draw on statistically generalizable samples (e.g. GEM's population-based research), most utilize convenience samples. As noted by Aldrich (1992), there is a bias against replication and confirmation and the publication of negative findings in social science and in entrepreneurship research, and this is also true for female entrepreneurship research. A recent review of 1046 articles published in the broad field of entrepreneurship research also indicates that there is progress on normal science dimensions (Edelman *et al.* 2009).

Second, progress in female entrepreneurship research can be considered with respect to the exploration reflecting a diversity of theory and methods. In this regard, the female entrepreneurship research has made progress with scholars exploring some new theories and methods. Two excellent methodological examples – albeit published in book form – are Ahl's (2004) discourse analysis and Bruni *et al.*'s (2005) ethnographies.

In her review, Fenwick (2008) criticized the field for an overfocus on individual psychological theories and a tendency to eschew new theories. As noted by Aldrich (1992), there is a paucity of ethnographies (Bruni *et al.* 2005 being an exception), lab experiments and computer simulations. Edelman *et al.* (2009) also found that entrepreneurship research broadly is highly methodologically diverse.

Finally, it is possible to examine female entrepreneurship research through a pragmatic lens. In this regard, recent research has explored issues considered important by stakeholders. These issues are not necessarily unique to women entrepreneurs, but may be critical for the broader population of all entrepreneurs.

WHERE CAN WE GO? PROMISING PATHS FOR FUTURE RESEARCH

Based on this summary of the literature and the assessment with respect to Aldrich's three perspectives, several promising directions for theoretical, methodological and practical directions for gender and new venture creation research can be suggested.

New Theories

First, with respect to new theories, there are possibilities to expand the diversity of theories, for example to include the following:

- *Institutional theory* describes how, in order to survive, firms must conform to certain cultural-cognitive, normative and regulative institutions (Scott 1995). Recently, scholars have developed an institution-based '5M' (markets, money, management, motherhood, meso/macro environment) framework to understand female entrepreneurship (Brush *et al.* 2009). Given the large variation in female entrepreneurial activity rates (GEM data), what institutions might be related to the establishment and growth of female-run firms? Are there certain institutions that drive entrepreneurial activity rates? Furthermore, do women's entrepreneurial activities lead to institutional changes?
- *Theory of practice* is concerned with 'entrepreneurship as practice', for example individuals pursuing entrepreneurial activities and the dual and complementary set of 'habitus' and 'field' which structure this activity (Honneth *et al.* 1986; Bourdieu 1998). Habitus refers to the dispositional 'mental structures' which are reproduced from

cognitive schema; field describes the relational 'world of objects' or network or configuration of four sets of capital: social, cultural, economic and symbolic. Elam (2008) outlines how females' strategic responses to local context, given personal social position and capital resources, enable an individual to maximize his/her legitimacy and convert this to other forms of capital. Key questions might include: What habitus and fields are related to certain types of female entrepreneurial activity rates? What types of capital do female entrepreneurs create and how?

- *Social capital, role status and social network theories* offer perspectives on the role of women's relationships to others. Women entrepreneurs have been said to have been disadvantaged through socialization processes (Fischer *et al.* 1993). Key questions might include: How do social networks influence women's paths from corporate to own ventures? Can social networks explain women's access to equity funding?
- *Social learning theory* (Bandura 1977) seeks to explain how people learn behaviour by observing others. If individuals observe positive, desired outcomes, they are more likely to model, imitate and adopt this behaviour. Key questions might include: In what ways are women influenced by male and female entrepreneurs? Are there certain observed behaviours which inhibit entrepreneurial activity?
- *Relational theory* describes how women's sense of self and personal development is shaped by relationships with others, particularly family members (Buttner 2001). Could relational theory explain women's choices regarding entrepreneurial aspirations, partners, timing, goals, industries and other key decisions?
- *Marxist feminism* is a type of feminist theory that describes how private property gives rise to economic inequality, dependence, political confusion and ultimately unhealthy social relations between men and women, and is at the root of women's oppression. Greer and Greene (2003, p. 19) call for Marxist feminism frameworks for examining: 'Are women entrepreneurs purposely limiting business size in an attempt to keep a viable balance between work and family obligations? Or are they held back from business expansion by family obligations and expectations? How do entrepreneurial men deal with the balance of work and family obligations and family expectations?'

New Data

With respect to the first and second viewpoints, it is possible to expand the repertoire of data available to rigorously test hypotheses. Currently, female entrepreneurship research is based on the following three data sources: self-employment and business ownership (national household surveys, OECD), new venture creation (GEM) and small firms (surveys and industry reports) (Parker 2009). There are many female entrepreneurship datasets in the public domain which have not been tapped. See Savych and Haviland (2005) and the Kauffman Foundation portal (http://research.kauffman.org) for a review of these. Furthermore, scholars should seek multiple dependent variables to develop a complete picture of the opportunity.

New (Qualitative) Methodologies

The first and second viewpoints could be further satisfied through the use of new qualitative methodologies. Most gender management research is positivist, based on datasets such as the above. Scholars could explore qualitative methods to unpack the context. For example, life history calendars (LHCs) are developed from archival data and interviews and are a useful means of facilitating respondents' memories of relevant and significant events (Freedman *et al.* 1988) and entrepreneurial careers. Action research describes the reflective process by which individuals work with others to address issues and solve problems. Action research in the entrepreneurship domain could take the form of working with large organizations and institutions (such as the United Nations, which is interested in developing female entrepreneurial capacity) to improve strategies, practice and knowledge through case studies and ethnographies. The new datasets and qualitative methods could easily be combined; for example, repertory grid interviews could elicit constructs which are then incorporated into a survey.

Focus on the Pragmatic

Finally, with regard to the third 'pragmatic' viewpoint, researchers could engage in conversations with entrepreneurs and policy makers about must-haves. A few promising future questions might include:

- *Venture capital:* As women constitute only 9 per cent of venture capitalists, key career-related questions surround the impact of the industry on women's introduction and development (or exit) and the impact of female venture capitalists on female entrepreneurs.
- *Business models:* What factors influence the development of business models by male and female entrepreneurs?
- *Growth aspirations:* Why is it that women aspire to smaller, slower-growing ventures?

- *Work–family balance:* What work and family conflicts impact women's entrepreneurial activity rates? What sets of activities can help to resolve these conflicts? What work–family balance factors might stimulate or thwart women's attempts to start and maintain high-growth firms?
- *Pedagogy:* What tools, conversations and other resources might female students need as they consider entrepreneurship?

Taken together, this roadmap of 'Where can we go from here?' shifts from traditional modes of research of female entrepreneurship and toward exploring complex dimensions and embracing women's perspective on enterprise. Further development of the field will expand our direct understanding of female entrepreneurship and entrepreneurship more generally.

ACKNOWLEDGEMENTS

We are grateful to the two editors for their invitation and to the anonymous reviewers for insightful comments.

NOTES

1. These top eight journals are *Entrepreneurship and Regional Development*, *Entrepreneurship Theory and Practice*, *Frontiers of Entrepreneurship Research*, *Journal of Business Venturing*, *Journal of Small Business Management*, *Journal of Small Business Strategy*, *Small Business Economics* and *Venture Capital*.
2. 480 citations as of 20 July 2009.
3. Thanks to Krishna Sankar for valuable research assistance.

REFERENCES

Ahl, H. (2004), *The Scientific Reproduction of Gender Inequality: A Discourse Analysis of Research Texts on Women's Entrepreneurship,* Copenhagen: Copenhagen Business School Press.
Aldrich, H. (1992), 'Methods in our madness? Trends in entrepreneurship research', in D.L. Sexton and J.D. Kasarda (eds), *The State of the Art in Entrepreneurship Research*, Boston: PWS-Kent, pp. 191–213.
Aldrich, H. and T. Baker (1997), 'Blinded by the cites? Has there been progress in entrepreneurship research?', in D.L. Sexton and R.W. Smilor (eds), *Entrepreneurship*, Chicago, IL: Upstart Publishing, pp. 377–400.
Aldrich, H.E. and M.A. Martinez (2001), 'Many are called, but few are chosen: An evolutionary perspective for the study of entrepreneurship', *Entrepreneurship Theory and Practice*, **25**(4), 41–56.

Allen, E., A.B. Elam, N. Langowitz and M. Dean (2008), *Global Entrepreneurship Monitor: 2007 Report on Women and Entrepreneurship*, Babson Park, MA: Babson College.

Anna, A.L., G.N. Chandler, E. Jansen and N.P. Mero (1999), 'Women business owners in traditional and non traditional industries', *Journal of Business Venturing*, **15**(3), 279–303.

Bandura, A. (1977), *Social Learning Theory*, New York: General Learning Press.

Bourdieu, P. (1998), *Practical Reason*, London: Polity Press.

Bruni, A., S. Gherardi and P. Poggio (2005), *Gender and Entrepreneurship: An Ethnographic Approach*, Abingdon, UK: Routledge.

Brush, C.G. (1992), 'Research on women business owners: Past trends, a new perspective and future directions', *Entrepreneurship Theory and Practice*, **16**(4), 5–30.

Brush, C.G. (2006), 'Women entrepreneurs: A research overview', in A. Basu, M. Casson, N. Wadeson and B. Yeung (eds), *The Oxford Handbook of Entrepreneurship*, Oxford: Oxford University Press, pp. 611–28.

Brush, C.G. and L. Edelman (2000), 'Women entrepreneurs: Opportunities for database research', in J. Katz and T. Lumpkin (eds), *Advances in Entrepreneurship, Firm Emergence and Growth: Research Databases in SME Research*, Greenwich, CT: JAI Press, pp. 445–84.

Brush, C.G., A. de Bruin and F. Welter (2009), 'A gender-aware framework for women's entrepreneurship', *International Journal of Gender and Entrepreneurship*, **1**(1), 8–24.

Buttner, E.H. (2001), 'Examining female entrepreneurs' management style: An application of a relational frame', *Journal of Business Ethics*, **29**(3), 253–70.

Buttner, E.H. and B. Rosen (1992), 'Rejection in the loan application process: Male and female entrepreneurs' reactions and subsequent intentions', *Journal of Small Business Management*, **30**(1), 58–66.

Buttner, E.H. and D.P. Moore (1997), 'Women's organizational exodus to entrepreneurship: Self reported motivations and correlates with success', *Journal of Small Business Management*, **35**(1), 34–46.

Bygrave, W.D. (1993), 'Theory building in the entrepreneurship paradigm', *Journal of Business Venturing*, **8**(3), 255–80.

Carter, N.M., W.B. Gartner, K.G. Shaver and E.J. Gatewood (2003), 'The career reasons of nascent entrepreneurs', *Journal of Business Venturing*, **18**(1), 13–39.

Carter, S., S. Anderson and E. Shaw (2001), *Women's Business Ownership: Review of Academic, Popular and Internet Literature*, Sheffield: Small Business Service.

Center for Women's Business Research (2008), *Top Facts about Women Owned Businesses*, Silver Spring, MD: Center for Women's Business Research.

Chaganti, R. and S. Parasuraman (1997), 'A study of the impact of gender on business performance and management patterns in small business', *Entrepreneurship Theory and Practice*, **21**(2), 73–5.

Chandler, G.N. and D.W. Lyon (2001), 'Issues of research design and construct measurement in entrepreneurship research: The past decade', *Entrepreneurship Theory and Practice*, **25**(4), 101–13.

Cromie, S. and S. Birley (1992), 'Networking by female business owners in Northern Ireland', *Journal of Business Venturing*, **7**(3), 237–51.

Dant, R.P., C. Brush and F.P. Iniesta (1996), 'Participation patterns of women in franchising', *Journal of Small Business Management*, **34**(2), 14–28.

Davidsson, P. and J. Wiklund (2001), 'Levels of analysis in entrepreneurship research: Current research practice and suggestions for the future', *Entrepreneurship Theory and Practice*, **25**(4), 81–100.

de Bruin, A., F. Welter and C.G. Brush (2006), 'Advancing cumulative knowledge on women's entrepreneurship', *Entrepreneurship Theory and Practice*, **31**(2), 1–25.

de Bruin, A., C.G. Brush and F. Welter (2007), 'Advancing a framework for coherent research on women's entrepreneurship', *Entrepreneurship Theory and Practice*, **31**(3), 323–39.

Dolinsky, A.L., R.K. Caputo, K. Pasumarty and H. Quazi (1993), 'The effects of education on business ownership: Longitudinal study of women', *Entrepreneurship Theory and Practice*, **18**(1), 43–53.

Edelman, L.F., T.S. Manolova and C.G. Brush (2009), 'Still blinded by the cites: Has there been progress in entrepreneurship research?', working paper presented at the Academy of Management.

Elam, A.B. (2008), *Gender and Entrepreneurship: A Multilevel Theory and Analysis*, Cheltenham, UK and Northampton, MA, USA: Edward Elgar Publishing.

Fasci, M.A. and J. Valdez (1998), 'A performance contrast of male- and female-owned small accounting practices', *Journal of Small Business Management*, **36**(3), 1–7.

Fenwick, T. (2008), *Women Entrepreneurs: A Critical Review of the Literature*, available at http://www.ualberta.ca/~tfenwick/ext/pubs/leaders.htm

Fischer, E.M., A.R. Reuber *et al.* (1993), 'A theoretical overview and extension of research on sex, gender, and entrepreneurship', *Journal of Business Venturing*, **8**(2), 151–68.

Freedman, D., A. Thornton, D. Camburn, D. Alwin and L. Young-DeMarco (1988), 'The life history calendar: A technique for collecting retrospective data', *Sociological Methodology*, **18**, 37–68.

Gartner, W.B. (1985), 'A conceptual framework for describing the phenomenon of new venture creation', *Academy of Management Review*, **10**(4), 696–706.

Gartner, W.B. (2001), 'Is there an elephant in entrepreneurship? Blind assumptions as theory development', *Entrepreneurship Theory and Practice*, **25**(4), 27–40.

Gatewood, E.J., N.M. Carter, C.G. Brush, P.G. Greene and M.M. Hart (2003), *Women Entrepreneurs, Their Ventures, and the Venture Capital Industry: An Annotated Bibliography*, Stockholm: ESBRI.

Greene, P.G., C.G. Brush, M. Hart and P. Saparito (2001), 'Patterns of venture capital funding: Is gender a factor?', *Venture Capital*, **3**(1), 63–83.

Greene, P.G., C.G. Brush and E.J. Gatewood (2006), 'Perspectives on women entrepreneurs: Past findings and new directions', in M. Minniti (ed.), *The Entrepreneurial Process*, Vol. 1, Praeger Perspectives Series, Westport, CT: Praeger Press.

Greer, M.J. and P.G. Greene (2003), 'Feminist theory and the study of entrepreneurship', in J.E. Butler (ed.), *New Perspectives on Women Entrepreneurs*, Greenwich, CT: Information Age Publishing.

Haynes, G.W. and D.C. Haynes (1999), 'The debt structure of small businesses owned by women in 1987 and 1993', *Journal of Small Business Management*, **37**(2), 1–19.

Honneth, A., H. Kocyba and B. Schwibs (1986), 'The struggle for symbolic order: An interview with Pierre Bourdieu', *Theory, Culture & Society*, **3**(3), 35–51.

Hoy, F. (1997), 'Relevance in entrepreneurship research', in D.L. Sexton and R.W. Smilor (eds), *Entrepreneurship 2000*, Chicago, IL: Upstart Publishing, pp. 361–76.

Kuhn, T. (1970), *The Structure of Scientific Revolutions*, Chicago, IL: University of Chicago Press.

Lavoie, D. (1984–85), 'A new era for female entrepreneurship in the 80s', *Journal of Small Business*, **2**(3), 34–43.

Low, M.B. (2001), 'The adolescence of entrepreneurship research: specification of purpose', *Entrepreneurship Theory and Practice*, **25**(4), 17–25.

Low, M.B. and I.C. MacMillan (1988), 'Entrepreneurship: Past research and future challenges', *Journal of Management*, **14**(2), 139–62.

Mallon, M. and L. Cohen (2001), 'Time for a change? Women's accounts of the move from organization careers to self employment', *British Journal of Management*, **12**(3), 217–30.

Minniti, M. (2009), 'Gender issues in entrepreneurship', *Foundations and Trends in Entrepreneurship*, **5**(7–8), 497–621.

Mone, M.A. and W. McKinley (1993), 'The uniqueness value and its consequences for organization studies', *Journal of Management Inquiry*, **2**(3), 284–96.

Orser, B.J., S. Hogarth-Scott and A.L. Riding (2000), 'Performance, firm size, and management problem solving', *Journal of Small Business Management*, **38**(4), 42–58.

Parker, S.C. (2009), *The Economics of Entrepreneurship*, New York: Cambridge University Press.

Reynolds, P., N. Bosma, E. Autio, S. Hunt, N.D. Bono and I. Servais (2005), 'Global

Entrepreneurship Monitor: Data collection design and implementation 1998–2003', *Small Business Economics*, **24**(3), 205–31.

Rialp, A., R. Rialp, D. Urbano and Y. Vaillant (2005), 'The born-global phenomenon: A comparative case study research', *Journal of International Entrepreneurship*, **3**(2), 133–71.

Savych, B. and A. Haviland (2005), 'A description and analysis of evolving data resources on small business', RAND Institute for Civil Justice, working paper.

Scott, W.R. (1995), *Institutions and Organizations*, Thousand Oaks, CA: Sage.

Sonfield, M., R. Lussier, J. Corman and M. McKinney (2001), 'Gender comparisons in strategic decision-making: An empirical analysis of the entrepreneurial strategy mix', *Journal of Small Business Management*, **39**(2), 165–73.

Starr, J.A. and M. Yudkin (1996), *Women Entrepreneurs: A Review of Current Research*, Wellesley, MA: Wellesley College, Center for Research on Women.

Terjesen, S. (2004), 'Female business owners: A review of the last decade of research', Academy of Management meeting.

Zahra, S.A., H.J. Sapienza and P. Davidsson (2006), 'Entrepreneurship and dynamic capabilities: A review, model and research agenda', *Journal of Management Studies*, **43**(4), 917–55.

6. Transgressive knowledge creation in entrepreneurship
Deborah Blackman and Miguel Imas

INTRODUCTION

In Chapter 3 Hans Landström and Fredrik Åström included a close examination of the seminal work of the doyen of new venture creation researchers, William Gartner, and his strong belief that the creation of an organization is a complicated and intricate process, influenced by many factors, which challenges us to develop research questions and methodologies that do justice to the complexity and heterogeneity of entrepreneurship and new venture creation. When they asked Gartner, in interview, what he thought we had learned about the process of new venture creation he replied:

> Honestly, we have learned very little. One reason is methodological concerns. For example, we have used very broad and crude ways of measuring the entrepreneurial processes, and we do not have a great deal of rich and detailed data on how people go about starting businesses over time – that is really a fundamental flaw in the area. (Ch. 3, p. 52)

In this chapter we will suggest that some of Gartner's key concerns can be addressed through a transgressive knowledge-based approach to researching entrepreneurship and new venture creation.

In an illuminating passage in *The Character of Physical Law* (1992), Physics Nobel Prize laureate Richard Feynman introduced us to the controversy of electrons' behaviour and the scientific knowledge produced to explain such complexity at the outset of quantum theory. Feynman pointed out that when electrons were first discovered they behaved exactly like particles or bullets, in a very simple way. Later, however, new research on electron diffraction contradicted this finding, suggesting that they behaved more like waves. This created confusion as to whether particles behaved like waves or vice versa. In the 1920s this confusion was partly resolved with the advent of the correct equation for quantum mechanics. And yet this controversy remains unresolved.

Feynmann described electrons' behaviour as 'inimitable': 'nothing people have seen before, as experience with things you have seen before is incomplete'. Knowledge, then, generated to explain such behaviours may have been misguided, the methods used inappropriate and the mathematical equations wrong, because they were based on preconceptions and were expected to fit into already classified systems.

We will argue that something similar may happen when trying to explain 'entrepreneurship' and 'new venture creation' behaviours and theory, the subject for this chapter. Discussion will focus, not upon what entrepreneurship and new venture creation are or are not, but upon how knowledge is created and dialogue utilized to generate interpretations of actions and behaviours, thereby developing or limiting the potential for alternative explanations. The aim is to suggest alternative ways of addressing questions which can engender more imaginative interpretations about researching new venture creation.

Initially, we consider the ways that research agendas are constructed in the management and organization literature which legitimize the field of management and, subsequently, new venture creation, and we will posit that the concept of transgression may need to be adopted in order to break the currently accepted boundaries. Underpinning these research agendas are the ideas of knowledge management and knowledge creation, which we then explore as we advocate that a reconsideration of knowledge is crucial if there are to be new understandings of new venture creation. Next we move to discuss different epistemological foundations, why they would lead to different outcomes in research and how different methodologies will favour some forms and not others. Lastly, we call for a move towards a range of transgressive approaches to knowledge that, in our view, would enable new knowledge to be created in new venture creation research.

RESEARCH AGENDAS IN THE ACADEMIC ARENA

A great deal of research takes place around the world in order to develop new theories and ideas that can contribute to an understanding of organizations in general and entrepreneurial organizations and individuals in particular. According to Tranfield and Starkey (1998) some of this research follows, on the one hand, the classical model whereby knowledge production occurs largely as a result of an (academic) agenda and is predominantly driven through, and categorized by, associated adjacent disciplines (mode 1). On the other hand, knowledge production requires trans-disciplinarity in which team-working and the harnessing and integration of different research agendas, rather than heroic individual endeavour, become the established norm (mode 2).

Many would argue that these differences encompass the range of management research currently being undertaken and that, whilst mode 2 might lead to implementation-focused research, working upon increasing entreprencurial effectiveness, mode 1 should lead to radical new ideas and alternative ways of working and thinking. In theory the strong focus on finding a one best way which can be adopted by all (Parker 2002) will be undermined by such research, owing to a tendency to pursue enquiry and not useful, applicable knowledge. Moreover, the wide range of alternative perspectives should enable radical new ideas to emerge.

However, the need to be accepted by peer reviewers and pressure to follow 'accepted' methodological practices (particularly when undertaking Ph.D. studies, applying for research funding or trying to get published in top entrepreneurship journals) may actually limit and hamper the originality of what is learned. This is because, although there needs to be a contribution to new knowledge, it usually has to be related to current knowledge (fads) and ideas. The process can become self-referential and the questions tend to be about effectiveness, suitability and application of certain ideas, rather than radical novelty. There is also, without necessarily meaning to be, a general trend to accept only certain types of methodology and to consider only some forms of knowledge acceptable (Hindle 2004).

At this point, we were reminded of the urban myth about someone who stops and asks for directions only to be told 'Well, I wouldn't start from here.' It seems that, if there are to be really new ideas for conducting entrepreneurial research which can trigger exciting new answers to the problems and difficulties faced by entrepreneurial organizations, we may need to start transgressing from somewhere else. This will necessitate a re-conception of the way that knowledge is both understood and used as the underpinning base of ideas creation within entrepreneurship. It should be clear that we are not proposing outright violation of the rules of research, or contraventions to the way that knowledge is understood in epistemological terms; rather we are proposing that, within the field of entrepreneurship, there should be encouragement to 'break the rules', lapse from currently accepted norms of thinking and challenge the received wisdom by rethinking the way that the knowledge being used to develop the field is created, analysed and applied.

A transgressive response to the way that we study and grasp the notion of new venture creation opens up the possibility of generating a novel and, potentially, radical way of conducting research in order to increase our understanding of this managerial-organizational economic phenomenon. The nature of knowledge, knowledge creation and (ultimately) knowledge transgression may enable entrepreneurial researchers to develop radically new ideas or at least reconsider current ones. We believe that this will contribute to the emerging fields of entrepreneurship, innovation and venture creation.

IMPLICATIONS OF THE CONCEPTIONS OF KNOWLEDGE

According to Quintas (Little and Quintas 2002) there are several reasons for having an increased understanding of knowledge and its importance, including: wealth being demonstrably and increasingly generated from knowledge and intangible assets; a rediscovery that people are the locus of much organizational knowledge; and recognition that innovation is key to competitiveness and depends on knowledge creation and application, together with the growing importance of cross-boundary knowledge transactions. Moreover, knowledge implies an understanding of our cultural milieu and of our organic structures embedded into social networks and emerging from encounters. Clearly it will be important to try to define and manage such an important concept, particularly if the view of entrepreneurship being about discovery, evaluation and exploitation of opportunities is adopted (Shane and Venkataraman 2000). Eckhardt and Shane (2003) emphasize entrepreneurship as a disequilibrium activity where opportunities are defined as 'situations in which new goods, services, raw materials, markets and organizing methods can be introduced through the formation of new means, ends or a means–ends relationship'. Klyver (Blackman and Hindle 2008) illustrates that entrepreneurship can be about either extending current relationships or making new ones, but something innovative must occur (Figure 6.1); if the activity is merely extending current practices within an existing context, then this is management but not entrepreneurship. In the other three squares of Figure 6.1 there is enough novelty for the activity to be classified as entrepreneurship and in two of them we are specifically confronting new venture creation. In this chapter we will address our arguments to the way knowledge transgressivity might inform new venture creation, but we believe that our arguments are just as applicable to the case where new means and ends relationships are created even if a new venture is not.

Entrepreneurial actions and decisions involve a creation or rearrangement of knowledge; moreover, they require an understanding of how knowledge is generated from both a theoretical and a praxis experience perspective. In terms of this chapter, it becomes clear that knowledge matters for two reasons: firstly, because without new knowledge new venture creation cannot occur; and, secondly, to understand new venture creation new knowledge and understandings of it must be created.

Actions involved

	Creation of new means and ends relationships	Maximizing existing means and ends relationships
New organizations	Change-oriented venture creation	Non-change-oriented venture creation
Existing organizations	Change-oriented corporate venturing	Traditional management

(Context)

Source: Klyver, in Blackman and Hindle (2008).

Figure 6.1 *Distinguishing the emergence and opportunity view of entrepreneurship*

Knowledge is difficult to define; indeed, philosophers have posed the question for hundreds of years, and there are still as many definitions as there are philosophers who attempt to define it. Interest in knowledge has led to many writings considering the idea, and most agree that a clear definition is difficult (Malhotra 1997; McInery and LeFevre 2000; Earl 2001). It helps to consider that:

> Knowledge is constituted by the ways in which people categorize, code, process and impute meaning to their experiences. . . . Knowledge emerges out of a complex process involving social, situational, cultural and institutional factors. The process takes place on the basis of existing conceptual frameworks and procedures and is affected by various social contingencies, such as skills, orientations, experiences, interests, resources and patterns of social interaction characteristic of the particular group or interacting set of individuals, as well as those of the wider audience. (Arce and Long 1992)

The key element here is the idea that knowledge is about creating new understandings. As a result it is more complex, being deeper and richer than mere data or information. Davenport and Prusak (1998) note that, within organizations, knowledge evidently becomes embedded in documents or repositories, but it is also embedded into organizational routines, processes, practices and norms leading to new behaviours. These two views are reflected in the proposition by Newell *et al.* (2002) that there are two different perspectives on knowledge, structural and processual, and that the decisions and actions taken which will emerge are dependent upon the perspective adopted by the researcher. In the structural view knowledge is perceived as a commodity, a set of facts that can be transferred from one place to another; it becomes something that can be tracked down, acquired, assessed, codified and distributed. In this perspective, knowledge is lodged in the view of the world as an objective external entity and acknowledged as a body of 'facts', truths which will explain the world. Because knowledge can apparently be acquired in a logical fashion by accurate information processing, many assume that research constitutes collecting such 'truths' and analysing them into patterns which will enable predictability and replicability in the future.

The evidence of such a perspective of knowledge can be found widely in new venture creation research, where there is a focus upon breaking ideas down in order to better predict how and why new venture creation should be undertaken or how entrepreneurs will behave. Many Ph.D. theses are about defining ideas into smaller and smaller parts or re-examining previously identified elements, in order to develop a 'truth' about a particular one. Knowledge is exemplified as rational, economic theorizing in which it is treated mostly as a predictable variable of what becomes 'factual' new venture creation. Moreover, the units of analysis used within research will lead to particular outcomes; currently there appears to be a focus upon the entrepreneur as an individual and the elements that make up a successful venture rather than, for example, new venture creation as a social phenomenon or the impacts of new venture creation upon different communities. This is not to say that there is no research in these areas but it is often found, not in the entrepreneurship or new venture creation literature or conference streams, but in critical management arenas, as it is not considered to be acceptable in the main entrepreneurial streams; the papers within the 2008 and 2009 Academy of Management conferences would support this position.

We posit that if new venture creation research adopted a more processual approach (Newell *et al.* 2002) the emerging ideas might be quite different. In the processual approach, knowledge is considered as being about relational, emotional and social, as well as psychological, processes. Nonaka and Konno (1998) describe socially based knowledge generation and note that participation in a social situation defines what knowledge is; it is described as useful only at a specific time and place if it is to be of value. Knowledge that is separated from its situation reverts to being information, to be communicated between situations. Once the information is communicated and becomes useful through the interpretations once more, it will then be knowledge again. The impact of such a dynamic and changing conception of knowledge upon new venture creation research and implementation is the focus of this chapter.

There is a range of scenarios that need to be contemplated when considering what is new venture creation and, consequently, what needs to be researched and what knowledge created. On the one hand, it may be said that knowledge is embedded within the cultural traditions of one place in which individuals have to 'learn' in order to cope and survive within their surroundings. For example, people living under harsh economic conditions have in most circumstances to learn and improvise the creation of innovative ideas to survive, that is, sell their products. On the other side of the spectrum, organizations strive to create 'products', objects with added new meaning that consumers may find more attractive than alternatives which can be used in a similar fashion. What matters here is that it can be argued that different aspects of new venture creation research will need to be accessed via different forms of knowledge, and the current methodologies being utilized may not encourage this. Consequently, understanding what knowledge might be and how it is created may become essential for developing better systems, theories and models of new venture creation.

It is not new to call for a range of ideas to be applied to a research area, nor is it new to imply that unless there is a range of ideas the whole cannot be understood. Mintzberg *et al.*'s (1998) call to consider different schools of strategic management, Bolman and Deal's (2003) reframing theories and Blackman *et al.*'s (2005) concerns as to the validity of learning organization knowledge were all based on the principle that if only a narrow aspect of a phenomenon is studied, or if only one way of studying something is adopted, then the whole will not be understood. Mintzberg *et al.* (1998), Gartner (2001) and Blackman *et al.* (2005) all used the tale of the 'Six blind men and the elephant' to illustrate this. In the story six blind men investigate the nature of an elephant by touch. Only by sharing their individual knowledge can they approach a complete and coherent understanding of the beast. We will argue that entrepreneurial research will only be able to complete the picture of the elephant if the knowledge developed becomes more transgressive.

TRANSGRESSIVE KNOWLEDGE AND NEW VENTURE CREATION

In order to underpin the importance of the recognition of the type of knowledge that needs to be in use let us consider Table 6.1. In this table we outline some orientations of epistemological thought and some of their attributes; from this some implications for methodology and its potential impact upon entrepreneurial research can be determined. We argue that at present the majority of entrepreneurial research is limited to the

Table 6.1 The relationships between epistemological orientations and knowledge outputs

Attribute	Epistemological orientation						
	Rationalism	Empiricism	Constructivism	Pragmatism	Scepticism	Postmodernism	Complexity
Source of knowledge	Reasoning from first principles.	Based on experience.	Constructed in social contexts.	Apparent utility, a precursor for action.	The problem of doubt.	Language and discourse.	Interactions between elements in a system.
Representation of the world	Emerges from logic and innate and a priori knowledge.	Emerges from the data.	Emerges from the patterns made with current ideas.	Expediency rather than a representation of reality.	Assumption that what is known may be false.	Meaning is constantly changing as language changes.	Holism, emergent from outcomes of non-linear interaction.
Focus of knowledge creation	Logical reasoning, Socratic dialogue.	Reflection on data and their relationship with what is outside the mind.	Interaction of information with its context and with the individual's pre-existing knowledge.	Posits an interactive relationship between human beings and the world by means of human action, experiment and experience.	Restoring the distinction between believing and knowing, which is blurred in constructed and pragmatic knowledge.	Understandings are derived from discourse as it takes place between participants.	Dynamics of interaction, self-organization, connections, holism and emergence.

Methodological techniques	Literature review and managed dialogues.	Surveys, observations, interviews and focus groups.	Interviews, participant observation and story gathering, case studies.	Focus upon what can be substantiated and used.	Gathering currently accepted knowledge, beliefs, etc. in order to find ways to challenge them.	Dialogue, unstructured interviews, group interviews, non-participant observation and recording dialogues.	Interactive dialogue.
Forms of analysis	Themes, questioning, making patterns linked to previous.	Grouping, ignoring outliers, statistics, developing norms.	Thematic, axial coding for important events, sense making multiple voices.	Sense making, can it be made useful?	Attempted falsification, challenging currently accepted norms or beliefs.	Narrative and discourse analysis, sense making.	Shared sense making with the participants.
Predominant approach and methodology	Theoretical construction.	Quantitative, positivist.	Qualitative, phenomenology, ethnography, biography.	Application, experimentation.	Falsification.	Qualitative ethnography.	Holism, complex case study.

Table 6.1 (continued)

Attribute	Epistemological orientation						
	Rationalism	Empiricism	Constructivism	Pragmatism	Scepticism	Postmodernism	Complexity
Limitations	May not recognize the phenomenon that needs to be explored and ignores it.	Data, current thinking frames the collection and interpretation of ideas.	Based upon current explicit and tacit knowledge.	Based upon a perception of utility.	If too global a scepticism all is doubted and it becomes unhelpful.	Understandings of the language and the meanings used for construction of knowledge.	Ability to recognize the system as a whole and remain focused on the system as the unit of analysis.

Source: Blackman and Kennedy (2009).

rationalist and empiricist orientations, although voices are being raised calling for an increase in constructivism via qualitative research (Hindle 2004). Rationalism is where new theories are developed either from a combination of current theories or as a result of the fact that there is a gap in the current understandings which is leading to unexpected outcomes. Such theoretical construction is usually a precursor to the undertaking of studies to test the new theory and can be found within the entrepreneurial discipline. What will matter is the form that the new data collection will take, and it is here that novelty can occur if the approach encourages it. Hindle's (2004) call for more qualitative work may begin to alter the focus of current research, and we support this initiative, but we also argue that the new forms will need to challenge the current mindset. Consequently, in terms of Table 6.1 we posit that, whilst scepticism should not necessarily be adopted as an orientation on its own, it may need to be adopted in a mild form as a framework around much of what is currently being done or is currently accepted. This will enable challenge to accepted theory and the development of space for novelty. Without this, the current mental models in place within the entrepreneurship discipline will frame the research, the analysis and, consequently, the findings that emerge. In addition to an increased focus on scepticism, we advocate a greater emphasis on orientations which focus less on finding a set of truths and more on the processes of interaction between events and human beings: social constructivism, postmodernism and complexity.

Social Constructivism

The first orientation we advocate, which is already being found within certain areas of entrepreneurship research but very little in the subfield of new venture creation, is social constructivism, a perspective that holds that all knowledge is constructed in social contexts and is constituted within the social practices of a community (Berger and Luckmann 1966). Individuals within the social context are seen not as passive receivers of information but as active constructors of meaning. Ortony (1993) outlines the constructivist approach thus: knowledge comes from the interaction of information with the context in which it is presented and, especially, with the individual's pre-existing knowledge. In this orientation, management knowledge is not a product of objective observations and facts, but rather creations of meaning that follow particular views of the world held by the community which constructs them (Berger and Luckmann 1966; Gergen 1992, 1994, 1997; Schwandt 1994). Gergen (1992, 1997) regards this paradigmatic shift as a fundamental break from what he describes as archaic forms of expression in the discipline of management which he considers as limited, monologic, defensive and dry. Instead, he suggests that, in order to be innovative and creative in the way we conceive knowledge, we must adopt an entirely different position that embraces multiple voices and narrative styles to communicate our findings, ideas or research, inciting us to transgress in this quest from the accepted 'scientific' or businesslike norms and scriptures imposed upon us to produce and to conceive knowledge. This change of emphasis to consider multiple voices would enable there to be greater emphasis on all the individuals within any entrepreneurial system, a concern voiced by Blackman and Hindle (2008) when they argued that the lack of focus upon human resource management within entrepreneurial research is currently a major weakness.

Postmodernism

Postmodern knowledge assumes that the world is constituted in language and we can only 'know' the world through the particular forms of discourses our language creates. Yet, as language is continuously in a state of flux, meaning is constantly slipping beyond our grasp and can thus never be lodged within one term (Hassard 1994). The notion of any single 'entrepreneurship' or 'new venture creation' concept as a well-defined and structured entity that can be clearly delineated and described completely disappears. Instead, there is transgressive instability in the concepts.

Dialogue becomes the force upon which this trangressivity in knowledge is acquired and then constantly produced and reproduced through networks of multiple voices. According to Bakhtin, we are constituted in dialogue, that is, verbal exchanges taking place between two or more individuals: two authors who express and contest their views of the world (see Bakhtin 1981, 1986). This dialogue is not fixed and singular, but continuously transforming in what he called a *heteroglossia*[1] of diverse and multiple voices. Heteroglossia, according to him, encapsulated our historical existence, our socio-ideological beliefs and social practices, which co-existed, at all times, between different epochs and between different groups, and were constantly renegotiated and reconstructed in the different dialogical instances of our lives (Bakhtin 1981). It is in this interplay, in what Bakhtin conceived as an in-between construction, that knowledge is fundamentally conceived, negotiated and renegotiated in the heteroglotic game. How we create or innovate knowledge, in other words, is to move away from a monoglotic world, apparently adopted by more traditional epistemological positions, to new venture creation knowledge or, in other words, to eschew the search for stable and well-defined structures that can account for the understanding of this phenomenon and embrace the unclear.

Complexity

This orientation primarily focuses upon holistic, descriptive accounts in which those involved witness emergent properties and make sense of them as part of the system as a whole. Complexity theories focus on the dynamics of interaction, self-organization, connection, holism and emergence (Anderson 1999). A complexivist view shifts the focus from assumptions of clear, linear relationships between action and effect, reductionism and direction, to the emergent outcomes of non-linear interaction. A new understanding of knowledge has evolved out of the recognition of its complexity and elusiveness, its situatedness, plurality and entwinement with human understanding and interaction (McElroy 2000). In terms of why this matters for entrepreneurial research, we argue that there are two aspects to consider. Firstly, the potential non-linearity of emergent experiences and incidents is very important in new venture creation; by concentrating on breaking the phenomena down it is likely that they will be less understood rather than more so. Consequently, methodologies that enable the researcher to develop understandings of the systems and emergent knowledge as a whole will deliver very different perspectives. Secondly, there needs to be a change in who develops the outcomes of the research. The need to reflect multiple voices has already been outlined in both social constructivism and postmodernism above, but in complexity it becomes important not only to reflect upon multiple voices but to actually include them in the development of the research outcomes, as they are the ones which are an active part of the system being studied. This will clearly influence the methods used, away from surveys and observation and towards active dialogue at all stages of the research process. This will also link with a pragmatic orientation. Again, we do not call for this theory to be developed as an approach on its own; however, it will link in with others in terms of determining not 'Is it true?', but 'Will it work as an explanation for now until we can create a better one?' Hence, combining pragmatism with complexity will encourage those undertaking the research not to break the system down but to maintain a picture of the system as a whole in terms of 'Is it actually creating and sustaining venture creation?'

APPLICATION: USING KNOWLEDGE TRANSGRESSIVITY IN NEW VENTURE CREATION RESEARCH

We will now build upon the proposition of the three epistemological orientations to consider how to make entrepreneurial knowledge creation

different in substantial and useful ways. Transgression knowledge creation emphasizes the ontological nature of all knowledge through dialogical flux, founded in social constructivist, postmodernist and complex
approaches to a field of study. It becomes distanced from scientific forms
of writing, researching and producing standardized, lineal forms of
knowledge that account for management and organization (see Burrell
1997). It transgresses and revolutionizes how to create and construct, with
others, knowledge, in this case on new venture creation. Following Rorty
(1980), once we dismiss notions of objectivity and scientific method in the
production of management knowledge and see them in a continuum with
creative forms of literature and art to generate meaning about new venture
creation, this will expand our understanding of our community of entrepreneurs; what may well emerge is a much wider range of accepted forms
of creating knowledge. Conventional research barriers are shattered, and
creativity and novelty, critical and central aspects of new venture creation behaviour, emerge to challenge the current status quo. The empirical
approach is replaced by a stance where the ontological interplay becomes
paramount to understanding what is new venture creation and how it is
constructed among the individual participants. What follows is an attempt
to provide some guidelines to methodology that will enable these new
ontologies.

> I believe nothing of any beauty or truth comes of a piece of writing without the
> author's thinking he has sinned against something – propriety, custom, faith,
> privacy, tradition, political orthodoxy, historical fact, literary convention, or
> indeed, all the prevailing community standards together. And that the work will
> not be realised without the liberation that comes to the writer from his feeling
> of having transgressed. (Doctorow 2003, p. 6)

Knowledge transgressivity implies an entirely new paradigmatic way of
understanding both entrepreneurship in general and new venture creation
specifically. As the concept itself suggests, it is the innovative, creative and
dynamic ways of generating ideas that can transform the way individuals
conceptualize frameworks and create/generate knowledge. Above all it
changes significantly how meaning is constructed. So how do we go about
constructing a new set of understandings of new venture creation?

One way is to adopt Deleuze and Guattari's ([1987] 2000) rhizome
notion as well as Eco's (1995) labyrinth ideas. In a knowledge-based
approach, understandings of entrepreneurship and new venture creation
should be rhizomic, because they can be constructed in such a way that
each part (narrated by an author or participant) can be connected to other
parts (narrated by other authors or participants), where there is no centre,
no periphery and no exit, and the process is potentially infinite (Eco

1995). Furthermore, it has neither beginnings nor ends and is the result of multiplicities, where there are no sequels, no one signification and no one author (Deleuze and Guattari [1987] 2000). It is no one tale; it has no plot, no central theme, no central manager-character and no structure.[2] In other words, the process of innovation/entrepreneurship/new venture creation becomes the association of all the parts, not the fragmentation of elements of them.

New venture creation knowledge creation might also benefit from the 'Tamarization' of knowledge creation. *Tamara* is a play that enacts a story taken from the diary of Aelis Mazoyer (Boje 2003). In *Tamara*, Boje (2003) explains, a dozen characters unfold their stories before a walking or running audience who can only follow one of these characters as each moves from room to room inside a house. Therefore, *Tamara* consists of many stories, and each story masks a multiplicity of stories that wandering and fragmented audiences had to follow (Boje 2003). *Tamara* is both rhizome and labyrinth, opening a multiplicity of storylines, and constructing and deconstructing[3] the story as the audience moves into one of the rooms.

Similarly, the creation and evolution of a new venture unfolds a multiplicity of stories, which appear fragmented, incongruent, contradictory and in flux to perplexed readers and audiences. These are stories where characters are not characters but authors,[4] because each one of them speaks in her/his own voice. Each one of them communicates her/his own entrepreneurial existence, her/his own organizational world, which undergoes constant metamorphosis (Deleuze and Guattari [1987] 2000). In this sense, any understanding should be conceived as polyphonic and *carnivalesque* (Bakhtin [1965] 1984). 'Carnival is not a spectacle seen by the people; they live in it, and everyone participates because its very idea embraces all the people. While carnival lasts, there is no other life outside it' (Bakhtin [1965] 1984, p. 17).

This reflects Burrell's (1997) organizational *pandemonium* of non-linear and chaotic interpretations, which are being renewed all the time. What becomes important is that any one understanding of new venture creation is, by its very nature, incomplete and this must be reflected in the research design in some way.

Finally, the entrepreneurial/new venture creation rhizome is a juxtaposition of micro-storias (Muir 1991; Boje 2001), which can be renamed here as micro-entrepreneurial-storias. Muir defines micro-storias as the stories of little people (e.g. Indigenous people, minorities, women, peasantry, day labourers, etc.), which are usually ignored and abandoned in mainstream research programmes, as they do not provide the 'big picture' (Boje 2001). These storias do not form a unitary discourse, a unique and grand history, but instead embrace the unconventional, the forgotten and the improper which we advocate in the writings on new venture creation. Micro-entrepreneurial-storias should destroy the sense of unity and coherence that exists in the classic representations of the genre, overcoming the desire to impose traditional plots and time structures on representations of new venture creation. This is exactly what Bill Gartner was seeking when he desired researchers in new venture creation to have greater respect for the vast heterogeneity of the process.

We want to stretch our imagination and the boundaries of the new venture creation genre further, in order to take both management writers and readers to a different plateau where there are infinite possibilities to explore. The view then is that the notion of new venture creation is always on the move, always forming new alliances with participants, readers and other interested parties, always changing its meaning and significance and, therefore, never allowing one conceptualization or one discourse or one voice to impose its grand idea/knowledge.

> Write to the nth power, the $n - 1$ power, write with slogans: Make rhizomes, not roots, never plants! Don't sow, grow offshoots! Don't be one or multiple, be multiplicities! Run lines, never plot a point! Speed turns the point into a line! Be quick, even when standing still! Line of chance, line of hips, line of flight. Don't bring the general in you! Don't have just ideas, just have an idea (Godard). Have short-term ideas. Make maps, not photos or drawings. Be the Pink Panther and your loves will be like the wasp and the orchid, the cat and the baboon. (Deleuze and Guattari [1987] 2000, p. 115)

CONCLUSION

Two main ideas derive from our discussion above. Firstly, knowledge is an essential and integral part of understanding new venture creation, in terms of both the research about it and also the act of undertaking new venture creation itself. Secondly, how knowledge is created, internalized and applied requires a more complex, interactive understanding, based on alternative orientations that will lead to new methodologies and new knowledge.

Our approach is distinct; we move away from traditional philosophical paradigmatic debate, as we regard it as an impediment, in one direction or another, to setting the basis upon which to construct 'model' representations of new venture creation. Rather, what for us constitutes a departure from the imposed constraint of philosophical traditions is to find a 'language' in which to describe and analyse what can be created and constituted as in-flux knowledge of entrepreneurial activity emerging from dialogue. Thus methodologically this should be addressed, not by exemplifying what an entrepreneur is like or in many cases appears to be, but by examining how ideas and knowledge are created in conjunction with others and within certain contexts. We consider that more 'voices' should be added in the investigation and mapping of entrepreneurial activity.

In this chapter we have offered new ideas that may significantly change the way that knowledge is defined, described and applied within new venture creation research, based on transgression knowledge and a paradigmatic shift in the way knowledge might be created. What we propose is to construct new venture creation research under a dynamic dialogical understanding of knowledge creation. Knowledge, as it is learned, understood and interpreted by all the agents that participate in the dialogue, allows for 'unique' configurations that cannot be explained in terms of a predictable process that can be followed, but only understood in a process of creation within the context of the events. We suggest that an increased focus upon social constructivism, postmodernism and complexity, combined with a greater awareness of scepticism and pragmatism, might increase the range and types of research undertaken about venture creation and entrepreneurship.

It is proposed that venture creation research needs to reflect knowledge which is not static; thus what we propose is to look for the dynamic understanding that happens or develops via the flux and complexity among actors (Bygrave 1989a, 1989b; Bruyat and Julien 2001). The way to do this is not only by identifying the language of the observer but also by observing the language construction of the participants. Consequently, we also look to communities which progressively have demonstrated an instinct for survival and the application of their entrepreneurial ideas to help and complement the communities in which they exist. We posit that new venture creation research should actively include voices that are currently absent in much extant scholarship and voices that are neglected in the traditional lexicon of business. We also posit that there needs to be a much greater focus upon an entire system and all the constituents within it. By concentrating on 'wholes' and the interactions both between parts of the systems and between systems themselves, it will be possible to gain a different understanding of the elements that create and sustain successful ventures.

Overall, some methodological approaches and foci have been suggested in order to offer alternative research strategies for new venture creation research. The need to break the potentially self-referential mould that may emerge if the same methodologies and methods are always used is outlined. The overall objective is to enable entrepreneurship researchers to be able to, if not comprehend the whole elephant, at least have a much clearer idea of the scope and size of it and the areas of understanding left to discover.

NOTES

1. Heteroglossia refers to simultaneous differences that exist in dialogue: a polyphony of voices in which each voice articulates his/her own view of the world (Bakhtin 1986; Morris 1994).
2. Chia (1999) has suggested similar rhizomic ideas to explain change and transformation in organizations.
3. No fixed meaning (Derrida [1966] 1996).
4. See Deetz (2003), who suggests that authoring can be seen as possibilities for creativity and an enriched social life, and the potential for unobtrusive forms of control. This point may also be associated with the work done by Shotter and Cunliffe (2003).

REFERENCES

Anderson, P. (1999), 'Complexity theory and organization science', *Organization Science*, **10**(3), 216–32.
Arce, A. and N. Long (1992), 'The dynamics of knowledge: Interfaces between bureaucrats and peasants', in Norman Long and Ann Long (eds), *Battlefields of Knowledge: The Interlocking of Theory and Practice in Social Research and Development*, New York: Routledge, pp. 211–46.
Bakhtin, M.M. ([1965] 1984), *Rabelais and His World*, Bloomington: Indiana University Press.
Bakhtin, M.M. (1981), 'Discourse in the novel', in M.M. Bakhtin (ed.), *Dialogic Imagination: Four Essays*, Austin: University of Texas Press, pp. 259–422.
Bakhtin, M.M. (1986), *Speech Genres and Other Late Essays*, translated by V.W. McGee, Austin: University of Texas Press.
Berger, P. and T. Luckmann (1966), *The Social Construction of Reality*, London: Penguin.
Blackman, D. and K. Hindle (2008), 'Would using the psychological contract increase entrepreneurial business development potential?', in R. Barrett and S. Mayson (eds), *International Handbook of HRM and Entrepreneurship*, Cheltenham, UK and Northampton, MA, USA: Edward Elgar Publishing, pp. 382–97.
Blackman, D. and M. Kennedy (2009), 'Knowledge management and effective university governance', *Journal of Knowledge Management*, **13**(6), 547–63.
Blackman, D., C. Connelly and S. Henderson (2005), 'Beyond all reasonable doubt? Epistemological problems of the learning organisation', *Philosophy of Management*, **5**(3), 47–65.
Boje, D.M. (2001), *Narrative Methods for Organizational and Communication Research*, London: Sage.
Boje, D.M. (2003), 'Using narrative and telling stories', in D. Holman and R. Thorpe (eds), *Management and Language*, London: Sage, pp. 41–53.
Bolman, L. and T. Deal (2003), *Reframing Organizations*, San Francisco: Jossey-Bass.
Bruyat, C. and P.A. Julien (2001), 'Defining the field of research in entrepreneurship', *Journal of Business Venturing*, **16**(2), 165–80.
Burrell, G. (1997), *Pandemonium: Towards a Retro-Organization Theory*, London: Sage.
Bygrave, W.D. (1989a), 'The entrepreneurship paradigm (I): A philosophical look at its research methodologies', *Entrepreneurship Theory and Practice*, **14**(1), 7–26.
Bygrave, W.D. (1989b), 'The entrepreneurship paradigm (II): Chaos and catastrophes among quantum jumps?', *Entrepreneurship Theory and Practice*, **14**(2), 7–30.

Chia, R. (1999), 'A "rhizomic" model of organizational change and transformation: Perspective from a metaphysic of change', *British Journal of Management*, **10**, 209–27.

Davenport, T.H. and L. Prusak (1998), *Working Knowledge: How Organizations Manage What They Know*, Boston: Harvard Business School Press.

Deetz, S. (2003), 'Authoring as a collaborative process through communication', in D. Holman and R. Thorpe (eds), *Management and Language*, London: Sage, pp. 121–38.

Deleuze, G. and F. Guattari ([1987] 2000), 'Rhizome', in N. Lucy (ed.), *Postmodern Literary Theory: An Anthology*, Oxford: Blackwell, pp. 92–120.

Derrida, J. ([1966] 1996), 'Structure, sign and play in the discourse of the human sciences', in P. Rice and P. Waugh (eds), *Modern Literary Theory: A Reader*, London: Arnold, pp. 223–42.

Doctorow, E. (2003), 'The call of the word', *Guardian Review*, 31 May, 4–6.

Earl, M.J. (2001), 'Knowledge management strategies: Toward a taxonomy', *Journal of Management Information Systems*, **18**(1), 215–33.

Eckhardt, J.T. and S.A. Shane (2003), 'Opportunities and entrepreneurship', *Journal of Management*, **29**(3), 333–49.

Eco, U. (1995), *Reflections on the Name of the Rose*, London: Minerva.

Feynmann, R.P. (1992), *The Character of Physical Law*, London: Penguin Books.

Gartner, W.B. (2001), 'Is there an elephant in entrepreneurship? Blind assumptions in theory development', *Entrepreneurship Theory and Practice*, **25**(4), 27–39.

Gergen, K.J. (1992), 'Organization theory in the postmodern era', in M. Reed and M. Hughes (eds), *Rethinking Organization*, London: Sage, pp. 703–23.

Gergen, K.J. (1994), *Realities and Relationships: Soundings in Social Construction*, Cambridge, MA: Harvard University Press.

Gergen, K.J. (1997), 'Social psychology as social construction: The emerging vision', in C. McCarty and A. Haslam (eds), *For the Message of Social Psychology: Perspectives on Mind in Society*. Oxford: Blackwell, pp. 113–28.

Hassard, J. (1994), 'Postmodern organizational analysis: Toward a conceptual framework', *Journal of Management Studies*, **31**(3), 303–25.

Hindle, K. (2004), 'Choosing qualitative methods for entrepreneurial cognition research: A canonical development approach', *Entrepreneurship Theory and Practice*, **28**(6), 575–607.

Little, S. and P. Quintas (2002), *Managing Knowledge: An Essential Reader*, London: Sage.

McElroy, M.W. (2000), 'Integrating complexity theory, knowledge management and organizational learning', *Journal of Knowledge Management*, **4**(3), 195–203.

McInery, C. and D. LeFevre (2000), 'Knowledge managers: History and challenges', in C. Prichard, R. Hull, M. Chumer and H. Willmott (eds), *Managing Knowledge: Critical Investigations of Work and Learning*, New York: Macmillan Business, pp. 1–19.

Malhotra, Y. (1997), 'Knowledge management, knowledge organizations and knowledge workers: A view from the front lines', BRINT.

Mintzberg, H., B. Ahlstrand and J. Lampel (1998), *The Strategy Safari*, London: Pearson Education.

Morris, P. (1994), *The Bakhtin Reader: Selected Writings of Bakhtin, Medvedev, Voloshinov*, London: Arnold.

Muir, E. (1991), 'Introduction: Observing trifles', in E. Muir and G. Ruggiero (eds), *Microhistory and the Lost People of Europe*, Baltimore/London: Johns Hopkins University Press, pp. 7–11.

Newell, S., M. Robertson, H. Scarborough and J. Swan (2002), *Managing Knowledge Work*, London: Palgrave.

Nonaka, I. and N. Konno (1998), 'The concept of "ba": Building a foundation for knowledge creation', *California Management Review*, **40**(3), 40–54.

Ortony, A. (1993), *Metaphor and Thought*, Cambridge: Cambridge University Press.

Parker, M. (2002), *Against Management: Organisation in the Age of Managerialism*, London: Polity.

Rorty, R. (1980), *Philosophy and the Mirror of Nature*, Oxford: Blackwell.

Schwandt, T.A. (1994), 'Constructivist, interpretivist approaches to human inquiry', in N.K. Denzin and Y.S. Lincoln (eds), *Handbook of Qualitative Research*, London: Sage.

Shane, S. and S. Venkataraman (2000), 'The promise of entrepreneurship as a field of research', *Academy of Management Review*, **25**(1), 217–26.

Shotter, J. and A.L. Cunliffe (2003), 'Managers as practical authors: Everyday conversations for action', in D.J. Holman and R. Thorpe (eds), *Management and Language: The Manager as a Practical Author*, London: Sage, pp. 1–12.

Tranfield, D. and K. Starkey (1998), 'The nature, social organization and promotion of management research: Towards policy', *British Journal of Management*, **9**(4), 341–53.

7 What does the economic literature contribute to understanding new venture creation?

John Legge

ECONOMISTS

Put simply, new venture creation has not attracted the interest of economists; and the assumptions that they commonly use render new venture creation almost invisible. Baumol (1968) described the sole role of the entrepreneur in then contemporary economics as an inscrutable but indivisible resource that prevented firms expanding indefinitely: a sort of lead weight lowered on to the cost curve to ensure that total unit costs rose with increasing output before any firm could satisfy an entire market.

The dominant form of economics is based on the neoclassical model which makes extensive use of the calculus and hence assumes continuous variables. The most common assumption underlying neoclassical economic analysis is that markets are competitive and firms are infinitesimally small price takers. An infinitesimally small object has no structure; and so the structure of firms as well as their creation and disappearance is disregarded in any work relying on the competitive assumption.

IO economics, building on the work of Chamberlin ([1933] 1960) and Robinson (1933) on imperfect competition, might be a more promising place to look for a theory of new firm formation; but one looks in vain. An assumption that IO economics carries across from late classical economics is the idea of the representative firm: that all firms may be treated as if they were identical as long as each of the properties of these representative firms equalled the average of each of the properties of the real firms so represented. This assumption underlies the structure–conduct–performance (SCP) paradigm, which asserts that industry structure determines firm conduct, which in turn determines firm performance. If all firms serving a market are identical or, with the paradigm at its most relaxed, the firms can be divided into a small number of subsets, all the members of each subset being identical, there aren't and can't be any new firms in the mixture.

Firm creation gets a brief mention in the purported proof that there can be no abnormal returns under monopolistic competition: the assumption here is that, if firms in a monopolistically competitive market are earning abnormally high profits, further firms will be created spontaneously until only normal profits are available. Assumptions about spontaneous creation do not encourage the study of real firm emergence.

Martin, in his highly regarded text (2001), notes that the standard assumption of IO economics is that a market gap attracts entry, which leads to the further assumption that there will be orderly entry into an emerging industry until all firms are at their minimum efficient scale, after which entry will cease. He reflects that actual case studies do not show such behaviour, but rather that an emerging market is like a busy building with a revolving door: many firms enter, some leave promptly, others leave after spending some time in the lobby, but very few make it to the lifts and a place in the penthouse suite.

Schumpeter was well aware of the unreality of contemporaneous economic analysis:

> The first thing to go is the traditional conception of the modus operandi of competition. Economists are at long last emerging from the stage in which price competition was all they saw. As soon as quality competition and sales effort are admitted into the sacred precincts of theory, the price variable is ousted from its dominant position. However, it is still competition within a rigid pattern of invariant conditions, methods of production and forms of industrial organization in particular, that practically monopolizes attention. But in capitalist reality as distinct from the textbook picture, it is not that kind of competition which counts but the competition from the new commodity, the new source of supply, the new type of organization (the largest-scale unit of control for instance), competition which commands a decisive cost or quality advantage and which strikes not at the margins of the profits and the outputs of the existing firms but at their foundations and their very lives. This kind of competition is as much more effective than the other as a bombardment is in comparison with forcing a door, and so much more important that it becomes a matter of comparative indifference whether competition in the ordinary sense functions more or less promptly; the powerful lever that in the long run expands output and brings down prices is in any case made of other stuff. Schumpeter (1942, pp. 84–5)

Unfortunately, Schumpeter's optimism was misplaced: even most of those economists who discard the assumption of perfect competition still cling to the assumption of 'a rigid pattern of invariant conditions, methods of production and forms of industrial organisation' (Martin 2001).

Harvey Leibenstein (1968) devoted some effort to explaining the role of the entrepreneur and critiquing the orthodox explanations of (or failures to acknowledge) the entrepreneur's role. He is far better known among economists for his description of X-[in]efficiency, and although his work was accepted by prestigious journals and he received generous tributes on his retirement his work on entrepreneurship does not appear to have had much lasting effect on orthodox economic academia (see for example

Baumol 1968). As an example of unintended consequences, the ongoing explosion in senior executive remuneration has been given economic respectability by principal–agent theory (Keser and Willinger 2007), which in turn was developed to solve the 'problem' of X-inefficiency.

Leibenstein focused on the role and environment of the entrepreneur and suggested, perhaps contentiously, that the elimination of X-inefficiency would also eliminate entrepreneurial opportunities by pre-empting them with intra-firm action.

Baumol (1993, 2004) has made a number of attempts to fill the gap described in Baumol (1968). Our opinion is that Baumol has been over-impressed by the aspect of Schumpeter's archetypical entrepreneur: a complete critique of his contribution would take a chapter; but in brief Baumol (especially 2004) has made unrealistic assumptions about the efficacy of competition in real economies, and the reasons he gives for *Übermensch* entrepreneurs becoming robber barons rather than warring barons are not convincing. In particular Baumol neglects the legal changes in late-seventeenth- and eighteenth-century England that made entrepreneurship in the modern sense possible (Legge and Hindle 2004, pp. 3–11).

The division of economics into two sub-disciplines, microeconomics to deal with industries and macroeconomics to deal with national economics as systems, tends to ensure that new venture formation stays 'below the radar' of the economics profession at large. The recent rise to prominence of behavioural economics has led to a powerful critique of conventional microeconomics without any focus on entrepreneurs and innovators.

Grossman and Helpman (1994) are associated with a series of attempts to extend standard microeconomic analysis to include innovation; but they use a context of established firms, and by carrying forward the standard microeconomic assumptions of perfect knowledge (so all consumers instantly recognize the superiority of the innovator's product) and perfect credit markets (so that an innovative firm can instantly expand its output to supply the entire market previously served by an arbitrary but possibly large number of former competitors) they assume away much of what is generally accepted to be crucial in the entrepreneurial studies literature. In particular, they largely ignore the difficulty entrepreneurs face in obtaining finance for an innovative proposal and the finite speed with which knowledge of an innovation and its superiority diffuses through the population of potential purchasers.

Paul Romer (1990) took a macroeconomic approach to the study of economic growth, and while he developed a consistent explanation of the macroeconomic conditions under which innovative new ventures might prosper he did little to investigate the specific factors affecting particular new ventures.

Piero Sraffa, the founder and sole member of the Anglo-Italian school of economic thought, made a crucial breakthrough (1926) by pointing out that the effort involved in sales and marketing was both significant and an indirect expense. His work has since tended to be studiously ignored in mainstream economic academia.

ECONOMIC FACTORS AFFECTING NEW VENTURES

There are a few loose straws in the marketing and economic literature which may be woven into a consistent narrative: what follows is a start.

The work of Avinash Dixit on investment under uncertainty showed that, when entry to a market involves an irreversible investment, as for example in marketing, investors will demand a high return a priori to minimize the risk of an actual loss. Dixit (1992) modelled revenue, which is an analogue of gross margin; but real businesses have fixed and semi-variable costs, and should unforeseen events lead to the gross margin failing to cover fixed costs for an extended period investors will not merely suffer a poor return on their money: they will suffer a total loss.

At least some of his colleagues recognized the significance of Dixit's work, leading to an invitation to contribute to the prestigious *Journal of Economic Perspectives* (1992) and the publication (with R. Pindyck) of the masterly work *Investment under Uncertainty* (1994). Unfortunately this work has not had the attention that it deserves in the mainstream economics discourse. Even finance economists have been very slow to recognize it: if we look at two popular textbooks, Ross *et al.* (2007) fail to mention Dixit's work, and Pierson *et al.* (2009) give it a short and somewhat misleading mention.

Entrepreneurship scholars can, however, use Dixit's work to examine the factors influencing new venture creation and survival.

Consider a stylized venture capital firm which raises money with a promise of an 18 per cent return to its investors. It then invests an equal amount in each of five firms, which it then monitors for five years before harvesting them. At that point it discovers that one investment is wholly lost, three can be recovered without any additional return, and one must pay for all. A little fiddling with the numbers reveals that the successful firm must return 57 per cent per year in order to provide an overall return of 20 per cent, leaving 2 per cent for the venture capital firm after paying out the required 18 per cent to its clients.

A little further fiddling shows that, for reasonable estimates of the risk-free rate, the volatility parameter, σ, for the successful firm must be over

90 per cent per year.[1] Since the venture capitalists do not know a priori which of the five investee firms will produce a satisfactory return they must apply the same high hurdle rate to each of them; that is, only firms whose verified business plans project a 57 per cent per year or better return over five years can expect venture capital support.

Dixit's result is based on the assumption of a geometric random walk of the logarithm of the firm's value. While this is an acceptable assumption a priori (and, with a much lower volatility parameter, an acceptable if approximate assumption for well-established firms), the actual value of a new venture may follow a random walk but the volatility should be expected to decline.

The performance of a new venture is the result of the complex interaction of a number of factors. These will include:

- the fraction of potential purchasers exposed to its product who will buy it;
- the fraction of those who buy it who will recommend it and, if the product is consumed in the course of use, replenish their supplies;
- the fraction of its marketing budget incurred by the firm in presenting its product to each potential purchaser;
- the absolute size of the potential market;
- the contribution from each completed sale.

Thanks to the work of the late F.M. Bass and others (Bass 1969; Mahajan *et al.* 1990; Legge 2002) it is possible, given a sales history, to deduce parameter values representing each of the above factors and, given estimates of these parameter values, to prepare a sales projection. The uncertainty in a new venture's value as at the date that it commences active marketing is a consequence of the uncertainty in each of the parameter values.

The launch of a new venture can be considered as an experiment intended to reveal the characteristic parameters of a particular market's response to a particular product or product set. The value of the parameter reflecting the prompt response to sales and marketing can be deduced to a satisfactory precision from quite early sales data and the management accounts; the other critical parameters emerge more slowly, with the absolute market size one of the last to be revealed.

Since the planner of a new venture will be operating on behalf of its entrepreneur and may actually *be* that entrepreneur, the line between justified confidence and excessive optimism is easily breached. In particular, the necessary sales and marketing budget is frequently drastically underestimated. Garnsey and Heffernan (2005) show in a longitudinal study that very few new firms achieve a level of growth that matches their entrepreneurs' expectations. An inadequate marketing budget may well be the proximate cause of many such disappointments; but it is possible that, had a realistic marketing budget been included in the pro forma accounts shown to investors, the venture would not have appeared attractive to them and may never have been commenced.

The cost, in terms of sales and marketing effort, of persuading one potential purchaser to give an unfamiliar product a trial will normally exceed the contribution earned on the sale of that product and may exceed the purchase price. When an inventor attempts to become an entrepreneur this fact is often very unwelcome. Whatever the statistics and however deep an expert's experience, inventors are likely to assert that their product is unique, not merely in its specifications and performance, but in the enthusiasm with which the market will greet it as well.

Once a purchaser has used a product and found that the product met or exceeded the expectations aroused by the sales and marketing effort that purchaser may become a regular purchaser if the product is consumed in use and may recommend the product to others. Sales triggered by recommendation and the regular purchases made by satisfied customers do not involve sales and marketing effort beyond the cost of the distribution channel and are the sole source of profits and enterprise value. As Drucker succinctly put it: 'The purpose of a business is to create a customer' (1955).

New ventures with an inadequate sales and marketing budget (or an adequate but incompetently managed one) may find their contribution from sales inadequate to cover their fixed costs; they will certainly fail to grow as rapidly as their business plan projected, if at all. If the product itself was attractive, their limited success will become a signpost for less entrepreneurial but better capitalized rivals to enter the market and replace the entrepreneurial firm entirely.

ECONOMIC CONTRIBUTORS TO OUR UNDERSTANDING OF NEW VENTURES

Table 7.1 sets out some key aspects of new venture formation and cross-relates it to the work of various schools of economists.

THE STYLIZED NEW VENTURE

Each new venture must start with an innovation (Schumpeter 1934) which gives its products a cost or quality advantage over the products (including services) offered by rival firms. As an essential precursor to entering

Table 7.1   *Key aspects of new venture creation and various schools of economics*

	Schumpeter	Sraffa	Dixit	Bass	IO economics	Partial equilibrium (Marshall)	General equilibrium (Walras)	New growth theory
Purposive, profit-seeking activity	Y	Y	Y	Y	?	N	N	Y
Relies on innovation	Y				N	N	N	Y
Contributes to economic growth	Y	(1)			N	N	N	Y
High levels of uncertainty lead to high expected returns			Y		N	N	N	N
Sales and marketing not a direct expense		Y			N	N	N	N
Market (share) growth occurs at finite rate				Y	N	N	N	N

Note: (1) Sraffa's (1960) work as extended by Kurz (2008).

business the firm must obtain control over sufficient resources to manufacture or deliver the product as appropriate; in general these will not, at the start of the entrepreneurial process, be owned by or under the control of the entrepreneur (Stevenson *et al.* 1989).

Once the product is ready to be offered to a market the entrepreneur must deploy sales and marketing resources to bring the product to the attention of potential customers and entice them to make a trial purchase. If the product proves to meet the entrepreneur's claims the potential customers will become actual ones, prepared to repurchase the product (if it is a frequently purchased good or service) and/or recommend it to their friends and colleagues (if it is an infrequently purchased good or service such as a durable good or a 'special' holiday).

If a significant fraction of those who try the product do *not* decide to repurchase and/or recommend it the venture will fail at that point, since the cost of the sales and marketing effort needed to secure a trial purchase exceeds the earned margin on that sale. If and only if a significant fraction of trial purchasers become customers intending to repurchase and/or recommend the product, will sales grow and deliver a positive gross margin; if the market is sufficiently deep and early competition weak the venture as a whole will become profitable.

At any point before a new venture enters a market there are a number of sources of uncertainty, many of which cannot be removed except by offering its products to the market and observing the response of potential customers. These include:

- The direct costs of production and delivery cannot be determined exactly without producing and delivering the product; and the actual costs may not leave a sufficient margin to the achievable price to deliver eventual profitability.
- The response of potential customers to ownership and use of the product cannot be known with certainty before they have the opportunity to own and use it.
- The actual number of potential customers cannot be determined with confidence until the product has been on the market for a significant time.
- Other firms, whether new or established ventures, may launch competing products that limit or even destroy the potential market for the entrepreneur's product.

The cumulative effects of these factors amount to an a priori risk or uncertainty of approximately $90\%/year^{1/2}$ as at the date of initial market entry, leading prudent investors to deny support to any entrepreneur who:

- fails to describe his or her proposed venture with a convincing and compelling business plan; and
- fails to project an investor return of the order of 60 per cent per year; and
- fails to offer his or her early investors a method of crystallizing their gains within a reasonable time frame.

Entrepreneurs who pass these tests, secure finance and launch a successful new venture will be entitled to what remains, if anything, after the investors have secured their returns.

CONCLUSION

By far the greatest part of the body of economic literature deals with either the allocation of a fixed set of resources between competing demands or the determination of prices and quantities. These are interesting topics, but far less interesting to students of entrepreneurship than the *creation* of resources. A new firm, or at least a new firm that doesn't promptly collapse, must involve the creation of a new resource, and so the new firm and its early development are not considered proper objects of economic study by the great majority of academic economists.

The work of some economists nevertheless sheds light upon certain aspects of entrepreneurship and new venture formation.

Adam Smith's legacy has become a sort of economic bible: every reader can find a quotation to support a personally selected point of view. One aspect of his legacy is sadly neglected among today's academic economists: his tireless collection of facts and his determination to build his theorizing around them.

Joseph Schumpeter tried valiantly to establish entrepreneurship and new venture formation as legitimate topics of discourse in economic academia and, like Smith, he based his theories around observations. He went beyond Smith in his deployment of analytic tools to expose the irrelevance of most contemporaneous economic publication.

Piero Sraffa made two key contributions to our understanding of entrepreneurship and new venture formation: he recognized that sales and marketing expenditure were not direct costs and that their effect was to render most models of competition moot; and he completed the work of the classical economists on price determination, creating the foundation upon which Kurz was to produce an analytic proof of the role of innovation in producing economic growth and development.

Harvey Leibenstein carried Schumpeter's work into the mainstream economic literature, but most economists are more likely to refer to his work on X-efficiency, if they refer to him at all.

William Baumol is another economist who has published on the subjects of entrepreneurship and new venture formation, but his work carries too much orthodox, static equilibrium baggage to be of great value to entrepreneurship scholars.

Paul Romer, Elhanan Helpman, Gene Grossman and the new growth theorists forced the subject of economic growth and development back into the mainstream economic agenda; while their work has not completely displaced equilibrium studies it provides a base from which to challenge the conclusions of such studies within economic academia.

Avinash Dixit and Robert Pindyck developed a comprehensive theory of investment under uncertain conditions, including a simple validation of empirically set hurdle rates and a more complete approach to venture formation, operation and dissolution. Because of Dixit's eminence as an economist his work has not been challenged, but its more awkward conclusions are widely ignored. Dixit (1992), in which he developed his formula for determining hurdle rates, has only 624 citations according to Google Scholar. Dixit and Pindyck (1994) has a healthier 6898 citations.

Frank Bass was a marketing professor who studied at an intensive econometrics programme, so most economists would treat his work as marginal; but he did provide a satisfactory account of the product life cycle. Unfortunately he developed an excessive attachment to the idea that his 'coefficient of innovation' was a population property rather than an artefact of sales and marketing effort, rendering his work useless in practice unless modified (Legge 2002; Legge and Hindle 2004).

In summary, familiarity with the economic literature can be useful to scholars of entrepreneurship concerned with specific issues, but many of the most important aspects of entrepreneurship study will draw little or no insight from conventional economics.

NOTE

1. Technically it is σ^2 that has a per year dimension; volatility has a dimension $t^{-1/2}$, a matter of some concern to mathematical purists.

REFERENCES

Bass, F.M. (1969), 'A new product growth model for consumer durables', *Management Science*, **15** (5), 215–27.

Baumol, W.J. (1968), 'Entrepreneurship in economic theory', *American Economic Review* (Papers and Proceedings), **58** (5), 64–71.

Baumol, W.J. (1993), 'Formal entrepreneurship theory in economics: existence and bounds', *Journal of Business Venturing*, **8** (3), 197–210.

Baumol, W.J. (2004), 'On entrepreneurship, growth and rent-seeking: Henry George updated', *American Economist*, **48** (1), 9–16.

Chamberlin, E.H. ([1933] 1960), *The Theory of Monopolistic Competition*, Cambridge, MA: Harvard University Press.

Dixit, A.K. (1992), 'Investment and hysteresis', *Journal of Economic Perspectives*, **6** (1), 107–32.

Dixit, A.K. and R.S. Pindyck (1994), *Investment under Uncertainty*, Princeton, NJ: Princeton University Press.

Drucker, P.F. (1955), *The Practice of Management*, London: Heinemann.

Garnsey, E. and P. Heffernan (2005), 'Growth setbacks in new firms', *Futures*, **37**, 675–697.

Grossman, G.M. and E. Helpman (1994), 'Endogenous innovation in the theory of growth', *Journal of Economic Perspectives*, **8** (1), 23–44.

Keser, C. and M. Willinger (2007), 'Theories of behavior in principal–agent relationships with hidden action', *European Economic Review*, **51** (6), 1514–33.

Kurz, H.D. (2008), 'Innovation and profits: Schumpeter and the classical heritage', *Journal of Economic Behaviour and Organisation*, **67** (1), 263–78.

Legge, J.M. (2002), 'Adapting and extending the Bass model to forecast sales of frequently repurchased products', *Proceedings of the 16th ANZAM Conference*, Melbourne: La Trobe University.

Legge, J.M. and K.G. Hindle (2004), *Entrepreneurship: Context, Vision and Planning*, Basingstoke: Palgrave-Macmillan.

Leibenstein, H. (1968), 'Entrepreneurship and development', *American Economic Review*, **58** (2), 72–83.

Mahajan, V., E. Muller and F.M. Bass (1990), 'New product diffusion models in marketing: A review and directions for research', *Journal of Marketing*, **54** (1), 1–26.

Martin, S. (2001), *Advanced Industrial Economics*, 2nd edn, Oxford: Blackwell.

Pierson, G., B. Brown, S. Easton, P. Howard and S. Pinder (2009), *Business Finance*, 10th edn, Sydney: McGraw-Hill.

Robinson, J. (1933), *The Economics of Imperfect Competition*, London: Macmillan.

Romer, P.M. (1990), 'Endogenous technological change', *Journal of Political Economy*, **98** (5), Part 2: The Problem of Development: A Conference on the Institute for the Study of Free Enterprise Systems, pp. S71–102.

Ross, S., S. Thompson, M. Christensen, R. Westerfield and B. Jordan (2007), *Fundamentals of Corporate Finance*, 3rd edn, Sydney: McGraw-Hill.

Schumpeter, J.A. (1934), 'The theory of economic development', in *An Inquiry into Profits, Capital, Credit, Interest and the Business Cycle*, translated by R. Opie, Cambridge, MA: Harvard University Press.

Schumpeter, J.A. (1942), *Capitalism, Socialism and Democracy*, New York: Harper & Row.

Sraffa, P. (1926), 'The laws of returns under competitive conditions', *Economic Journal*, **36** (144), 535–50.

Sraffa, P. (1960), *Production of Commodities by Means of Commodities*, Cambridge: Cambridge University Press.

Stevenson, H.H., M.J. Roberts and H.I. Grousbeck (1989), *New Business Ventures and the Entrepreneur*, 3rd edn, Homewood, IL: Irwin.

8 Modelling the innovative new venturing process in terms of dialectical systemic thinking

Matjaž Mulej and Miroslav Rebernik

INTRODUCTION

Not all innovation processes require the creation of a new venture. Not all new venture creation is based on the introduction and dissemination of an innovation. This chapter concerns the situation where actors consciously choose to introduce an innovation by means of creating a new venture so that the two activities are intricately intertwined. For this situation we will contribute a systems theory perspective in order to point to the need for creative cooperation of different disciplines, so that they would better use their capabilities by making synergies among several of them. We will set out the dialectical system, which means a synergy or system of all crucial viewpoints and helps thinkers, decision makers and other actors attain the requisite holism. How important requisite holism is in the issue of new venture creation becomes clear when we observe the difficulty of venture survival (Shepherd *et al.* 2000; Delmar and Shane 2004; Rebernik *et al.* 2008; Širec and Rebernik 2009).

The chapter is organized as follows. We first provide a brief summary of the holistic focus of systems thinking. We next provide a closer focus on dialectical systems thinking and the related law of requisite holism/realism. Then we apply dialectical systems thinking and the law of requisite holism to innovative new venture creation, which results in the articulation of a four-stage process model. We conclude that Mulej's dialectical systems theory offers a helpful conceptual and practical approach to the creation of new ventures based on introducing and disseminating innovations.

A BRIEF SUMMARY OF THE HOLISTIC FOCUS OF SYSTEMS THINKING

Systemic thinking is unavoidable for mastering all preconditions of innovation involving new venture creation quoted or discussed in this chapter. It has been and is a millennia-old attribute of successful people and the root cause of their being different from the less successful ones. A theory about it was created in the mid-twentieth century.

We are talking about human thinking style. Edward de Bono, the world-famous author on creative thinking, said: 'Thinking is the most important human behaviour' (de Bono 2003). We would add that holistic and creative thinking is what he must have had in mind – and rightly so. This is what systems theory has been created for (Davidson 1983). Ludwig von Bertalanffy, a philosopher, historian of art and theoretical biologist (Drack and Apfalter 2007), hence an interdisciplinary thinker, is the father of the general systems theory, the oldest of the well-known systems theories, which are now abundant (François 2004). He found, some seven to eight decades ago, that the human way of fighting human problems is also the cause of human problems. Humankind, millennia ago, developed the attitude that humans have dominion over nature, rather than being a part of nature and adapting to our natural environment. Since then, and especially in the twentieth century, we have – as humankind – developed a vast array of insights into the laws of nature and the methods/technologies and techniques of using them. We benefit from them; we have never lived a better life, by our own criteria. But we can no longer really understand and master our lives, because we – as humankind – know so much that we – as individuals – must be narrowly specialized. And we do not live as humankind, but as individuals and groups. The whole is fragmented into parts, which might no longer be able to become a whole.[1]

So, Bertalanffy (quoted in Elohim 1999) believed that the overall fate of the world depends on the adoption by humanity of a new set of values, based on a general systems *Weltanschauung* (worldview). He wrote:

> We are seeking another basic outlook: the world as organization. This [outlook] would profoundly change the categories of our thinking and influence our practical attitudes. We must envision the biosphere as a whole . . . with mutually reinforcing or mutually destructive interdependencies. [We need] a global system of mutually symbiotic societies, mapping new conditions into a flexible institutional structure and dealing with change through constructive reorganization.

Bertalanffy advocated that we dare to broaden our loyalty from nation to globe, that we become patriots of the planet, endeavouring to think and act primarily as members of humanity and that we must begin protecting the individual and cultural identity of others. He advocated a new global morality: 'an ethos, which does not center on individual goods and individual value alone, but on the adaptation of Humankind, as a global system, to its new environment'. The need for this new morality, he said, was imperative:

We are dealing with emergent realities; no longer with isolated groups of men, but with a systematically interdependent global community: it is this level of [reality] which we must keep before our eyes if we are able to inspire larger-scale action, designed to assure our collective and hence our individual survival. (Davidson 1983, quoted from Elohim 1999)

Quoting from Bertalanffy's Foreword (Bertalanffy 1979, p. VII):

Systems science . . . is predominantly a development in engineering sciences in the broad sense, necessitated by the complexity of 'systems' in modern technology. . . . Systems theory, in this sense, is pre-eminently a mathematical field, offering partly novel and highly sophisticated techniques . . . and essentially determined by the requirement to cope with a new sort of problem that has been appearing.

He goes on to point out that what may be obscured in these technical developments of the field – important as they are – is the fact that systems theory is a broad view which far transcends technological problems and demands, a reorientation that has become necessary in science in general and in the gamut of disciplines. It heralds a new worldview of considerable impact. However, development of the field involves a heavy irony. These days, the student of 'systems science' receives a technical training which makes systems theory – originally intended to overcome current over-specialization – into merely another of the hundreds of academic specialisms.

Bertalanffy (1979) makes three key points about the need to emphasize generality in general systems theory. First, it presents a novel paradigm in scientific thinking: the concept of system can be defined and developed in different ways as required by the objective of research, reflecting different aspects of the central notion. Second, general systems theory, then, involves scientific explorations of 'wholes' and 'wholeness' which, not so long ago, were considered to be metaphysical notions transcending the boundaries of science. Systems problems are problems of interrelations of a great number of variables. Third, models, conceptualizations and principles, such as the concepts of information, feedback, control, stability and circuit theory, far transcend specialist boundaries and are of an interdisciplinary nature.

These generic features of systems theory together constitute the 'uncommon sense' Bertalanffy argued for (Davidson 1983). He was fighting the common current practices of one-sidedness, because they were dangerous and still are, as a growing trend. The authority on creativity de Bono might say that Bertalanffy has been arguing for lateral rather than vertical thinking (de Bono 2006). Systems thinking, in most of its versions, was and is about fighting the narrow, over-specialized vertical thinking that can only follow prefabricated rules, for instance in solving crosswords. Systems or lateral thinking requires creative thinking along an unknown path. What is required is both types of thinking where each is appropriate. Lateral thinking must become a normal human habit alongside and in combination with vertical thinking. Let us return to Bertalanffy.

> What is to be defined and described as a system is not a question with an obvious or trivial answer. It will be readily agreed that a galaxy, a dog, a cell and an atom are real systems; that is, entities perceived in or inferred from observation, and existing independently of an observer. On the other hand, there are conceptual systems such as logic, mathematics (but e.g. also including music) which essentially are symbolic constructs; with abstracted systems (science) as a subclass of the latter, i.e. conceptual systems corresponding with reality. However, the distinction is by no means as sharp and clear as it would appear. . . . The distinction between 'real' objects and systems as given in observation and 'conceptual' constructs and systems cannot be drawn in any commonsense way. (Bertalanffy 1979, pp. XXI–XXII)

All this underpins our understanding of the term *system* (Mulej 1979, p. 10). Systems are mental pictures of real or abstract entities as objects of human thinking; they are concepts that represent something existing from a selected perspective, viewpoint or aspect. In mathematical formal terms, a system is a round-off entity consisting of elements and relations, which makes it holistic. In terms of contents, a system depends on its authors' selected viewpoint; hence, it does not comprise all attributes of the object under consideration, but only the selected part of them. This fact makes a system both holistic (formally, with no contents, or inside the selected viewpoint only) and one-sided (owing to the unavoidable selection of a viewpoint).[2]

Objects exist, and humans watch and manipulate them with different levels of holism. Total holism makes the object and the system as someone's mental picture of the object totally equal, but it reaches beyond human natural capacity. This is why humans often become specialized and limited to single viewpoints, causing humans to limit consideration of any object to a one-viewpoint system. By cooperation, normally an interdisciplinary one that includes several essential professions in a synergetic effort, a team can attain more holism – by a dialectical system. Both a system and a dialectical system exist inside the human mental world, in human thinking and feeling; they can be expressed for other humans and other living beings to receive information about humans' thinking and feeling in models. Thus, according to Bertalanffy (implicitly), a total holism is what systems thinking is all about in order to cover totally everything. Experience has shown that humans are not able to attain this level, not only because of bounded rationality but also because 1) we all are unavoidably specialized in single small fragments of humankind's entire knowledge and 2) we hardly learn and practise interdisciplinary creative cooperation aimed at more holism in our education.

What matters, too, is the fact that Bertalanffy used the wording 'systems teaching' rather than 'systems theory' in his original German version. This can be read as a crucial difference: teaching includes influence over people, while theory does not, but offers a generalized knowledge for people to use, if they care to. As we can see from François (2004), there are many systems theories, but only the dialectical systems theory speaks of influencing people (Mulej 1975, 1977, 1978, 1979; Mulej and Ženko 2004a, 2004b; Mulej *et al.* 1992, 2000, 2007).

DIALECTICAL SYSTEMS THINKING AND THE RELATED LAW OF REQUISITE HOLISM/REALISM

The European Union Communication (EU 2000) summarized the essence of systemic thinking with application to innovation in the following context. Humans who are living now are living in the time in which innovation has become more frequent and unavoidable than ever before. The most advanced areas of the world – Europe, North America, Australia, New Zealand, Japan and the four Pacific Rim tigers: Singapore, Hong Kong, Taiwan and South Korea – contain the 20 per cent of humankind who are living on innovation much more than the other 80 per cent are. The innovative society and economy require humans to master much more entanglement than ever before:

- There are no longer local markets hidden from the global market.
- There is no longer the likelihood that many humans will live without permanent renewal of their skills.
- There are no longer markets in which supply is not bigger than demand, except for the least advanced areas in which close to a billion people are hungry, while in the other areas about a billion people are too fat to be healthy, and except for the most demanded novelties, be they suggestions, potential innovations or innovations.
- There are no longer many areas in which humans can live with no innovation and therefore with no requisitely holistic thinking, called systems thinking in systems theory.
- Still, there are very few humans around the world who are capable of teaching holistic thinking and permitted to teach it in curricula. The role of narrow specialization, which is unavoidable but not sufficient for success, is so strong that people hardly see that the

requisitely holistic thinking makes specialization of any profession much more beneficial than any specialization alone. Nobody, whatever their profession, can live well without cooperation with people of other professions. Over-specialization kills, Bertalanffy rightly warned.

A good fifty years after the authors of systems theory succeeded in making this theory known, and after politicians of the world succeeded in using it (informally) by establishing the United Nations Organization – at least on paper – as the most holistic political organization of humankind, the EU found it necessary to explicitly link a 'systemic' view with innovation. In its communication (EU 2000, p.6), the EU, after reminding readers of its previous documents enhancing innovation, states:

> The Action Plan [First Action Plan for Innovation in Europe, 1996, based on Green Paper on Innovation, 1995] was firmly based on the 'systemic' view, in which innovation is seen as arising from complex interactions between many individuals, organizations and environmental factors, rather than as a linear trajectory from new knowledge to new product. Support for this view has deepened in recent years.

If this has to be stated explicitly in such documents, the question arises:

- Are we humans capable of interdisciplinary cooperation that we need almost every moment?
- What is the theoretical basis for those who are not currently capable of it to learn?

The empirical experience and references-based answer reads:

- Very few humans are by their nature and education capable of interdisciplinary cooperation, because specialists teach specialists to be specialists, including being proud of their specialization. This teaching is fine, but not enough: it may cause hiding from reality behind the walls of one's specialization and lacking respect for other specializations and their need for each other as well as for their capacity to solve real problems in interdisciplinary creative cooperation much better than in separation (Ackoff 2001, 2003; Gigch 2003).
- The theoretical basis to learn the skills of interdisciplinary cooperation stems from the original authors of systems theory and cybernetics. But many forget that the founders of systems theory and cybernetics had created their answers to the burning problems of their and our time in an interdisciplinary approach. This is where

Mulej's dialectical systems theory (DST) came in a good three decades ago to fill the gap.

● The well-intended and well-applied versions of systems theory which describe a part of reality inside the viewpoint of one or another traditional, specialized, scientific discipline do not match the well-stated EU definition of 'systems view'. Thus they help people solve other problems, but not the one of holism of thinking, decision making and action as a precondition of the survival of humankind and the planet on which we live and/or of success in any human action (Geyer *et al.* 2003).

In Table 8.1 our definition of holistic thinking (Mulej *et al.* 1992, reworked in 2007) is displayed.

A dialectical system comprises in a network all crucial viewpoints in order to help the observer attain a requisite holism (Figure 8.1), once a total, that is, real, holism with all viewpoints, synergies and attributes is reaching beyond the human capacity.

Inside the authors' (usually tacitly!) selected viewpoint, one tends to consider the object dealt with on the basis of limitation to one part of the really existing attributes only. When specialists of any profession use the word *system* to call something a system inside their own selected viewpoint, it makes a system fictitiously holistic. It does not include all existing attributes that could be seen from all viewpoints and all their synergies (Table 8.2).

The essence of the concept of the dialectical system and related law of requisite holism/realism is well expressed by Wilby (2005, p. 388), although she leaves open the question of viewpoints selected and thereby determining the boundaries of study:

> The goal of holistic study is not to look at 'everything'. Instead it is to make a decision about what is relevant to the study and what is not and to know and understand why those choices were made. The biases and interests affect the choice of what is likely to be included and excluded (i.e. what is in the system as opposed to what is relegated in the environment of the system).

What Wilby calls holistic, we call requisitely holistic.

Why is requisite holism important? There are scientists attempting to say that their discipline offers the only unique and unifying basis for dealing with systems. They do not speak of worldview, as Bertalanffy does, but of professional/scientific disciplines. Can they be right? Yes, in their own perspective they can. Can these be sufficient for holism? They can be so rarely, exceptionally. Nobody can be really holistic: teams can perhaps be requisitely holistic with interdisciplinary creative cooperation.

Table 8.1   Dialectical system of basic attributes of requisite holism/realism of thinking, decision making and action

Interdependent actual general groups of real features' attributes	Interdependent attributes of the requisitely holistic consideration of real features	Considered attributes of thinking about real features	Attributes of participants of consideration at stake	Surfacing of all these attributes in a given case
Complexity	Systemic.	Consideration of attributes of the whole that parts do not have.	Interdisciplinary team.	The final shared model resulting from research as a dialectical system of partial models.
Complicatedness	Systematic.	Consideration of the parts' attributes that the whole has not.	One-discipline group or individual.	Partial models resulting from one-viewpoint-based investigation.
Relations – basis for complexity	Dialectical.	Consideration of interdependences of parts that make parts unite into the new whole – emerging (in process) and synergy (in its outcome).	Ethics and practice of interdependence – path from one-discipline approach to interdisciplinary teamwork.	Shared attributes and complementary different attributes, which interact to make new synergetic attributes, i.e. from systematic to systemic ones.
Essence – basis for requisite realism and holism of consideration	All essential.	Consideration that selection of the systems of viewpoints must consider reality in line with the law of requisite holism for results of consideration to be applicable – by reduction of reductionism.	Capability of researchers to deviate from reality as little as possible in order to understand reality, including systemic, systematic and dialectical attributes of it.	Findings applicable in practice, although resulting from theoretical considerations.

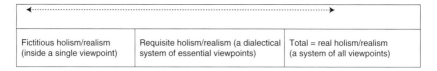

Fictitious holism/realism (inside a single viewpoint)	Requisite holism/realism (a dialectical system of essential viewpoints)	Total = real holism/realism (a system of all viewpoints)

Figure 8.1   The selected level of holism and realism of consideration of the selected topic between the fictitious, requisite and total holism and realism

Table 8.2   Relation between reality and holism/realism of human consideration of it

Level of realism of consideration of the selected topic	Level of simplification of consideration	Viewpoints of consideration taken into account	Components taken into account in consideration	Relations taken into account in consideration
Existing object to be dealt with	None.	All existing.	All existing.	All existing.
Dialectical system	Small, requisite.	All essential.	All essential.	All essential.
One-viewpoint system	Big owing to specialization.	Single, selected by specialization.	Selected inside the boundaries set by the selected viewpoint.	
Model of the one-viewpoint system	Big owing to specialization and modelling aimed at clear presentation.	Single, selected by specialization and simplified to be clear.	Selected inside the boundaries set by the selected viewpoint and shown in a simplified, modelled way.	

A brief summary of the law of requisite holism may thus read:

The law of requisite holism says that one needs always to try to do what many, but not all, have the habit of doing in their thinking, decisions and actions – doing one's best to avoid the exaggeration of both types: 1) the fictitious holism, which observers cause by limiting themselves to one single viewpoint in consideration of complex features and processes; 2) the total holism, which observers cause by no limitation to any selection of a system of viewpoints in consideration of complex features and processes. Instead, the middle ground between both exaggerations should be covered, which can be achieved by using a 'dialectical system', made by the author(s) as a system, entity or network of all essential and only essential viewpoints.

For requisite holism to be achieved three preconditions, at least, matter:

1. Both specialists and generalists are needed, as teams that feel ethics of interdependence and cooperate.
2. They include professionals from all and only essential professions or disciplines.
3. Their values are expressed in their ethics of interdependence and practised in a creative team, task force or session(s) based on an equal-footed cooperation rather than top-down one-way commanding.

Requisitely holistic thinking cannot include the global attributes only, because they make a part of the really existing attributes only, although they matter very much and tend to be subject to oversight by specialists. Neither can holistic thinking include the parts' attributes only, although they matter very much and tend to be subject to focus by specialists of single disciplines and professions. Oversight of relations, especially interdependences causing influences of parts over each other, may not be forgotten about in holistic thinking; specialists who have not developed the habit of considering specialists different from themselves tend to make crucial oversights in this respect. This experience means that they are not realistic.

THE APPLICATION OF DIALECTICAL SYSTEMS THINKING TO INNOVATIVE NEW VENTURE CREATION

How can this understanding of systems thinking inform understanding of the invention–innovation–new venture creation process? We believe there are four stages in the evolution from raw idea to realized, innovative new venture. We will set out the following concepts:

1. A new venture starts as an idea intended to become an outcome of the invention–innovation process in the form of establishment of the new venture. This is a complex and complicated attempt that rarely succeeds, unless all the crucial attributes are considered for the attempt to match the law of requisite holism (see for greater detail than is provided here Mulej and Kajzer 1998; Rebernik and Mulej 2000; Mulej 2007). Let us take a quick look at the attempt to create an innovation. We will see that no single scientific discipline alone can assure success, although many of them may be crucial, but they must also be networked into a dialectical system of all crucial viewpoints (e.g. Mulej

Idea →	Invention →	Suggestion →	Potential innovation →	Innovation → (diffusion)
Unclear potential	Promising a benefit	Recorded as promising a new benefit	Capable of yielding a benefit	Providing and yielding a benefit (to many)
Scientific research and applied development			Production and market management	
Scientists (for basic knowledge) and technologists (for applied knowledge)			Entrepreneurs, managers (with co-workers) and (many) customers (for final benefit)	
Interdependent complex phases of a complex process: all essential, none self-sufficient → need for requisite holism by (informal) systemic thinking				

Source: Ženko *et al.* 2008.

Figure 8.2   Summary of the invention–innovation–diffusion process

1974; for an explanation in English see Mulej *et al.* 2007; for a case in English see Potočan and Mulej 2007).

2. The basic phases of an invention–innovation–diffusion process include (Figure 8.2):

a. Creation of ideas concerning what new benefit could, perhaps, be created.

b. Division of the collected created ideas into the groups of not promising ideas and inventions that are promising ideas.

c. Selection of inventions in the groups of forgotten-about inventions and suggestions as the recorded inventions called suggestions.

d. Selection of suggestions in the groups of suggestions left aside for later consideration, suggestions to be sold and suggestions worked on as projects in order to develop potential innovations from them. The latter might later, but do not yet, create benefit to the potential users of them and therefore do not yet yield benefit such as revenue and profit to owners or creators.

e. After the thoughts, decisions and actions in phases a and b have taken place with the owners or creators and managers of their organizations, the decision as to whether or not a potential innovation will become an actually implemented innovation is up to its users, customers or buyers. From the viewpoint of owners, creators or managers now, after the phases of ideas management, research (both in a research department and else-where), development (both in a development department and elsewhere) and production (including human resources, finance, material and other supply management, legal issues, etc.), in

---

Innovation = (invention suggestion X entrepreneurship and entrepreneurial spirit X requisite holism X management X co-workers X suppliers X competitors X customers X innovation-friendly values, culture, ethics and norms X natural environment X socio-economic environment and other outer, i.e. objective, conditions X random factors, such as luck)

Note: X denotes interdependence.

Figure 8.3 Equation of interdependent preconditions of innovation

   this phase marketing, public relations and sales management are crucial.
f. Ideas, invention suggestions, potential innovations and innovations can be used 'in-house' or sold elsewhere. In both cases, as many users, customers or buyers of the potential innovation as possible should be persuaded and attracted. This topic is handled in the diffusion-of-novelty phase of the invention–innovation–diffusion process. This phase can follow every phase mentioned above.

The above insight into the invention–innovation–diffusion process demonstrates that this is a complex and complicated issue. So do data from surveys of practice showing that less than 5 per cent of innovation projects succeed (Chesbrough 2003; Nussbaum *et al.* 2005; Chesbrough *et al.* 2006; *Economist* 2006, 2007; Huston and Sakkab 2006; IBM 2006; McGregor 2006; Nussbaum 2006; Jangtchi 2007) and less than 1 per cent of ideas about inventions become innovations and successful ventures.

Owing to the above facts one must consider:

1. The 'innovation formula' to underline the complexity to be considered. The innovation and successful new venture (as an outcome of the invention–innovation process) result from synergy of many factors. If one is missing there is no long-term successful venture (Figure 8.3).
2. The related systems, that is, requisitely holistic monitoring, perception, thinking, emotional and spiritual life, decision making and action.
3. The resulting process from vision definition to the reality of successful working of the new venture.

CONCLUSION

A successfully created new venture can be considered a type of the invention–innovation–diffusion process resulting in innovation if it transforms an invention into a new benefit for its users, authors and owners. New ventures succeed in a similarly small percentage as other innovative attempts do. Requisitely holistic monitoring, perception, thinking, emotional and spiritual life, decision making, communication and action have normally been a better basis for success than the one-sidedness of specialists, who are inflexible and too narrow to succeed without interdisciplinary creative cooperation. According to experience, this capability is difficult for many specialists to attain. Systems theory, as embodied in the EU's definition of it in connection with innovation, can help them, to a certain but limited extent. While other systems theories are helpful for other problems, Mulej's dialectical systems theory has in 35 years of development and application proved to offer a helpful conceptual and practical approach to the creation of new ventures based on introducing and disseminating innovations.

NOTES

1. The Nobel Prize for Peace 2007 proves that awareness about this fact is growing, as does the Bali conference on climate change and related activities. Data are clear: since 1950 the population on the planet Earth has grown 2.5 times and its consumption of natural resources has grown seven times, while the planet Earth is not growing, but getting depleted very quickly. Humans will either start behaving in terms of systems thinking and requisite holism or leave the Earth as a dying planet to our children or, in the best-case scenario, to our grandchildren (Brown 2008; Taylor 2008; Korten 2009).
2. Therefore, in terms of contents, no system (as a mental picture of the object under consideration from a selected viewpoint) is holistic, but limited to one part of the really existing attributes of the object or topic under consideration. A system can anyway be composed of two kinds of smaller systems: a) subsystems cover attributes owing to which they differ from each other (such as countries of a continent, or production units of a factory, or bonds from blood vessels, etc.); b) partial systems cover attributes which the different parts share (such as a number of uniting organizations of a continent, human resources issues of an office or factory, etc.).

REFERENCES

Ackoff, L.R. (2003), 'Iconoclastic management authority advocates a "systemic" approach to innovation', interview by Robert J. Allio (sent to M. Mulej by email, 11 July 2003, from Ackoff Center: acasa@seas.upenn.edu).

Ackoff, L.R. (2001), 'Interaction among departments is crucial', *Kansas City Star*, 30 July, interview by Diane Staffors (received by M. Mulej by email from John Donges, jdonges@seas.upenn.edu).

Bertalanffy, L.V. (1979), *General Systems Theory: Foundations, Development, Applications*, rev. edn, New York: Braziller.

Brown, L.R. (2008), *Plan B 3.0: Mobilizing to Save Civilization*, New York and London: Earth Policy Institute, W.W. Norton.

Chesbrough, H.W. (2003), *Open Innovation: The New Imperative for Creating and Profiting from Technology*, Boston, MA: Harvard Business School Press.

Chesbrough, H.W., W. Vanhaverbeke and J. West (2006), *Open Innovation: Researching a New Paradigm*, Oxford, New York: Oxford University Press.

Davidson, M. (1983), *Uncommon Sense: The Life and Thought of Ludwig von Bertalanffy, Father of General Systems Theory*, Los Angeles: J.P. Tarcher.

de Bono, E. (2003), 'Creative thinking', Talk to the 3rd New Moment Ideas Campus, Piran, August 2003, New Moment Ideas Company, Ljubljana (taped by N. Mulej and her team).

de Bono, E. (2006), 'Lateralno razmišljanje' [Lateral thinking], *New Moment*, **30**.

Delmar, F. and S. Shane (2004), 'Legitimating first: Organizing activities and the survival of new ventures', *Journal of Business Venturing*, **19**(3), 385–410.

Drack, M. and W. Apfalter (2007), 'Is Paul Weiss' and von Bertalanffy's systems thinking still valid today?', *Systems Research and Behavioral Science*, **24**(5), 537–46.

Economist (2006), 'The new organisation: A survey of the company', 21 January, 1–20.

Economist (2007), 'Something new under the sun: A special report on innovation', 13 October, 1–24.

Elohim, J.L. (1999), 'A message from Professor Elohim', poster at the 11th WOSC Conference, Uxbridge.

EU (2000), *Communication from the Commission to the Council and the European Parliament: Innovation in a knowledge-driven economy*, COM(2000) 567 Final, Brussels: Commission of the European Communities.

François, C. (2004), *International Encyclopedia of Systems and Cybernetics*, 2nd edn, Munic: Saur.

Geyer, F., B. Hornung *et al.* (2003), The Fourth International Conference on Sociocybernetics: Sociocybernetics – the Future of the Social Sciences: Society from Ancient Greece to Cyberspace and Beyond. Abstracts and Program, ISA, RC 51, Kerkyra, Corfu, 30 June – 5 July, 2003.

Gigch, J.P.v. (2003), 'The paradigm and the science of management and of the management science disciplines', *Systems Research and Behavioral Science*, **20**(6), 499–506.

Huston, L. and N. Sakkab (2006), 'Connect and develop: Inside Procter & Gamble's new model for innovation', *Harvard Business Review*, **84**(3), 1–9.

IBM (2006), *The Global Innovation Outlook*, Armonk, NY: IBM.

Jangtchi, G.ur. (2007), 'Erfolgreich Produkte entwickeln 2007: Ideenmanagement und Kreativität; Kernkompetenzen und Markenbildung; Open Innovation und Netzwerkansätze', seminar, Ausseninstitut, Montanuniversität Leoben.

Korten, D.S. (2009), *Agenda for a New Economy: From Phantom Wealth to Real Wealth*, San Francisco: Berrett-Koehler.

McGregor, J. (2006), 'The world's most innovative companies', *Business Week*, 24 April, 63–76.

Mulej, M. (1974), 'Dialektična teorija sistemov in ljudski reki', *Naše gospodarstvo*, **21**(3–4), 207–12.

Mulej, M. (1975), 'Dialektična teorija sistemov', lecture notes, University of Ljubljana, Faculty of Sport, MA course on systems theory. (A few articles in Slovene journals soon followed.)

Mulej, M. (1977), 'A note on dialectical systems thinking', *International Cybernetics Newsletter*, p. 63.

Mulej, M. (1978), 'Toward the dialectical systems theory', in R. Trappl, P. Hanika and F. Pichler (eds), *Progress in Cybernetics and Systems Research*, Vienna: OeSGK.

Mulej, M. (1979), *Ustvarjalno delo in dialektična teorija sistemov* [Creative work and the dialectical systems theory] (in Slovenian), Celje: Razvojni center.

Mulej, M. (2007), 'Systems theory: A worldview and/or a methodology aimed at requisite holism/realism of humans' thinking, decisions and action', *Systems Research and Behavioral Science*, **24**(3), 347–57.

Mulej, M. and S. Kajzer (1998), 'Ethics of interdependence and the law of requisite holism', in M. Rebernik and M. Mulej (eds), *STIQE '98: Proceedings of the 4th International Conference on Linking Systems Thinking, Innovation, Quality, Entrepreneurship and Environment*, Maribor: Institute of Systems Research Maribor *et al.*

Mulej, M. and Z. Ženko (2004a), *Dialektična teorija sistemov in invencijsko-inovacijski management. (Kratek prikaz)*, Maribor: Management Forum.

Mulej, M. and Z. Ženko (2004b), *Introduction to Systems Thinking with Application to Invention and Innovation Management*, Maribor: Management Forum.

Mulej, M., G. de Zeeuw, R. Espejo, R. Flood, M. Jackson, Š. Kajzer, J. Mingers, B. Rafolt, M. Rebernik, W. Suojanen, P. Thornton and D. Uršič (1992), *Teorije sistemov*, Maribor: Univerza v Mariboru, Ekonomsko-poslovna fakulteta.

Mulej, M., R. Espejo, M. Jackson, Š. Kajzer, J. Mingers, P. Mlakar, N. Mulej, V. Potočan, M. Rebernik, A. Rosicky, B. Schiemenz, S. Umpleby, D. Uršič and R. Vallee (2000), *Dialektična in druge mehkosistemske teorije (podlaga za celovitost in uspeh managementa)*, Maribor: Univerza v Mariboru, Ekonomsko-poslovna fakulteta.

Mulej, M., V. Čančer, A. Hrast, K. Jurše, Š. Kajzer, J. Knez-Riedl, N. Mulej, V. Potočan, B. Rosi, D. Uršič and Z. Ženko (2007), *The Law of Requisite Holism and Ethics of Interdependence: Basics of the Dialectical Systems Thinking (Applied to Innovation in Catching-Up Countries)*, available at www.gesi.ar

Nussbaum, B. (2006), 'On Inside innovation', *Businessweek, Supplement*, June.

Nussbaum, B., R. Berner and D. Brady (2005), 'Special report. Get creative! How to build innovative companies. and: A creative corporation toolbox', *Business Week*, August, 51–68.

Potočan, V. and M. Mulej (eds) (2007), *Transition into an Innovative Enterprise*, Maribor: University of Maribor, Faculty of Economics and Business.

Rebernik, M. and M. Mulej (2000), 'Requisite holism, isolating mechanisms and entrepreneurship', *Kybernetes*, **29**(9/10), 1126–40.

Rebernik, M., P. Tominc and K. Pušnik (2008), *Premalo razvojno usmerjenih podjetij: GEM Slovenija 2007*, Maribor: University of Maribor, Faculty of Economics and Business, IPMMP, available at www.gemslovenia.org.

Shepherd, D., E. Douglas and M. Shanley (2000), 'New venture survival: Ignorance, external shocks, and risk reduction strategies', *Journal of Business Venturing*, **15**(5/6), 393–410.

Širec, K. and M. Rebernik (eds) (2009), *Dynamics of Slovenian Entrepreneurship: Slovenian Entrepreneurship Observatory 2008*, Maribor: Faculty of Economics and Business.

Taylor, G. (2008), *Evolution's Edge: The Coming Collapse and Transformation of Our World*, Gabriola Island, BC: New Society Publishers.

Wilby, J. (2005), 'Combining a systems framework with epidemiology in the study of emerging infectious disease', *Systems Research and Behavioral Science*, **22**(5), 385–98.

Ženko, Z., M. Mulej, V. Potočan, B. Rosi and T. Mlakar (2008), 'A model of making theory as invention to become an innovation', in M. Mulej, M. Rebernik and B. Bradac (eds), *STIQE 2008: Proceedings of the 9th International Conference on Linking Systems Thinking, Innovation, Quality, Entrepreneurship and Environment*, Maribor: University of Maribor, Faculty of Economics and Business, IPMMP and Slovenian Society for Systems Research (with honorary co-sponsorship of the European Academy of Sciences and Arts, Salzburg, Austria, and IFSR – International Federation for Systems Research, Vienna, Austria), pp. 145–52.

9 Social networks and new venture creation: the dark side of networks

Kim Klyver, Majbritt Rostgaard Evald and Kevin Hindle

INTRODUCTION

Since the beginning of the 1970s there has been an increased focus on social networks in a wide variety of organizational research. This has resulted in exponential growth of publications in the area (Borgatti and Foster 2003). In their review of social networks in organizational research, Borgatti and Foster (2003) argue that attention mostly has been directed toward positive consequences of network structure, rather than causes. This might be due to many reasons, but most likely this has to be due to the fact that the field is young and has strong aims to achieve legitimacy. The close association between social networks and social capital might also explain a possibly excessive attention to positive aspects. Social capital is often argued to be the value created and stored in social networks, and often social capital studies seek to explain variation in performance as a function of social network composition. Thus this focus has caused a sometimes undue fascination with the positive aspects of social networks. It may be argued that most studies so far have focused relatively more on positive opportunities provided by network structure rather than network constraints (Adler and Kwon 2002). One important 'spillover' effect of an overly sanguine view of what social networks contribute concerns research in new venture creation in the entrepreneurship field. Research into new venture creation has focused predominantly on which activities a single entrepreneur or team of entrepreneurs are creating in the process of new venture creation. This sets the primary focus on the positive achievements an entrepreneur can gain by activating his or her personal network to obtain valuable resources. What Adler and Kwon (2002) call 'downsides' and others call the 'dark side' of the social network phenomenon in general is therefore also applicable when the spotlight turns to how social networks influence the new venture creation process. The main purpose of this chapter is, therefore, to discuss academic achievements of research on social networks and new venture creation and specifically address the need to direct attention toward the often neglected detrimental consequences of networks in new venture creation research.

In the following section we define new venture creation. Subsequently we discuss how a network can influence the behaviour of individuals and which perspectives of the literature concerning networks and new venture creation should become focal for researchers. Then assumptions made in the body of research concerning networks and new venture creation are discussed, followed by a literature review of the 'dark side' of social networks. We end with a call for more research on the dark side of social networks, specifically with regard to new venture creation.

NEW VENTURE CREATION IN THE FIELD OF ENTREPRENEURSHIP

A contentious discussion takes place in entrepreneurship research concerning the definition and operationalization of entrepreneurship. Broadly, this discussion can be divided into two perspectives. The first perspective (the opportunity perspective) argues that entrepreneurship is about discovery, evaluation and exploitation of opportunities (Shane and Venkataraman 2000), whereas the second perspective (the emergence view) regards entrepreneurship as 'firm emergence' or 'firm creation' (Gartner 1993). In this chapter, both perspectives are appreciated, but our approach to entrepreneurship leans a little more to the emergence perspective, as is to be expected when the core subject matter is new venture creation. Central for new venture creation research is to uncover the initial stages of organization emergence, including getting an idea, evaluating it as a real opportunity, and conceptualizing the opportunity to an entrepreneurial project so that it can be exploited by materializing the opportunity to a new and emerging organization. By defining entrepreneurship as an emergence process, entrepreneurship can be seen as synonymous with the shaping of new structures, because new ventures typically are characterized by the extent to which they display formal structure, administrative procedures and objectives. However, an important boundary exists, as conventional organization theory 'begins at the place where the emerging organization ends' (Katz and Gartner 1988, p.429). This means that research into new venture creation in the entrepreneurship field primarily concentrates on the process that leads to the creation of a new venture, while organization theory primarily focuses on what happens when the organization has been created and is further developed.

Research in new venture creation is sometimes pictured as one out of many sequences a new venture goes through during its life cycle. Examples of such sequences are 'initiation' (Kroeger 1974), 'conception' and 'gestation' (Reynolds 1997) or 'idea', 'opportunity' and 'project' (Fayolle 2003). Common to most sequential models is to view the entrepreneurial process as a linear and forward-moving process. However, Fayolle (2003) divides the entrepreneurial process into various sequences, allowing relapse from later phases to earlier ones to occur. In addition, the phases do not necessarily develop in the outlined order. Some entrepreneurs, for example, formally establish an organization before they have evaluated to what extent the idea represents a real opportunity. Finally, the process can stop at any given level. For example, a new organization may never come into existence. Fayolle's model shows that new venture creation does not only consist of one single step – namely from a situation 'without a new venture' to a situation 'with a new venture'. On the contrary, it is possible to talk about a number of steps on the way toward a new and independent venture. Because of the fluid crossing between the situation 'without a new venture' and the situation 'with a new venture', it is in practice hard to decide when a new venture is created.

A central problem is, however, that the above-mentioned sequence models do not catch what triggers or activates the new venture creation process. As far back as 1985 Gartner had already tried to provide valuable insight into different variables that constitute the process of new venture creation by recognizing the need to explain new venture creation as a multi-dimensional process that takes place as a result of an interaction between four components: individual(s), the environment, the organization and the process. The dominance of each variable during the new venture creation process was however not explained, as the literature of entrepreneurship at that point in time suggested that differences among entrepreneurs and among their ventures were as great as the variation between entrepreneurs and non-entrepreneurs and between new firms and established firms (Gartner 1985, p. 696). Since then only a few attempts to exactly identify what triggers new venture creation or what sub-processes lead up to new venture creation have been discussed and suggested (Davidsson and Honig 2003). A model worth mentioning is the process model of new venture creation suggested by Bhave (1994), which focuses on how new venture creation can be stimulated either externally or internally. As such, the model captures the sub-processes of initiating a new venture in that some individuals consciously chase the creation of a new venture while others seem to end up as entrepreneurs as a result of external factors. Another way to uncover the new venture creation process is illustrated in models that combine the theory of network and new venture creation (Hite and Hesterly 2001). For instance, Davidsson and Honig (2003) concluded that social capital especially was a strong predictor for creating a new venture. The findings showed that 'entrepreneurs would be well advised to develop and promote networks of all sorts, particularly interfirm and intrafirm relations' (Davidsson and Honig 2003, p. 303).

Thus, broad consensus has emerged among entrepreneurship scholars that networks play a central role in successful firm emergence. The advantage with a network approach is no doubt that it captures the emergent processes of organizing by focusing on the evolving nature of linkages between units and exchange processes between actors (Gartner *et al.* 1992). A concrete model that captures this dynamic and ever-evolving process is suggested by Larson and Starr (1993). The model 'depicts the dynamics underlying the acquisition of resources, the formation of exchange relationships, and the inherent trial-and-error discovery and learning process of new venture creation' (Larson and Starr 1993, p. 4). Thus 'the process describes the transformation of exchange relationships from a set of relatively simple, often single-dimensional dyadic exchanges into a dense set – a network – of multidimensional and multilayered organizational relationships' (Larson and Starr 1993, p. 4). To know more about how network theory can be approached to enhance our understanding of the new venture creation process, we continue with a discussion on how a network can influence the behaviour of individuals. We also offer a further critique of extant research in this area.

NETWORK INFLUENCES ON THE BEHAVIOUR OF INDIVIDUALS

Theory of the particular relationship between entrepreneurship and networks is based on traditional social network theory. The traditional theory was originally developed in the field of sociology but has since expanded to a number of disciplines in the social sciences, including organization theory and entrepreneurship theory. The crucial argument in social network theory is that networks influence the behaviour of individuals. Lin (2001) mentions four fundamental ways in which networks influence the behaviour of individuals. Networks 1) provide persons with information that can be used in relation to the situations which they face, 2) influence other persons in the network by influencing decisions and actions that are to be made, 3) create social legitimacy for persons within a network structure to get access to resources, and 4) develop and strengthen the identities of the persons.

The theory of entrepreneurship and network has primarily focused on the resources that can be obtained through networks. Hoang and Antoncic (2003) write:

> Interpersonal and interorganizational relationships are viewed as the media through which actors gain access to a variety of resources held by other actors.

> With the exception of work on the role of networks to access capital . . . most research has focused on the entrepreneur's access to intangible resources. . . . A key benefit of networks for the entrepreneurial process is the access they provide to information and advice. (Hoang and Antoncic 2003, p. 169)

The resources which can be provided through social networks are often referred to as *social capital*. Social capital refers to the means and resources that the entrepreneur benefits by through his or her personal contacts and acquaintances.

Even though social network theory has a long history, the interest in networks within entrepreneurship is relatively recent. Birley (1985), Aldrich and Zimmer (1986) and Johannisson (1988) made the first contributions. These contributions can be seen as a backlash to the research dominated by the psychological approach in which the entrepreneur was treated as an individual without consideration of the environments and contexts that the individual was part of. On the contrary, as mentioned, in the theory of entrepreneurship and networks, an entrepreneur's network is considered a medium through which the entrepreneur can gain access to different resources. The individual and his or her environments are in this way in play at the same time in entrepreneurial network theory. Moreover, the importance of the network not only is related to the start-up of a new venture but is valid throughout the entire life cycle of the venture (Hoang and Antoncic 2003).

SOCIAL NETWORKS AND NEW VENTURE CREATION

In general, two main arguments and one synthesis can be found in research into the relationship between social networks and new venture creation. The first argument could be termed the 'heterogeneity' argument. Here it is argued that individuals can more efficiently obtain valuable resources and benefits from access to variation and diversity. Scholars have elaborated on the argument on two levels: the relationship level and the network level. Granovetter (1973) is a strong advocate for the 'heterogeneity' argument and focuses on the relationship level. He argues that the strength of ties impacts the nature of resources individuals can obtain from them. According to Granovetter (1973), individuals are more likely to obtain valuable resources – or information – from weak ties, as these weak ties are more likely to circulate in a higher volume and variety of social networks and therefore to possess different and wider-ranging resources. The argument is supported by Burt (1992). He argues that the typical disadvantage with strong network ties is that they involve closely related individuals who, accordingly, possess similar information. As a consequence, many ties in such a network become redundant (from a utility perspective), as they do not add any new resources or information. Burt (1992) does, however, take the argument further to the network level and argues that what he calls *structural holes* in a network are important in order to obtain valuable resources and information. Structural holes emerge when certain people in a network are not connected. This has the consequence that some people become central and can act as bridges to resources and information. Individuals who have networks with many structural holes are more likely to access non-redundant resources and information.

The second perspective is basically the opposite and could be termed the 'homogeneity' argument. According to this argument, individuals obtain benefits from consistency, cohesion and minimal variation. The nature of disagreement between the two arguments is the kind of benefits or resources they focus on. The 'heterogeneity' argument focuses on resources that basically are available to everyone. However, people are limited in their access, owing to asymmetric information distribution. Thus, through their position in the network, they overcome some of these barriers of asymmetric information. The 'homogeneity' argument, on the other hand, focuses on resources and information that are only shared with certain others (Krackhardt 1992). Here resources and information do not travel from person to person just because a direct or indirect relationship exists. The relationship needs to contain certain properties, for example trust. Examples of the kind of resources the homogeneity argument is interested in include emotional support or sensitive market information. On the relationship level, it is therefore argued that, among strong relations, trust and mutual obligations are more likely to develop. And, based on these properties of the relationship, individuals are more likely to obtain emotional support and network contacts are more likely to share sensitive information. On the network level, it is argued that dense and cohesive networks, often based on trust and mutual obligations among relations, decrease the uncertainty of exchange and increase the ability to cooperate (Coleman 1988b, 1990). Aldrich and Zimmer (1986) talk about a collective action capacity developed through trust and common norms.

The main difference between the two arguments is thus that, while the heterogeneity argument stresses that weak ties and networks consisting of many structural holes are essential in order to obtain network benefits, the homogeneity argument stresses the importance of strong ties and cohesive networks. Accordingly, there seems, superficially at least, to be a battleground between the heterogeneity argument and the homogeneity argument. However, this is not necessarily the case. Many scholars have tried to bind the two arguments together in a synthesis. Proponents of the synthesis perspective argue that it is a matter of balance rather than a battle (Uzzi 1996), and this balance depends on the situation and nature of the challenges individuals are facing. In different situations, individuals need access to different kinds of resources. Lin wrote (2001, p. 27):

> For preserving or maintaining resources (i.e., expressive actions), denser networks may have a relative advantage. . . . On the other hand, searching for and obtaining resources not presently possessed (e.g., instrumental actions), such as looking for a job or a better job, accessing and extending bridges in the network should be more useful.

Following this synthesis, individuals need to activate a network with a balance between cohesion and variance that fits their resource needs. As their resource needs change, they develop their network according to the new requirements.

Several models, primarily stage models, attempt to describe how the entrepreneur's network develops during the entrepreneurial process. In the very early stages of new venture creation when the entrepreneur looks for an opportunity, the entrepreneur needs non-redundant market information in order to be able to create or discover a new opportunity. Therefore the entrepreneur is interested in a network consisting of many different persons – a network with many structural holes and in which the entrepreneur has weak ties to other persons (Klyver and Hindle 2007). When the entrepreneur has identified an opportunity and is about to start the new venture, there is suddenly a need for other resources. In this stage, there is a demand for advice and support to be able to make the final decision about starting, and there might be a need for supply of capital. For that reason, the aim is a closer network consisting of many strong ties, including many family members (Evald *et al.* 2006). After the venture is started and the entrepreneur moves forward in the life cycle of the venture, some of the persons in the network are being replaced. At this stage, it is crucial to the entrepreneur to be established in the market and, consequently, the entrepreneur needs access to market information again. Therefore the network will once again change to a network consisting of many different persons – a network with structural holes and a network with more weak ties, for instance to new acquaintances (Larson and Starr 1993; Evald *et al.* 2006). It appears that the network changes during the entrepreneurial process and that these changes can be related to the problems the entrepreneur is confronted with and thus the resources the entrepreneur needs. However, as argued at the beginning of the chapter, the dark side of the nexus between social network and new venture creation has been neglected in the research so far. Attention is mainly focused on positive achievements an entrepreneur or team of entrepreneurs can gain by activating their personal networks to get valuable resources. Hence prior research rests on a range of assumptions.

ASSUMPTIONS MADE IN RESEARCH ON THE NEXUS BETWEEN NETWORK AND NEW VENTURE CREATION

In most studies on social networks in new venture creation a rational choice approach is taken. Within this approach, individuals – being managers, entrepreneurs or employees – are perceived as purposive actors who include people in the network on a criterion of utility in terms of the resources those others can bring in support of the individual's tasks. The people in the network are supporters who provide mostly tangible resources such as advice and funds, and perhaps also some less tangible resources such as legitimacy and emotional support. In this conceptuality, the business sphere is isolated from other spheres of life, meaning that any acts in the business life can be separated from other spheres and will not have any consequences. The relationship between the ego and actors in the network is typically specific (namely supportive), affectively neutral, contractual and short-term. The 'other' people are carefully selected by the ego actor in order to avoid constraints in the network. Thus four assumptions can be identified:

- Individuals are purposeful actors.
- Networks are selected.
- Relationships are specific.
- The business sphere is isolated from other life domains.

We believe that these assumptions might not be realistic. At least, this is the argument provided by what might be called 'the embedded perspective'. First, previous research into individuals' rationality shows clearly a lack of rationality or at least that only bounded rationality prevails. Individuals interact with others not only because they try to obtain benefits, but also because human interaction is part of being human! Second, it may be presumed that networks can have a history as well as a present selection mode. Individuals carry with them a 'stable core' of personal associations, some of which are inherited or acquired accidentally rather than purposively chosen. This core is more or less unchangeable. Third, some relationships between people tend to be diffuse (not only supporting, but also detracting), affective, trusting and long-term in contrast to being specific. Fourth, decisions and actions in the business sphere can have huge impacts in other spheres of life. Research on family business, specifically on how business and family spheres interfere and conflict with each other, illustrates this. Thus it seems as though many previous studies on social networks and organizational behaviour have been under-socialized and have not taken sufficient account of the influence from people's past and current contexts. It seems more realistic to assume the following:

- Individuals are not only purposeful actors.
- Part of the network is derived from the past.
- Relationships are also diffuse.
- Different spheres in life are mixed together.

These four new assumptions have profound implications for how social networks might influence organizational behaviour. Specifically, two limitations to the previously described 'balancing' act between cohesion and variance through network activation can be identified.

The life individuals have lived sets limits to people whom these individuals can 'choose' from when they are developing their networks. An individual's life history has a major role in determining the range and nature of those who can reasonably be expected to form part of that individual's network. In this sense, history opens or closes the window of opportunity on network participation. So individuals simply cannot choose to network with everyone – they need some sort of past direct or indirect connection. As individuals are different in nature and have lived different lives, some have a huge reservoir of potential network members to choose from, whereas others have a far more limited range of choice.

Now let us bring in the consideration, discussed earlier, that some relationships are diffuse and different spheres of life are all mixed together and another limitation on network choice possibilities emerges. Individuals develop mutual obligations with certain people – especially people close to them. These mutual obligations might contrast with their intentions and will potentially interfere with their 'free' choice. At least they have to consider how potential personal choices may influence people with whom they have mutual obligations. A classic 'for instance' is that it is for many people necessary to consider their spouse's opinion before they take any huge final vocational decisions that might affect family life. They cannot, without profound personal consequences, just exclude (read 'not select') this part of the network. Mutual obligations potentially constrain individuals' freedom of choice. They need to consider how their decisions affect those with whom they feel mutually obligated. From these diffuse mutual obligations emerges the 'stable core', the largely unchangeable network we have previously discussed. With or without individuals' willingness this core influences individuals' decisions. Changes in the core often have huge consequences.

Recognizing these two limitations on how people in organizational contexts can choose to network, we are moving into what we have previously termed 'the dark side' of the social network phenomenon when it comes to new venture creation. Below is a short review of the extant literature.

PREVIOUS RESEARCH ON THE DARK SIDE OF SOCIAL NETWORKS

Studies on the dark side of social networks have taken two main paths: a sociometric approach and an egocentric approach. The sociometric literature can further be divided into studies that focus on how being embedded in a certain community constrains community members and, second, how social capital on a community level can be used to achieve outputs that may be viewed as beneficial by the individual protagonist but detrimental by other members of the community.

An important contribution concerning how communities constrain community members is referred to by Portes (1998), who mentions Geertz's (1963) study of successful entrepreneurs in Bali who experienced excessive claims from other less successful kinsmen about jobs and loans. Owing to strong norms of mutual assistance, Geertz found, otherwise promising businesses were turned into less successful businesses, at least from an economic perspective. Portes and Sensenbrenner (1993) found a similar mechanism in their study. They found that entrepreneurs obtained benefits from cohesive networks to launch their business, but later this same cohesive network constrained their ability to exploit new opportunities, owing to obligations resulting from network associations. Portes (1998) also refers to different studies that provide evidence of downward-levelling norms. Here an individual's success outside his or her group undermines group cohesion, since the cohesion basically is grounded in the perception that success outside its bonds is impossible. Thus people experiencing success outside their group can be viewed by some as violating their social heritage, and their behaviour is perceived as disrespectful. Studies that support such downward-levelling norms include Bourgois' (1995) study of Puerto Rican crack dealers in the Bronx, Stepick's (1992) study of Haitian American youth in Miami, and Matute-Bianchi's (1986, 1991) study of Mexican-American teenagers in Southern California, as well as Foley's (2003, 2008) study of Indigenous entrepreneurs in Australia.

Another concept also dealing with constraints emerging from community norms is 'mixed embeddedness'. It was developed by Kloosterman *et al.* (1999) in their study of immigrant businesses in the Netherlands. They developed the concept as a reaction to Granovetter's (1985) concept of embeddedness, arguing that Granovetter's concept is too narrow. Mixed embeddedness tries to capture the role of co-ethnic networks simultaneously with immigrants' relations to their host society. Some of the main conclusions from the studies on mixed embeddedness are that immigrant individuals have problems breaking out from the traditional niches among which their community belongs, not only because of community embeddedness but also because of the economic and institutional conditions in the host society.

In studies of ethnic groups and communities, another dark side aspect of social capital has also been identified (Waldinger 1995). Here it is emphasized that the same strong ties that help people within a group are excluding people outside the group. Waldinger's (1995) study of how white ethnics controlled the construction trades and the fire and police unions in New York is an often cited example, but another example includes Coleman's (1988a, mentioned in Portes 1998 and Portes and Landolt 1996) study of Jewish merchants' monopoly of the New York diamond trade.

The above examples focus on the constraining mechanism social networks potentially have on their members. However, as mentioned, studies on the dark side of social networks also include those situations where the benefits of social networks are used in order to achieve things not desirable for society. This is essential. Putzel (1997), for instance, argues that the high level of trust in Germany and Japan also might have made them particularly susceptible to fascism. Ostrom (1997) reminds us that 'cartels and organized crime are networks of relationships that lower overall productivity while generating disproportional benefits for a few beneficiaries' (Ostrom 1997, p. 162). Nee and Nee's 1972 study of Chinatown inhabitants in San Francisco (mentioned in Portes and Landolt 1996) reveals that, even though communities may help community members in launching successful businesses and protect them from outside discrimination, this also has its downsides. The community is led by a family clan which uses the control of business opportunities to seize central control in many other aspects of life.

Also in the debate between the homogeneity argument and the heterogeneity argument discussions on the dark aspects of networks prevail. For instance, Gargiulo and Benassi (2000) perceive cohesive networks as the dark side, using the phrase 'trapped in your own net' because of their finding that managers with cohesive networks were less likely to adapt their networks to new requirements.

In other studies, it has been argued that individuals, owing to their bounded rationality, develop inefficient social networks. For instance, Gargiulo and Benassi (2000) talk about relational inertia. Hence it is argued that individuals, even though they do not expect to gain anything from the relationship, stay in these mutual exchange relationships endlessly. Thus bounded rationality does seem to cause the inefficient development of social networks. In this regard, a finding by Uzzi (1997) is interesting even though the focus is on organizations and not individuals. Uzzi argues that embedded transactions are more functional than arm's length transactions up to a point. An inverted U-relationship between embeddedness and performance seems to exist. While embedded transactions are superior to unembedded ones, it still remains possible for an organization to depend too much on embedded ties. If an unbalanced number of an organization's relationships are embedded, then the organization becomes trapped by these relationships.

Also Adler and Kwon (2002) make us aware of the risk associated with building social networks. They argue that establishing and maintaining relationships may not be beneficial when the time spent is adequately taken into consideration. Using longitudinal data from the Australian Bureau of Statistics, Watson (2007) found that small business owners' benefits from networking take the form of a reversed U-shape curve. In the beginning, increased networking increases performance. However, when a certain level of networking is reached, the time spent does not cover the additional benefits obtained. Watson, therefore, argues that only a certain level of networking activity is beneficial.

Finally, power disadvantages can be perceived as a dark side of social networks. Normally, power to influence others is something that is highlighted as a benefit of social networks (Sandefur and Laumann 1998). However, the power relationship might be reversed, in the sense that someone's power advantage is another's power disadvantage. Further, as argued by Ahuja (1998), the information benefits gained from having many direct ties with many other ties simultaneously create a power disadvantage, as the focal actor is no longer an essential actor in its ties' network – they have many other relations to rely on too.

A CALL FOR MORE RESEARCH ON THE DARK SIDE OF SOCIAL NETWORKS IN NEW VENTURE CREATION

We have shown that there is some extant research attention paid to studies on the dark side of social networks, but, we argue, not nearly enough. We join other scholars who have emphasized the importance of further research in this area. For instance, Portes (1998) argues it is important to emphasize the less desirable consequences of social capital for two reasons: first, to avoid a perception of social capital as an unmixed blessing and, second, to make sociological research in this area more dispassionate and keep it away from moralizing statements. Adler and Kwon (2002) also encourage research into the dark side of social capital: 'social capital research would benefit from a more systematic assessment of risks as well as benefits. We need to understand better the downsides of social capital both for the focal actor and for others' (p. 35).

In this chapter we have tried to advance this call for research into the dark side of social networks as they affect new venture creation. The focus on the benefits of social networks in entrepreneurship and new venture creation research is strong and, in common with sociology and organizational theory, entrepreneurship research has a great need for a more sophisticated perspective. The need for better, more balanced, less sanguinely biased research on the role of networks in new venture creation research is urgent. The key to improved future research is the need to take a starting point based in the more empirically realistic assumptions about networking outlined by the embedded perspective. Here it is argued not only that individuals are purposeful actors but that part of individuals' networks is derived from the past, that relationships are diffuse and that different spheres in life are mixed together. Using these assumptions as the starting-point, the vital study of the effects of social networks on new venture creation can generate improved research and provide the field with a more empirically realistic approach.

REFERENCES

Adler, P.S. and S.-W. Kwon (2002), 'Social capital: Prospects for a new concept', *Academy of Management Review*, **27**(1), 17–40.
Ahuja, G. (1998), *Collaboration Networks, Structural Holes and Innovation: A Longitudinal Study*, San Diego, CA: Academy of Management Meeting.
Aldrich, H.E. and C. Zimmer (1986), 'Entrepreneurship through social networks', in D.L. Sexton and R.W. Smilor (eds), *The Art and Science of Entrepreneurship*, New York: Ballinger, pp. 3–23.
Bhave, M.P. (1994), 'A process model of new venture creation', *Journal of Business Venturing*, **9**(3), 223–42.
Birley, S. (1985), 'The role of networks in the entrepreneurial process', *Journal of Business Venturing*, **1**, 107–17.
Borgatti, S.P. and P.C. Foster (2003), 'The network paradigm in organizational research: A review and typology', *Journal of Management*, **29**(6), 991–1013.
Bourgois, P. (1995), *In Search of Respect: Selling Crack in El Barrio*, New York: Cambridge University Press.
Burt, R.S. (1992), *Structural Holes: The Social Structure of Competition*, London: Harvard University Press.

Coleman, J.S. (1988a), 'The creation and destruction of social capital: Implications for the law', *Notre Dame Journal of Law, Ethics & Public Policy*, **3**, 375–404.

Coleman, J.S. (1988b), 'Social capital in the creation of human capital', *American Journal of Sociology*, **94**(1), 95–120.

Coleman, J.S. (1990), *Foundation of Social Theory*, Cambridge, MA: Harvard University Press.

Davidsson, P. and B. Honig (2003), 'The role of social and human capital among nascent entrepreneurs', *Journal of Business Venturing*, **18**(3), 301–31.

Evald, M.R., K. Klyver and S.G. Svendsen (2006), 'The changing importance of the strength of ties throughout the entrepreneurial process', *Journal of Enterprising Culture*, **14**(1), 1–26.

Fayolle, A. (2003), 'Research and researchers at the heart of entrepreneurial situations', in C. Steyaert and D. Hjorth (eds), *New Movements in Entrepreneurship*, Cheltenham, UK and Northampton, MA, USA: Edward Elgar Publishing, pp. 35–50.

Foley, D. (2003), 'An examination of Indigenous Australian entrepreneurs', *Journal of Developmental Entrepreneurship*, **8**(2), 133–52.

Foley, D. (2008), 'Indigenous (Australian) entrepreneurship', *International Journal of Business and Globalisation*, **2**(4), 419–36.

Gargiulo, M. and M. Benassi (2000), 'Trapped in your own net? Network cohesion, structural holes, and the adaptation of social capital', *Organization Science*, **11**(3), 183–96.

Gartner, W.B. (1985), 'A conceptual framework for describing the phenomenon for new venture creation', *Academy of Management Review*, **10**(4), 696–706.

Gartner, W.B. (1993), 'Words lead to deeds: Towards an organizational emergence vocabulary', *Journal of Business Venturing*, **8**(3), 231–9.

Gartner, W.B., B.J. Bird and J.A. Starr (1992), 'Acting as if: Differentiating entrepreneurial from organizational behavior', *Entrepreneurship Theory and Practice*, **16**(3), 13–31.

Geertz, C. (1963), *Peddlers and Princes*, Chicago: University of Chicago Press.

Granovetter, M.S. (1973), 'The strength of weak ties', *American Journal of Sociology*, **78**(6), 1360–80.

Granovetter, M.S. (1985), 'Economic action and social structure: The problem of embeddedness', *American Journal of Sociology*, **91**(3), 481–510.

Hite, J.M. and W.S. Hesterly (2001), 'The evolution of firm networks: From emergence to early growth of the firm', *Strategic Management Journal*, **22**(3), 275–86.

Hoang, H. and B. Antoncic (2003), 'Network-based research in entrepreneurship: A critical review', *Journal of Business Venturing*, **18**(2), 165–87.

Johannisson, B. (1988), 'Business formation: A network approach', *Scandinavian Journal of Management*, **4**(3/4), 83–99.

Katz, J.A. and W.B. Gartner (1988), 'Properties of emerging organizations', *Academy of Management Review*, **13**(3), 429–41.

Kloosterman, R., J. van der Leun and J. Rath (1999), 'Mixed embeddedness: (In)formal economic activities and immigrant businesses in the Netherlands', *International Journal of Urban and Regional Research*, June, 253–67.

Klyver, K. and K. Hindle (2007), 'The role of social networks at different stages of business formation', *Small Enterprise Research: The Journal of SEAANZ*, **15**(1), 22–38.

Krackhardt, D. (1992), 'The strength of strong ties: The importance of philos in organizations', in N. Nohria and R.G. Eccles (eds), *Networks and Organizations: Structure, Form, and Action*, Cambridge, MA: Harvard Business School Press, pp. 216–39.

Kroeger, C.V. (1974), 'Managerial development in the small firm', *California Management Review*, **17**(1), 41–7.

Larson, A. and J.A. Starr (1993), 'A network model of organization formation', *Entrepreneurship Theory & Practice*, **17**(2), 5–15.

Lin, N. (2001), *Social Capital: A Theory of Social Structure and Action*, New York: Cambridge University Press.

Matute-Bianchi, M.E. (1986), 'Ethnic identities and patterns of school success and failure among Mexican-descent and Japanese-American students in a California high school', *American Journal of Education*, **95**, 233–55.

Matute-Bianchi, M.E. (1991), 'Situational ethnicity and patterns of school performance among immigrant and non-immigrant Mexican-descent students', in M.A. Gibson and J.U. Oghu (eds), *Minority Status and Schooling: A Comparative Study of Immigrants and Involuntary Minorities*, New York: Garland, pp. 205–47.

Ostrom, E. (1997), 'Investing in capital, institutions, and incentives', in C. Clague (ed.), *Institutions and Economic Development: Growth and Governance in Less-Developed and Post-Socialist Countries*, Baltimore: Johns Hopkins University Press, pp. 153–81.

Portes, A. (1998), 'Social capital: Its origins and application in modern sociology', *Annual Review of Sociology*, **24**, 1–24.

Portes, A. and J. Sensenbrenner (1993), 'Embeddedness and immigration: Notes on the social determinants of economic action', *American Journal of Sociology*, **98**(6), 1320–50.

Portes, A. and P. Landolt (1996), 'The downside of social capital', *American Prospect*, **26**, 18–22.

Putzel, J. (1997), 'Accounting for the "dark side" of social capital: Reading Robert Putman on democracy', *Journal of International Development*, **9**(7), 939–49.

Reynolds, P.D. (1997), 'Who starts new firms? Preliminary explorations of firms-in-gestation', *Small Business Economics*, **9**(5), 449–62.

Sandefur, R.L. and E.O. Laumann (1998), 'A paradigm for social capital', *Rationality and Society*, **10**(4), 481–501.

Shane, S. and S. Venkataraman (2000), 'The promise of entrepreneurship as a field of research', *Academy of Management Review*, **25**(1), 217–26.

Stepick, A. (1992), 'The refugees nobody wants: Haitians in Miami', in G.J. Grenier and A. Stepick (eds), *Miami Now*, Gainesville: University of Florida Press, pp. 57–82.

Uzzi, B. (1996), 'The sources and consequences of embeddedness for the economic performance of organizations: The network effect', *American Sociological Review*, **61**(4), 674–98.

Uzzi, B. (1997), 'Social structure and competition in inter-firm networks: The paradox of embeddedness', *Administrative Science Quarterly*, **42**, 35–67.

Waldinger, R. (1995), 'The "other side" of embeddedness: A case study of the interplay between economy and ethnicity', *Ethnic and Racial Studies*, **18**, 555–80.

Watson, J. (2007), 'Modeling the relationship between networking and firm performance', *Journal of Business Venturing*, **22**(6), 852–74.

10 Entrepreneurial commitment and new venture creation: a conceptual exploration

Alain Fayolle, Olivier Basso and Erno T. Tornikoski

INTRODUCTION

The act of new venture creation does not relate to one single decision. Inaugural decisions and founding 'ruptures' often result from a long and winding path. Comparable in that sense to the act of artistic creation, the act of new venture creation is not suited to simplifying causal analysis.

In light of this, numerous works conducted in the field of new venture creation have attempted to explain the emergence of the phenomenon, and more particularly the pivotal moment when the creation process is set in motion. This is how Shapero and Sokol (1982) designed a model based on the notions of 'desirability' and 'feasibility' of the project, combined with a factor of displacement that acts as a triggering event. The notion of displacement refers to the effect of a perceived disruption or radical change in one's personal life. The introduction of a discontinuity precipitates the decision to act entrepreneurially and serves as a catalyst for the trigger. This event, the sudden occurrence of which incurs imbalance in the individual's life, may be perceived by the actor as either a positive displacement (discovery of an opportunity) or a negative one (professional dissatisfaction or lay-off).

Following these precursor works, the concept of 'intention' appeared, which in turn led to a number of theoretical models.

Using intention relies on the assumption that founding a business is both an intentional and a planned act (Krueger and Carsrud 1993). Since the beginning of the 1990s, the application of the theory of planned behaviour (Ajzen 1991) to the field of new venture creation has made it possible to renew the approaches and models based on intention. However, this approach has several limitations as regards the nature of the phenomenon studied. Intention constitutes, under certain conditions, an acceptable predictor of human behaviour, but must not be confused with the behaviour itself, a fortiori when the phenomenon studied is as complex as new venture creation (Gartner 1989; Bruyat 1993; Bruyat and Julien 2001).

The study of the antecedents of intention and its formation certainly contributes to extending our knowledge of the phenomenon, but this approach does not make it possible to understand the process that leads an individual to actually start a venture creation process.

Drawing on the theory of planned behaviour, Krueger and Carsrud (1993), in order to overcome this limitation, added exogenous variables that act as triggering factors, inhibitors or accelerators between intention and behaviour (in their model behaviour corresponds to taking action). However, their model presents another limitation linked to the initial postulate. Even if we accept that new venture creation is an intentional and planned behaviour, we do not know exactly at which point in the process intention actually appears consciously. Indeed, intention may precede the trigger of the process, as shown by Krueger and Carsrud (1993), but it may also appear after the process of new venture creation has been triggered. Intention therefore corresponds to the moment when the individual acknowledges where he or she is going. His or her behaviour becomes reflexive.

Bruyat (1993) overcomes these difficulties by proposing a dynamic model of new venture creation structured around the concept of commitment.

The individual's commitment to a new venture creation process thus becomes a determining variable in understanding the actual point in time when the entrepreneurial process is set in motion and how the new organization emerges. Commitment may be partial or total. Commitment is considered total when a stage has been reached in the process that makes going back impossible. Once fully committed to the process, the individual will go through with his or her project, as disengagement costs will appear too high.

We define commitment as the moment when the individual starts devoting most of his or her time, energy and financial, intellectual, relational and emotional resources to his or her project. Once committed to the process, the individual no longer considers the possibility of going back: the investments made would make opting out far too difficult and would be experienced as a personal failure.

The present chapter is exploratory and provides an overview of the advancement of the research in progress: our objective is to better understand the phenomenon of commitment to a new venture creation process. In order to do so, we will use the main psycho-social theories of commitment, starting with an analysis of the concepts and theories developed in the field of both social and cognitive psychology. We then look at the notion of commitment within the field of entrepreneurship by analysing the most prominent works devoted to the subject and also by looking into two concrete cases. We use psycho-social approaches in analysing the two cases and propose two perspectives to better understand the formation and persistence of entrepreneurial commitment before presenting the initial elements of a potential model of entrepreneurial commitment.

COMMITMENT, ESCALATION OF COMMITMENT AND COMMITMENT THEORIES

A review of the literature reveals the existence of numerous works that have led to the elaboration of theories on commitment in the fields of social psychology (Kiesler and Sakumara 1966; Kiesler 1971; Joule and Beauvois 1989, 2002) and cognitive psychology (Festinger 1957; Staw 1981). These concepts have been applied to the fields of management and company administration, especially in the contexts of commitment to work (Meyer and Allen 1997; Mowday 1998), new product development projects (Royer 1996; Schmidt and Calantone 2002) or software development projects (Keil 1995; Abrahamsson 2002).

Commitment is related to decision and action. Festinger (1964) defines commitment as a decision that directly influences future behaviours. In 1971 Kiesler laid the foundations of the social psychology of commitment. For Kiesler (1971, p. 81), commitment is what 'binds the individual to his or her behavioural acts'. Contrary to popular wisdom, people are not committed through their ideas or feelings, but through their actions or behaviours. To feel committed, individuals must feel they are the initiators of the given behaviour. As a result, individuals may be committed in various degrees. People are committed through their actions, and only the decisions made with a certain degree of freedom lead to perseverance. The perception of external pressure, or of a threat, will weaken all the more the strength of a commitment resulting from a 'freely consented' decision.

Most psychologists define commitment as the force that stabilizes the behaviour of individuals (Kiesler 1971; Brieckman 1987), a force that gives individuals the strength to pursue whatever course of action they have undertaken, despite the obstacles met and whatever the attractiveness and potential of alternative options (Dubé *et al.* 1997).

According to Beauvois and Joule (1981), in any given situation, the more the individual acts, the more he or she commits himself or herself. They also consider that the likelihood of an activity leading to the individual's commitment is directly linked to the individual's feeling of freedom. Individuals must feel they have a certain amount of freedom (real or perceived) when making a decision for the ensuing actions to lead to commitment. In a nutshell, the notion of commitment relates to a process that develops over time and leads individuals to preserve the consistency of their actions or the coherence of their decisions.

Commitment corresponds to a position that it is difficult to opt out of (Becker 1960); we can even say it corresponds to an irrevocable choice (Secord and Backman 1974) or a constraint that prevents any change in behaviour (Gerard 1965).

The notion of escalating commitment completes the notion of commitment and often overlaps with it. The escalation of commitment corresponds to the propensity of individuals to persist, sometimes in an apparently incoherent manner, with a decision or a course of action, despite the existence of negative feedback and the great uncertainty ('halo effect') that affects the plausibility of future success (Staw 1981). Sabherwal *et al.* (1994) even speak about being 'too committed' to explain this unreasonable obstinacy. Escalation of commitment may concern the individual, the group or the organization (Caldwell and O'Reilly 1982). Commitment escalation has been studied in various fields of application: researchers have used this perspective to address subjects such as the war in Vietnam, urban planning policies and software development projects (Staw 1981; Simonson and Staw 1992).

Beauvois and Joule (1981) attempt to explain the reasons for the escalation: 'We are only committed through our actions. We are not committed through our ideas, our feelings, but by our actual behaviour. The individual rationalizes his or her behaviours by endorsing, retrospectively, ideas designed to justify them.' This type of reconstruction of past behaviour *ex post* will be progressively internalized and contribute to convincing the individual that his or her new opinion is well founded. To a certain extent, this perspective undermines the simplistic intention models that put forward intention as preceding and explaining the behaviour. Here intention is reinterpreted and reconstructed a posteriori. The act comes first. It shows how the 'intention–decision–action' logic must give way to more complex perspectives: the efforts to justify one's decisions, the retroactive influence of the outcomes of the actions undertaken, the capacity to look at a given situation from a different point of view and so on all reveal the complexity of the processes at work.

Consequently, other analysis frameworks must be used to better understand the notion of commitment. An analysis of the literature on the subject highlights three main approaches that show similarities.

The Theory of Cognitive Consistency and Dissonance

This theory originated with the precursor works of Festinger (1957), who at the time spoke of 'simultaneous existence of elements of knowledge (cognition) which, in one way or another, are conflicting (dissonance), which motivates the individual to make efforts to make them concordant (reduction of dissonance)'.

The central postulate is based on the stability of individuals' cognitive systems. When individuals behave in a way that does not fit with their system of beliefs, the imbalance induced is such that they will do anything in their power to restore the balance of their cognitive system. In this case, individuals have a choice of two alternatives: they alter either their behaviour or their attitudes.

Dissonance results from internal conflicts that occur between acquired opinions and discordant new elements. Festinger (1957) identifies several types of cognitive dissonance: they may result from prior decisions that need to be justified, from actions the results of which are unexpected, or from the excessive amount of effort required to reach a given objective.

This theory also relates to the phenomenon of self-justification, which results from the individuals' desire to appear rational (to themselves or others) in their every act or decision: 'Individuals will bias their attitudes on the experimental task in a positive direction so as to justify their previous behaviour' (Festinger and Carlsmith 1959). This link between the theory of self-justification and escalation of commitment is also acknowledged by Brockner (1992).

Beauvois and Joule's Theory of Commitment[1]

In line with the works of Festinger and Lewin, two French researchers in psycho-sociology from the University of Grenoble have chosen to focus on what they call the 'decision traps', which translate into three phenomena:

1. *The 'freezing effect':* the decision to behave in such or such a way freezes out the system of possible alternatives by making the individual focus exclusively on what is directly linked to his or her decision. The notion of 'freezing effect' translates the individual's commitment to the decision made. Once we have made a decision, we are bound to this decision and, in a way, prisoner of it.
2. *The 'escalation of commitment':* a behavioural tendency of the individual to stick to his or her initial decision even though this decision is clearly questioned by the facts. The individual shows the need and the will to persist in his or her actions in order to prove the rational character of the initial decision taken.
3. *The 'unnecessary expenditure' and 'dead end':* it is an 'unnecessary expenditure' to the extent that individuals put themselves through an unnecessary and unproductive course of action because they have

committed themselves to doing so (financially, materially, etc.), and a 'dead end' because individuals voluntarily put themselves through tough situations in which the goals set are no longer achievable.

In this perspective, all goes to show that individuals, committed through their initial choices, would rather sink with the ship than admit and rectify an initial error of assessment, judgement or appreciation. This is where the notion of self-justification finds its relevance. This behaviour leads to useless actions and costs and may lead the individual to continue with a process whatever the consequences and whatever the costs. The commitment theory developed by these authors relies heavily on the individual's feeling of freedom and the nature of the acts accomplished or to be accomplished. According to Beauvois and Joule, the feeling of freedom accounts for the perseverance in a decision. 'Perseverance' here translates as a tendency to persist repeatedly in a course of action, which leads to a stereotypical behaviour, because the individual is incapable of the mental or behavioural changes necessary to inhibit the ongoing activity.

The actions considered may be split into two main categories. First we may distinguish 'non-problematic' actions that are compatible with our cognitive system and induce as a result a greater resistance to change and a strong commitment. In contrast, constrained or 'problematic' actions often lead to U-turns: people are led to alter their decisions, except when they have been costly to make. In the latter case, positions are more rigid and commitment is rather weak. When an individual has been forced to make a decision, indeed, there is often a boomerang effect that goes against the desired effect.

The Escalation of Commitment Theory

This stream of research owes a great deal to the works published by Staw and his associates (Staw 1976, 1981; Staw and Ross 1987; Simonson and Staw 1992). Staw (1981, p. 578) focuses on global courses of action, not isolated acts: 'many most difficult decisions an individual must make are choices not about what to do in an isolated instance but about the fate of an entire course of action'. He also underlines the fact that individuals have a tendency to persist in a given course of action, which provokes the escalation of commitment. This phenomenon can be explained by the need of all individuals to rationalize their behaviours. Staw (1980) distinguishes two types of rationalization, retrospective and prospective: 'the individual seeks to appear competent in previous as opposed to future actions', and the behaviour models based on the subjective expected utility theory examine the principle of prospective rationality. The combination of these two rationalization factors brings an added difficulty to the understanding of decision-making processes.

Staw (1981) highlights four factors of escalation:

1. internal justification (self-justification) or external justification, which he explains thus: 'to prove to others that they were not wrong in an early decision and the force for such external justification could well be stronger than the protection of self-esteem';
2. persistence of the action;
3. perceived probability of the result;
4. perceived value of the result.

For Staw (1981), commitment is a complex process, subjected to multiple and sometimes conflicting forces. His theoretical model based on the four types of determinants presented above is still often used in empirical research today.

COMMITMENT TO A PROCESS OF NEW VENTURE CREATION: THE STATE OF CURRENT RESEARCH AND TWO CASE STUDIES

Our exploratory research is mainly interested in the concept of commitment in the context of a new venture creation by an individual who does it for the first time, without any particular experience. Here we consider commitment as a result, a posture or a state, as opposed to its process dimension, which may vary in degree. It corresponds to the moment when the individual starts devoting most of his or her time, energy and financial, intellectual, relational and emotional resources to his or her project. The possibility of going back is no longer an option, as, in light of the investments made, giving up would be too difficult and would be considered as a failure. Commitment therefore corresponds to a phase in the process, without which the process could not be completed in the best possible conditions.

The Notion of Commitment in the Field of Entrepreneurship

To the best of our knowledge, commitment theories have been little used in entrepreneurship research. The notion of commitment itself is not perceived homogeneously. Bruyat (1993, 2001) structures his thesis around this concept. He describes commitment as a set of actions or decisions that are spread over time. Actions and decisions are joined in the process, and it is difficult to identify a traditional sequence of events (collection of data, analysis and deliberation, decision and action). The new business founder described by Bruyat has a bounded rationality and progressively commits himself or herself to the process until total commitment. This escalation of commitment leads to a stage of near irreversibility (except if the individual opts out) and leads individuals to focus increasingly on their projects. Going back therefore becomes very difficult, even impossible, given the costs of disengagement (financial resources consumed, social costs through the partners involved, costs in terms of career, psychological costs and cognitive dissonance). This commitment process that leads to full commitment may be incremental or revolutionary, depending on the resistance to change in particular. It is therefore important to distinguish several forms of commitment. The analysis model proposed by Bruyat (1993, 2001) relies on the theory of catastrophes and provides a visual representation of the phenomenon.

Gaillard-Giordani (2004) addresses the question of commitment within the context of the relation between investors and entrepreneurs. The perspective adopted is financial, and the approach focuses mainly on the mutual commitment of the actors involved in the entrepreneurial process. The perspective developed by this author relies on the exchange of mutual and credible commitment; and these exchanges participate in the sense making and realization of the project. The types of commitment examined in this work relate to knowledge and resources that are specific to the process. While Bruyat considers commitment as an individual variable, it appears mainly in its collective dimension in Gaillard-Giordani's doctoral research. Both authors nevertheless concur on the importance they give to the issue of commitment.

In the Anglo-Saxon literature, commitment theories seem to be applied to the field of entrepreneurship in a totally different perspective. Commitment is no longer perceived as an essential element (phase or act) of the process, but as a psychological factor susceptible to divert the entrepreneur from the right decision paths, considering that the right decision paths should be dominated by the – often economic – rationality of the actor. The reduction of cognitive dissonances and the escalation of commitment are considered as possible cognitive biases. This appears more particularly in the works of McCarthy *et al.* (1993), which attempt to analyse to what extent the decisions of financial reinvestment are influenced by rational processes or variables of commitment escalation. The results show that entrepreneurs who started their own business are more prone to commitment escalation than entrepreneurs who took over an existing business. Moreover, entrepreneurs who have too much self-confidence are those who exhibit the most significant escalation of commitment.

Our Research Method

The two case studies presented here correspond to situations of new venture creation that we were able to observe almost in their entirety by being in regular contact with the actors.

We used several methods of data collection: interviews with the project bearers (with extensive note taking), working documents produced by the individuals, and interviews with other parties involved in the project (mainly experts in new venture creation and stakeholders). In each case the data were collected over periods of time spanning several years.

We develop below the reasons why we chose the case study method for our exploratory research.

Case studies involve documenting a phenomenon by using several techniques of data collection. The various data sources help build a case destined to be analysed from a specific perspective, around a given issue (Hamel *et al.* 1991), which corresponds to our objective here.

Moreover, this research method is particularly relevant for our investigation, in that it takes into account the time, context and circumstantial dimensions of the 'stories' we are concerned with. Some researchers, like Mintzberg for instance, have already tried to legitimize the research works that deal with a limited number of cases: 'What, for example, is wrong with samples of one? Why should researchers have to apologize for them?' (Mintzberg 1979, p. 583). For this author, researchers must go beyond statistical approaches and interpret the data, thus breaking away from the statistical weight of scientific replication, the objective being to discover new elements, even if their scope remains limited.

In order to reach this goal, various techniques are called upon: the perspective is that of a convergence of approaches. Hamel (1997) underlines this clearly: 'Indeed, the case study, by definition, calls upon various techniques, be they observation, semi-directive interviews, and one or the other technique of contents analysis. . . . The variety of the methods used is in line with the idea of comparing several angles of study or analysis' (p. 103). Later, this author talks about 'data triangulation', which aims to compare different points of view, to weave a network which will outline the case pattern, its internal logic: 'Various methods are used in order to place the object of study under various lights, in the hope that they will reveal all its dimensions' (p. 104). The types of data collected 'may thus overlap and shed light upon one another in order to throw light on the case concerned' (p. 105).

Collecting the data is an essential part of the case study process. Several possible data sources can be used. Yin (1994) identified six of them (p. 80), with their advantages and drawbacks: documentation, archives, interviews, direct observation, participant observation, and technical and cultural artefacts. For the work presented here, we used and cross-analysed the first five sources cited above.

Presentation of Two Commitment Cases

Case A dates back to the late 1980s, whereas case B is from the mid-1990s. We have always stayed in touch with the main actors of these two situations of new venture creation.

Case A

AF is an engineer in a consultancy firm specializing in the market of central and local administrations. He likes his job and his working environment. He does not feel any dissatisfaction as regards his professional life and does not feel threatened in his job. In 1986, then aged 32, during a conversation with a colleague he happens to mention his desire to set up his own firm one day. He then discovers that this person has the same desire. Over the following days and weeks, this becomes a recurrent topic of their conversations; an idea emerges, takes shape and progressively takes on more and more importance in the life of AF and his colleague. They start devoting time to the project and expand the team by inviting other people to join them on the project. The process is therefore triggered. While working on the project, the main actors remain in their employed positions. A market study is carried out and positive contacts are made with potential clients. Despite the fact that the activity they have in mind does not compete with their employer's activities, in order to avoid their employer learning about the project accidentally AF decides to inform his superior as soon as possible, even though at this point he is not yet certain they will go through with their new venture creation project. In AF's mind, this is an ethical issue, but it is a risky step to take in terms of career, especially if the project ends up being scrapped. On the one hand are the certainties and comforts of a paid job and on the other the attractiveness of new venture creation with its inherent uncertainties. AF clearly has the impression, at this point in time, that he will give up what he has got to go chasing after shadows, but letting his employer know about his project is an indispensable step in pursuing his project. He therefore requests an appointment with his hierarchy and lets them know about his project. At the end of the interview, which went well, AF is convinced that a decisive step has just been taken and that going back would be very difficult from then on. AF has just committed himself to the process of new venture creation. His firm (MC) would be effectively created five months after this interview and to this day continues developing IT solutions for the management of industrial SMEs, somewhere in the south of France.

Case B

In 1995, RC is 28 and has just finished an MBA programme in a major French school of management. RC is an engineering graduate and comes from a university background that does not predispose him to the career of entrepreneur. After completing technical studies, he worked for a large American company in France for a few years. During the MBA programme, RC enrolled in an optional entrepreneurship course and discovered a world that was entirely new to him. He recognizes that this course generated rather quickly within him the intention to create a business. However, he decided to complete his MBA programme in an English university and graduated with a double degree, following which he was all set to find, without too much effort, a good and well-paid job corresponding to his new qualifications. RC therefore starts looking for a job, while at the same time becoming interested in the idea of setting up his own business. He becomes particularly keen on a rather crazy and passionate idea in the wine sector. He starts talking about it to his fellow students and his teachers and especially to the teacher who was in charge of the new venture creation elective. The wine trade, whatever the quality of the concept developed, is a very tough sector with low margins and intense competition, and therefore the first reactions are rather discouraging. However, RC decides to hold on to his idea, and for three months leads his job search in parallel with his study of a venture creation project in the wine sector. He goes to recruitment interviews, while meeting wine professionals to refine his project. This could have gone on for ever, but RC starts to realize he is diluting his time and energy into two projects of a contradictory nature. He has to choose. He decides to stop his job search for a while and devote all his time and energy to his new venture creation project. As time passes, he realizes the significance of the decision he has made. We often met with RC during this period of his life, and we are convinced that this decision dramatically increased his commitment to the process. A year later RC created the business that he still runs today.

ANALYSIS OF THE CASES AND PROPOSITIONS

We first analyse both cases from the perspective of psycho-social theories on commitment, which leads us to underline the limitations of these theories as regards our preoccupations. We then discuss our results further and make two propositions to orient future research.

Analysis of the Two Cases from the Psycho-sociological Perspective

In both cases, the individuals are confronted with two possible alterna-tives. For A, the alternatives are either 'I stay with the company that employs me (and I give up on my project and put it aside, at least for a while)' or 'I resign in order to eventually set up my own business (in which case, I must inform my employers as soon as possible)'. For B, the alternative is either 'I look for a paid job (and I devote most of my time and resources to this project)' or 'I focus all my attention on my venture creation project (and I will go back to looking for a paid job if this does not work out)'. In both cases, the individuals are faced with what we can call 'decisive' choices. Both subjects perceive the potential results of the decisions considered (going through with it, or not) as bearers of change in their life patterns. The retention of one alternative – persistence with the status quo or the decision to set up a business for one, and looking for a new job or setting up a business for the other – will affect their existence in the long term. These structuring choices are perceived as pivotal periods, the consequences of which will shape radically and lastingly the life of the actors.

What happens once the choices are made is aptly described by the theories of self-justification and escalation of commitment: what they aim to explain, above all, is not so much why, how or when an individual commits himself or herself to the process, but why he or she remains com-mitted. The initial steps do not so much constitute the major difficulty, but staying constant in this movement or persisting with this path does.

For A as much as for B, the freezing effect leads the actors to focus exclusively on the path they have chosen. From then on, for A and for B, it will become difficult not to persevere with their future decisions and actions, in order to rationalize the whole process. Self-justification and escalation of commitment theories can also explain why, even if conflicting feedback arises, challenging the validity of their creation project, individu-als A and B may still persist with their decision and may even reinforce it further.[2]

The choices made by A and B are of a different nature and a priori do not seem to bear the same weight. For A, declaring his intentions to his hierarchy amounts to taking the risk of being forced to resign. For B, it is rather a question of opting (or not) for a new venture creation project that seems unlikely to happen at a later time in his life. Other decisions and actions were taken before these choices, and other decisions and actions will be taken after. So why did these choices bear so much significance – in our view – to the extent that they very likely caused a decisive evolution of these individuals' commitment? Why these choices and not others?

In both cases, the dynamic of commitment appears to be a subtle and fragile reality that seems to relate more to evolution than revolution. Commitment here relates to a transition period, a process during which a new situation is progressively structured, and it is often during transition periods that ambiguity, paradoxes and tensions are at their most intense.

In both cases, the progression of commitment that leads to irreversibility – since aborting the process would be considered by the individual as a failure – happens long before its legal registration. The projects in themselves were still rather hazy at that stage. However, we may also envisage that commitment happens later in the creation process: at the time of legal registration, or even later, if the business founder has kept a paid job for instance.

Research Propositions: Two Conditions of Entrepreneurial Commitment

Commitment as an implication process may take various shapes and is not suited to a single modelling approach. By *implication process* it is meant that individuals in the course of their action devote more and more of their time and financial, intellectual and emotional investments to their projects. The nature of the path leading to commitment thus appears contrasted: for some individuals, commitment is progressive and spreads over a long period of time, without it being possible to identify a decisive moment. Such a representation seems to correspond to the observations we made about cases A and B. However, for other individuals whom we have been able to observe through our practice of entrepreneurial support, commitment occurs as a sudden rupture. For instance, giving up one's career in order to set up a business represents a major change of direction and a major career change for the individual.

In light of this, the process that leads an individual to commit to a new venture creation process can be seen as an incremental or radical change process. This implies that two conditions, illustrated by our cases, can be considered as necessary[3] for the commitment to take place. Firstly, the act of new venture creation must be preferred (to any other alternative) and, secondly, resistance to change must be overcome.[4] In both cases, of course, these are individual perceptions, and there may be some significant cognitive biases in estimating the risks, among other things. The desirability of entrepreneurial action involves psychological and social aspects as well as financial ones.

Condition 1: the venture creation project must be preferred
Some projects abort because the entrepreneur is unable to gather the necessary means, for example financial resources, permits, means of

production, support from a partner, and so on. The project must therefore be abandoned, even though it was what the entrepreneur preferred.

If the individual is not forced to abandon the project, commitment occurs when the venture creation action (a specific project, whether detailed or not) is perceived as being preferable to the current situation (employee, unemployed, student, etc.) or to any other potential change (e.g. change of employer). The act of new venture creation is perceived as preferable to the current situation as soon as there is an increase in the attractiveness of the new venture creation and/or when there is a decrease (or indeed a sharp drop) in the attractiveness of the current situation.

Most theoretical models of venture creation retain this aspect as essential.[5] They describe the formation of this preference as the result of environmental factors and factors specific to the entrepreneur. We will not, however, be considering these factors in further detail at this point. Instead, the preference, resulting from a push–pull situation, is assessed on the basis of criteria relating to the desirability and feasibility of the act of venture creation. The individual's cognitive limitations must also be considered. The emergence of the preference is a complicated process, made even more complex by several factors, such as 1) the potential diversity of the criteria to be considered, 2) the fact that the criteria are not independent of one another, 3) the difficulty of measuring them (they are perceptions, not 'objective' facts), 4) the evolution of the perceptions over time, 5) the non-linearity of the functions linking some of the criteria to the preference (sigmoidal curves, parabolic curves, etc.), and 6) the fact that it is impossible to formalize these links by a classical preference function (additive model). Only one factor may trigger opting-out. In other words, the emergence of preference is a system and as such it resists oversimplified approaches.

Condition 2: resistance to change must be overcome
The preference for a venture creation project, translated by a need and desire for change, will only lead to actual change if the actor is able to overcome his or her resistance to change.

Strangely enough, this is not discussed as such in entrepreneurship literature, probably because entrepreneurs are often considered to have different attitudes to risk to the general public (they are often perceived as daredevils). However, empirical research does not appear to have produced key findings in support of this.

Consideration of resistance to change adds to the complexity of analysing commitment processes but, as we shall see later, also helps to explain their diversity. Without going into detail, and without claiming to cover every possibility, we draw from our practical experience in new venture creation support and derive five situations in which resistance to change can be analysed.

Firstly, there is resistance to change due to habits and inertia in reasoning and behaviour. This is particularly important where individuals have devoted most of their past commitment to an employed position without ever considering venture creation (cognitive dissonance, family role model). Secondly, resistance to change may also be due to fear of the unknown. Uncertainty may be related to a specific project or a lack of knowledge of what creating and managing a small business or proposed venture actually involves. Thirdly, resistance to change may also be due to the perceived irreversibility of the new situation. In some cases, individuals believe (accurately) that, if their projects should fail, it would be impossible for them to go back to their previous jobs or indeed to any other job; failure, even if not immediate, would therefore be disastrous. Fourthly, resistance to change may be due to the perceived opportunity costs and/or significant irreversible costs; the potential entrepreneur gives up an enjoyable situation, devotes less time to family and leisure activities, commits most of the family heritage, cuts back on his or her lifestyle, and so on. Finally, resistance to change can be due to a lack of resources or advice and, more generally, environmental hostility to venture creation.

Here again, the 'hiding hand'[6] plays a significant role in dissimulating or exaggerating certain problems. Entrepreneurs who take action often overestimate their chances of success and underestimate the problems they are likely to encounter. Resistance to change in the venture creation process varies in intensity. For example, resistance to change is weaker: if the individual has been exposed early in life to the idea of venture creation (parents or entrepreneurial role models); if he or she has a social network and lives in an environment (family, friends, education) which is relevant and conducive to venture creation; if his or her current situation is unsatisfactory; and, finally, if the project involves only a low degree of uncertainty for the individual (duplicate creation, broad experience of the sector and of management) or if it can be implemented gradually, without engaging significant irreversible costs.

These various points are not independent, but overlap to some extent and form part of an overall system. Accordingly, the preference for new venture creation and resistance to change are not independent. Because of the complexity of the system, we have attempted to highlight a thread that could eventually be further formalized for specific applications. In our model, we assume that the entrepreneur's full commitment does not occur unless 1) the venture creation project is preferred to the status quo or any other alternative option and 2) the would-be entrepreneur is able to overcome his or her resistance to change. These are the two necessary conditions for the formation of entrepreneurial commitment.

Now that we have established the conditions necessary for the formation of entrepreneurial commitment, we can raise further questions related to the formation of entrepreneurial commitment. For example, why are some choices so significant, in that they trigger a decisive change in the entrepreneurial commitment process? Why these choices and not others? Clearly, in addition to the two necessary conditions for the formation of entrepreneurial commitment, we need to add a more dynamic vision of the reality.

Toward a New Representation of the Entrepreneur's Commitment

Analysis of the semantic definition of the term *commitment* encompasses and articulates the theoretical elements developed above. Commitment refers initially to a deliberate binding by promise or contract. The example of the pledge (legal or romantic) is a good illustration of this situation: the subject who makes a pledge thus generates an obligation for himself or towards others. To commit oneself means to place oneself deliberately in a situation that then generates responsibilities and implies choices that are predetermined by the initial decision.

This negative definition of commitment perceived as surrendering part of one's freedom can also be found in the psycho-sociological approaches developed previously. It is worth remembering that they particularly insist on the deliberative dimension of this subjection.

However, commitment and escalation of commitment approaches essentially describe situations in terms of traps or manipulations whereby the individual surrenders his or her freedom. Cartesian criticism[7] of promises is relevant here: to promise means to commit oneself; it means taking today the resolution to accomplish one or several actions in the future. It means deciding today what one will be tomorrow, without knowing anything about what the future holds and the situations one will be confronted with.

But commitment cannot be reduced to the sole destructive dimension of the actor who perseveres in his or her choices: it may also be seen as a structuring and productive phenomenon, conducive to positive effects for the individual. Its creative force manifests itself in the construction of a professional path, the writing of a book, the constitution of a couple, and so on. The actor thus chooses to follow a path in which the initial step (a degree, for instance) naturally leads to opting for other actions that are linked and that complete the movement thus initiated.

The theory of the decision trap with uncontrollable consequences should not detract from the positive side of commitment: it leads to the creation of a new state in which the subjects invest themselves. The language of finance meets the language of psychology: committing capital to a business means investing. To commit oneself means to invest oneself.

Commitment is thus analysed as the process that crystallizes a significant choice (here new venture creation), while being merely the more or less long-term consequence of a series of committing actions. Indeed, the set of minor decisions taken by an individual may be reread as the progressive concrete realization of a project. This only becomes obvious to the subject a posteriori, when he or she thinks back over the path he or she has taken.

To summarize our position, commitment is the result of an action that necessarily leads to more actions. In this regard, commitment is a binding act: the actor's freedom or the degree of his or her freedom will be reduced. Why? Because what subjects accept when committing themselves includes two dimensions: on the one hand, they take part in a series of almost irreversible actions (constraining nature of the process) and, on the other hand, commitment relates to other actions that reach beyond what subjects can perceive at the time when they commit themselves (gamble on the future). However, this constraining process is also what enables the subject to create a new path. For instance, the act of starting a family implies responsibilities and offers a new dimension to one's life: the choice of an individual life is abandoned; the creation of a state of dependency is chosen (parental responsibility) and corresponds to a life-changing decision.

New venture creation is also a life-changing decision. The dynamic of commitment can vary in intensity; it may be progressive or immediate. One of the difficulties concerns the heterogeneity of the situations: we have until now considered commitment as resulting from a deliberate choice, not a constrained one. However, new venture creation does not always result from a free choice. It seems relevant here to distinguish *a minima* two, or even three, possible configurations. Constrained new venture creation corresponds to a professional choice for want of a better alternative: the individual is out of a job or looking for a change and does not necessarily have a choice other than starting his or her own business in order to find a new activity. On the contrary, 'deliberate and embraced' new venture creation refers to a conscious professional choice and the existence of a project. This duality strongly relates to the distinction drawn in the Global Entrepreneurship Monitor project between 'necessity' and 'opportunity' forms of new venture creation. Finally, even though this status is uncertain, some businesses seem to be created randomly: in this case, it is often a chance meeting or an idea that constitutes the turning point that leads to the individual's commitment.

These few exploratory remarks remind us that the paths taken by business founders often reflect the complexity of unique and individual stories. Beyond the key stages (identifying an idea, finding resources, clients and funding, and legal registration), the sequence of events is anything but linear: what happens is the emergence (or not) of a new pattern leading to a commitment situation characterized by the irreversibility of the choice of becoming an entrepreneur (in the sense of new venture creator).

From a methodological point of view, the difficulty lies in combining an objective 'ballistic' approach that reflects the sequence of events that shape the entrepreneur's path with an approach based on the construction of meaning by the actors concerned. Indeed, preference and resistance forces only exist in relation to the representation that individuals have of them at a given point in time.

The techniques of life-story analysis could help us define a terminology of the would-be entrepreneur's commitment: ups and downs, interruptions, regressions, alterations, bifurcations and so on all correspond to a logic at a given moment in time that determines the position of the 'mobile entity' (the entrepreneur) on a commitment scale as regards his or her project. As the commitment process cannot be measured from a linear perspective (increase or decrease of commitment level), a real understanding of the phenomenon requires a new modelling of entrepreneurs' paths.

This analysis must go beyond the examination of variations in the subject's motivations; it must shed a light on the genesis and the constitution of a fundamental choice – new venture creation – by integrating the constitutive dimensions of this life path, that is to say the tangible facts and the actor's representations.

The paths taken by business founders are no different from personal life paths taken by any individual: they are strewn with events, periods of crisis, and crossroads that lead them to make choices and sometimes opt for drastic changes. What must be done therefore is to identify the 'ingredients' used in the decision-making process, by using several variables (structural, contextual, relational and individual), as well as various interacting temporalities. Maybe this is precisely what causes the type of 'rupture' or bifurcation that new venture creation represents in an individual's life (new job, new life).

We have presented here the prolegomena of a model whose ambition is to combine these two dimensions by confronting the factuality of the various stages (constitutive moments) with the reconstruction of the factors that determined the choices. The model should also propose a more precise definition of new venture creation: if it cannot be reduced to the legal creation of an activity, then what is it exactly? When does it actually happen? How is it linked with the commitment that leads to it? In the early stages of our reasoning, it seems that ambiguity remains as to the exact nature of commitment: is it the process or the result? Does commitment as a result coincide with the creation of the new business? This circular definition may be resolved thanks to an objective analysis of the time that the actor spends building his or her company. An entrepreneur's real commitment translates into the actual place that the project occupies in his or her professional life (allocated time and resources and absence of commitment to any other alternative). Psychological commitment also includes the total commitment of resources, which automatically excludes any other project.

CONCLUSION

As a psychological construct, commitment is at the heart of several explanatory theories of behaviour. These behavioural approaches focus on its emergence and dynamic and often share some common ground. Commitment and escalation of commitment theories explain the deliberate entry of individuals, sometimes without their realizing (especially in the case of manipulation), into a complex mechanism resulting from an initial decision, even if the subject was not aware of its significance at the time.

Other works, such as agency theory (Keil 1995) or the theory of catastrophes (Bruyat 1993), can be used successfully in combination with psycho-sociological approaches in analysing the complex process that leads an individual to create a new business.

To test the relevance of this parallel between commitment and new venture creation, we examined, from the perspective of the theories mentioned above, two cases of new venture creation. Indeed, we were able to make numerous observations and gather extensive data about these experiences by studying the whole venture creation process. In view of this, it appears that psycho-sociological theories are useful in understanding the individuals' persistence in their decision and the escalation of commitment. In other words, they make it possible to better understand the reasons why individuals' decisions, at a given point in time, commit them to a choice that will lead them further and further in the process, until the business is created and the new activity developed.

However, these theories do not clarify the nature of this particular moment and the nature of the choice, embedded in a flow of actions and decisions, the heterogeneity of which is well illustrated in our two case studies. They also provide little information on the formation of commitment and its evolution until its almost irreversibility in the context of new venture creation.

The notion of commitment seems nonetheless very important in understanding the new venture creation process. Commitment could amount to a change of phase in the process, with key consequences on the future of the project or of the nascent organization. The concept therefore calls for particular treatment and must be placed within a different representation of the new venture creation process that takes into account the richness and diversity of the situations. Several elements have been put forward to constitute a new model: the career path logic, the analysis of life-story narratives, the identification of a link between the events and the actor's interpretation of them, and so on; all outline the first lineaments of an ambitious model. The multiform and chaotic characteristic of the commitment process is undeniable: we know that numerous individuals who work on venture creation projects, alone or with support entities, have not reached this stage yet, and may never reach it. This last possibility may come as a surprise to external observers who did not doubt the strength of the individuals' apparent commitment and who were unable to recognize the early warning signs or to explain the reasons for their abandonment of a project that seemed imminent.

Hence there is substantial importance in studying the concept of commitment further within this particular framework and context. A better understanding of the dynamics of commitment should improve the quality of the support given to entrepreneurs. Improving operational knowledge of the commitment phenomenon should, at a more global level, enable the actors of venture creation support to better allocate incubating and support resources, by reserving them for projects that meet the relative conditions of commitment (acquired or latent).

NOTES

1.   See especially Beauvois and Joule (1981) and Joule and Beauvois (1989, 2002).
2.   We were able to observe such situations in both cases.
3.   These two conditions are also put forward by Bruyat (1993).
4.   In both cases, resistance to change is perceptible: change in one's satisfactory professional situation in the case of A, and change of career path for B, despite his predispositions, which were reinforced following his MBA.
5.   See for example Shapero (1975), Shapero and Sokol (1982) and Bird (1988, 1992). The theory of planned behaviour, originally proposed by Ajzen (1991, 2002), and its applications in the field of entrepreneurship (Krueger and Carsrud 1993; Autio *et al.* 1997; Tkachev and Kolvereid 1999) also provide an interesting theoretical basis to explain how the preference could be formed.
6.   Hirschman (1967) explains that one of the motors for action is the individual's ignorance of what awaits him or her when action is taken. The term *hiding hand* is a play on words with Smith's *hidden hand*.

7. Descartes, *Discourse on Method*, part III:

> And I placed *in the class of extremes especially all promises by which somewhat of our freedom is abridged*; not that I disapproved of the laws which, to provide against the instability of men of feeble resolution, when what is sought to be accomplished is some good, permit engagements by vows and contracts binding the parties to persevere in it, or even, for the security of commerce, sanction similar engagements where the purpose sought to be realized is indifferent: but *because I did not find anything on earth which was wholly superior to change*, and because, for myself in particular, I hoped gradually to perfect my judgments, and not to suffer them to deteriorate, *I would have deemed it a grave sin against good sense, if, for the reason that I approved of something at a particular time, I therefore bound myself to hold it for good at a subsequent time, when perhaps it had ceased to be so, or I had ceased to esteem it such.*

REFERENCES

Abrahamsson, P. (2002), 'The role of commitment in software process improvement', academic dissertation, University of Oulu, Finland.

Ajzen, I. (1991), 'The theory of planned behavior', *Organizational Behavior and Human Decision Processes*, **50**(2), 179–211.

Ajzen, I. (2002), 'Perceived behavioral control, self-efficacy, locus of control, and the theory of planned behavior', *Journal of Applied Social Psychology*, **32**, 1–20.

Autio, E., R.H. Keeley, M. Klofsten and T. Ulfstedt (1997), 'Entrepreneurial intent among students: Testing an intent model in Asia, Scandinavia and USA', *Frontiers of Entrepreneurship Research*, Babson Conference Proceedings, www.babson.edu/entrep/fer

Beauvois, J.L. and R.V. Joule (1981), *Soumission et idéologies: Psychosociologie de la rationalisation*, Paris: Presses Universitaires de France.

Becker, H.S. (1960), 'Notes on the concept of commitment', *American Journal of Sociology*, **66**(1), 32–40.

Bird, B. (1988), 'Implementing entrepreneurial ideas: The case for intention', *Academy of Management Review*, **13**, 442–54.

Bird, B. (1992), 'The operation of intention in time: The emergence of the new venture', *Entrepreneurship Theory and Practice*, **17**(1), 11–20.

Brieckman, P. (1987), *Commitment, Conflict and Caring*, Englewood Cliffs, NJ: Prentice Hall.

Brockner, J. (1992), 'The escalation of commitment to a failing course of action: Toward theoretical progress', *Academy of Management Review*, **17**(1), 39–61.

Bruyat, C. (1993), 'Création d'entreprise: Contributions épistémologiques et modélisation', these pour le doctorat ès sciences de gestion, Université Pierre Mendès France de Grenoble.

Bruyat, C. and P.-A. Julien (2001), 'Defining the field of research in entrepreneurship', *Journal of Business Venturing*, **16**(2), 165–80.

Caldwell, D.F. and C. O'Reilly (1982), 'Response to failure: The effects of choice and responsibility on impression management', *Academy of Management Journal*, **25**(1), 121–36.

Dubé, L., M. Jodoin and S. Kairouz (1997), 'Development and validation of three-factor model of commitment: From dynamic process to personal disposition', manuscrit soumis pour publication, Université de Montréal.

Festinger, L. (1957), *A Theory of Cognitive Dissonance*, Stanford, CA: Stanford University Press.

Festinger, L. (1964), *Conflict, Decision and Dissonance*, Stanford, CA: Stanford University Press.

Festinger, L. and J.M. Carlsmith (1959), 'Cognitive consequences of forced compliance', *Journal of Abnormal and Social Psychology*, **58**(2), 203–10.

Gaillard-Giordani, M.L. (2004), 'Les modalités transactionnelles et relationnelles de la création et du financement des nouvelles organisations: La dynamique des engagements et des désengagements', thèse pour le doctorat en sciences de gestion, Université de Nice Sophia Antipolis.

Gartner, W.B. (1989), 'Some suggestions for research on entrepreneurial traits and entrepreneurship', *Entrepreneurship Theory and Practice*, **14**(1), 27–38.

Gerard, H.B. (1965), 'Deviation, conformity and commitment', in R.P. Steiner and M. Fishbein (eds), *Current Studies in Social Psychology*, New York: Holt, Rinehart and Winston, pp. 263–77.

Hamel, J. (1997), *Etude de cas et sciences sociales*, Paris: L'Harmattan.

Hamel, J., S. Dufour and D. Fortin (1991), *Case Study Methods*, Newbury Park, CA: Sage.

Hirschman, A. (1967), *Development Projects Observed*, Washington, DC: Brookings Institution.

Joule, R.V. and J.L. Beauvois (1989), 'Une théorie psycho-sociale: La théorie de l'engagement', *Recherche et Applications en Marketing*, **4**(1), 79–90.

Joule, R.V. and J.L. Beauvois (2002), *Petit traité de manipulation à l'usage des honnêtes gens*, Grenoble: Presses Universitaires de Grenoble.

Keil, M. (1995), 'Escalation of commitment in information systems development: A comparison of three theories', *Academy of Management Best Paper Proceedings*, 348–52.

Kiesler, C.A. (1971), *The Psychology of Commitment*, New York: Academic Press.

Kiesler, C.A. and J. Sakumara (1966), 'A test of a model of commitment', *Journal of Personality and Social Psychology*, **3**(3), 349–53.

Krueger, N.F. and A.L. Carsrud (1993), 'Entrepreneurial intentions: Applying the theory of planned behaviour', *Entrepreneurship and Regional Development*, **5**(4), 315–30.

McCarthy, A.M., F.D. Schoorman and A.C. Cooper (1993), 'Reinvestment decisions by entrepreneurs: Rational decision-making or escalation of commitment?', *Journal of Business Venturing*, **8**(1), 9–24.

Meyer, J.P. and N.J. Allen (1997), *Commitment in the Workplace: Theory, Research, and Application*, London: Sage.

Mintzberg, H. (1979), 'An emerging strategy of "direct" research', *Administrative Science Quarterly*, **24**(4), 582–9.

Mowday, W.H. (1998), 'Reflections on the study and relevance of organizational commitment', *Human Resource Management Review*, **8**(4), 387–401.

Royer, I. (1996), 'L'escalade de l'engagement dans le développement de produits nouveaux', *Recherche et Applications en Marketing*, **11**(3), 7–22.

Sabherwal, R. *et al.* (1994), 'Why organizations increase commitment to failing information systems projects?' working paper, Department of Decision Science and Information Systems, Miami, FL.

Schmidt, J.B. and R.J. Calantone (2002), 'Escalation of commitment during new product development', *Journal of the Academy of Marketing Science*, **30**(2), 103–18.

Secord, P.F. and C.W. Backman (1974), *Social Psychology*, New York: McGraw-Hill.

Shapero, A. (1975), 'The displaced uncomfortable entrepreneur', *Psychology Today*, **9**(6), 83–8.

Shapero, A. and L. Sokol (1982), 'The social dimensions of entrepreneurship', in C.A. Kent, D.L. Sexton and K.H. Vesper (eds), *Encyclopedia of Entrepreneurship*, Englewood Cliffs, NJ: Prentice Hall, pp. 72–90.

Simonson, I. and B.M. Staw (1992), 'De-escalation strategies: A comparison of techniques for reducing commitment to losing courses of action', *Journal of Applied Psychology*, **77**(4), 419–26.

Staw, B.M. (1976), 'Knee-deep in the Big Muddy: A study of escalating commitment to a chosen course of action', *Organizational Behavior and Human Performance*, **16**(1), 27–44.

Staw, B.M. (1980), 'Rationality and justification in organizational life', in B.M. Staw and L. Cummings (eds), *Research in Organizational Behavior*, Greenwich, CT: JAI Press.

Staw, B.M. (1981), 'The escalation of commitment to a course of action', *Academy of Management Review*, **6**(4), 577–87.

Staw, B.M. and J. Ross (1987), 'Understanding escalation situations: Antecedents, proto-types, and solutions', in B.M. Staw and L.L. Cummings (eds), *Research in Organizational Behavior*, Greenwich, CT: JAI Press, pp. 39–78.
Tkachev, A. and L. Kolvereid (1999), 'Self-employment intentions among Russian students', *Entrepreneurship and Regional Development*, **11**(3), 269–80.
Yin, R.K. (1994), *Case Study Research: Design and Methods*, London: Sage.

PART III

DATA AND
MEASUREMENT

11 Are we there yet? Measurement challenges in studying new ventures
Phillip H. Kim and Howard E. Aldrich

INTRODUCTION

In the fall of 1999, John Kim met with two colleagues for dinner to discuss the possibility of starting a new business (Morse and Lim 2006). As a ten-year veteran of IBM Korea and KPMG, Kim perceived an opportunity to develop a web-based 'back office' software solution targeted at the business-to-business market in South Korea. Kim and his colleagues spent the rest of 1999 exploring this potential business concept. By February 2000, they had filed the necessary papers with the Korean National Tax Service to register their new company, NeoGenius, as a legally recognized entity. They also secured office space, purchased computer equipment, and used their personal savings as initial capital for NeoGenius. During the spring and summer of 2000, the founders of NeoGenius formed partnerships with other established software vendors, filed patents and raised additional angel funding. In November 2000, Kim and his start-up team launched NeoSite, NeoGenius's flagship software product.

As highlighted by the NeoGenius case, entrepreneurs navigate around multiple start-up challenges as they guide their emerging organizations through a series of phases and transitions (Hannan and Freeman 1989; Reynolds and Miller 1992; Ruef 2005). From an evolutionary perspective, business creation is not simply a discrete event, but should more accurately be viewed as a multi-dimensional process based on the achievement of start-up milestones over some period of time (Katz and Gartner 1988; Aldrich and Ruef 2006). These planning, execution or operational milestones may occur sequentially, as commonly taught in entrepreneurship courses or postulated in research on founding processes (Delmar and Shane 2004; Shane and Delmar 2004; Eckhardt *et al.* 2006). However, entrepreneurial efforts may also unfold in ways that do not follow linear or path-dependent processes, especially if founders need to find creative ways to overcome their resource constraints (Baker and Nelson 2005).

Thus, for scholars, the emergent and evolutionary nature of business creation poses challenges to theory development and empirical investigations. Theoretically, what factors explain the underlying processes, staged or non-linear, that lead to the creation of new businesses? Do these explanations vary based on different levels of analyses? Methodologically, how do we measure business creation as a multi-staged event at multiple levels? What measures enable us to know when a new firm has been created?

To address these questions, we propose that the study of firm emergence should be based on the same properties that define existing organizations. We acknowledge that no single approach answers all questions concerning new venture creation and so we advocate creative solutions that combine theoretically interesting and methodologically consistent strategies. We begin with a brief review of common approaches for measuring when new firms come into existence. We then propose a more comprehensive model to track the emergence of new firms and conclude with potential applications and extensions of our approach.

CURRENT APPROACHES

In this section, we review the strengths and weaknesses of two current approaches to defining firm emergence: 1) overuse of single indicators of emergence and 2) heavy reliance on participants' perceptions of the creation process. First, the most common approach for identifying new business entities has been to use single indicators, a practice followed in organizational ecology, business strategy, sociological and economic studies of self-employment, and economic geography and regional planning. In the organizational ecology literature, for example, scholars studying population vital rates have relied on a single event to indicate when organizations enter the risk set. Given the broad historical sweep of time needed for population-level studies, interviews with founders are simply impractical. Instead, researchers must rely on key organizing events from archival data sources to select an appropriate founding event (Hannan and Freeman 1989). Consequently, what is considered a founding event often differs across organizational populations – the commencement of production for automobile manufacturers (Carrol and Hannan 2000) versus legal registration for day care centres (Baum and Oliver 1992).

Similarly, management and finance researchers who focus on organizational growth most often rely on their data sources for founding definitions, rather than beginning with their own definition. Bamford *et al.* (2004) reviewed sampling frames in studies spanning over two decades of research and found a significant number of studies that used samples of firms based on arbitrarily assigned periods of time (e.g. 'less than five years old'). Sociologists and economists have used reports of self-employment status in longitudinal panel data as a proxy for new business creation (Evans and Leighton 1989; Arum and Mueller 2004; Sørensen 2007). These scholars assume that transitions into self-employment from some other occupation or labour market status indicate the start of new businesses. Finally, economic geographers and regional planning scholars have relied on business registration and census data to count new start-ups within particular regions (Plummer and Headd 2008).

As an alternative approach, entrepreneurship researchers have often used founders' perceptions, or those of other participants, to define a firm's beginning. Carter *et al.* (1996), for example, asked nascent entrepreneurs if their businesses were operating, if they were actively organizing, or if they had abandoned their start-up efforts. In their examination of the relationship between business plans and successful start-up attempts, Honig and Karlsson (2004) used a self-reported indicator of operating status to measure whether a new firm was successfully founded. Researchers who mark organizational founding with this method must assume that their respondents are using a definition of organizational founding commonly accepted for their business type or industry. Without this assumption, researchers who want to interpret what 'founding' actually means for respondents need supplementary information from them about how they defined organizational founding. Researchers also encounter biases of over- and under-confidence when entrepreneurs estimate their achievements (Forbes 2005).

Despite the shortcomings of these two approaches, single indicators based on founders' reports are useful when research questions focus on events that occur well after the initial founding. For example, in their study on founding team characteristics, Burton and Beckman (2007) were interested in top management team dynamics long after the initial founding period had passed. Thus they measured firm age using a single indicator acquired through interviews with founders. Nonetheless, if an investigator is interested in the dynamics surrounding the initial founding process, then relying on a single indicator, especially one based solely on respondents' perceptions, may well be misleading. Therefore, as an alternative approach to single-indicator strategies, we propose a multi-dimensional emergence framework, based on Aldrich (2007) and Katz and Gartner (1988).

A MULTI-DIMENSIONAL EMERGENCE FRAMEWORK

An emergence framework integrates multiple events, tracks the multi-dimensional nature of the organizing process, and accommodates non-linear organizing pathways. By relying on multiple events, an emergence approach limits selection biases that result from using samples of young firms based on arbitrarily designated founding events. Our proposed general framework applies across industries and avoids relying solely on founders' perceptions and other cognitively based conceptions of organizational founding.

We define organizational emergence in terms of three dimensions: goal orientation, boundedness and inter-organizational exchange. The first dimension of organizational emergence, goal orientation, refers to the development of each organization's intended purpose and defining target outcomes (Aldrich 2007). Newly operating organizations can signal their orientation to particular goals in several ways, such as transforming ambiguous business concepts into a viable product or service, creating an organizational identity, educating external stakeholders through marketing of their products and services, and establishing priorities for mobilizing resources through awareness of their financial needs. By pursuing these self-directed goals, founders reveal their 'entrepreneurial orientation' through their emerging firms' autonomy (Lumpkin and Dess 1996).

The second dimension, boundedness, reflects the degree to which emerging organizations distinguish themselves from other organizations within their environment. Boundary maintenance activities allow new firms to stand on their own, apart from their founders (Aldrich 2007). Organizational boundaries can emerge through intentional actions undertaken by founders as well as through fulfilling requirements set by the organizations' environments. For example, responding to legal requirements established by the state also enables emerging organizations to gain their own identity. Firm registration processes vary across nations, and entrepreneurs can establish organizational boundaries much more easily in countries with minimal requirements than in those in which governmental authorities impose major restrictions (Djankov *et al.* 2002). Intentional actions may involve the separation of resources and liability between founders and their emerging organizations, and nations vary in the extent to which founders are shielded from liability created through their firms' actions. Some economic historians argue that a key step in the development of the modern corporation was the enactment of strong laws limiting the liability of the owners and top management of corporations. Founders can create access to their emerging organizations for other actors in the organizations' environments such as potential creditors, suppliers and customers.

Lastly, inter-organizational exchange refers to the processes by which organizations develop routines to engage other organizational actors within their environments (Scott and Davis 2007). Because most organizations require external resources to accomplish their goals, organizations initially depend on other actors in their environments (Aldrich and Pfeffer 1976). Activities associated with this dimension of organizational emergence involve transactions of resource inputs and production outputs with other actors in the organizational environment. Beginning with few founding members, some emerging organizations eventually resemble bona fide groups, which stand out for their dependence on their immediate environmental context through stable but permeable boundaries (Putnam and Stohl 1990).

Emerging organizations are highly dependent on their surroundings, so founders initially rely on their personal social networks to develop transactional relationships with other organizational actors (Aldrich and Ruef 2006). Entrepreneurs may attempt to expand the reach of their network by seeking endorsements and introductions. For emerging organizations that survive and become established, the initial informal network of relationships may evolve into the core of a future inter-organizational exchange network (Brass *et al.* 2004). When such networks achieve some degree of permanence and continuity, we say that they have become 'institutionalized'.

To capture the emergent qualities of this framework, we view these three dimensions – goal orientation, boundedness and inter-organizational exchange – as latent variables linked to observable start-up milestones and activities. Taken together, they can be used to create a measurement model useful for testing theories of new venture creation. Thus our measurement model accommodates multiple events that can occur during the start-up process and retains the multi-dimensional characteristics of the emergence process. With latent variables, we can also track emergence as a continuous process spanning a much longer period beginning with founders' initial activities associated with their start-up efforts. By defining these dimensions as continuous measures, we can describe organizational emergence as a process with a range of intermediate thresholds. Thus fully emergent organizations would exhibit characteristics along all three dimensions. When used in a structural equations modelling framework, our proposed measurement model can be used as an outcome to test if certain founder characteristics or founding conditions affect the likelihood for organizational emergence, similar to the regression models with single-event outcomes used in prior research. Kim (2006) developed such a model of organizational emergence using the Panel Study of Entrepreneurial Dynamics (PSED) dataset.

CONTRIBUTIONS, CHALLENGES AND CONCLUSIONS

We highlight two contributions to entrepreneurship and organizational research by using an emergence framework. First, by disaggregating the founding process into distinct stages, researchers can probe more closely at transitions between stages and the factors that affect such transitions. Researchers can improve the precision with which they examine the determinants of entrepreneurial entry and their impact on organizing, growth and survival. Using a structural modelling framework, researchers can further investigate the impact of exogenous factors (such as resource availability or environmental conditions) on transitions between multiple stages. In these models, organizational emergence acts as an intervening variable and is modelled with other outcome measures, such as new venture performance and survival. This approach enables researchers to avoid selection biases when their sampling designs do not include all actors at risk (Aldrich and Ruef 2006).

Second, the emergence framework suggests new interpretations of existing accounts of founding processes and complements existing research on other stages of the founding process, such as the emergence of organizational communities (Chiles *et al.* 2004). Furthermore, theorizing and measuring the activities that occur during the organizing stage in a comprehensive model provide opportunities to join macro-level theoretical propositions of organizational founding with micro-level foundations and processes (Ruef 2005). For example, the internal dynamics of a founding team may be heavily influenced by the status characteristics members bring into the team from the larger society. Research on knowledge-intensive start-ups in Sweden shows, for example, that men are more likely to leave start-ups in which they are a minority than in which they are a majority whereas, by contrast, women do not seem to be affected by their proportions within a start-up (Hellerstedt 2008).

As researchers develop and pursue more sophisticated methodologies for understanding founding processes, we highlight several issues that call for further exploration. First, we believe that selection pressures force most founders to abandon their start-up efforts, requiring researchers to employ sampling strategies that capture founders early in the start-up process to understand how founding efforts unfold. Although we have explanations for how founding milestones may reflect some type of sequential ordering (Delmar and Shane 2004; Shane and Delmar 2004; Eckhardt *et al.* 2006), theoretical explanations of learning and feedback during the creation process remain underdeveloped; Parker (2006) is one exception.

Second, we need an approach for measuring organizational emergence that preserves the complexity of the process. In the chaotic conditions surrounding initial efforts, founders must mobilize sufficient resources, secure appropriate legal recognition, create awareness among potential customers, and negotiate favourable terms with suppliers – all actions devoted to transforming their entrepreneurial intentions into established, viable organizations. Because these start-up activities are highly interdependent, founders are unlikely to follow a linear developmental trajectory (Weick 1979; Aldrich and Ruef 2006). Founders, in some cases, may delay certain activities or pursue multiple organizing pathways concurrently because of unexpected contingencies or limited resources (Baker *et al.* 2003). Founders may also repeat organizing activities already once accomplished, such as making improvements to product designs, to generate multiple feedback loops during the founding process (Chiles *et al.* 2004). Measurement models must capture such complexity.

Third, entrepreneurship scholars are often under pressure to come up with unified and coherent 'best' solutions to the problems they study. More so than in other fields, in entrepreneurship, pressures from practitioners weigh heavily upon the kinds of problems chosen for study and upon the way research results are reported. Our proposed approach suggests that we should resist overly simple one-size-fits-all solutions. Instead, there may be multiple answers to the question of when an organizing effort actually results in a 'new firm'. The answer may depend upon which dimension of the founding process is being investigated and where in the founding process the organizing effort is studied.

In this chapter, we have addressed the theoretical and methodological challenges associated with determining when new firms are created. We reviewed the strengths and weaknesses of prior approaches and discussed how to align theoretical questions more closely with empirical measures. We suggest that future new venture creation research integrate measurement approaches to better reflect the multi-dimensional nature of the founding process.

REFERENCES

Aldrich, H.E. (2007), *Organizations and Environments*, classic edn, Stanford, CA: Stanford Business Books.

Aldrich, H.E. and J. Pfeffer (1976), 'Environments of organizations', *Annual Review of Sociology*, **2**, 79–105.

Aldrich, H.E. and M. Ruef (2006), *Organizations Evolving*, London: Sage.

Arum, R. and W. Mueller (2004), *The Reemergence of Self-Employment: A Comparative Study of Self-Employment Dynamics and Social Inequality*, Princeton, NJ: Princeton University Press.

Baker, T. and R.E. Nelson (2005), 'Creating something from nothing: Resource construction through entrepreneurial bricolage', *Administrative Science Quarterly*, **50**(3), 329–66.

Baker, T., A.S. Miner and D.T. Easly (2003), 'Improvising firms: Bricolage, account giving and improvisational competencies in the founding process', *Research Policy*, **32**(2), 255–76.

Bamford, C.E., T.J. Dean and T.J. Douglas (2004), 'The temporal nature of growth determinants in new bank foundings: Implications for new venture research design', *Journal of Business Venturing*, **19**(6), 899–919.

Baum, J.A.C. and C. Oliver (1992), 'Institutional embeddedness and the dynamics of organizational populations', *American Sociological Review*, **57**(4), 540–59.

Brass, D.J., J. Galaskiewicz, H.R. Greve and W. Tsai (2004), 'Taking stock of networks and organizations: A multilevel perspective', *Academy of Management Journal*, **47**(6), 795.

Burton, M.D. and C.M. Beckman (2007), 'Leaving a legacy: Position imprints and successor turnover in young firms', *American Sociological Review*, **72**(2), 239–66.

Carroll, G. and M.T. Hannan (2000), *The Demography of Corporations and Industries*, Princeton, NJ: Princeton University Press.

Carter, N.M., W.B. Gartner and P.D. Reynolds (1996), 'Exploring start-up event sequences', *Journal of Business Venturing*, **11**(3), 151–66.

Chiles, T.H., A.D. Meyer and T.J. Hench (2004), 'Organizational emergence: The origin and transformation of Branson, Missouri's musical theatres', *Organizational Science*, **15**(5), 499–519.

Delmar, F. and S. Shane (2004), 'Legitimating first: Organizing activities and the survival of new ventures', *Journal of Business Venturing*, **19**(3), 385–410.

Djankov, S., R. La Porta, F. Lopez-de-Silanes and A. Shleifer (2002), 'The regulation of entry', *Quarterly Journal of Economics*, **117**(1), 1–37.

Eckhardt, J., S. Shane and F. Delmar (2006), 'Multistage selection and the financing of new ventures', *Management Science*, **52**(2), 220–32.

Evans, D.S. and L.S. Leighton (1989), 'Some empirical aspects of entrepreneurship', *American Economic Review*, **79**(3), 519–35.

Forbes, D.P. (2005), 'Are some entrepreneurs more overconfident than others?', *Journal of Business Venturing*, **20**(5), 623–40.

Hannan, M.T. and J. Freeman (1989), *Organizational Ecology*, Cambridge, MA: Harvard University Press.

Hellerstedt, K. (2008), 'The composition of new venture teams: Its dynamics and consequences', Ph.D. thesis, Jönköping University, Stockholm.

Honig, B. and T. Karlsson (2004), 'Institutional forces and the written business plan', *Journal of Management*, **30**(1), 29–48.

Katz, J. and W.B. Gartner (1988), 'Properties of emerging organizations', *Academy of Mangement Review*, **13**(3), 429–41.

Kim, P.H. (2006), 'Organizing activities and founding processes of new ventures', Ph.D. thesis, Department of Sociology, University of North Carolina at Chapel Hill.

Lumpkin, G.T. and G.G. Dess (1996), 'Clarifying the entrepreneurial orientation construct and linking it to performance', *Academy of Management Review*, **21**(1), 135–72.

Morse, E.A. and D.S.K. Lim (2006), *NeoGenius Co., Ltd (Case)*, London, ON: Ivey Publishing.

Parker, S.C. (2006), 'Learning about the unknown: How fast do entrepreneurs adjust their beliefs?', *Journal of Business Venturing*, **21**(1), 1–26.

Plummer, L.A. and B. Headd (2008), *Rural and Urban Establishment Births and Deaths Using the U.S. Census Bureau's Business Information Tracking Series*, Washington, DC: Small Business Administration.

Putnam, L.L. and C. Stohl (1990), 'Bona fide groups: A reconceptualization of groups in context', *Communication Studies*, **41**(3), 248–65.

Reynolds, P.D. and B. Miller (1992), 'New firm gestation: Conception, birth and implications for research', *Journal of Business Venturing*, **7**(5), 405–18.

Ruef, M. (2005), 'Origins of organizations: The entrepreneurial process', in L.A. Keister (ed.), *Research in the Sociology of Work*, Greenwich, CT: JAI Press, pp. 63–100.

Scott, W.R. and G.F. Davis (2007), *Organizations and Organizing: Rational, Natural, and Open System Perspectives*, Upper Saddle River, NJ: Pearson Prentice Hall.

Shane, S. and F. Delmar (2004), 'Planning for the market: Business planning before marketing and the continuation of organizing efforts', *Journal of Business Venturing*, **19**(6), 767–85.

Sørensen, J.B. (2007), 'Bureaucracy and entrepreneurship: Workplace effects on entrepreneurial entry', *Administrative Science Quarterly*, **52**(3), 387–412.

Weick, K.E. (1979), *The Social Psychology of Organizing*, Reading, MA: Addison-Wesley.

12 The new venture mortality myth
Jonathan Levie, Gavin Don and Benoît Leleux

INTRODUCTION

In this chapter, we demonstrate the following: in advanced economies of the world: a) new businesses do not suffer a high failure rate; b) most people overestimate the chances of new firm failure; and c) fear of failure reduces entrepreneurial entry. Taken together, they suggest that new venture creation rates are lower than they would be if the true rate of new venture failure was widely known.

Official statistics tend to exaggerate enterprise churn, and it is common practice to assume that enterprise discontinuations are failures. A UK example of the weaknesses of sales tax registration, company incorporation data and business bank account data as measures of business failure is provided by the following case of a real business that trades as Young Company Finance. YCF was founded by Equitas, a partnership, in January 1998. At the outset it incorporated (measurable as a Companies House start-up), registered for value added tax (measurable as a VAT start-up) and opened two bank accounts (measurable as two parallel bank start-ups). In 1999 it opened a new bank account (a third bank start-up). In 2000 YCF Ltd sold its business and assets to Jonathan Harris, who incorporated a company to acquire them (a second Companies House start-up), opened a bank account (a fourth bank start-up) and registered for VAT (second VAT start-up). In due course, YCF Ltd, now a cash shell, closed its three bank accounts (three bank closures), deregistered for VAT (first VAT closure) and then removed itself from the company register (first Companies House closure). None of these closures constituted a failure.

Official statistics have become better at tracking new enterprise appearances and persistence, and increasingly warnings are posted in technical notes attached to the statistics about confusing discontinuation with failure. Most people, however, still believe new business failure rates are high. In the next section, we attempt to summarize what is known about persistence of new enterprises in official records across time, and the nature of discontinuations, including what proportion of enterprise discontinuations could be described as business failures. Then we review general beliefs about new business failure rates and find them to be much higher than research would suggest is justifiable. Finally, using the case of the UK as an example, we estimate the effect on the nascent entrepreneurship rate of this misperception of high new business failure rates.

NEW BUSINESSES DO NOT SUFFER A HIGH FAILURE RATE

In 1978, in a *Journal of Small Business Management* article entitled 'It's easier to slay a dragon than kill a myth', Michael Massel revealed widespread misinterpretations of Dun & Bradstreet's rate of failure statistics. At the time, popular textbooks and published academic articles were estimating 'failure rates' of new ventures at 90 per cent, despite the fact that it was impossible to estimate rates of failure by firm age given the data available. In the 30 years since that article, many researchers have tried to convince the public that new business failure rates are lower than commonly thought (Shapero 1981; Birch 1988; Watson and Everett 1993; Duncan 1994; Kirchhoff 1994, Chapter 8; Gibb 2000; Stanton and Tweed 2009). During this time, journalists have periodically 'discovered' the business mortality myth (Szabo 1988; Anon. 1993; James 1993; Selz 1994; Donald 2007).

Probably the most comprehensive cross-national set of new business survival rates (or, more correctly, one-year persistence rates) has been collected by the OECD Entrepreneurship Indicators Programme. Table 12.1 shows the one- to five-year persistence rates for new employer enterprises and all enterprises in OECD countries in 2005. On average, over 80 per cent of enterprises that enter a country's official records in one year are still recorded as persisting to the next year. The rate of persistence drops by another 10 per cent or so after two years and by roughly another 10 per cent after three years. Five-year persistence rates are just over 50 per cent on average. Figures for other years (from 1998 to 2006) compiled by the OECD were very similar.

The median life of a typical new enterprise in an annual cohort, at around five years, is longer than the median tenure of a new job in Canada or the UK (Heisz 1996; Macaulay 2003) and around the same as the median spell in self-employment in the US (Evans and Leighton, 1989). Yet job turnover rates are not normally described as job failure rates. While some people leave their job because they have failed in their job, many leave voluntarily to take up better positions elsewhere. The vast majority of enterprises are vehicles to provide a job for their owners, plus perhaps one or two others. Seen in this light, an enterprise discontinuance rate of 50 per cent after five years is around what one would expect, and is neither high nor low.

Table 12.1   One- to five-year percentage persistence in official records of new enterprises in OECD countries, 2005

Enterprise type*	One-year persistence rate		Two-year persistence rate		Three-year persistence rate		Four-year persistence rate		Five-year persistence rate	
	A	B	A	B	A	B	A	B	A	B
Austria	80.5									
Canada	85.2		73.3		62.9		57.6		50.5**	
Czech Republic	84.5	78.1		61.1		54.0		47.2		
Denmark	79.6									
Finland	75.1	83.0		66.7		58.5		52.6		48.2
Hungary	73.5	77.5		66.2		61.6		52.4		46.3
Italy	83.8	87.0		75.4		65.9		61.2		55.1
Luxembourg	90.0	88.3		73.9		65.5		57.3		51.4
Netherlands	57.3	84.9		73.1		63.9		59.2		53.6
New Zealand	73.5		58.7							
Portugal		78.9								
Slovak Republic	91.3	95.1		72.8		58.9		52.7		53.8
Spain	81.3	84.6		71.9		65.2		58.1		51.7
Sweden		96.9		85.8		78.4		70.7		64.4
United Kingdom		96.4		81.2		64.4		52.6		43.9
United States			80.0				53.4			
Bulgaria	69.0									
Estonia	82.5									
Latvia	94.9									
Lithuania	90.6									
Romania	88.9									
Slovenia										
Average	81.3	86.4	70.7	72.8	62.9	63.6	57.6	56.4	53.4	52.0
Standard deviation	9.5	7.2	10.9	7.2		6.5		6.5		5.9
No. of countries	17	11	3	10	1	10	1	10	1	9

Notes:
*   A: Employer enterprises; B: All enterprises.
**   2006 estimate.

Source: OECD Entrepreneurship Indicator SBDS business demography statistics, http://stats.oecd.org/Index.aspx?DataSetCode=SBDS_BDI (accessed 24 July 2009).

The countries covered by the OECD study have completely different enterprise registration systems. In some countries, it is virtually impossible to trade without registering first. In others, laissez-faire rules, particularly for smaller start-ups. The fact that the OECD enterprise discontinuance rates are so similar across these different regimes increases the credibility of the overall pattern. However, these data cannot be assumed to reflect the rate of those new businesses that have not failed since inception. An unknown number of 'enterprises' are set up for temporary legal reasons or to exploit temporary market opportunities or to be sold in a relatively short time frame. That is, they are not intended to have a long life. Enterprises may also switch legal status (from partnership or sole trader status to limited liability status or through a trade sale), thus creating false discontinuances in official records.

The extent of these false deaths has been investigated by several researchers. Phillips (1993) concluded from a review of the literature that the rate of business dissolutions in the US was four to eight times the rate of business failure, where business failure was defined in the narrow sense of the business stopping and leaving unpaid debts or filing for bankruptcy. However, owners may cease operations without leaving unpaid debts, but see the stoppage as a failure in that it did not provide them with an adequate return given their other options.

Headd (2003) cited an unpublished US Census Characteristics of Business Owners database which showed that 29.1 per cent of the owners whose businesses closed felt the business was successful (versus unsuccessful) at closure. This, however, does not adequately cater for ventures which might be sold for capital gain even though they were making operating losses at the time of the sale.

Research in 2002 by Barclays Bank of current and previous UK business owners (drawn from a face-to-face survey by BMRB International Ltd of a representative sample of 1994 adults aged 15 or over between 30 May and 12 June 2002) found that 48 per cent of the firm closures they surveyed were voluntary (rising to 58 per cent for 35- to 54-year-olds), a further 6 per cent sold the business to another business and 23 per cent to an individual, and only 5 per cent of the firms closed owing to insolvency or bankruptcy. Table 12.2 gives a complete breakdown of the reasons for closure reported in the Barclays survey.

An earlier study on business closures for HSBC bank (Stokes and Blackburn 2002) distinguished between a business closure, which they defined as a situation in which a business entity discontinues in its existing form, and an owner's exit, which is the act of departure from business ownership by the business owner. They received 388 responses (a 14 per cent response rate) to a survey of exited or closed business owners. Stokes

Table 12.2   Why do businesses close in the UK?

Sold to another individual	23%
Sold to another business	6%
Business failed (owing to insolvency or bankruptcy)	5%
Business closed voluntarily	48%
Changes in legislation forced closure (i.e. IR 35)	2%
Business still operating and has involvement	5%
Business passed to family member	3%
Illness	3%
Retirement	1%
Other	5%

Source: Barclays Bank, http://www.altassets.net/pdfs/BarclaysQ2200225-9-02.pdf

and Blackburn presented a typology of closures, where approximately half of closed businesses are discontinued because either they have failed financially (20 per cent) or they no longer meet their owners' objectives (30 per cent). However, half are effectively continued as either they are sold on (35 per cent) or they represent closures for technical reasons which reopen (15 per cent) under a different legal form. The proportions for the Barclays study are similar: 30 per cent sold, 15 per cent still going or passed on to a family member, and 50 per cent closed voluntarily (this would include those that no longer meet the owners' objectives and those reopening). The main difference is that, in the HSBC study, around 20 per cent of the firms were identified as having failed financially, whereas in the Barclays study 5 per cent were identified as technical failures; the equivalent for the HSBC study was 4 per cent. The gap can be explained by the difference in definitions. The HSBC study included owners' perceptions of business failure, whereas the Barclays study recorded only legal bankruptcy or insolvency.

Given the similarity in results between these different studies, we can be reasonably confident that they represent approximately the UK population. In summary, no more than 5 per cent of business closures are bankruptcies or liquidations. A further 15 per cent or so are considered financial failures by their owners. Around a third of 'closures' are not closed but sold on, while a further 15 per cent are reopened in a different legal form. The remainder (less than a third) are closed not because they are financial failures but because they no longer fulfil the objectives of their owners, who wish to do something else. A large-scale study of US small businesses by Kirchhoff (1994) found similar results; after eight years, 54 per cent of start-ups still survived, 28 per cent under the original owners and 26 per cent under new owners. Of the remainder, 18 per cent closed with losses to creditors and 28 per cent closed without losses to creditors.

The Global Entrepreneurship Monitor (Bosma *et al.* 2009, pp. 23–5) asked over 150 000 people aged 18–64 in 43 countries in 2008 if they had discontinued a business in the last 12 months, by selling, shutting down or otherwise discontinuing an owner/management relationship with the business, and if so what was the main reason for doing so. On average, about one-third of the businesses that were discontinued by an owner continued in another form or with different ownership. On average across the 18 developed countries, financial problems were cited by just over 40 per cent of the owners as the most important reason for discontinuing the business. Only 33 per cent cited 'business not profitable', with the other financial problem category being 'problems raising finance'. Primary reasons for discontinuation cited by almost 60 per cent of the respondents in these 18 countries included 'an incident', 'personal reasons', 'retirement', 'exit was planned in advance', 'other job or business opportunity' and 'opportunity to sell'. It is difficult to make a case for why any of these reasons could be considered a 'failure' of the business.

MOST PEOPLE OVERESTIMATE THE CHANCES OF NEW FIRM FAILURE

Despite all these data that show that new firm failure rates in advanced economies are relatively low, there is still a widespread perception in the media and in the public mind that new firms have a high mortality rate. A Google search on 26 and 27 July 2009 of the exact phrases 'of businesses fail in their first year', 'of new businesses fail in their first year' and 'of small businesses fail in their first year' revealed 301 percentage failure rate estimates on identifiably different websites (duplicates were omitted from analysis). The distribution of estimates of business failure rates in these web pages is shown in Figure 12.1. The mean percentage failure rate quoted was 57 per cent; the median was 50 per cent and the mode was 50 per cent. Only 67 of the 301 quotes were attributed. There were 190, or 63 per cent, of the estimates at 50 per cent, and almost all of these also quoted an estimate of 95 per cent in five years.

The most frequent source cited was the US Small Business Administration, which was cited 45 times as the source of one-year failure rates (33 of these were 50 per cent, one was 70 per cent, eight were 80 per cent and three were 90 per cent). In two of the latter, the following mathematically impossible statistic was claimed: '[The] SBA reports that nearly 90% of new businesses fail in their first year and nearly half fail

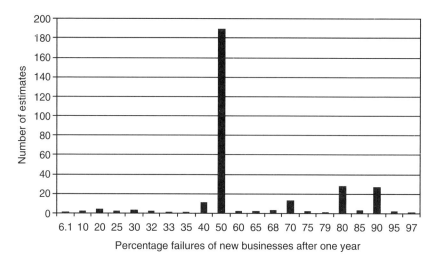

Source: Search on 26 and 27 July 2009 of all Google hits of the exact phrases 'of businesses fail in their first year', 'of new businesses fail in their first year' and 'of small businesses fail in their first year'. Total number of identifiably separate estimates: 301.

Figure 12.1   Distribution of estimates of one-year new business failure rates on the world wide web

within the initial three years.' Clearly, however, the 50 per cent estimate dominated. It stems from the following passage, taken from the US Small Business Administration website, which has been replicated in hundreds of educational and consultancy websites, blogsites, newspaper and magazine articles and books, not just in the United States, but across the world: 'Starting a small business is always risky, and the chance of success is slim. According to the U.S. Small Business Administration, over 50% of small businesses fail in the first year and 95% fail within the first five years'.

A Google search of these exact sentences together on 5 November 2005 generated 482 hits. Minor variants of the wording generated hundreds of further instances. On 27 July 2009, a non-exact search of the second sentence generated 601 000 hits. Where the reference is supplied (which is rare), it is given as the SBA website's web page with the address http://www.sba.gov/starting_business/startup/areyouready.html. This web page was changed in early 2005 on the instructions of the SBA's chief statistician (Brian Headd, email personal communication, 16 August 2005) and for a time no longer contained these sentences. More recently, the SBA website was reorganized, and they reappeared, but with the statistics altered to read 'roughly 50% of small businesses fail within the first five years' on a new 'Get Ready' web page aimed at prospective

entrepreneurs: http://www.sba.gov/smallbusinessplanner/plan/getready/
SERV_SBPLANNER_ISENTFORU.html.

These web pages did not cite a specific document as the source of the quoted failure rate statistic, and failure is not defined. We have been unable to trace the original source of these statistics, although the quotation suggests they come from a study conducted or sponsored by the SBA. Elsewhere in the SBA website, only survival rates of employer firms (from Knaup and Piazza 2007) are mentioned.

The second most frequent source of failure rate estimates was Michael Gerber's *The E-Myth Revisited* (Gerber 1995), with eight quotes of his attribution to the US Department of Commerce of a new business failure rate of 40 per cent in the first year, 80 per cent in the first five years, and 80 per cent of the remainder in the second five years. That would leave only 4 per cent of the original cohort that had not failed! According to Phillips (1993), however, the US Department of Commerce ceased publishing business dissolution data after 1963 because they were unreliable.

Only one source quoted the OECD business survival statistics, but these authors quoted the inverse of the survival rates as if they were failure rates, and highlighted the one anomalous number in the dataset: 'Not surprisingly, a high proportion of businesses fail in their first year of operation: 10%–20% across most of the reporting countries, but as high as 40% in the Netherlands' (Giovannini and Schramm 2008).

In a UK study which was designed to study the prevalence of myths about entrepreneurship among UK adults, Allinson *et al.* (2005) present evidence that suggests that those who are entrepreneurially engaged are more likely to believe that new firm failure rates are very high than those who are not entrepreneurially engaged. During focus group research involving 178 individuals in eight English regions, they found that the

> biggest myth to emerge . . . related to perceived rates of business failure . . . most people believed the likelihood of failure to be relatively high – that in the region of three out of four new businesses were likely to collapse in their first year. The perception was widespread, though no one could cite a reliable source for the information when challenged. (p. 16)

In the second stage of the study, in a large sample of 1002 UK adults, which was not representative of the population but stratified by seven different categories of engagement with entrepreneurship, 56 per cent thought that 50 per cent or more of new businesses would fail within a year of start-up, and 20 per cent, or one-third of these, thought that three-quarters or more would fail in the same time period. Correcting for the stratified nature of the study, this suggests that 51 per cent of the UK population would think that 50 per cent or more of new businesses

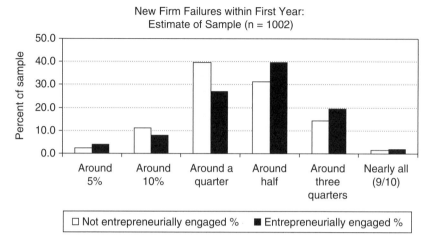

Source: Allinson *et al.* (2005).

Figure 12.2   Estimated new firm failures within the first year in the UK

would fail within a year of start-up, and 18 per cent, or over one-third of these, would think that three-quarters or more would fail in the same time period.[1] This distribution is quite similar to the distribution of estimates on websites shown in Figure 12.1.

Interestingly, those who had given no recent thought to starting a business, a category that constitutes around 70 per cent of the UK population, according to the 2003 UK Household Survey of Entrepreneurship, had lower failure rate estimates than other groups. Forty-seven per cent of the former (n = 301) thought at least 50 per cent would fail in the first year compared with around 60 per cent for other, more entrepreneurially engaged groups (n = 701). The distributions of the answers of these two groups are significantly different (chi-square statistic = 22.296, df = 5, p < .001). The answers of those who are not entrepreneurially engaged were approximately normally distributed around the range of categories presented to the respondents, but those who had at least some degree of engagement all had right-skewed distributions (see Figure 12.2). One interpretation of this difference would be that people who are entrepreneurially aware or engaged are conscious of presumed high new firm failure rates, while those who were not interested may not have had a rate in mind, but used the range provided as a cue.[2]

The Allinson *et al.* (2005) survey also asked respondents to choose from five different estimates of new firm survival rates within three years. These ranged from category 1 ('around 25%') to category 5 ('around 75%').

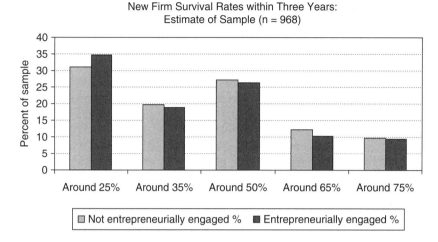

New Firm Survival Rates within Three Years:
Estimate of Sample (n = 968)

Source: Allinson *et al.* (2005).

Figure 12.3 Estimated new firm survival rates within three years

Allinson *et al.* quote VAT registration and deregistration statistics to suggest that respondents aware of the 'true' rate would have chosen category 4 (the 'around 65%' category), and one would expect an informed sample to produce a right-skewed distribution. However, 80 per cent of the sample chose category 1, 2 or 3, with fully one-third choosing category 1, producing a left-skewed distribution. As Figure 12.3 shows, there were no differences between those who were not engaged and others in the distribution of estimates. This suggests that most people in the UK believe that new firm survival is low over a three-year period.

In our review of new business failure rate estimates on the world wide web, we have found that the myth of high failure rates has been perpetuated by poor-quality referencing of empirical evidence, misinterpretation of empirical evidence and stating of assumptions without any referencing. These practices have been used by the following:

- promoters of books on how to achieve success and avoid failure in business;
- journalists in search of stories that provoke interest with a mixture of greed (how to get rich against all odds) and fear (of failure);
- successful entrepreneurs who believe they have won out against incredible odds and are therefore not just lucky but, somehow, 'special';
- business advisers and trainers who wish to justify their work;

- suppliers of business equipment and services such as IT, business rescue, insurance and credit rating[3] who wish to sell their services; and
- academics who wish to justify their business research.

In some cases, the writers quote sources such as the US SBA or Department of Commerce that no one would suspect of perpetuating false statistics. In other cases, the statistics appear to be simply made up on the spot to support an argument. All writers have clearly chosen statistics that fit their cause, since a more detailed review of the literature would have revealed plenty of evidence that the statistic they quote is at odds with the consensus of current research findings. Recent examples of each of these myth perpetuators from the US are given in Table 12.3. They include web-based marketing material from large businesses, including Microsoft (attributing a 40 per cent failure rate in the first year to the US Department of Commerce) and Cisco (attributing an 80 per cent failure rate in the first year to the US SBA).

In her study of the perpetuation of a different myth in the management literature – the myth that expatriate postings have a high failure rate – Harzing (2002) found that four citation violations were 'particularly influential in creating and maintaining the myth'. These were the use of unreliable sources, the misrepresentation of the content of source articles, the use of empty references[4] and the use of out-of-date references. The same practices are evident in the perpetuation of the new venture mortality myth. Indeed there are many examples of multiple violation of referencing best practice.

An example that combines all four violations is a statistic quoted by Stern and Henderson (2004) in a top-ranked journal (*Strategic Management Journal*): '50–70 percent of new firms fail within their first 5 years and over 80 percent in their first decade' (p. 488). Stern and Henderson quote Aldrich and Auster (1986) as the source of this statistic. While Aldrich and Auster do not explicitly quote that statistic in their paper, the 'over 80% in 10 years' statistic is similar to a calculation (mentioned in Aldrich and Auster 1986) by Starbuck and Nystrom (1981) of 81 per cent discontinuance of corporations after ten years, using data from the 1940s reported by Crum in 1953. Aldrich and Auster noted that the data had 'severe . . . limitations' and that Starbuck and Nystrom's calculations produced a 'crude estimate'. The 80 per cent in ten years statistic also mirrors a statistic of estimated discontinuances of new businesses that appears in Dickinson (1981, p. 18), attributed to Department of Commerce data quoted in Hollander (1967, p. 106).

Another source of the new business mortality myth is misinterpretation

Table 12.3   Selected recent US examples of perpetuation of the business mortality myth

Author	Year	Profession of author or original quoted source	Quotation
Fountain	2005	Adjunct professor, Case Western Reserve University; online at www.weatherhead.case.edu/about/news/detail.cfm?idNews=721	'We know that a vast majority – over 80% of businesses – fail in their first year.'
Microsoft	2005	Business brochure for Microsoft Retail Management System; online at www.envision-inc.net/downloads/Rachael_Boutique.pdf	'The United States Department of Commerce statistics on small businesses show that 40 percent of new businesses fail by the end of their first year. Eighty percent fail in their first five years.'
Morse	2007	Managerial accounting textbook, Chapter 3, page 72	'About 80 percent of all new businesses fail in the first five years.'
Candy Express	2009	Franchisor's website, www.candyexpress.com/HTML/usfranchise.html	'According to the Department of Commerce statistics almost 70% of all "independent" businesses fail within the first five years. Franchises have nearly a 95% annual success rate.'
Nevada Corporate Planners	2009	Home page, www.nvinc.com	'95% of all new businesses fail in the first five years, losing all their assets.'
Kurtzman and Rifkin	2005	Business book authors	'Every year hundreds of new firms come into existence. Of these, nine of ten will fail, often within the first year of operation. And the majority will cease to exist within five years' (inside front flap).
Office of vice-president	2009	University at Buffalo, www.research.buffalo.edu/stor/incubator	'A study done by Inc. Magazine and National Business Incubator Association (NBIA) revealed that 80 percent of new businesses fail within the first five years. When a startup is affiliated with an incubator, however, 87 percent survive.'

Table 12.3   (continued)

Author	Year	Profession of author or original quoted source	Quotation
Cisco	2009	Business brochure for Cisco products, www. cisco.com/en/US/ solutions/. . ./bwtv_ episode_10.html	'According to the Small Business Administration, 80 percent of small businesses fail in the first year.'

of the data that are available (Massel 1978). James (1993) quotes David Birch as tracing the source of the 'four out of five small firms fail' myth to a misinterpretation of Dun & Bradstreet studies showing that almost all businesses that fail are small. He quoted Birch as saying: 'It's like being on the end of a whisper chain . . . it's a myth everyone agrees to.'

Reynolds and White (1997) note that not all discontinuances of firms are undesirable, and that it may be better to describe firms as persistent or discontinued rather than 'successful or failed' or 'dead or alive' (p. 130). However, others have not been so discerning. For example, in his influential book *Understanding the Small Business Sector*, Storey (1995, p. 80) commented:

> The term 'failure' is often considered to have a perjorative connotation, imply-
> ing either that the business should never have been started in the first place, or
> that the person who ran the business was not competent to do so, or that the
> business left behind significant unpaid debt. In fact, none of these connota-
> tions need apply, and the reader can choose any of the four terms ['death',
> 'failure', 'cease to trade' or 'closure'] to apply to a business which has ceased
> to trade. In many senses the term 'failure' is used solely because of ease and
> recognition.

Compared with the agnostic (some might say lax) approach to nomen-
clature of Storey, Shane (2008) presents what might be described as a
committed (some might say single-minded) view. He writes: 'Most new
businesses fail. Pretty much all studies agree on that. The only question is
how long it takes for a majority of them to go out of business (and why)'
(p. 98). To Shane, closure means failure (p. 100). In his support, he cites
Headd (2003) as the source of a study 'of new employer and non-employer
firms founded between 1989 and 1992 that went under within four years
[that] showed that 70.1 percent of the founders felt that their start-up effort
was unsuccessful' (p. 100, italics in original). This citation misrepresents
the original Headd article in three ways. The first is that the study was of

firms that went under. In fact, it was based on two government databases that recorded closure, not failure. Second, the CBO data actually showed that 29.1 per cent of the owners whose businesses closed felt the business was successful at closure, while the BITS data recorded 50 per cent of new employer firms as surviving four years or more. Headd concluded from this (p. 58) that, 'Contrary to what is commonly believed, not all closures are failures. [After four years] only one-third of new businesses (33 percent) closed under circumstances that owners considered unsuccessful.'

Twisting a sensationalist business mortality headline out of facts of low business mortality is not uncommon in the media. Here is an example from the UK, in which statistics are quoted that clearly demonstrate low levels of business failure, yet a sub-editor and business services provider treat them as if they were high. The headline (from *Newcastle Chronicle & Journal*, dated 8 February 2003) reads: 'Gloomy year as business failure rates soar'. The story reads:

> The full year total of over 16,000 was 9pc up from the 14,972 insolvencies in 2001. But the DTI said the number of companies going bust represented only 1.1pc of all active companies. Simon Appell, of corporate rescue specialist Kroll, said: 'The figures offer grim reading for UK businesses and there is no sign of any light at the end of the tunnel.'

By any standard, a failure rate of 1 per cent per annum is low. Yet the newspaper and a 'corporate rescue specialist' repeatedly used emotive language to give the impression of a worryingly high failure rate. The notion that new firms have high failure rates remains so entrenched that many media columnists and academics don't bother to check or state statistics, as in these examples:

1. 'I haven't checked the government statistics recently, but we all know the number of small businesses that fail each year is very high, especially in the first year of operations' (Faletra 2005, p. 152).
2. 'A myth of the dot-com stock meltdown is that high tech and Internet companies are failing at a higher rate than ever before. This simply isn't true. The failure rate of startup companies has always been high in excess of 90 percent. This just happens to be the first time the rest of us have been allowed to share in the carnage' (Cringely, 15 March 2001, PBS website).

In summary, most people, including highly reputable academics known for insisting on evidence-based arguments, appear to believe that new businesses have a high failure rate, and this myth is perpetuated by those with vested interests in the myth.

FEAR OF FAILURE REDUCES ENTREPRENEURIAL ENTRY

There is considerable evidence from the Global Entrepreneurship Monitor that a high percentage of the population worldwide say they are put off from starting a business by the fear of failure (Bosma *et al.* 2009). Self-reported fear of failure has been shown to have a negative and statistically significant effect on an individual's propensity to start a business in the UK, after controlling for a set of demographic and attitudinal factors (Levie 2007). In the UK, successive Global Entrepreneurship Monitor UK reports have shown fear of failure among the non-entrepreneurially active (those not actively trying to start or running their own business) over the period 2002 to 2008 ranging from 36 to 38 per cent (Levie and Hart 2009). This tends to be somewhat below the G7 nation average but above the US average. Fear of failure appears to be higher among women than men, and higher among younger working-age adults than older working-age adults.

We do not know whether GEM respondents are saying they would not start a business because they are afraid of the consequences should it fail, such as personal failure, bankruptcy or loss of property, or because they think the probability of a new business failing is high and therefore they would not start one. Possibly, both the perceived risk of failure and the perceived consequences of failure are implicit in the responses.

Other surveys have also tried to probe this issue. For example, in the Flash Eurobarometer Entrepreneurship Surveys 2004 and 2007, respondents were asked 'If you were to set up a business today, which are the two risks you would be most afraid of?' Respondents were given a choice from a list of personal rather than business risks. Table 12.4 shows the results for the EU25, UK and US. Half of European respondents mentioned the risk of going bankrupt, while uncertainty of income came second. Around 40 per cent of UK respondents were also concerned about losing their property, presumably if they went bankrupt.

When respondents to the 2007 Flash Eurobarometer survey were asked if they believed that one should not start a business *if there is a risk it might fail*, 48 per cent of EU respondents agreed, compared with 19 per cent of US respondents. Clearly, perceived risk of failure is higher in Europe than in the US. Arguably, therefore, false perception of high new business failure may matter more in Europe than in the US.

Fear of failure appears to be most prevalent among those who have no intention of starting a business (so-called 'avoiders'), while belief in a high failure rate seems to be highest among those who are thinking of starting a business or are already engaged in entrepreneurial activity. This makes sense in that the latter are more likely to remember (mis)quotes of high

Table 12.4   If you were to set up a business today, which are the two risks you would be most afraid of?

Year	2004			2007		
Percentage choosing this risk	EU25	UK	US	EU25	UK	US
The possibility of going bankrupt	45	47	36	51	49	41
The uncertainty of your income	34	38	38	38	41	41
The risk of losing your property	35	47	21	36	43	27
Job insecurity	17	15	14	19	18	19
The need to devote too much energy or time to it	15	18	22	17	18	26
The possibility of suffering a personal failure	15	16	16	18	19	19
DK/NA	5	4	11	7		5

Source: EOS Gallup Europe (2004, 2007).

new firm failure rates they may come across. According to the 2004 UK Household Survey of Entrepreneurship, commissioned by the UK Small Business Service, 58 per cent of avoiders agreed that 'the chance that your business might fail' was a barrier to them starting a business, compared with 36 per cent of those who were 'thinking' about starting a business.

It seems reasonable to suppose that, if people knew the chance of failing is low and also knew that the proportion of bankrupts who are bankrupt because their business failed is also low (see Tribe 2006), they would recalibrate the odds and be more likely to start. There is some evidence from the psychology literature on risk to support this. For example, Weber and Milliman's (1997) research on risk perception and risky choice suggests that decision making in risky choices is affected by the perceived riskiness of different choice alternatives rather than personal attitudes to risk. And, according to Fox and Tversky (1995), 'people prefer to bet on known rather than unknown probabilities'. However, as Fox and Tversky point out (pp. 586–7), 'the decision to undertake a business venture . . . [is] commonly made in the absence of a clear idea that these actions will be successful'. Heath and Tversky (1991) found that people preferred to bet on vague beliefs in situations where they feel especially competent or knowledgeable, although they prefer to bet on chance if they do not feel like that.[5] This supports the findings of Cooper *et al.* (1988) on perception of risk among entrepreneurs, and suggests that a false belief of a high failure rate is likely to keep people off the general notion of starting a business, that is, reinforce an avoidance mentality. It is less likely to put people off starting a business for which they have a specific idea, because they are thinking about the specific risks involved in their venture, not in terms of general probabilities. It may have most effect, then, on the in-between group, the 'thinkers'.

The proposition that the destruction of the new firm failure rate myth might elicit greater entrepreneurial activity among 'thinkers' than 'avoiders' or 'doers' is supported by the findings of Allinson *et al.* (2005): 'when told that [their estimated] proportions [of firms failing] were incorrect, and that a far greater number of businesses survived, most focus group participants were ready to believe it and found it an encouraging prospect' (p. 16). In stage two of the Allinson *et al.* study, when those who had overestimated the failure rate were informed that the 'true' rate of new firm failure in the first year was 10 per cent, 55 per cent of those who were 'thinking' of starting a business were more positive about their prospects of starting a business than previously, compared with only 25 per cent of those who had no intention of starting a business and 30 per cent of those who had started a business. This suggests that the new firm failure rate myth has a significant and detrimental effect on over half of those thinking about starting a business, by reducing the perceived feasibility and the perceived desirability of this activity.

In the GEM 2005 UK data, 12 per cent of the working-age population were thinkers (using the same definitions as Allinson *et al.*). About 12 per cent of thinkers agreed they had the skills to start a business and thought there were good opportunities to start a business in their local area but were afraid to start a business in case it might fail. This is 1.44 per cent of the working-age population, or almost half of the 3.1 per cent who were actively trying to start a business in the UK in 2005. Using the Allinson *et al.* results as a guide, 55 per cent of these, or 0.79 per cent of the working age population, should feel much more positive about their business prospects, potentially lifting the nascent entrepreneurship rate by 0.79/3.1 or 25 per cent, if false belief in high failure rates is indeed the barrier to start-up activity for these thinkers.

In 2005, 72 per cent of the GEM UK sample of the working-age population were avoiders, 4.7 per cent of whom reported start-up skills and perceived good opportunities but feared failure. If avoiders knew the true fear of failure, and if this was the only criterion holding them back, then using the Allinson *et al.* finding that 25 per cent of avoiders felt much better about their business prospects, this could produce an additional $0.72 \times 0.047 \times 0.25 = 0.85$ per cent of the population becoming nascent entrepreneurs, lifting the nascent entrepreneurship by 0.85/3.1 or 27 per cent, around the same yield as for thinkers. Of course, this is not the only barrier to avoiders. Forty-one per cent of avoiders reported that one of the biggest barriers to them starting a business was getting finance for the business. These are 2.2 per cent of avoiders who have skills and good opportunities and do not see money as a major barrier but fear failure. If these avoiders knew the true fear of failure, and if this was the only criterion holding them back, another $0.72 \times 0.022 \times 0.25 = 0.4$ per cent of the population might become nascent entrepreneurs. This would lift the nascent entrepreneurship population by 0.4/3.1 or 13 per cent.

Overall, combining the potential yield from thinkers and avoiders for whom the principal barrier to starting a business appears to be fear of failure, it appears that widespread knowledge of the true failure rate of new firms could lift the UK nascent entrepreneurship rate by around a third.

CONCLUSION

In advanced economies, new businesses appear to have high survival rates, with a declining rate of attrition for the first five years from around 80 per cent to around 50 per cent of the original cohort. This estimate may be subject to fluctuations by economic cycle and industry, which is beyond the scope of this chapter. But few new enterprises go bankrupt or stop leaving debts in their first year or two (Phillips 1993). A portion, perhaps a third, of discontinuations do actually continue in another guise, while perhaps another third of discontinuations could be seen as failures to make a go of it. The remainder are cessations for non-financial reasons. Thus the true failure rate is much lower, perhaps two to three times lower depending on how one defines business failure, than the inverse of the survival rate.

These data suggest that interpreting 'not survived' as 'failed' and 'not successful' as the inverse of 'successful' is mistaken at best, disingenuous at worst. By making these terms equivalent, some academics and others with vested interests in heightening fear of failure have exaggerated the failure statistics, creating a very real fear of failing among a significant segment of the population and reducing nascent entrepreneurship rates.

The theoretical concept of 'liability of newness', coined by Stinchcombe in 1965, is still supported in the academic literature (Aldrich 1999), despite empirical evidence of liability of adolescence (Bruderl and Schussler 1990; Fichman and Levinthal 1991) and liability of ageing (Ranger-Moore 1997) and calls for the concept of liability of newness to be laid to rest (Barron *et al.* 1994, p. 414).[6] It appears to have exerted a powerful effect on the profession, and perpetuated the new business failure myth.

Aldrich (1999) uses the Darwinian metaphor of 'struggle' to depict the competition between new organizations and the resulting high failure rate for new businesses. We take issue with the use of the term 'struggle' in this context. In our view, humans are forward-thinking beings and, because most people believe that new businesses have a high failure rate, 'struggle' will take place mainly at the nascent stage, in the entrepreneur's mind, as she shapes the business conceptually and tests her assumptions through such activities as building prototypes, talking with customers, seeking funding and so on. PSED studies that track cross-sections of nascent entrepreneurs over time suggest that, after seven years, only around one-third of nascents have actually started a business (Reynolds 2007, p. 56). Once the new business has been started, closure rates are low, rates of 'failure to make a go of it' are lower and technical business failure rates are very low.

The perception of high new firm failure rates causes misallocation of resources by government agencies, banks, entrepreneurs and investors. For example, we might expect a higher level of informal investment in new firms if the true rate were more widely known. The 2004 GEM Global Executive Report (Acs *et al.* 2005) demonstrated a wide divergence in assumed returns and probability of returns between informal investors and nascent entrepreneurs. Informal investors, other than angel investors, tended to assume that they would have low returns and a low probability of any return. Entrepreneurs and angel investors, however, expected high returns and high probability of returns. The difference can be explained using the theoretical lens of decision making under uncertainty developed by Tversky and colleagues outlined above. Looking through that lens, we would expect informal investors, knowing little about the specifics of the business but believing that new firms had a high rate of failure, to assume the worst, as indeed they appear to have done. Entrepreneurs and angel investors, however, were focused on the specific business and its prospects, and calculated the odds of success very differently.

In another example, the UK government has recently attempted to mitigate the effect of bankruptcy, in the belief that risk of bankruptcy puts people off from starting businesses and that business failure is a major cause of bankruptcy. The latter is a commonly held view, even among experts in insolvency law (Milman 2005, p. 18). Indeed, one journalist expressed this confusion between business failure and personal bankruptcy by commenting that the Enterprise Act 2002 changes to personal bankruptcy proceedings were enacted to 'make it easier for companies to go bankrupt' (Stuart 2005).

Governments around the world encourage people to think about starting a business. At least some of this effort is unproductive because it results in people discovering and dwelling on the (false) high new business failure rate. A campaign to apprise people of the facts of the matter could produce a significant lift to nascent entrepreneurship rates. Removing the new firm failure rate myth might also reduce the assumption of some bankers that new firm lending is high-risk because of a high new firm failure rate[7] (Ford 1996) and thus encourage more entrepreneurs to consider this form of finance.[8] Finally, the presumed purpose of enterprise training and incubation facilities might shift resources from trying to prevent failure to helping clients to be more successful (Bee 2004).

NOTES

1. Calculated using the sample proportions cited by Allinson *et al.* (2005, p. 6).
2. As only 13 per cent of the focus group sample had never thought about self-employment, it is not surprising that the responses of the focus group were so skewed to the right of the failure rate range offered in the second-stage survey.
3. Massel's principal conclusion in his 1978 paper was 'the rate of failure in United States industries that are covered by Dun and Bradstreet data is minimal and should not be accorded great attention or emphasis' (p. 49). The journal's editor appended this footnote to Massel's conclusion: 'In strong disagreement with this statement, Rowena Wyant of D&B points out that this failure data *should* be accorded attention and emphasis because 'they represent the most severe impact upon the economy and pinpoint the most vulnerable industries and locations in a specific time period'.
4. According to Harzing (2002), 'empty references are references that do not contain any original evidence for the phenomenon under investigation, but strictly refer to other studies to substantiate their claim. Other authors subsequently use these empty references to substantiate their claims rather than going back to cite the original source.'
5. For other evidence supporting this, see Fox and Tversky (1995, p. 587).
6. The consensus of these researchers is that, controlling for size, there is a liability of ageing, not of newness.
7. For example, Richard Banks, managing director, wholesale banking, Alliance & Leicester, is quoted as stating at an analysts, meeting in 2003 that 'something like half small business startups fail in the first three years' (*Fair Disclosure Wire*, Waltham, 2 August 2005), while Richard Cracknell, head of franchising at Barclays, was quoted in a *Financial Times* article as saying 'Almost 90% of franchisees are still trading after three years compared to less than 50 percent of ordinary startups' (Peter 1999, p. 1).
8. Evidence from several recent studies (Fraser 2004; Harding *et al.* 2006) suggests that a very low percentage (around 4 per cent) of entrepreneurs fail to secure bank funding if they ask for it.

REFERENCES

Acs, Z.J., P. Arenius, M. Hay and M. Minniti (2005), *Global Entrepreneurship Monitor 2004 Executive Report*, London: London Business School and Babson Park, MA: Babson College.

Aldrich, H. (1999), *Organizations Evolving*, London: Sage.

Aldrich, H. and E.R. Auster (1986), 'Even dwarfs started small: Liabilities of age and size and their strategic implications', in B.M. Staw and L.L. Cummings (eds), *Research in Organizational Behavior*, Greenwich, CT: JAI Press, pp. 165–98.

Allinson, G., P. Braidford, M. Houston and I. Stone (2005), *Myths Surrounding Starting and Running a Business*, London: Small Business Service.

Anonymous (1993), 'The incredible shrinking failure rate', *Inc.*, **15**(10), 58.

Barron, D.N., E. West and M.T. Hannan (1994), 'A time to grow and a time to die: Growth and mortality of credit unions in New York city, 1914–1990', *American Journal of Sociology*, **100**(2), 381–421.

Bee, E. (2004), 'Small business vitality and economic development', *Economic Development Journal*, **3**(3), 7–15.

Birch, D. (1988), 'Live fast, die young', *Inc.*, **10**(8), 23–4.

Bosma, N., Z. Acs, E. Autio, A. Coduras and J. Levie (2009), *Global Entrepreneurship Monitor 2008 Executive Report*, London: Global Entrepreneurship Research Association.

Bruderl, J. and R. Schussler (1990), 'Organizational mortality: The liabilities of newness and adolescence', *Administrative Science Quarterly*, **35**(3), 530–47.

Cooper, A., C. Woo and W. Dunkelberg (1988), 'Entrepreneurs' perceived chances for success', *Journal of Business Venturing*, **3**, 97–108.

Crum, W. (1953), *The Age Structure of the Corporate System*, Berkeley: University of California Press.

Dickinson, R. (1981), 'Business failure rate', *American Journal of Small Business*, **6**(2), 17–25.

Donald, C. (2007), 'Study explodes myth of business failure', *Scotsman*, 15 December.

Duncan, J.W. (1994), 'The true failure rate of start-ups', *D&B Reports*, **43**(1), 1.

EOS Gallup Europe (2004), Flash Eurobarometer 160: Entrepreneurship, Wavre, Belgium: EOS Gallup Europe for the European Commission.

EOS Gallup Europe (2007), Flash Eurobarometer 192: Entrepreneurship, Wavre, Belgium: EOS Gallup Europe for the European Commission.

Evans, D. and L.S. Leighton (1989), 'Some empirical aspects of entrepreneurship', *American Economic Review*, **79**(3), 519–35.

Faletra, R. (2005), 'Keeping the failure rate low', *CRN*, 27 June, p. 152.

Fichman, M. and D.A. Levinthal (1991), 'Honeymoons and the liability of adolescence: A new perspective on duration dependence in social and organizational relationships', *Academy of Management Review*, **16**(2), 442–68.

Ford, J.K. (1996), 'The risk of lending to new firms may not be insurmountable', *Commercial Lending Review*, **12**(1), 56–7.

Fox, C.R. and A. Tversky (1995), 'Ambiguity aversion and comparative ignorance', *Quarterly Journal of Economics*, **110**(3), 585–603.

Fraser, S. (2004), *Finance for Small and Medium-Sized Enterprises: A Report of the 2004 UK Survey of SME Finances*, Coventry: Warwick Business School.

Gerber, M.E. (1995), *The E-Myth Revisited: Why Most Small Businesses Don't Work and What to Do about It*, New York: HarperCollins.

Gibb, A.A. (2000), 'Academic research and the growth of ignorance. SME policy: Mythical concepts, myths, assumptions, rituals and confusions', *International Small Business Journal*, **18**(3), 13–35.

Giovannini, E. and K. Schramm (2008), 'Where companies grow: Finally a way to measure countries' entrepreneurs', available at http://online.wsj.com/article/SB122833686657976713.html

Harding, R., D. Brooksbank, M. Hart, D. Jones-Evans, J. Levie, M. O'Reilly and J. Walker (2006), *GEM United Kingdom 2006 Report*, London: London Business School.

Harzing, A.W. (2002), 'Are our referencing errors undermining our scholarship and credibility? The case of expatriate failure rates', *Journal of Organizational Behavior*, **23**(1), 127–48.

Headd, B. (2003), 'Redefining business success: Distinguishing between closure and failure', *Small Business Economics*, **21**(1), 51–61.

Heath, C. and A. Tversky (1991), 'Preference and belief: Ambiguity and competence in choice under uncertainty', *Journal of Risk and Uncertainty*, **4**(1), 5–28.

Heisz, A. (1996), 'Changes in job tenure and job stability in Canada', Statistics Canada working paper, p. 95.

Hollander, E. (1967), *Failure of Small Business*, Praeger: New York.

James, A. (1993), 'Debunking the failure fallacy', *Fortune*, **128**(5), 21.

Kirchhoff, B.A. (1994), *Entrepreneurship and Dynamic Capitalism*, Westport, CT: Praeger.

Knaup, A.E. and M.C. Piazza (2007), 'Business employment dynamics data: Survival and longevity, II', *Monthly Labor Review*, **130**(9), 3–11.

Levie, J. (2007), 'Immigration, in-migration, ethnicity and entrepreneurship', *Small Business Economics*, **28**(2), 143 69.

Levie, J. and M. Hart (2009), *Global Entrepreneurship Monitor United Kingdom 2008 Report*, Birmingham: Aston Business School.

Macaulay, C. (2003), 'Job mobility and job tenure in the UK', *Labour Market Trends*, **111**(11), 541–50.

Massel, M. (1978), 'It's easier to slay a dragon than kill a myth', *Journal of Small Business Management*, **16**(3), 44–9.

Milman, D. (2005), *Personal Insolvency Law, Regulation and Policy*, Aldershot: Ashgate Publishing.

Peter, J. (1999), 'Potential franchisees must do their homework well', *Financial Times*, Surveys edn, 22 June, p. 1.

Phillips, B.D. (1993), 'The influence of industry and location on small firm failure rates', in S. Birley, W.D. Bygrave, F.S. Hoy, N.C. Churchill and W.E. Wetzel (eds), *Frontiers of Entrepreneurship Research, 1993*, Babson Park, MA: Babson College.

Ranger-Moore, J. (1997), 'Bigger may be better, but is older wiser? Organizational age and size in the New York life insurance industry', *American Sociological Review*, **62**(6), 903–20.

Reynolds, P.D. (2007), 'New firm creation in the United States: A PSED I overview', *Foundations and Trends in Entrepreneurship*, **3**(1).

Reynolds, P.D. and S. White (1997), *The Entrepreneurial Process: Economic Growth, Men, Women, and Minorities*, Westport, CT: Quorum Books.

Selz, M. (1994), 'For business survival, bigger isn't necessarily better – small companies boast the lowest failure rates in D&B survey', *Wall Street Journal*, 21 October, B2.

Shane, S. (2008), *The Illusions of Entrepreneurship: The Costly Myths that Entrepreneurs, Investors, and Policy Makers Live By*, London: Yale University Press.

Shapero, A. (1981), 'Numbers that lie', *Inc.*, **3**(5), 16.

Stanton, P. and D. Tweed (2009), 'Evaluation of small business failure and the framing problem', *International Journal of Economics and Business Research*, **1**(4), 438–53.

Starbuck, W. and P. Nystrom (1981), 'Designing and understanding organizations', in P. Nystrom and W. Starbuck (eds), *Handbook of Organization Design*, New York: Oxford University Press, pp. ix–xxii.

Stern, I. and A.D. Henderson (2004), 'Within-business diversification in technology-intensive industries', *Strategic Management Journal*, **25**(5), 487–505.

Stinchcombe, A.L. (1965), 'Social structure and organizations', in J.G. March (ed.), *Handbook of Organizations*, Chicago: Rand-McNally, pp. 142–93.

Stokes, D. and R. Blackburn (2002), 'Learning the hard way: The lessons of owner-managers who have closed their businesses', *Journal of Small Business and Enterprise Development*, **9**(1), 17–27.

Storey, D.J. (1995), *Understanding the Small Business Sector*, London: Routledge.

Stuart, J. (2005), 'Bankruptcy "It's an easy way out. I can start afresh"', *Independent*, 16 February.

Szabo, J.C. (1988), 'Survival rates for start-ups', *Nation's Business*, **76**(10), 8.

Tribe, J. (2006), *Bankruptcy Courts Survey 2005 – A Pilot Study. Final Report*, Kingston upon Thames: Centre for Insolvency Law and Policy, Kingston University London.

Watson, J. and J.E. Everett (1993), 'Defining small business failure', *International Small Business Journal*, **11**(3), 35–48.

Weber, E.U. and R.A. Milliman (1997), 'Perceived risk attitudes: Relating risk perception to risky choice', *Management Science*, **43**(2), 123–44.

13 Comprehensive Australian Study of Entrepreneurial Emergence (CAUSEE): design, data collection and descriptive results

Per Davidsson, Paul Steffens and Scott Gordon

INTRODUCTION

The Comprehensive Australian Study of Entrepreneurial Emergence (CAUSEE) is a research programme that aims to uncover the factors that initiate, hinder and facilitate the process of emergence of new economic activities and organizations. It is widely acknowledged that entrepreneurship is one of the most important forces shaping changes in a country's economic landscape (Baumol 1968; Birch 1987; Acs 1999). An understanding of the process by which new economic activity and business entities emerge is vital (Gartner 1993; Sarasvathy 2001). An important development in the study of 'nascent entrepreneurs' and 'firms in gestation' was the Panel Study of Entrepreneurial Dynamics (PSED) (Gartner *et al.* 2004) and its extensions in Argentina, Canada, Greece, the Netherlands, Norway and Sweden. Yet while PSED I is an important first step towards systematically studying new venture emergence, it represents just the beginning of a stream of nascent venture studies – most notably PSED II is currently being undertaken in the US (2005–10) (Reynolds and Curtin 2008).

CAUSEE employs and extends the research approach of PSED and to some extent the Global Entrepreneurship Monitor (GEM) (Reynolds *et al.* 2003, 2005). Essentially we identify individuals involved with a nascent firm from a screening interview of the adult population. We then conduct an extensive interview with them about their new venture annually over four years (2008–11). While CAUSEE benefits greatly from the progress that has been made in previous research on nascent entrepreneurship and is partially harmonized with the ongoing PSED II study in the US, it is much more than a mere replication study. The most important extensions to and/or departures from the PSED II are as follows:

1. Since high-growth firms are relatively rare in any random sample of new firms, we include a non-random over-sample of 'high-potential' firms.

2. We incorporate additional theory-driven content, including packages related to effectuation, bricolage, the resource-based view, venture newness and venture relatedness.
3. We include an equally sized sample of young firms that allows us both to compare the progress of young firms with that of our nascent cohort over the same period and identical factor conditions and also combine the two samples to study some processes of entrepreneurial emergence over a longer time frame.
4. We select the venture as the primary unit of analysis, whereas PSED uses a mixture of new venture and individual.
5. We study entrepreneurial emergence within an Australian context.

The purpose of the current chapter is to explain and rationalize the CAUSEE design and to present some preliminary, descriptive results from the first wave of the data collection.

PROJECT CONCEPTUALIZATION

One major aim of the research is to identify a statistically representative sample of ongoing venture start-up efforts. These start-up efforts are subsequently followed over time through repeated waves of data collection so that insights can be gained also into process issues and determinants of outcomes. The overarching research approach was originally developed by Reynolds and collaborators for PSED and is a central development in entrepreneurship research for the following reasons:

1. The approach largely overcomes the under-coverage of the smallest and youngest entities and the non-comparability across countries that typically signify available business databases from statistical organizations. Avoiding under-coverage and non-comparability allows for describing and comparing the prevalence of entrepreneurial activity in different economies. The more comprehensive studies of nascent entrepreneurship also overcome the lack of data on many interesting variables that restrict the usefulness of 'secondary' datasets.
2. The approach overcomes the selection bias resulting from including only start-up efforts that actually resulted in up-and-running businesses. This is achieved by screening a very large, probabilistic sample of households in order to identify those individuals who are currently involved in an ongoing start-up effort. The potential criticality of this is demonstrated by the fact that studying only those processes that

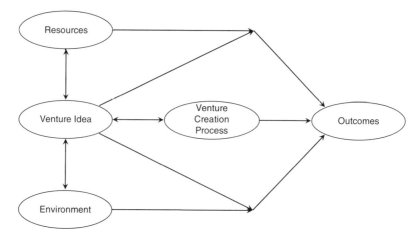

Figure 13.1   The components and fit of the process of emergence of new organizations and activities

result in successfully established firms is equivalent to exclusively investigating winners when studying gambling.[1]

3. The approach largely overcomes hindsight bias and memory decay resulting from asking survey questions about the start-up process retrospectively, and gets the temporal order of assessment right for causal analysis.

Figure 13.1 provides an overview of the main components of the CAUSEE study and the relationships between these key elements. CAUSEE adopts a process view of new venture creation, whereas processes are central in the research model. Important antecedents are the nature of the venture idea itself, the resources that the founders bring to the venture (including their own human and social capital) and the business/market environment. Indeed, it is not only these three elements separately, but aspects of their fit, that is considered important (Davidsson 2005b). Finally, the project examines many types of outcomes, including progress, survival and financial measures.

Several outcomes exemplify the relative success of this research approach. First, the PSED has triggered a well-funded follower in the ongoing PSED II study (Reynolds and Curtin 2008), as well as counterpart studies in a number of countries, including Canada (Menzies *et al.* 2002), the Netherlands (van Gelderen *et al.* 2005), Norway (Alsos and Kolvereid 1998) and Sweden. This has – apart from all other forms of dissemination – resulted in at least 70 articles published in peer-reviewed journals (Davidsson and Gordon 2009), including the best cited papers since 2000 in the leading European (Delmar and Davidsson 2000), as well as the leading North American (Davidsson and Honig 2003), journals in entrepreneurship. The Global Entrepreneurship Monitor has led to two special issues of the *Small Business Economics* journal (in 2005 and 2007) and is without doubt the most influential policy research project by far in the area of new and small business. As a case in point, at the time of this writing a Google search for 'Global Entrepreneurship Monitor' yields 93 700 hits, which is even higher than another very well-known international research programme, the World Values Survey, which stops at 92 400. Davidsson (2006) and Davidsson and Gordon (2009) provide reviews of previous academic research based on PSED, GEM and related studies, while Reynolds (2007) provides an overview of results of the original PSED study conducted in the US.

WHAT DISTINGUISHES CAUSEE FROM ITS FORERUNNERS?

While benefiting greatly from the progress that has been made in previous research on nascent entrepreneurship (Davidsson 2006; Davidsson and Gordon 2009), CAUSEE has several unique features. CAUSEE has been designed as a venture-level study. This means that the interviewee is regarded as a resource and informant for the venture. The characteristics and contributions of other founders (when present) are as important as the respondent's, and when the respondent no longer works on the start-up it is still a valid case as long as somebody else does.

PSED and related studies have been somewhat limited in terms of the theoretical underpinning and measurement scales incorporated into the survey design (Davidsson 2006). This is largely due to the very large size of the team that was involved in its development (Davidsson 2005a) and to the – essentially sound – ambition to give a realistic overview of the many factors involved in the process of starting different kinds of businesses (cf. Reynolds 2007). As a consequence of trying to represent many factors, PSED-style studies are restricted to the use of relatively simple measures that, at best, serve as proxies for these complex issues. In response, CAUSEE, while still comprehensive, aims at covering fewer aspects in a more theory-driven fashion and with more carefully developed and validated operationalizations of theoretical constructs.

One of the great strengths of the PSED approach is that it allows – for the first time – the study of representative samples of emerging firms. This is a prerequisite for statistical generalizations and for developing an understanding of what types of ventures make up the empirical population of business start-ups. However, the sampling approach has limitations for other purposes. A random sample of business start-ups is dominated by relatively modest, 'me-too' start-ups in mature industries. While this category of firm should not be dismissed as unimportant (Davidsson *et al.* 1998) there is the risk that the sample will not generate a sufficiently large (i.e. statistically analysable) group of high-tech, high-growth and/ or high-potential firms, that is, the types of firms that according to some studies generate almost all the effect of start-ups on job creation and economic development (Birch *et al.* 1995; Wong *et al.* 2005). Generating a sufficiently large sample of high-potential firms via random contacts with households would be exceedingly expensive. As a second best, CAUSEE makes a comprehensive effort to obtain a theoretically valid representation of high-potential nascent and young firms. We do this via contacts with a very large number of organizations that are likely to be in contact with such ventures. This will allow analysis of the special features of this category in comparison with that of a random sample of start-ups. The strategy and process behind this sampling effort are reported elsewhere (Davidsson *et al.* 2008).

Another unique feature of CAUSEE relative to previous studies within the PSED paradigm is that it includes not only the sample(s) of nascent firms, but also an equally sized sample of young firms, that is, firms which have been operational and trading for three years or less. The inclusion of the 'young firms' sample has several advantages. First, it gives leverage to the significant investment needed to identify the nascent sample. Thus, the generation of the 'young firms' sample comes at almost no extra cost (the repeated interviewing of them, however, is costly). Second, the two samples in combination will provide a picture of entrepreneurial emergence over a longer time horizon. The processes involved in the development of young firms are both theoretically and empirically different from the transition of nascent firms into actual firms (Gartner *et al.* 2004; Davidsson 2006). Consequently, inclusion of the young firms allows us to investigate important economic issues, such as growth and internationalization, which could not be effectively investigated among nascents since most of them will not show much growth or internationalization within the four-year time span of the study. Third, the inclusion of both groups allows quasi-longitudinal comparisons at early stages of the project, before longitudinal data on the nascent firms' development have been obtained. Fourth, the nascent sample will allow appropriate corrections for survival bias that would not be possible if the young firms sample was studied alone.

Another distinguishing factor is, obviously, that CAUSEE builds on Australian empirics. The Australian participation in GEM has suggested that Australia's level of entrepreneurial activity – measured in this way – stands up relatively well in international comparison and that at any given point in time more than 1.2 million adult Australians are either (part-) owners of a recently started business or actively involved in an ongoing business start-up (Hindle and O'Connor 2006). However, the GEM surveys only give rudimentary information about the characteristics and goals of these ventures (although we know they are modest in a majority of cases), and their development is not followed over time. Hence, little information is gained about what leads to successful completion of a start-up process.

In sum, CAUSEE represents a clear 'first' in Australia and has a number of unique design features also in relation to its closest international counterparts or predecessors. The most important of these are: a) a clear focus on the venture level of analysis; b) emphasis on theory testing and high quality in operationalizations; c) inclusion of a sample of 'young firms' alongside the ongoing start-ups ('nascent firms'); and d) the addition of a judgement-based over-sample of 'high-potential firms' in both categories. These unique features strengthen CAUSEE's potential for contributions to scholarship and practice.

MAIN CONTENTS AND FOCI OF THE CAUSEE RESEARCH

Figure 13.1 provides a graphical overview of the core concepts and relationships investigated in the CAUSEE research. Table 13.1 lists the main sections of the Wave I questionnaire that follow after successful screening (see next section). Table 13.1 also indicates the degree of harmonization with the PSED II study. Together Figure 13.1 and Table 13.1 provide a good overview of the main contents of the research.

Conspicuous in its absence in Figure 13.1 is a box labelled 'The Individual'. This is because of the venture-level perspective that CAUSEE employs. The characteristics of the founder may only be part of the human social capital at the venture's disposal, and these are seen as resources just as are financial and other resources that are also captured by the questionnaire contents. Hence, it is the 'Resources' concept that deserves a separate box in the figure, mirrored by the 'Team Resources' and 'Sources of Funding and Advice' sections in the questionnaire. Important theoretical sources for this section are the resource-based view of the firm (Barney 1991) and recent theorizing about bricolage, that is, the use of frugal and creative tactics for acquiring and combining resources, often for new use (Baker and Nelson 2005). Hence the questionnaire contains separate

Table 13.1   Sections in the CAUSEE Wave I interview schedule

Section	Purpose	Applies to	Harmonized with PSED II
Classifying the venture	Categorizing the venture on a number of dimensions	All ventures	Mostly
Gestation activities	Initiation and completion of certain activities typical for start-ups, inclusive of time stamps for these events	Nascent ventures	Yes
Activities	Similar to above but adapted to young firms and without time stamps	Young firms	N/A
Business idea newness	Degree of four types of newness (product, market, process, type of buyer)	All ventures	Unique to CAUSEE
Business idea relatedness	Degree of relatedness to prior knowledge; available resources; opportunities	Nascent ventures	Unique to CAUSEE
Business idea change	Different types of changes of the idea and reasons for these changes	Nascent ventures	Unique to CAUSEE
Effectuation	Behaviours reflecting theoretical effectuation principles	All ventures	Unique to CAUSEE
Team resources	The investment of human, social, financial and other resources	All ventures	Partly
Resource advantages	Identification of particular resource strengths and weaknesses (RBV)	All ventures	Unique to CAUSEE
Bricolage	Use of frugal tactics for acquiring and combining resources	All ventures	Unique to CAUSEE
Sources of funding and advice	Use and relative importance of different sources	All ventures	Unique to CAUSEE/ funding info simplified in CAUSEE
Future expectations	Assessing the founders' views on the firms' future development	All ventures	Partly

sections covering these issues. Some early findings on resource assessment are reported in Steffens *et al.* (2008).

It has recently been observed that entrepreneurship research has hitherto paid too little attention to the characteristics of the venture idea (often referred to as 'the opportunity'; see Shane and Venkataraman 2000). In response, the CAUSEE research will thoroughly investigate the newness and relatedness of the venture idea (Dissanayake *et al.* 2008), as well as how it changes over time (Davidsson *et al.* 2006). Consequently these areas are covered in separate sections of the questionnaire. Basic classifications of the type of venture idea along different dimensions are also made in the section 'Classifying the Venture'.

The environment is not given much room in the questionnaires but enters the research via knowledge of what industry and region (type) the ventures belong to. Non-survey data about the characteristics of regions and industries can be added to the dataset.

As regards process, a very important part of the survey is the time-stamped gestation activities that we investigate. This has been one of the most fruitful parts of previous studies of nascent entrepreneurship (Davidsson 2006). Our main theory-testing effort concerning process will be a systematic empirical test of Sarasvathy's (2001) theory of effectuation, which also has its separate questionnaire section. CAUSEE offers an opportunity to systematically test this theory on a large, representative sample for the first time, applying a measuring instrument that has been carefully developed for this purpose. Other sections also capture process issues, for example 'Bricolage' and 'Venture Idea Change'.

Assessment of outcomes is a tricky matter in studies of nascent and young firms. Because the ventures are at early (and slightly different) stages, traditional performance measures may not be relevant or available. In addition, it is not always the case that abandonment of the start-up is a worse outcome than is continuation, and similar issues arise for other outcomes on supposed 'better–worse' scales (see Davidsson 2006, 2008). CAUSEE will employ a range of outcome variables, such as the pace of progress in the process, reaching certain milestones like first sales or profitability, levels of sales, employment and profitability, growth, and so on. This is an area where design work is still ongoing for implementation in later waves.

As indicated by the graphical representation of the framework, entrepreneurship research has moved beyond simplistic, direct, additive and linear relationships. Issues of fit and interdependence between the different components will consequently be a key interest in the project (Shane and Venkataraman 2000; Davidsson 2004a). Detailed ideas about these contingencies have recently been elaborated in Davidsson (2005b).

DATA COLLECTION AND SAMPLE SELECTION METHODS

The primary dataset for CAUSEE comprises random samples of 'nascent firms' (N = 625) and 'young firms' (N = 561) obtained by screening 30 105 adults. Smaller supplementary, non-random samples of high-potential ventures of both nascent firms (N = 102) and young firms (N = 113) were also generated. Below we describe the processes employed to identify start-up efforts and qualify them for the various samples.

Eligible cases that agreed to participate proceeded through a 40- to 55-minute-long telephone interview. They will then be re-contacted for follow-up interviews every 12 months for four years. When a venture has been terminated, an 'exit interview' is performed and the case is dropped from subsequent waves. Among the non-eligible cases every 50th respondent was selected for inclusion in a control group (N = 506) to allow for basic socio-demographic comparisons.

Random Samples

Identifying a random sample of ongoing business start-ups – young and emerging firms – is a very challenging task. Business registers are not available that capture the youngest start-up efforts or all the established smallest firms. The pioneering PSED and GEM studies developed an approach to identify such start-up efforts by screening a random sampling of the adult population using random digit dialling (RDD).

To determine that a firm qualifies as a nascent start-up effort, the screening interview attempts to establish that a start-up is not just a dream or a wish, but an idea that is actively worked upon. At the same time, it should be in the start-up process and not an operational business. Hence, the criteria must exclude cases that are either under- or over-qualified (Shaver *et al.* 2001; Reynolds 2007). Likewise, the (non-overlapping) criteria for eligibility as a 'young firm' must establish the firm is in an operational but not mature stage.

The samples are obtained in the following way. First, the household is selected via RDD. After it has been ascertained that the respondents are over 18 years old and living in the household, their gender is recorded and they are directed to a screening interview that has been refined over the years within the PSED–GEM research paradigm. The effects of the exact wording of the screening items – which can be profound – have been thoroughly examined by Reynolds (2009). We use the PSED II screening procedure, which tends to be inclusive rather than exclusive of 'marginal' cases. However, while our treatment of eligible 'nascent' cases is identical to the PSED II study, we have adapted the screening mechanism to also capture 'young firms' with equal precision.

Figure 13.2 gives an overview of the screening questions and sequence (other than items 1–3, the wording is not necessarily verbatim). We start by asking all respondents three initial screening questions. In most cases

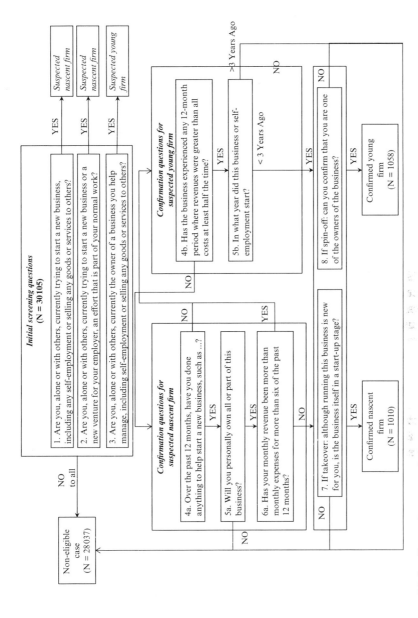

Figure 13.2 *Screening procedure*

225

the response to all of these is 'no', in which case they are excluded as non-eligible for the study. Other respondents are then asked a series of more detailed questions to confirm eligibility. If item 1 or 2 is answered 'yes' the case is initially treated as a 'suspected nascent firm'. Those that answer 'yes' only to item 3 are treated as a 'suspected young firm'. If the respondent is involved in separate nascent and young firms we give priority to the nascent case. This is determined with an additional question and instruction item not included in the figure. Also excluded from the figure is the selection of respondents for the control group.

- *Suspected nascent firms.* If 4a (confirming active activity to start a business over the last 12 months) is answered 'no', the case is not eligible in this category and instead transferred to 'suspected young firms' to check if it is eligible under this category. Otherwise it continues to 5a, where it must affirm intended (part-)ownership to stay eligible. Item 6a (actually two items) identifies if the firm is already substantially trading. If so, the case is over-qualified and instead transferred to the 'suspected young firm' sequence. Otherwise, the case is tentatively qualified as a nascent firm.
- *Suspected young firm.* If the minimum trading requirement is confirmed (4b: a 12-month period where revenues are greater than costs half the time) and the business started in 2004 or later (5b), the case is treated as a tentatively confirmed young firm. If 4b is not confirmed the case is transferred to 4a and tested for eligibility as a nascent firm. Under certain circumstances cases can get into a loop and arrive at 4b for the second time. This question is then skipped and they go directly to 5b. If that question is not affirmed the case is deemed ineligible.

Both types of (tentatively) confirmed cases are then asked what type of start-up the firms represent in terms of origin and governance. Those that report takeover or spin-off are asked additional questions to reconfirm that the case is eligible by age and ownership stake criteria. For eligible cases the screening interview is concluded with transfer either to immediate continuation with the full interview (preferred) or to making an appointment for re-contact.

Early in the full interview the cases are further classified on a number of dimensions. Two classifications are particularly important, as they determine the eligibility or wording of a range of other questions later in the interview. These classifications concern whether the venture is mainly oriented towards provision of products or services, and whether it is a solo or team effort. If the respondent confirms the firm sells/will sell 'mainly services', they thereafter get the 'services' version of questions, whereas all other answers (including 'both equally', 'don't know' and 'refused') lead to the more generic 'products' wording. Solo versus team is assessed through a sequence of questions that first determines whether any other owner is involved, whether any other owner is a 'romantic' partner, and the total number of (prospective) owners. This makes it possible to make the important distinction between 'romantic' and other teams (Ruef *et al.* 2003) and to apply appropriate wording and question content for solo, partner and multi-person team cases. Owing to the venture-level focus of CAUSEE this is critically important, because not only are the respondent's beliefs, attitudes and qualities important but also those of other individuals who have an influence on the venture. In this regard, CAUSEE differs from PSED II even when the 'same' questions are included.

For example, where PSED II asks all respondents 'Which of the following two statements best describes your preference for the future size of this business: I want this new business to be as large as possible, or I want a size I can manage myself or with a few key employees?' CAUSEE asks respondents representing team start-ups 'Which of the following two statements best describes the preference your start-up team has for the future size of this business: We want this new business to be as large as possible, or we want a size we can manage ourselves or with a few key employees?' Similarly, where PSED II asks 'Which came first for you, the business idea or your decision to start a business – or did they occur together?', in team cases CAUSEE first asks 'Was it you or another team member who first came up with the idea for this business?' and words the following question (when applicable) differently as 'Which came first for the person behind the idea for the business; was it the business idea or your decision to start a business – or did they occur together?'

DESCRIPTIVE RESULTS

Below we present selected Wave I results based on a dataset comprising the random samples of both nascent and young firms. Table 13.2 shows the breakdown of the CAUSEE. Results for both nascent and young firms from the main sample are analysed (and contrasted where applicable). Cases from the high-potential over-sample are not included. Of the approximately 30 000 participants (N = 30 105) who completed the short telephone screener interview, over 2000 (N = 2068) qualified as either nascent or young firms in approximately equal measure. The participation rate for those who qualify is high, with 60 per cent of those qualified to participate completing the questionnaire (N = 1186).

Table 13.2   CAUSEE Wave I sample breakdown

Sample and prevalence	Total	
	N	%
Participants screened	30 105	
Qualified to participate	2 068	6.9
Nascent firms	1 010	3.4
Young firms	1 058	3.5
Completed questionnaires	1 186	57.4
Nascent firms	625	61.9
Young firms	561	53.0

The main focus of the CAUSEE project is to examine the characteristics and strategies of nascent and young Australian firms, and how these relate to eventual outcomes. The project will be able to report more about outcomes in following years when more becomes known about the fate of the businesses it follows. Here we provide an overview of the characteristics of Australian nascent firms (NF) and young firms (YF), and where possible compare these with international findings.

It is also possible to contrast characteristics of NF and YF. This allows tentative interpretations about the success of groups of firms. By way of example, if we find that a greater percentage of NF than YF are solo (single-owner) businesses then we might initially assume that solo businesses are more likely to fail to become operational young firms than partner or team businesses. However, there are in fact four possible reasons for this difference:

1. *Survival differences:* As above, solo NFs are less likely to survive to become YFs.
2. *Rate of progress differences:* Solo start-ups remain in the nascent phase for a longer time on average than partner or team firms and therefore have a greater chance of being included as NFs in the survey.
3. *General-level changes over time:* More solo NFs are started now than when the YFs were started.
4. *Firm-level changes over time:* Some solo firms add owners in the process of developing into a YF.

These four possible explanations exist whenever we observe differences between NF and YF. Consequently, it is important to interpret such differences with caution. In NF–YF comparisons below we apply the interpretations we find to be the most plausible. Later CAUSEE results that use longitudinal data will give more definitive answers to what process is driving the observed differences between NF and YF.

Level of Entrepreneurial Activity

Although assessing and comparing the level of independent entrepreneurial activity in the country is not the main purpose of CAUSEE (unlike the Global Entrepreneurship Monitor) a few observations on level of activity deserve mention. First, we have noted above that our random sampling procedure identified 3.4 and 3.5 per cent of the respondents as involved in NF and YF efforts, respectively, in total giving a prevalence rate of 6.9 per cent. These figures indicate a lower prevalence rate than what has usually been found for Australia in the GEM research: 12.0 per cent in 2006, 11.6 per cent in 2003 and 11.3 per cent in 2000 (Hindle and Rushworth 2000, 2003; Hindle and O'Connor 2004; Klyver *et al.* 2007). Recent US data suggest that at least in part this difference can be explained by subtle differences in sampling and screening criteria (Reynolds 2007, 2009). By way of international comparisons, PSED II identified 1571 NF cases from a sample of 31 845 (4.9 per cent) adults in the US, indicating a higher prevalence rate than CAUSEE while using closely harmonized procedures (Reynolds and Curtin 2008). The CAUSEE prevalence rate for NFs is clearly higher than reported for 1998 in the Swedish PSED counterpart study despite its somewhat less demanding criteria for inclusion (Delmar and Davidsson 2000). Overall, our findings are consistent with the major impression from the GEM studies that the level of independent entrepreneurial activity in Australia is relatively high compared to other 'developed' or 'Western' countries. Our comparison with PSED II, however, suggests that the number of start-up efforts in relation to the size of the population is not quite as high as in the US.

What Types of Firms Are Started?

In this age of large multinationals, global franchising systems and omnipresent Internet it may be easy to think that traditional, independent, brick-and-mortar business start-ups are a dying breed. That would be a false conjecture. Our data show that the vast majority of our cases – 88 per cent – are independent new businesses started by an individual or a team. Only some 5 per cent are franchises or multilevel marketing (MLM) initiatives. A similar percentage of businesses are partly backed by existing businesses. There are no marked differences between the NF and YF categories in these regards (Figure 13.3). Neither do Australian results differ markedly from those obtained in the US, except for the higher level

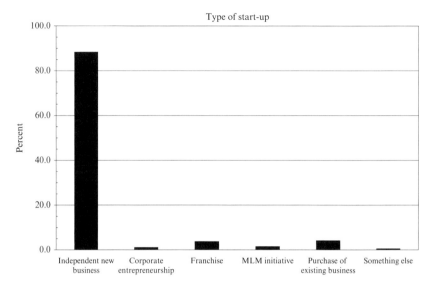

Figure 13.3   Type of start-up

of multilevel marketing programmes in the US. When interpreting these data it should be remembered that cases are included only if a) the activity of the firm is new and b) the respondent is or is going to be an owner or part-owner of the business.

As regards online business, approximately 80 per cent of the young firms have no online sales at all, and less than 7 per cent generate more than 50 per cent of their revenue via the Internet. The online sales plans of the nascent firms are considerably higher (Figure 13.4), but it may still come as a surprise that more than half plan for no online sales and less than 10 per cent are trying to set up a purely online business.

The difference between NF and YF is large and important. As discussed above, it may be interpreted as showing that:

1. There is a real increase in Internet-orientated business occurring over time;
2. The expectations of Internet sales for NFs may not match the reality of actual Internet sales once they develop into YFs; or
3. There is a difference between those who try and fail and those who succeed in setting up a business and make it survive its early years.

Subsequent CAUSEE findings using data from several points in time and following the fate of the NFs will be able to determine which effect is the

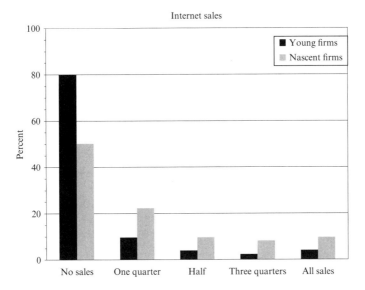

Figure 13.4   Percentage Internet sales

stronger. In this case we believe all three effects are likely to be in operation. It appears plausible that there is an increasing trend for the proportion of businesses relying on Internet sales. NFs may also be naively
optimistic concerning their ability to generate Internet sales. Finally, the
difference in Internet sales is also likely linked to differences in the industry make-up of the NFs versus YFs (reported below), which in turn may
reflect differential survivability across industries.

It is important to note that the somewhat low figures for online sales
do not necessarily reflect a lack of 'Internet savvy' in these businesses.
Responses to other questions reveal that 84 per cent of the NFs either
already have or plan to set up their own website, and 70 per cent either
already have or plan to join some Internet-based community or network
for the purpose of furthering their start-up effort. Across NFs and YFs
some 50 per cent have used Internet-based sources of business advice.
The use and rated importance of such sources are somewhat higher for
the NFs, confirming an increasing role for the Internet among Australian
start-ups over time.

To the extent that some might regard venture capital start-ups entering
the market with a war chest of millions of dollars as in any sense 'typical',
the CAUSEE data provide a good reality check. Members of this stereotypical category – while possibly important on a 'per firm' basis – are
so unusual that they are close to non-existent in a random sample of

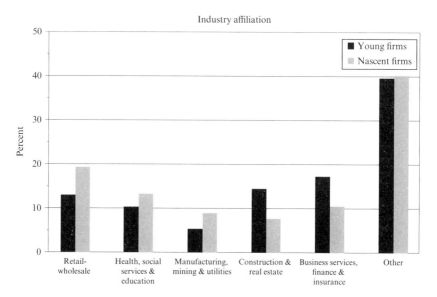

Figure 13.5   Percentage industry affiliation

start-ups. In our sample of 1057 firms we find just two such firms – one NF and one YF. Indeed, findings in the US are similar. As pointed out by Reynolds and Curtin (2008) the total annual number of VC deals in the US is in the 2000–3000 region, so only a few hundred would involve start-ups. This should be contrasted to the annual number of start-up attempts in the US, which count in the millions. Consequently, VC-backed start-ups are close to non-existent in the PSED II random sample of some 1000 nascent firms as well.

A profile of the industries in which Australian firms are being started is displayed in Figure 13.5 in aggregated form. The following discussion is based on a finer delineation into 16 industries. The industries that account for more than 10 per cent of either NFs or YFs are retailing, consumer services, health, education and social services, construction and business consulting/services. Manufacturing accounts for 5.9 per cent of the start-ups, similar to the 4.5–6.5 per cent reported for the US (Reynolds and Curtin 2008). The Australian industry distribution for NFs is similar across the board to that reported for the US (PSED and PSED II do not report YF figures).

Figure 13.5 reveals sizeable and important differences between the NF and YF categories. In particular, the proportion of NF is much higher than YF in retailing and manufacturing. The tendency is similar (but weaker) for consumer services and health, education and social services. Again, there are different possible interpretations. Arguably, manufacturing is a special case among those that have over-representation among NFs. It may be that manufacturing firms are more complex (and ambitious) businesses to set up and that the start-up process therefore takes longer. This alone could produce the observed pattern even if the manufacturing start-ups are as successful at getting started and surviving as the average start-up. However, the result may also reflect a higher tendency for manufacturing start-ups to give up in the process owing to the cost and complexity of getting such firms going. One plausible interpretation of the pattern for retailing is that many dream of starting their own firm in this industry but fail to actually get it going or fail to sustain if for very long. This may be due to having low entry barriers while having to deal with large numbers of small-ticket, price-sensitive customers. The same would apply to large parts of consumer services and health, education and social services as well.

The same pattern for retailing is strongly supported by US data, which also have the percentage of retailing NFs about twice that of the sector's share of established firms (Reynolds and Curtin 2008). The NF versus YF difference we have identified is a warning signal for those who wish to start their own firm in retailing or other low-entry-barrier, high-price-competitiveness industries.

In contrast, construction and business consulting/services show a marked higher prevalence of YF compared with NF. The construction and business services start-ups deal with fewer and less price-sensitive customers; presumably the founders often have one or more important customer contacts established already when they set out to found their firms.

Growth and Innovation Orientation

Despite reporting relatively high prevalence rates compared with other countries, the GEM project reports have voiced pessimism about entrepreneurship in Australia (Hindle and Rushworth 2002; Hindle and O'Connor 2004). For example, Hindle and O'Connor (2004) conclude that: 'Australia consistently displays relatively high rates of business participation, especially in the start-up phase, but growth intentions (through both export and technology) and incorporation of innovation are low despite a high claimed level of opportunity motivation.'

While the CAUSEE data in part confirm this view, comparative analysis with the US reveals that this is not a distinctly Australian phenomenon. Indeed Australian firms are on a par with, or more advanced than, their US counterparts. Throughout our analyses one should realize that in the vast majority of cases we are talking about very small businesses. A minority have any employees at all at this early stage. About two-thirds in both categories are still located in a residence or personal property. Similarly,

Table 13.3   Relative potential/sophistication for US and Australian start-ups

	US: PSED (NF)	US: PSED II (NF)	AUS: CAUSEE (NF)	AUS: CAUSEE (YF)
Wants maximum growth rather than manageable size	22%	22%	25%	16%
Considers the business to be 'hi-tech'	36%	24%	31%	27%
Claims R&D expenditure will be a major focus	29%	25%	45%	24%
Firm has moved to own, dedicated premises	14%	9%	10%	18%
Legal form is some type of limited liability company	20%	17%	18%	26%
Has hired employee(s)	14%	7%	14%	38%

about 50 per cent in both categories are sole traders rather than some more advanced legal form, and most founders have limited growth aspirations. However, it is true for any country that in numbers a random sample of business start-ups will be dominated by relatively modest businesses. Besides, Apple, Google and IKEA also once resided in homes or the iconic garage. An important question is whether Australia stands out from other countries in this regard – and if it stands out negatively.

In Table 13.3 some comparative indicators have been compiled. The PSED and PSED II data were sourced from Reynolds and Curtin (2008). It should be noted that the most relevant comparison is that between PSED II and CAUSEE-NF, which are very similar in terms of sampling and time period. CAUSEE-YF should not be compared to the US data, which only refer to nascent firms.

The findings indicate Australian start-ups on average appear somewhat more sophisticated or ambitious than their US counterparts and are certainly no less advanced. The self-assessment nature of some of the questions may have led to biased (probably exaggerated) estimates. However, as the US and Australian respondents have received exactly the same questions this limitation of the data can hardly explain any group differences. Unpublished data from the Swedish PSED counterpart study also confirm that Australian founders' growth aspirations are high in comparison.

The NF versus YF differences within the CAUSEE data perhaps suggest a higher degree of realism by YFs, which display lower figures for growth aspirations and technological sophistication. The difference may also be partially due to start-up cohorts becoming more 'advanced' over time. Still another reason that partially explains this difference is that more ambitious projects have a lower probability of getting to or surviving an operational stage (that is, to 'graduate' from nascent to young firms). While this would be a cause for concern it does not appear to be a uniquely Australian problem; similar tendencies have been observed before in other countries (Davidsson 2006; see also Gimeno *et al.* 1997). Finally, what looks like a trend towards US start-ups becoming *less* advanced over time (PSED II versus PSED) is probably due to the sampling criteria being in some respects more inclusive in PSED II. That is, the latter study (like CAUSEE, which shares the same design differences to the original PSED) is likely to include a higher proportion of 'marginal' businesses, increasing the number of identified start-ups but bringing down the proportion of the overall sample that is more progressive or advanced.

The Founders and Their Motivations

An important first insight about business founders is that the group is not dominated by lone wolfs. Just over 50 per cent of both NFs and YFs are involved in efforts that have more than one owner. This is similar to what has been found in the US (Ruef *et al.* 2003) and Sweden (unpublished).[2] Those who believe 'multiple-owner start-up' translates to a well-balanced team with members carefully selected for their complementary functional business specializations are up for another reality check. In the CAUSEE data well over half of the multiple-owner start-ups are founded by spouses or de facto couples (Ruef *et al.* 2003).

Figure 13.6 displays the proportion of solo, partner (any two owners) and team (three or more owners) start-ups. This figure reveals an unexpected and somewhat surprising finding: the proportion of team start-ups is much smaller among YFs compared with NFs, implying that team start-ups may be less likely to succeed. This appears to run counter to the general conclusion in the literature, which is that team start-ups tend to be more successful – and other parts of our data support that notion. Yet it turns out that, when we ask our YF founders (the only group ready to report such outcomes) about their satisfaction with the business's performance in terms of net profit, sales, cash flow and value growth, the team founders are consistently more satisfied than the other groups. The solution to this apparent paradox may be that team-based start-ups are more complex and more conflict prone and therefore make slower progress and/or are more likely to dissolve before getting to an operational stage. This would explain the lower occurrence of team start-ups in the YF group. Once started, the team start-ups appear to benefit from their greater human and

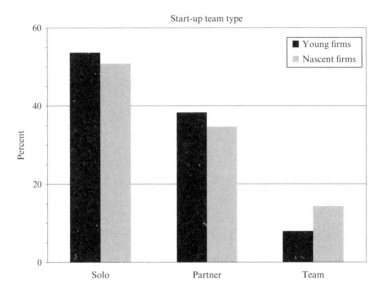

Figure 13.6   Solo, partner or team start-up

other resources and therefore conform to the above-average performance generally found in earlier research.

Knowing that many ventures have more than one founder we focus on the individual founders–respondents in the remainder of this section. However, where applicable we have asked the respondent to answer on behalf of the team.

While Australian business founders come in all ages there is a peak around the age of 40. The unweighted average age among both NFs and YFs is 43 years, which is significantly younger than the control group not involved in business start-ups (mean age 49). At least based on the unweighted data the mean age appears slightly higher than in comparable samples in the US and Sweden (see Delmar and Davidsson 2000; Reynolds and Curtin 2008); however, both report proportions in age classes rather than mean age, so an exact comparison is not possible.

One could speculate that business founding as a further career in retirement would be comparatively frequent within Australia given its relatively early retirement and lump sum payout of superannuation funds. This does not seem to be the case, however. The vast majority of founders (82 per cent) come out of employment or self-employment. Further, while 19 per cent are over 55 years only 7 per cent are above 65, and among nascent firm founders less than 3 per cent describe themselves as retired, which is far less than the control group figure of 27 per cent. While many international studies have pointed out unemployment as a major driver of firm foundation this is not the case currently in Australia. Less than 3 per cent of the NF founders are unemployed. This is equal to the control group figure, so we find no heightened tendency among the unemployed to found their own businesses.

This notion is also supported by responses to a subjective question about the motivation to found the new business. We asked whether the decision was driven mainly by perception of opportunity or mainly by sense of necessity (lacking other alternatives for gainful employment). Over 70 per cent of founders say the start-up was opportunity driven, while only 9 and 13 per cent of NF and YF respectively see it as born out of necessity. The remainder allow for a bit of both or volunteered an answer suggesting that although not exactly forced by necessity they are seeking better alternatives to an existing job. This dominance of opportunity-driven business foundings in the CAUSEE data mirrors what has previously been reported from the GEM project (Hindle and Rushworth 2003; Hindle and O'Connor 2004, 2006). The proportion of NF claiming pure necessity motives reported for the US by Reynolds and Curtin (2008) is 12 per cent.

It is also commonly believed that business founders first decide that they want to go into business for themselves or start a company. Then, it is assumed, they search for and evaluate several alternative business ideas before they settle for one, which they further develop and eventually create their business around. Bhave (1994) found that an alternative process was also common. In this second model it is a specific opportunity, rather than a long-nurtured dream to have their own business, that triggers the decision to found a firm. Consequently, no search for alternative business ideas is involved; either a start-up is attempted around the one, triggering opportunity or no start-up is attempted. CAUSEE data suggest that the 'business idea as trigger' process is much more common than is the sequence where the decision to start a business comes first (Figure 13.7). Only 16 per cent of the NFs claim the decision to start a business came first. However, while this process sequence was the least common also among the YFs it is substantially more common in that group (25 per cent). This may reflect either a positive effect of a stronger commitment to making firm start-up a reality or that selecting a venture idea based on analysis of several alternative ideas makes it easier to get up and running and/or survive.

Figure 13.8 shows that female participation in start-up activity in Australia is relatively high although not on a par with that of men. The 43 per cent of Australian NFs that are female is at least equal to what is found in the US (although the form of reporting used by Reynolds and Curtin 2008 makes exact comparison difficult). The proportion of females is definitely higher than that reported for Sweden, a country with very high

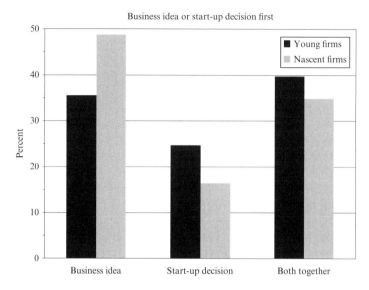

Figure 13.7   Which happened first, business idea or decision to start?

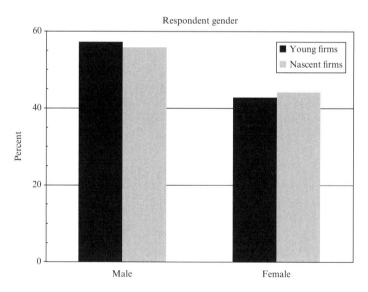

Figure 13.8   Proportion male and female founders

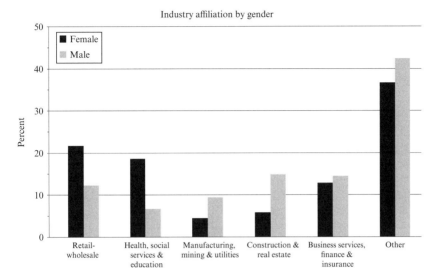

Figure 13.9   Industry affiliation by gender

female participation in the workforce and a reputation for relatively high gender equality in general (see Delmar and Davidsson 2000).

Figure 13.9 shows that there are marked differences in the industry distribution of start-ups by gender. Comparing these results with those displayed in Figure 13.5 leads to an important finding: women are over-represented in those industries that have a low survival rate of NF (i.e. an over-representation of YFs compared to NFs). Conversely, women are under-represented in some of the industries with a higher survival rate. This suggests many women business founders are active in industries where successful establishment and survival of the business are relatively difficult. It also suggests that what may erroneously be interpreted as female underperformance in a less careful analysis is in reality an industry effect. The interpretation that the NF–YF industry proportion differences are an industry effect rather than a gender effect is supported in our data by the fact that the NF–YF gender proportion difference is small and not statistically significant despite the 'industry handicap' female founders as a group face. This interpretation is also consistent with multivariate analyses in earlier research – including an Australian study – that, while women are under-represented among business founders as well as in the small minority of rapidly growing firms, there is no general underperformance by females once they have entered the process of founding a firm (Du Rietz and Henrekson 2000; Watson 2002; Davidsson 2006).

We also find that business venturing is well dispersed across the diverse Australian population. There are no statistically significant differences in the ethnic composition of NFs versus YFs versus control group members. All groups are dominated (81–84 per cent) by people of European descent, other tested categories being Indigenous Australian (2–4 percent), Asian (3–5 per cent), Middle Eastern (0.5–1 percent), mixed ethnicity (3–4 per cent) and other (6–7 per cent). Neither is there any marked tendency for immigrants or those with parents born outside Australia to be differently represented among business founders, except for a somewhat peculiar over-representation of people with one, and only one, parent (usually the mother) born overseas among the NFs (15 per cent compared with 10 per cent for YF and the control group). It is hardly evidence that deserves elaborate interpretations.

Finally, it is worth pointing out that higher-educated individuals are over-represented as business founders. The data reveal 37 per cent of the business founders are university graduates, which is higher than in the control group (27 per cent) and higher than in the PSED II study in the US (approximately 33 per cent; Reynolds and Curtin 2008). In addition, a large proportion of the founders have previous experience from owning and running businesses. Just over 50 per cent of the NFs and YFs combined were started by individuals or teams that had previous experience from starting a firm. This evidence on education and experience again challenges earlier concerns about the 'poor quality' of Australian start-ups.

An even larger share of business founders, 57 per cent, had at least one parent who had been running their own business. This is considerably higher than in the control group, where 45 per cent reported such parental role model experience. The CAUSEE figure is also slightly higher than international comparisons: 52 and 53 per cent for the US PSED and PSED II, respectively (Reynolds and Curtin 2008) and 50 per cent in Sweden (Delmar and Davidsson 2000). While PSED II does not have a control group, PSED is about the only study ever reported where there is no over-representation of business founders among those who have a self-employed parent (Davidsson 2004b; Kim *et al.* 2006). Swedish PSED results reported by Delmar and Davidsson (2000), by contrast, indicate an even stronger parental role model effect (50 per cent and 37 per cent) than what we find for Australia (57 per cent and 45 per cent).

Sources of Funding and Advice

The CAUSEE questionnaire captures considerable amounts of information about the financial and knowledge resources accessed and used by start-ups. In this section we focus mainly on a set of questions regarding the sources of funding and advice that are used by firms and whether each source is of major or minor importance for them (we will also take glimpses at other parts of the questionnaire).

As regards funding, we have noted already that venture capital funding is close to non-existent in this random sample of start-ups. Those who build their expectations on close familiarity with the small business sector – or the venture capital industry – rather than popular media images may not be surprised by that fact. Yet it may come as a surprise that a majority of firms – as many as 55 per cent – plan to realize the start-up without any outside funding at all. Although aversion to outside control is a well-known characteristic of many small firm owner-managers (Sapienza *et al.* 2003), the strength of this finding is nonetheless surprising. There may be several explanations. First, we have noted that many start-ups are very modest, tiny-scale efforts that may not require much in the way of start-up capital. Second, some founders may underestimate their need for funding, not least the need for working capital once they start trading. Third, we have noted that many founders have run businesses before; many of those presumably are in control of funds from prior business success that can cover the start-up costs. Finally, many founders apply creative, iterative and incremental strategies – known under labels such as 'effectuation' (Sarasvathy 2001), 'financial bootstrapping' (Winborg and Landstrom 2001) and 'bricolage' (Baker and Nelson 2005) – that may make it possible for them to reach impressive results with seemingly very small financial inputs. These are themes that the CAUSEE design covers and have been reported elsewhere (Senyard *et al.* 2010; Steffens *et al.* 2009, 2010).

Table 13.4 presents data on the use of various sources of funding for the start-ups. The wording of the question and response alternatives varied slightly between NFs and YFs. They are both asked whether each source of funding is a major source (more than 20 per cent of funding needs), minor or not used at all. However, for YFs we ask 'within the past 12 months' whereas for NFs we ask 'since the earliest days'. Also we ask about the 'founders' (NFs) as against 'owners' (YFs). Therefore, while the data are roughly comparable, formal statistical testing or far-reaching interpretation of any differences is not advisable.

What is most striking about the data in Table 13.4 is the very limited use of many sources. Representatives of some sources of funding may be surprised at what a small share of the potential market they serve (or are 'invited' to serve). Striking is also the relatively small differences between NF and YF. They are very similar other than the higher use of personal savings by NFs and to some extent the higher use of customers and suppliers by YFs – both a natural drift as the firms enter an operational stage.

Table 13.4   Sources of funding

Source	Not used		Minor source		Major source	
	NF	YF	NF	YF	NF	YF
Personal savings	13	25	15	24	72	51
Personal credit card	55	53	25	28	21	19
Money from another business that the founders also own	85	96	6	2	9	2
Government grants	93	94	5	5	2	1
Delayed payment terms from suppliers	87	78	8	13	5	9
Advance payment from customers	86	78	9	14	5	8
Loans from family members	86	91	9	6	5	2
Loans from friends, employers or colleagues	95	96	4	3	1	1
Founders' personal secured bank loans	83	84	4	6	12	11
Founders' other personal loans, overdraft or other credit facilities from a bank	85	84	9	9	6	6
Secured bank loans to the business itself	92	91	3	4	5	6
Other loans, overdraft or other credit facilities from a bank to the business itself	94	92	5	6	1	2
Loans from any other organization to the business itself	96	94	3	3	1	2
Equity from family members	95	91	4	6	1	2
Equity from friends, employers or colleagues	98	99	1	1	1	0
Equity from other private investors ('business angels')	98	99	1	1	1	0
Equity from venture capital firms or any other organizations	100	100	(one case each among NF and YF, respectively)			

Note: Entries in percentages. Entries may not sum to 100 horizontally because of rounding error.

In most cases firms do not seem to undergo revolutionary change in their funding sources from 'inception' through early life.

Only one source – personal savings – is used by more than 50 per cent of all start-ups. Despite (in)famous references to the '3 Fs' – friends, family

Table 13.5   Sources of advice

Source	Not used		Minor source		Major source	
	NF	YF	NF	YF	NF	YF
Family members	50	51	25	31	25	18
Friends, employers or colleagues	36	38	36	39	28	23
External investors like venture capitalists or 'business angels'	100	92	0	7	0	1
Board members other than those categories already mentioned	85	92	10	6	5	1
Bank staff member	85	87	13	11	2	2
Potential/actual customers	38	46	38	32	24	22
Potential/actual suppliers	56	63	27	25	17	12
Chartered accountant	61	48	25	35	15	17
Lawyer	79	79	14	16	7	5
Consultant at government agency or not-for-profit organization	73	80	18	15	8	5
Independent tax consultant	81	74	14	21	4	5
Other commercial consultant	85	85	11	12	3	3
Internet websites or communities	49	56	30	28	21	16
Other business media (print and TV/radio)	60	63	31	29	9	8

Note: Entries in percentages. Entries may not sum to 100 horizontally because of rounding error.

and fools – the instances of loan or equity funding from such sources are few. Only single-digit percentages of firms use such sources as major providers of funding (meaning 20 per cent or more of funding needs). Among 'bank products', credit card debt is by far the most used, and even among the YFs personal loans and overdrafts appear in total a more important source of funding than business loans and overdraft facilities. It can be noted, though, that personal bank loans rank third on the list of sources of major importance. In another part of the questionnaire the nascent firm founders were asked whether they had opened a bank account for the business. Close to 40 per cent said they had done so and another 47 per cent planned to do so, while 9 per cent reported they were using an existing account for the business's purposes.

With that let us turn to sources of (business) advice. The use of different sources for advice is displayed in Table 13.5.

Here we see a more diverse use of sources in many cases compared to the funding analysis. Yet many providers may still be surprised at the high levels of non-use. For example, some 75–85 per cent report not using

Table 13.6   Nascent firm's advice and networking activities

Activity	Yes	No, but will in the future	No, not relevant
Has retained accountant?	46	41	13
Has retained lawyer?	17	33	51
Has become member of trade/industry association?	16	46	38
Has contacted (government or NGO) business assistance organization?	34	38	28
Has joined Internet-based network?	21	49	31
Has joined face-to-face business network or service club (e.g. Rotary, Lions)?	13	35	52

Note: Entries in percentages. Entries may not sum to 100 vertically because of rounding error.

government agency or NGO consultants, tax consultants or other commercial consultants. Again the patterns for NFs and YFs are similar. The relative importance of family members, and to some extent friends as well, is lower for YFs, arguably a natural and expected development. Somewhat surprisingly, YFs do not rate customers and suppliers important to a higher extent than do NFs. As we have noted already, NFs are more Internet-intensive than are the YFs. We may note that this is not associated with a difference in the mean age of the founders between the categories.

Chartered accountants are the most important type of paid consultant by a considerable margin – ranking fourth in 'popularity' in Table 13.5. In another part of the questionnaire we asked the NF founders whether they had yet retained an accountant and a lawyer for the business. We also asked about other potential sources of contacts and advice – joining associations and networks for the purpose of helping develop the business. The results are reported in Table 13.6.

The perceived importance of accountants again stands out in these data, with only 13 per cent regarding it not relevant to retain an accountant. By contrast, 51 per cent of the founders do not believe they need to retain a lawyer for the purpose of this business. Notable also is the relatively low use of trade/industry organization membership and joining formal, face-to-face business networks. The latter especially is a cause for concern, as this has been singled out in previous research as one of the strongest contributing factors for taking the emerging firm to an operational stage (Davidsson and Honig 2003).

SUMMARY

The Comprehensive Australian Study of Entrepreneurial Emergence (CAUSEE) is the largest study of new firm formations ever undertaken in Australia. The project aims to find out what factors initiate, hinder and facilitate the process of establishing new, independent businesses. For this purpose, the project follows the development of two categories over time: ongoing start-up efforts (nascent firms) and operational firms that started trading in 2004 or later (young firms). In this chapter we have outlined our data collection methods and reported selected, descriptive findings from the first wave of data collection in this multi-wave, four-year study.

CAUSEE relies heavily on its forerunners, most notably the PSED studies and to a lesser extent GEM and the concurrent PSED II study. Most importantly, the screening process to identify nascent firms and several parts of the survey are harmonized with PSED II. This said, CAUSEE has several unique features: a) it includes a random sample of young firms (up to three years old at first contact); b) it includes a non-random over-sample of 'high-potential' nascent firms and young firms; c) it focuses consistently on the venture level of analysis; d) the questionnaire contents incorporate several theoretically driven scales, some newly developed, such as effectuation, bricolage, venture idea newness, venture idea relatedness and a resource-based view, that have not previously been part of a study of this type; and e) the empirical context, Australia, is new for this type of longitudinal study.

Below we reiterate some of the more important findings:

1. Our results are consistent with the conclusion in previous research that in quantitative terms entrepreneurial activity, measured as the prevalence of owner-managed young firms and ongoing start-up attempts, is relatively high in Australia. However, our data suggest the numbers in relation to the size of the population are lower than in the US.
2. The typical start-up is a 'traditional', fully independent, brick-and-mortar business. Few are franchises or otherwise backed up by an existing business; 80 per cent of young firms have no online sales (although Internet use is higher for other purposes and increasing over time); most are at this early stage sole proprietorships that are run from home and do not yet have any employees; and only a minority of businesses are strongly growth oriented or highly sophisticated in technological terms. However, it is true for any country that the average start-up is relatively modest, especially at the early stages.
3. Our analyses show that Australian start-ups in fact compare well to start-ups in the US in that many firms are founded by experienced

and highly educated founders and the firms they found are at least as growth oriented and technologically sophisticated. If anything, Australian start-ups on average appear more progressive than their US counterparts.

4. Start-up efforts in industries like construction or business services seem much more likely to get their businesses up and running than do those that try to set up firms in retailing, consumer, health or educational services, or manufacturing. That is, to the extent the founders can choose, industry selection is a critical success factor.

5. More than 40 per cent of Australian business founders are women, which makes the female participation in business start-ups comparatively high – on a par with the US and higher than many other countries.

6. However, many women founders go for industries that are relatively tough to succeed in, like retailing and consumer services. Despite this there is no indication of female underperformance – once in the process they appear to do no worse or better than men.

7. Teams with three or more founders seem much less likely to get their start-ups to an operational stage. Once up and running, however, they perform better than solo entrepreneurs. It thus appears that being a team adds complexity and conflict potential that may make the effort come out stillborn, but once up and running the team start-ups seem to benefit from having a broader knowledge, resource and network base.

8. The range of funding sources commonly used is narrow. Most start-up businesses rely heavily on personal savings and credit card debt for funding. Not only bank loans but also contributions from family and friends are relatively low in frequency. Venture capital-backed start-ups make up a minuscule share of the population of business start-ups.

9. The range of sources used for information and advice is broader and includes widespread use of Internet-based sources. Accountants are by far the most important paid consultants. The low emphasis founders put on joining face-to-face business networks for the purpose of furthering their start-up effort is a cause for concern, as previous research has pointed to this as one of the strongest contributing factors for bringing the start-up to an operational stage.

Elsewhere we have reported more detailed analyses of specific sections of the CAUSEE contents, including a descriptive analysis of the high-potential sample (Davidsson *et al.* 2008), bricolage and firm progress (Senyard *et al.* 2009), effectuation and venture idea newness (Garonne and Davidsson 2009), venture newness and relatedness (Dissanayake *et al.*

2008), bricolage and the resource-based view (Steffens and Senyard, 2009; Steffens *et al.* 2009) and habitual entrepreneurs (Gordon and Steffens 2009). When additional waves of data have been collected the analyses will also turn to more direct assessment of developments over time in nascent and young firms rather than relying on the assumption that a comparison of these two groups reflects changes over time.

ACKNOWLEDGEMENTS

We gratefully acknowledge the significant financial support that made this study possible. The CAUSEE/FEDP research is funded by Australian Research Council grants DP0666616 and LP0776845 as well as contributions from industry partners BDO Kendalls and National Australia Bank, NAB.

NOTES

1. From such a study one would, among other things, conclude that: a) gambling is profitable (for the gamblers); b) the more you bet, the more you win; and c) the higher risks you take (i.e. the more unlikely winners you pick), the more you win. While true for winners these conclusions are, of course, blatantly false for the population of gamblers (cf. the population of start-up attempts) (Davidsson 2004a).
2. Importantly, this does not mean that a majority of *start-up efforts* are team-based in either country. Because the sampling mechanism samples households, team start-ups with owners from different households have higher sampling probability than solo start-ups and those started by several members of the same household.

REFERENCES

Acs, Z.J. (ed.) (1999), *Are Small Firms Important? Their Role and Impact*, Dordrecht: Kluwer.
Alsos, G.A. and L. Kolvereid (1998), 'The business gestation process of novice, serial and parallel business founders', *Entrepreneurship Theory and Practice*, **22**(4), 101–14.
Baker, T. and R.E. Nelson (2005), 'Creating something from nothing: Resource construction through entrepreneurial bricolage', *Administrative Science Quarterly*, **50**(3), 329–66.
Barney, J. (1991), 'Firm resources and sustained competitive advantage', *Journal of Management*, **17**(1), 99–120.
Baumol, W.J. (1968), 'Entrepreneurship in economic theory', *American Economic Review*, **58**(2), 64–71.
Bhave, M.P. (1994), 'A process model of entrepreneurial venture creation', *Journal of Business Venturing*, **9**(3), 223–42.
Birch, D. (1987), *Job Creation in America: How Our Smallest Companies Put the Most People to Work*, New York: Free Press.
Birch, D., A. Haggerty and W. Parsons (1995), *Who's Creating Jobs?*, Boston, MA: Cognetics.

Davidsson, P. (2004a), *Researching Entrepreneurship*, New York: Springer.

Davidsson, P. (2004b), 'Role models and perceived social support', in W.B. Gartner, K.G. Shaver, N.M. Carter and P.D. Reynolds (eds), *Handbook of Entrepreneurial Dynamics: The Process of Business Creation*, Thousand Oaks, CA: Sage, pp. 179–85.

Davidsson, P. (2005a), 'Paul Davidson Reynolds: Entrepreneurship research innovator, coordinator and disseminator', *Small Business Economics*, **24**(4), 351–8.

Davidsson, P. (2005b), 'The types and contextual fit of entrepreneurial processes', *International Journal of Entrepreneurship Education*, **2** (listed as academic year 2003/4)(4), 407–30.

Davidsson, P. (2006), 'Nascent entrepreneurship: Empirical studies and developments', *Foundations and Trends in Entrepreneurship*, **2**(1), 1–76.

Davidsson, P. (2008), 'Interpreting performance in entrepreneurship research', in P. Davidsson (ed.), *The Entrepreneurship Research Challenge*, Cheltenham, UK and Northampton, MA, USA: Edward Elgar Publishing, pp. 189–212.

Davidsson, P. and B. Honig (2003), 'The role of social and human capital among nascent entrepreneurs', *Journal of Business Venturing*, **18**(3), 301–31.

Davidsson, P. and S.R. Gordon (2009), 'Nascent entrepreneur(ship) research: A review', unpublished manuscript, Queensland University of Technology, available at eprints.qut.edu.au

Davidsson, P., L. Lindmark and C. Olofsson (1998), 'Smallness, newness and regional development', *Swedish Journal of Agricultural Research*, **28**(1), 57–71.

Davidsson, P., E. Hunter and M. Klofsten (2006), 'Institutional forces: The invisible hand that shapes venture ideas?', *International Small Business Journal*, **24**(2), 115–31.

Davidsson, P., P. Steffens, S. Gordon and J. Senyard (2008), *Characteristics of High-Potential Start-Ups: Some Early Observations from the CAUSEE Project*, Project report, Brisbane: Queensland University of Technology, available at http://www.causee.bus.qut.edu.au/results/

Delmar, F. and P. Davidsson (2000), 'Where do they come from? Prevalence and characteristics of nascent entrepreneurs', *Entrepreneurship & Regional Development*, **12**(1), 1–23.

Dissanayake, S., S. Gordon and P. Davidsson (2008), 'Understanding venture idea newness, relatedness and change among nascent entrepreneurs', paper presented at AGSE International Entrepreneurship Research Exchange, Melbourne, Australia.

Du Rietz, A. and M. Henrekson (2000), 'Testing the female underperformance hypothesis', *Small Business Economics*, **14**(1), 1–10.

Garonne, C. and P. Davidsson (2009), 'Effectuation and newness: An intertwined relationship?', in Babson College Entrepreneurship Research Conference (BCERC), 4–6 June 2009, Boston, MA.

Gartner, W.B. (1993), 'Words lead to deeds: Towards an organizational emergence vocabulary', *Journal of Business Venturing*, **8**(3), 231–9.

Gartner, W.B., K.G. Shaver, N.M. Carter and P.D. Reynolds (2004), *Handbook of Entrepreneurial Dynamics: The Process of Business Creation*, Thousand Oaks, CA: Sage.

Gimeno, J., T.B. Folta, A.C. Cooper and C.Y. Woo (1997), 'Survival of the fittest? Entrepreneurial human capital and the persistence of underperforming firms', *Administrative Science Quarterly*, **42**(2), 750–83.

Gordon, S.R. and P.R. Steffens (2009), 'Why, how, what for? Motivations, actions and expectations in habitual entrepreneurship', Babson College Entrepreneurship Research Conference, 4–6 June 2009, Wellesley, MA.

Hindle, K. and S. Rushworth (2000), *GEM: Yellow Pages Global Entrepreneurship Monitor Australia, 2000*, Melbourne: Swinburne University of Technology.

Hindle, K. and S. Rushworth (2002), *Sensis GEM Australia, 2002*, Melbourne: Swinburne University of Technology.

Hindle, K. and S. Rushworth (2003), *Westpac GEM Australia: A Study of Australian Entrepreneurship in 2003*, Melbourne: Westpac Corporation and Swinburne University of Technology.

Hindle, K. and A. O'Connor (2004), *Westpac GEM Australia: A Study of Australian*

Entrepreneurship in 2004, Melbourne: Westpac Corporation and Swinburne University of Technology.

Hindle, K. and A. O'Connor (2006), *National Entrepreneurial Activity Summary: A Summary of Key Observations from the 2005 GEM Australia National Adult Population Survey*, Australian Graduate School of Entrepreneurship Research Report Series 3, Melbourne: Swinburne University of Technology.

Kim, P.H., H.E. Aldrich and L.A. Keister (2006), 'Access (not) denied: The impact of financial, human, and cultural capital on entrepreneurial entry in the United States', *Small Business Economics*, **27**(1), 5–22.

Klyver, K., G. Hancock and K. Hindle (2007), *Entrepreneurial Participation in Australia in 2006: A Summary of Salient Data from the 2006 GEM Australia National Adult Population Survey*, Australian Graduate School of Entrepreneurship Research Report Series, 4(1), Melbourne: Swinburne University of Technology.

Menzies, T.V., Y. Gasse, M. Diochon and D. Garand (2002), 'Nascent entrepreneurs in Canada: An empirical study', paper presented at the ICSB 47th World Conference, San Juan, Puerto Rico.

Reynolds, P.D. (2007), 'New firm creation in the US: A PSED overview', *Foundations and Trends in Entrepreneurship*, **3**(1), 1–151.

Reynolds, P.D. (2009), 'Screening item effects in estimating the prevalence of nascent entrepreneurs', *Small Business Economics*, **33**(2), 151–63.

Reynolds, P.D. and R.T. Curtin (2008), 'Business creation in the United States: Panel Study of Entrepreneurial Dynamics II initial assessment', *Foundations and Trends in Entrepreneurship*, **4**(3).

Reynolds, P.D., W.D. Bygrave and E. Autio (2003), *GEM 2003 Global Report*, Kansas, MO: Kauffman Foundation.

Reynolds, P.D., N. Bosma, E. Autio, S. Hunt, N. De Bono, I. Servais, P. Lopez-Garcia and N. Chin (2005), 'Global Entrepreneurship Monitor: Data collection design and implementation 1998–2003', *Small Business Economics*, **24**(3), 205–31.

Ruef, M., H.E. Aldrich and N.M. Carter (2003), 'The structure of organizational founding teams: Homophily, strong ties, and isolation among U.S. entrepreneurs', *American Sociological Review*, **68**(2), 195–222.

Sapienza, H.J., M.A. Korsgaard and D.P. Forbes (2003), 'The self-determination motive and entrepreneurs' choice of financing', in J. Katz and D. Shepherd (eds), *Cognitive Approaches to Entrepreneurship Research: Advances in Entrepreneurship, Firm Emergence, and Growth*, Oxford: Elsevier/JAI Press, pp. 107–40.

Sarasvathy, S. (2001), 'Causation and effectuation: Towards a theoretical shift from economic inevitability to entrepreneurial contingency', *Academy of Management Review*, **26**(2), 243–88.

Senyard, J.M., T. Baker and P. Davidsson (2009), 'Entrepreneurial bricolage: Towards systematic empirical testing', Babson College Entrepreneurship Research Conference (BCERC), 4–6 June 2009, Boston, MA.

Senyard, J., T. Baker and P. Steffens (2010), 'Entrepreneurial bricolage and firm performance: The moderating effects of firm change and innovativeness', paper presented at the Academy of Management Conference, Montreal, 6–11 August.

Shane, S. and S. Venkataraman (2000), 'The promise of entrepreneurship as a field of research', *Academy of Management Review*, **25**(1), 217–26.

Shaver, K.G., N.M. Carter, W.B. Gartner and P.D. Reynolds (2001), 'Who is a nascent entrepreneur? Decision rules for identifying and selecting entrepreneurs in the Panel Study of Entrepreneurial Dynamics (PSED) [summary]', in W.D. Bygrave, E. Autio, C.G. Brush, P. Davidsson, P.G. Greene, P.D. Reynolds and H.J. Sapienza (eds), *Frontiers of Entrepreneurship Research 2001*, Wellesley, MA: Babson College.

Steffens, P.R. and J.M. Senyard (2009), 'Linking resource acquisition and development processes to resource-based advantage: Bricolage and the resource-based view', Babson College Entrepreneurship Research Conference, 4–6 June 2009, Boston, MA.

Steffens, P., P. Davidsson and S. Gordon (2008), 'Operationalising the resource based view for nascent and young firms: Development of a scale for resource advantages and disadvantages', paper presented at AGSE International Entrepreneurship Research Exchange, Melbourne.

Steffens, P.R., J.M. Senyard and T. Baker (2009), 'Linking resource acquisition and development processes to resource-based advantage: Bricolage and the resource-based view', 6th AGSE International Entrepreneurship Research Exchange, 4–6 February 2009, University of Adelaide.

Steffens, P., T. Baker and J. Senyard (2010), 'Betting on the underdog: Bricolage as an engine of resource advantage', paper presented at the Academy of Management Conference, Montreal, 6–11 August.

van Gelderen, M., A.R. Thurik and N. Bosma (2005), 'Success and risk factors in the pre-startup phase', *Small Business Economics*, **24**(4), 365–80.

Watson, J. (2002), 'Comparing the performance of male- and female-controlled business: Relating outputs to inputs', *Entrepreneurship Theory and Practice*, **26**(3), 91–100.

Winborg, J. and H. Landstrom (2001), 'Financial bootstrapping in small businesses: Examining small business managers' resource acquisition behaviors', *Journal of Business Venturing*, **16**(3), 235–54.

Wong, P.K., Y.P. Ho and E. Autio (2005), 'Entrepreneurship, innovation and economic growth: Evidence from GEM data', *Small Business Economics*, **24**(3), 335–50.

PART IV

NVC THROUGH CONTEXTUAL LENSES

14 Cultural context as a moderator of private entrepreneurship investment behaviour
Fredric Kropp, Noel J. Lindsay and Gary Hancock

INTRODUCTION

Entrepreneurship is the driver of modern Western economic activity. If opportunities can be identified and properly exploited, entrepreneurial activity can create jobs and wealth for the entrepreneurs and investors, as well as for society as a whole. In many countries, more jobs are created by entrepreneurial business ventures than by any other form of private sector economic activity. For example, nearly 6 million people start a business every year in the US alone (Kauffman 2008).

Numerous ingredients are required to help transform an idea into a viable exploitable opportunity: the right people with the right capabilities, intellectual and social capital and luck, just to name a few. In addition to all of the other components, adequate financial resources are required to bring the opportunity to fruition. Entrepreneurial business ventures (EBVs) go through many stages, and each stage has different financial requirements for different purposes (see Churchill and Lewis 1983; Friesen and Miller 1984; Scott and Bruce 1987). Although not without controversy, the stage model can be useful in identifying different needs and sources of funds.

For example, it has been argued that the establishment and development stages of an EBV can be characterized by the seed, start-up and early-growth stages. In the seed stage, resources are needed to investigate and research the business concept and to determine if the idea is the basis for a viable opportunity. Financial resources are needed for research and development and for the basics, for example paying rent, purchasing materials and providing the entrepreneur with enough funds to survive. By far the biggest sources of funding for these activities are personal savings, followed by credit card debt and secured bank loans. More than three-quarters of start-ups, 78.5 per cent, tap into personal savings (Timmons and Spinelli 2009).

As EBVs move into the start-up and early-growth phases, financial resources are needed to produce and market a product or service. Working capital is required to purchase materials, hire employees and meet the costs of going to market. At this point, self-funding becomes more difficult and cash flows are typically inadequate to cover costs. Entrepreneurs need to reach out to other investors. Although there are exceptions, typically professional venture capital (VC) investors are not yet interested in providing funding. It is too early. The ventures are perceived as being too high a risk without the assurance of adequate returns to compensate for the risk. Informal relation-based investors, friends and family, are the main source of external funds and, in some cases, arm's length business angel (BA) investors. For example, the percentage of equity-financed new ventures in Australia that accepted finance from friends or relatives is consistently above 83 per cent (O'Connor and Hindle 2006; Hancock *et al.* 2007).

If EBVs survive the establishment and development stages, the next stage is the expansion stage, where they will invest in facilities, expand to new markets, develop new products and services, and add personnel and equipment amongst other activities. At this point, there is enough of a track record to attract additional rounds of angel investment and, perhaps, VCs, if the opportunity is deemed to be attractive and the team exceptional.

If the EBVs make it through this stage, VCs and/or other financial institutions become involved in the bridging stage of taking the firm to an initial public offering (IPO) or in identifying other corporations suitable for mergers or acquisitions. Funding requirements can go from a few million to hundreds of millions of dollars.

The general pattern of funding is shown in Table 14.1. Friends and family are the major source of funding for early-stage local EBVs, BAs are the major source for local and national ventures in the development stage, and VCs are a major source of finance for more developed, higher-potential, expansionary ventures. Though there are exceptions and overlap, large-scale investment firms provide bridging finance to take ventures public and to assist in mergers and acquisitions.

NATIONAL CULTURE

The patterns of funding presented in Table 14.1 can and will be shaped by the cultural context of where the financing occurs. McCracken (1986, p. 72) describes the culturally constituted world as 'the world of everyday experience in which the phenomenal world presents itself to the individual's senses fully shaped by and constituted by the beliefs of his/her culture'.

Table 14.1   General patterns of funding

	Local EBVs	National EBVs	Multinational EBVs
Relationship investors (friends and family)	Major source for early-stage and smaller-scale ventures.	Possible but typically limited.	Only in rare cases with very high net worth individuals.
Business angels	Available for ventures in the establishment and development stages.	Available for ventures in the establishment and development stages.	Possible in more limited-scale ventures.
Venture capitalists	Typically only available for growth-oriented high-potential ventures that have proven themselves.	Typically only available for growth-oriented high-potential ventures that have proven themselves and that are within a reasonable travel-time distance.	Source of potential funding for high-potential ventures where a VC may have a local office and there is a reasonable travel-time distance.
Large-scale investment firms	Typically only available for IPOs and mergers and acquisitions.	Typically only available for IPOs and mergers and acquisitions.	Typically only available for IPOs and mergers and acquisitions.

Note: Patterns will vary by type of venture and stage of development.

Culture is defined as 'a set of shared values, beliefs and expected behaviors' (Hayton *et al.* 2002, p. 33). Culture is the collective programming of the mind that distinguishes people included in one category from those in another (Hofstede 1989). Culture can also be viewed as a collective mental knowledge developed by a group of people exposed to a similar context (Kroeber and Kuckhorn 1952; Geertz 1973). Patterns of behaviour are shaped by national culture, and the values, beliefs and assumptions of a group of people (Hofstede 1993).

Markus and Kitayama (1991) identify that there are major differences in motivation, values and cognition across cultures. Not all cultures foster entrepreneurial activity equally (McGrath *et al.* 1992). Previous research into entrepreneurship identifies that cultural characteristics shape entrepreneurial behaviour; for example, cultures that value risk taking are more entrepreneurial, whereas cultures that value conformity are less entrepreneurial (Hayton *et al.* 2002). Hayton *et al.* (2002) identify several studies that explored national culture and characteristics of entrepreneurs based on different research questions, including motivation, reasons for starting a business, differences between entrepreneurs and non-entrepreneurs, the moderating role of national culture between individual needs and work roles, cognitive scripts and entrepreneurial traits. Even within a country, different cultures may have different entrepreneurial patterns; for example, on a per capita basis, Asian people in the USA have more than four times the rate of business ownership of African-Americans (Busenitz and Lau 1996).

National culture is a 'central organizing principle of employees' understanding of work, their approach to it, and the way in which they expect to be treated' (Newman and Nollen 1996, p. 755). We extend Newman and Nollen's (1996) concepts of the 'organizing principles of employees' to organizing principles of entrepreneurs and financing in an attempt to look at the role of culture on private equity investment behaviour.

Newman and Nollen (1996) identify several studies of differences in national cultures based on international survey results, including Trompenaars (1993), Hofstede (1980, 1993) and Laurent (1986). Other studies include work by Bond (1988), Schwartz (1994), and Schwartz and Bilsky (1990), to name a few. In addition, numerous studies have examined cross-cultural values and business or marketing behaviours, for example Kahle (1986) and Thomas and Mueller (2000).

Hofstede (1980, 1983, 1993) identified five different dimensions that distinguish cultures: individualism–collectivism, power distance, masculinity–femininity, uncertainty orientation and time orientation, also known as Confucian dynamism. The work by Hofstede has dominated the field (Kirkman *et al.* 2006) and is justifiably well respected. In this chapter, however, we describe national culture using the Trompenaars model. The major reason for this decision is that, in addition to focusing on cultural differences and the effects they have on doing business and managing (Trompenaars and Hampden-Turner 1998; Trompenaars and Woolliams 2003), Trompenaars' work builds upon and enhances Hofstede's work.

The Trompenaars value structure identifies seven dimensions of cultural valuing: universalism–particularism, individualism–communitarianism (also known as individualism–collectivism), achievement–ascription orientation, neutral versus emotional, specific versus diffuse, attitudes to time and attitudes to the environment (Smith *et al.* 1996; Trompenaars 1996; Trompenaars and Hampden-Turner 1998). The first five dimensions relate to relationships with people. In this section, we will describe each of the seven dimensions. In subsequent sections, we will relate the dimensions to private equity investment behaviour.

Universalism versus Particularism

Universalist societies place a stronger emphasis on universal rules and obligations and 'apply rules and procedures universally to ensure consistency' (Trompenaars 1996, p. 55). Universalists treat people equally; particularists treat each case on its own merit (Trompenaars 1996). Particularist societies place a stronger focus on particular situations and relationships, encouraging adaptability and flexibility (Trompenaars 1996). Universalists tend to see one truth; particularists view multiple perspectives (French *et al.* 2001). Scandinavia, the US, Canada and the UK are more universalist; China, Korea and Venezuela are more particularist (Trompenaars 1996).

Individualism versus Communitarianism

This dimension is the most similar to Hofstede's (1980) individualism–collectivism dimension. Individualism–collectivism is one of the most important ways of differentiation between cultures (Triandis 1989). Self-reliance, independence and self-actualization are important in individualist cultures, whereas the collective self is more important in collectivist cultures (Triandis 1989). Status derives from individual achievements in individualist cultures compared to group membership for identity and status in collectivist cultures (Newman and Nollen 1996). The prime orientation to the individual is central to the individualist culture compared to the community in the communitarian culture (Trompenaars 1996). North America, Western Europe and Australia are examples of individualistic cultures; Korea, China and Japan are examples of communitarian cultures.

Achievement versus Ascription

The achievement–ascription dimension focuses on how status is awarded to individuals in a culture. Achievement-oriented cultures can be viewed as meritocracies where individuals are awarded status based on their achievement: in essence, by what an individual does rather than who he or she is (Trompenaars and Hampden-Turner 1998). In these cultures, authority is justified more by skill and knowledge (Trompenaars 1996). In contrast, status is granted in ascription-oriented cultures by factors such as age, gender, ethnicity, experience, education and professional qualifications (Trompenaars and Hampden-Turner 1998). In countries such as Kuwait or Saudi Arabia, there is a greater respect based on family background than in more egalitarian cultures such as Denmark or Norway. Though there are exceptions, Western European countries tend to be more achievement oriented (Trompenaars and Hampden-Turner 1998).

Neutral versus Emotional

This dimension is somewhat similar to Hofstede's masculine–feminine dimension. The amount of emotions expressed openly varies between cultures. In neutral cultures or organizations, the emotional expression tends to be controlled so issues can be considered more objectively; in affective countries emotions are expressed more freely (Trompenaars 1996). One of the questions Trompenaars asked respondents involved their willingness to show emotions openly. The most emotional countries were Kuwait, Egypt and Oman; the least were Ethiopia, Japan and Poland (Trompenaars and Hampden-Turner 1998).

Specific versus Diffuse

This dimension relates to our involvement in other people's lives, for example whether it is important to keep business separate from other aspects of life. In a specific-oriented culture, 'a manager segregates out the task-relationship she or he has with a subordinate and insulates this from other dealings' (Trompenaars and Hampden-Turner 1998, p. 83). Thus communication tends to be more direct and to the point, and principles are independent to the individual (Trompenaars and Hampden-Turner 1998). The relationship is more diffuse and holistic in a diffuse society, where interpersonal relationships are considered more important. Private life and business relationships are more interdependent. In general, the USA and Western Europe tend to be more specific and South-East Asia and Latin America tend to be more diffuse.

Attitude toward Time

Many people who have travelled to other cultures have experienced differences in perception or attitudes towards time. Early philosophers, such as St Augustine, adopted a subjective view of time, noting that it does not exist in reality but only in the mind's apprehension of reality. At a deeper philosophical level, there is a dichotomy between presentism and eternalism. Presentism conceptualizes that only the present exists and that the past and the future do not exist. Eternalism represents a belief that the past and future exist eternally.

Hall (1959) introduced the concept of monochronic and polychronic times. In monochronic societies, time is more linear and is something to be spent carefully, for example 'Time is money.' Interpersonal relationships are subordinate to time and people do one thing at a time, take time commitments seriously, emphasize promptness and are accustomed to short-term relationships. In contrast, polychronic people do many things at once, are committed to people and relationships, change plans more easily and often and may not pay as much attention to time.

Another time typology deals with time orientation from a past, present and future orientation (Trompenaars and Hampden-Turner 1998). In illustrating cultural time differences, Trompenaars and Hampden-Turner (1998, p. 10) state:

> With respect to time, the American Dream is the French Nightmare. Americans generally start from zero and what matters is their present performance and their plan to 'make it' in the future. This is *nouveau riche* for the French who prefer the *ancien pauvre*; they have an enormous sense for the past and relatively less focus on the present and future than Americans.

Any of these time typology orientations can be examined to distinguish cultures from each other.

Attitude toward the Environment

There are several interrelated aspects to individual and to culture-specific relationships. One of the key constructs is locus of control, developed by Rotter (1966), which refers to the extent that people perceive they can control their environment. People with a high locus of control believe that events are contingent on their own behaviour or enduring characteristics; people with low locus of control ascribe causality to external factors such as chance, fate or higher powers (Smith *et al.* 1997).

Those with a high locus of control have a dominating attitude towards the environment and tend to focus on the self and function. Individuals with a low locus of control may have a more flexible attitude and value harmony more (Trompenaars and Hampden-Turner 1998). Culturally, Western countries tend to have a higher locus of control.

National Culture Summary

Culture refers to human activity. Metaphorically, it is the lens through which we see things and give them meaning. It is based upon the environment in which we were raised, all the stimuli we experienced and the meanings ascribed to them, and the values and assumptions of our lives. Culture includes our norms, laws, ethics and patterns of behaviour. Thus it is almost impossible for a social system to be culture free. We do, however, believe that the influence national culture has on investment decisions will vary by the size of investment and the nature of the investors. For example, as will be developed later in this section, national culture may

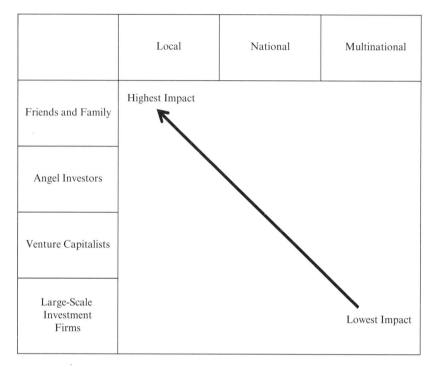

Figure 14.1   The impact of national culture on investment decisions

play a significantly stronger role on local relation-based investment deci-sions than on more global venture capital decisions. The role of culture is shown in Figure 14.1. Our overall conceptual model is depicted in Figure 14.2, which shows that both economic and non-economic factors influence the investment decision. Non-economic factors can influence the sense of obligation to invest.

INVESTORS IN ENTREPRENEURIAL FIRMS

Entrepreneurial firms are proactive and competitive, and are founded upon managed risk taking and product/market innovations (Miller 1983). They exhibit an entrepreneurial orientation that reflects proactiveness, innovativeness, measured risk taking, autonomy and competitive aggres-siveness behaviour (Lumpkin and Dess 1996). Developing an entrepre-neurial orientation in a business is important and, other things being equal, firms demonstrating a higher entrepreneurial orientation tend to be

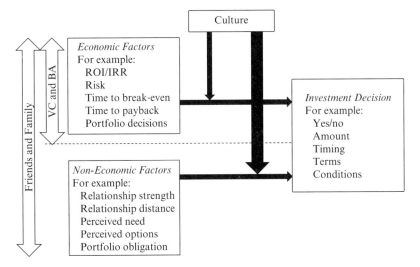

Figure 14.2   Role of culture in equity investment decisions

more successful contingent upon environmental and organizational contexts (Lumpkin and Dess 1996; Kropp *et al.* 2006, 2008).

Investors in entrepreneurial firms play an important role in helping them to establish and develop. To varying degrees, investors consider economic and non-economic factors before deciding to commit funds. Economic factors include expected returns on an investment as reflected in an investment's estimated internal rate of return (IRR) and time to break-even and payback period. Expected returns are associated with assessments of market and agency risk as well as potential profit. Market risk is related to unforeseen competitive conditions affecting market demand; agency risk is the degree of uncertainty that investor and/or entrepreneur interests may diverge from the requirements of the financing contract (Fiet 1995). VCs tend to view market risk as more threatening than agency risk, while BAs view agency risk as more threatening than market risk (Fiet 1995). Individual investment risk can be diversified by adopting a portfolio investment approach (Gompers and Lerner 2001).

Non-economic investment factors increase or decrease the sense of obligation to invest. Non-economic factors include the strength of the relationship between the investor and the nascent entrepreneur. This is inversely correlated with relationship distance. Arm's length investors have no or only weak relationships with entrepreneurs until they undertake due diligence. Friends and family have much stronger relationships with entrepreneurs with whom they invest.

The entrepreneurship literature distinguishes between opportunity-based entrepreneurs and necessity-based entrepreneurs (Bygrave *et al.* 2003; Maula *et al.* 2005). Opportunity-based entrepreneurs identify an opportunity, evaluate it and then exploit it, and this is based on a desire to be an entrepreneur. Necessity-based entrepreneurs become entrepreneurs because there are no other viable options. Some examples of necessity-based entrepreneurs include older workers who have been made redundant, people left behind by Hurricane Katrina because their businesses were destroyed (Kropp and Zolin 2008), and chronically unemployed people in third-world countries who attempt to establish businesses (Lindsay *et al.* 2009). We propose that necessity-based nascent entrepreneurs who have only limited options available to them will invoke a greater sense of obligation for financial support from friends and family than opportunity-based entrepreneurs who may have multiple options to choose from in determining their future.

As a preview of coming attractions, our conceptual model shows that economic considerations dominate for VCs and BAs when considering investment decisions. Both economic and non-economic considerations are important to friends and family, though non-economic factors will be most influential because they can heighten the sense of obligation to invest.

Culture moderates the relationships for all investors; however, we propose that it plays a stronger role for friends and family. Before delving into the role of culture, we outline some of the key factors in investments by VCs, BAs and friends and family investors. The impact of culture is described in a subsequent section, 'National culture and investment behaviour'.

Venture Capitalists

VC investment is an important ingredient in the success of entrepreneurial firms and, in 2007, in the USA alone, VC investment was $30.7 billion (Lefteroff 2008). VCs are professionals who invest institutional money. They raise this money primarily from pension funds and insurance companies (Gompers and Lerner 2001), although high net worth individuals may also invest (Harrison and Mason 2000). VCs pool the funds they raise so that they can invest in a variety of ventures (Freear *et al.* 2002). Sometimes they co-invest with other VCs. These activities are consistent with portfolio theory designed to diversify risk and maximize returns.

Investor willingness to commit monies to a particular VC fund depends upon the past performance by the fund's managers, perceived risk and expected returns, among other factors. Greater expected returns lead to a greater supply of VC fund investors. The demand for venture capital is generated by the number of entrepreneurial firms that can provide the expected rate of return that will meet the VC fund's minimum threshold (Gompers and Lerner 2001).

Most VC funds have a limited life of around 10–12 years, after which any remaining investments are liquidated and the fund dissolved, with net capital gains disbursed to investors (Gompers and Lerner 2001). This process provides an opportunity for VCs to terminate any 'living dead' investments, that is, underperforming firms in their portfolio. To ensure continuity, VCs usually raise a new fund every two to five years – contingent upon their track record and anticipated future investment performance (Gompers and Lerner 2001). VCs typically receive a management fee as well as a 'carried interest' which represents a share of the capital gains when an investment is sold (Gompers and Lerner 2001).

VCs provide a unique role in the capital market in that they act as financial intermediaries between fund providers and young entrepreneurial firms (Chan *et al.* 1990). In addition to providing finance, VCs usually assume an active, non-executive role in the firms in which they invest. Typically, VCs prefer not to be involved in day-to-day operational matters unless investments underperform.

Differences may exist among VCs in their source of funds, for example from the public or private sectors. Differences also exist in the type of investments pursued, the size of investments made, the stage of investment preferred and other factors. There is, however, a VC subculture founded upon common practices and behaviours that suggests a sense of VC homogeneity (Isaksson *et al.* 2004). Underpinning this subculture of VC investment is an invaluable VC general expertise set that complements their industry-specific expertise (Berglund *et al.* 2007).

Institutional theory provides insights into how VCs develop commonalities. Institutional theory suggests that organizational behaviour involves efforts to comply with conventional beliefs based on social and cultural norms (Scott 1995). Efforts to comply with beliefs increase in uncertain environments (DiMaggio and Powell 1983). Since VCs are immersed in uncertain environments, emphasis will be placed on VC conforming behaviour – particularly among younger VCs as they strive to emulate older, successful VC role models (Isaksson *et al.* 2004).

From an agency perspective, a principal–agency relationship exists between VCs and their investors (Van Osnabrugge 2000). VCs must demonstrate competent behaviour to keep investors happy and interested (Van Osnabrugge 2000; Mason and Harrison 2002). Thus, VCs need to have in place sophisticated rational financial investment processes and models that facilitate effective decision making and monitoring.

Business Angels

Although formal venture capital has a high profile in the media and in academic research, the level of BA finance far outweighs VC investment (Mason and Harrison 1993; Bygrave *et al.* 2003). Estimates suggest that, annually, angels invest between two to five times more money in entrepreneurial firms than VCs (Mason and Harrison 1993; Freear *et al.* 1994). Based on Lefteroff's (2008) estimate of $30.7 billion VC investment in the US in 2007, BA investment could well exceed $100 billion in the US.

BAs tend to be high net worth individuals who invest their own monies into early-stage, growth-oriented, entrepreneurial firms in expectation of financial returns (Van Osnabrugge and Robinson 2000; Freear *et al.* 2002). They tend to be experienced business or professional people and may have operated businesses previously (Van Osnabrugge 2000). As such, they exhibit an entrepreneurial orientation (Lindsay 2004).

Though BAs may invest several million dollars into a given venture, BAs typically make investments in entrepreneurial firms needing less than $500,000 (Van Osnabrugge 2000). Since BAs fund much smaller amounts than VCs, it is estimated that they fund between 30 and 40 times more entrepreneurial firms than VCs (Wetzel and Freear 1996). Unlike VCs, BAs are not beholden to investors and so owe an allegiance of professionalism only to themselves and the entrepreneurs in whom they invest (Van Osnabrugge 2000).

Freear *et al.* (1994) identify two types of high net worth investors in entrepreneurial firms: those with investment experience and potential investors with no investment experience. Experienced angel investors may act individually or cluster with other angel investors (Harrison and Mason 2000). Joining with other angel investors provides additional knowledge to assess investments, the possibility of reducing risk through shared investment and diversification, and an ability to create a pool of investment funds. Some angel investors, typically experienced investors, band together to create angel alliances that emulate professional VC behaviour (Freear *et al.* 2002). These groups of experienced angel investors form to fund larger deals and some second-round early-stage deals (Freear *et al.* 2002). These alliances play an important role to help to fill a gap in the market as VCs migrate upward seeking deals that require higher investment levels than were made in the past as well as preferring to invest in later-stage deals – all at the expense of smaller, earlier-stage investments (Freear *et al.* 2002).

Friends and Family: Relationship-Based Investors

The largest external source of venture financing, especially for early-stage ventures, comes from friends and family, also known as relation-based investors or altruistic investors. Unlike VCs or BAs who transact financial investments with entrepreneurs at arm's length for predominantly financial reasons, family and friends are connected with the entrepreneurs they are looking to finance. Though VCs or BAs may develop a close relationship with entrepreneurs they finance, these relationships are a *posteriori* rather than *a priori*. Family and friends are connected with the entrepreneurs they are looking to finance prior to the investment opportunity.

Friends and family, particularly close family, are often driven by philanthropic or altruistic motivations and the needs of the entrepreneur as well as financial considerations (Maula *et al.* 2005). Thus family and friends may be perceived as investing on the basis of the relationship rather than economic return on investment and may be viewed as more angelic than business angels (Lindsay *et al.* 2010).

Friends and family investment in an entrepreneurial business venture is a function of many factors, some of which are economic and some of which are non-economic. Risk equity is provided by people who are known to the entrepreneur by way of family, friends or other close acquaintances. The area of friends and family investment is a relatively under-researched topic. Research that has been conducted into financing ventures predominantly consists of empirical research into the formal capital market and the impact of public policy. To a great extent, research in the formal capital market does not capture the processes, motivations and characteristics of participants in the informal market.

Research conducted by Bygrave *et al.* (2003), based on the GEM project (see www.gemconsortium.org), concludes that informal investment from close family members, friends and neighbours of the entrepreneur was as much as 1.1 per cent of GDP worldwide. In addition, 3.4 per cent of the adult population of the surveyed countries were involved with informal investment in someone they knew (Bygrave *et al.* 2003). Behaviours and expectations of family investors are different to those of other investors (Erikson *et al.* 2003).

On the economic side, the motivations for friends and family investors are similar to those of arm's length investors: the desire to make a profit proportional to the risk associated with the investment – the higher the risk the higher the expected profit. Many of the other economic drivers are similar to those described for VCs and BAs, for example return on investment/internal rate of return, return on equity and risk balancing.

In a study examining loan contracts within a family group, Basu and

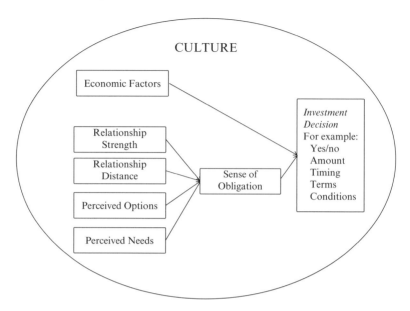

Figure 14.3   Conceptual model of friends and family investing

Parker (2001) identify the role of altruism in the investment process. This research provides an important transition between angel investing and friends and family investing. It is important to understand the context of finance between and within communities, because it can be significantly different.

On the non-economic side, there are several key factors that influence the sense of obligation that the relationship investor has to the entrepreneur. These factors include the strength and distance of the relationship, the perceived need of the entrepreneur, and options open to the entrepreneur in terms of other sources of finance (see Figure 14.3). Obligations will also arise out of an individual's culture and values (Kockelman 2007).

Investments between friends and family are made within a social construct. Social capital is accessed through social networks and enables or disables entrepreneurial activity. A social network provides an important mechanism through which business venture investment is conducted, and a focus on economic analysis alone provides an incomplete explanation of investment behaviour in early-stage ventures (Westland and Bolton 2003). This is particularly important when the investment is made within a family environment, owing to the added complexity evident in family business and the inherent family obligations that are present. Social networks and their impact on entrepreneurship can be both supportive and non-supportive to the entrepreneurial process, depending on their relationship with the entrepreneur (Klyver 2007). This concept was developed from Aldrich and Zimmer (1986), which identified different role sets in an entrepreneurial network.

The concentric circles model of responsibilities toward others (Brock 2005) states that people accept greater responsibilities for and more obligations towards others who are physically or affectively closer to them. All other things being equal, the closer the relationship, the more likely friends and family are to invest. For example, a parent is more likely to invest in a child than are cousins. The dyad, however, is not symmetrical. It is possible that a parent may be more likely to invest in a child's business than a child would be to invest in a parent's business. This asymmetrical obligation can be seen in the context of the difference between reliance and obligation. The extent to which one party relies on another has an influence on the obligation felt. In addition to the distance, for example parent–child, the strength of the relationship will be important. In a colloquial sense, some parents are closer to their children than others and vice versa. Again, all other things being equal, dyadic relationships that are stronger will be more likely to invest than those that are weaker.

Friends and family investors will consider both economic and non-economic factors in their investment decision process. They will weigh both economic and non-economic factors. Economic considerations will dominate in a situation when the relationship is distant or weak and if there is a lower sense of perceived obligation. Non-economic considerations will dominate in a situation when the relationship is close or strong and if there is a higher sense of perceived obligation.

The role of gender differences in the business start-up process has been studied extensively (Treichel and Scott 2006). Arenius and Autio (2006) find that women tend to obtain financing from friends and family more often than men, even though the propensity for female-controlled firms to seek external funding is significantly less than that of their male counterparts. Arguably, one of the reasons for this discrepancy is that females are often at a disadvantage in accessing external funds because they have a less developed social network in a business context than their male counterparts (Manolova *et al.* 2006).

NATIONAL CULTURE AND INVESTMENT BEHAVIOUR

A review of the venture capital and angel investment literature reveals that few studies specifically address cultural differences associated with investment behaviour. As stated earlier in this chapter, culture plays an important role in shaping values, attitudes, norms and behaviour. We explicitly acknowledge the importance of culture. Culture is important in the relationship between investors and entrepreneurs.

We argue, however, that the extent to which culture impacts investment behaviour depends upon the level of sophistication of investor behaviour, the focus on economic or non-economic objectives, the sense of obligation and the nature of the relationships between the investor and the entrepreneur, amongst other factors. Our premise is that national culture plays the greatest role with relation-based investors who invest primarily for altruistic reasons, a somewhat lesser role with angel investors (depending on their investment experience levels), and the least influential role with VCs who are professional investors. We discuss VCs first, followed by friends and family and, finally, angel investors.

Venture Capitalists

In describing subcultures of consumptions, an important construct in marketing, Schouten and McAlexander (1995, p. 43) identify that 'the most powerful organizing force in modern life are the activities and relationships that people undertake to give their lives meaning'. As participant observers, they used ethnographic research methods to study new Harley-Davidson riders. One of the more interesting findings from their study was that new bikers developed subcultures of consumption. In some ways Harley-Davidson riders, even those from different countries, were more like each other than they were like members of their own national culture.

We propose that venture capitalists have a culture or subculture of investment that bonds them and, in some ways, transcends national culture. Imagine, for a moment, that you were in a compartment in a train going from Paris to Barcelona and that there were eight VCs, each from a different country, sitting in the compartment. They would probably all speak English and would read the same publications, for example the *Financial Times* and the *Wall Street Journal*. They may have graduated from the same or similar MBA schools. Their understanding of the financial system is sophisticated and nuanced. Even though they come from different countries and cultures, their values are similar. They share a culture of VC investment.

Although there may be exceptions at the margins, VCs are primarily interested in economic considerations, including factors such as expected IRR, risk, ability and time to exit particular deals, overall portfolio performance and forecast versus actual returns to their investors as well as to themselves. Economic factors dominate the non-economic factors in VC decision making. Yet VCs must be cognizant of local customs, norms and regulations in order to function, since non-economic environmental factors can affect investment outcomes (for example, interest is proscribed in many Islamic countries).

VCs need to be aware of culture and comply with mechanistic artefacts of a nation, such as tax laws, common law and corporate regulatory influences. We argue, however, that the VC mindset – the culture of VC investment – transcends some national cultural differences. Since VCs do not operate in a vacuum, some aspects of a nation's culture may be more influential in affecting VC behaviour than others. Yet a review of the venture capital literature reveals that few VC studies specifically address cultural differences associated with investment behaviour even though there has been a range of studies undertaken in different countries – see, for example, Lu *et al.* 2006 (Singapore); Cumming 2007 (Australia); Li 2008 (USA); Patzelt *et al.* 2009 (Europe).

Most of the studies, however, are US-centric, and the results may not necessarily be generalizable to countries with different national cultures. The same can be said of non-US venture capital studies where national cultures may be different from the US culture. Although we believe that there is a shared culture of investment that can and will transcend some of the differences between national cultures, national culture still could affect VC investment behaviour. We examine some of the influences using Trompenaars' (1993) cultural dimensions.

Universalists place a stronger emphasis on universal rules, and particularists place a stronger emphasis on situations and relationships (Trompenaars 1996). Status derives from individual achievement in individualistic cultures and is focused on community in communitarian cultures (Trompenaars 1996). VCs are more likely to assess proposals more on merit in universalist cultures than in particularist cultures. Although VCs value relationships, they are used as part of the due diligence process to reduce VC investment risk. VC investment behaviour may be more self-interested in an individualist society than a collective society. In communitarian cultures, investment behaviour may be tempered by the ways in which the investment could benefit the community. This will particularly be the case where a national government provides significant support for VC funding. In total, however, these effects will be tempered by the VC culture of investment.

Achievement cultures tend to be more meritocracies; ascription cultures look at other factors such as family background and social status. In neutral cultures, emotions are not expressed as freely as in emotional cultures and issues are considered more objectively. In an achievement-neutral culture, VC investment and perception of VC performance will be based on analytic performance rather than on status or extraneous factors.

Specific cultures tend to segregate tasks and relationships; diffuse cultures are more holistic in considering the relationship. VC personal relationships and their interplay with business situations may play a role at the margins; however, ultimately, VCs are answerable to their investors. Although a personal relationship may provide an entrepreneur with an edge in getting a sympathetic initial VC hearing, deals are assessed on the basis of their merits. Thus, in general, there will be little or no difference in VC investment behaviour between those that operate in specific versus diffuse cultures that are achievement oriented.

Attitudes towards time will provide an important cultural context for VC investment behaviour; it is expected that VCs from any culture will be driven by the overarching need to perform and generate economic gains as soon as possible so as to impress their stakeholders. They may, however, have different time frames for minimal payback. For example, present-oriented cultures may have less patience than past- or future-oriented societies. VCs in monochronic cultures, where time is perceived as linear, may proceed faster with investment decisions than those in polychronic cultures that are not focused on getting things done as quickly. These attitudes will be tempered by the culture of investment that places a higher value on timeliness and rational economic criteria.

The attitude toward the environment cultural dimension will have a greater influence within nations than across nations, and this will be related to VC experience. New entrants to the VC industry with limited experience may feel less in control than their more experienced counterparts. Once VC investment success has been experienced and reinforced with subsequent successes (while learning from failures), it is expected that a higher VC locus of control will be exhibited. This can occur within any national culture. Thus it is expected that the attitude toward the environment cultural dimension will not significantly differentiate VCs from diverse cultures.

In summary, we expect that some dimensions of national culture will exert greater influence on VC investment and capital-raising behaviour than others. Those exerting greatest influence include the universalism versus particularism, individualism versus communitarianism, and achievement versus ascription cultural dimensions. Even those dimensions will be tempered by the VC culture of investment.

Friends and Family

Unlike VCs, friends and family are bound by national culture. Their values, ideals and behaviours are shaped by national culture. Although they may be part of a subculture of consumption, they are not part of a culture of investment that transcends their own culture. Though many individual relation-based investors may have business or financial acumen, there is a substantial proportion of people in the category who do not have a business foundation. As a group, relation-based investors are less sophisticated than angel investors or venture capitalists. In support of this, it has been estimated that 85–95 per cent of the businesses in which friends and family invest never reach a liquidity event.[1]

As depicted in Figure 14.3, their behaviour resides in the cultural milieu. Since they are relation-based investors, they place substantially more weight on non-economic factors, in particular the distance of relationships, the strength of relationships, perceived options that the entrepreneur could take rather than having her or his own business, and the perceived needs of the entrepreneur. In the next section, we discuss these elements and relate them to some of the dimensions of national culture developed by Trompenaars (1996).

Distance and strength of relationship
We distinguish between distance of relationship and strength of relationship. Within the bounds of the family, there are some relationships that are closer (e.g. parent–child or brother–sister) and others that are more distant (e.g. cousin–cousin). The strength of relationship relates to the emotional bond between the parties. For example, one dyad of parent–child could have a strong relationship and another could have a weak relationship. In contrast, two friends might be unrelated (a distant relationship) but have very strong emotional bonds. Colloquially, close friends may speak of each other in terms of 'I love him like a brother' or 'I love her like a sister'.

We propose that, all other things being equal, closer relationships will have a higher perceived sense of obligation to invest in a friend or family member's venture. We also propose that, all other things being equal, stronger relationships will have a higher perceived sense of obligation to invest in a friend or family member's venture. The perceived sense of obligation is shaped by the national culture of the investor.

Trompenaars (1996) identified that universalists place a stronger emphasis on universal rules and particularists place a stronger emphasis on situations and relationships. Trompenaars (1996) also distinguishes between individualism, where status derives from individual achievement, and communitarianism, where the focus is on the community. We propose, all other things being equal, that there would be a higher sense of obligation to invest in particularist communitarian cultures, like Korea, than in universalist individualist cultures, like Sweden, as they are more relationship based.

In an achievement-oriented, neutral, specific culture, decisions are based more on objective factors such as past performance in a role-defined situation. Ascriptive cultures look at other factors such as family background and social status. Similarly, diffuse cultures are more holistic, considering the relationship. As more non-economic factors are considered in ascriptive, emotional and/or diffuse cultures, the strength and closeness of relationships play a larger role in the perceived obligation to invest.

Attitudes towards time are different in different national cultures. Present-oriented cultures are more focused on the task and will place less emphasis on relationships than past- or future-oriented cultures. Similarly, monochronic cultures place a greater emphasis on task and polychronic cultures place a greater emphasis on relationship. All other things being equal, friends and family in past-oriented and polychronic cultures will feel a greater obligation to invest in EBVs than friends and family in present-oriented and monochronic cultures.

People with a higher locus of control believe that they are more able to shape the environment than people with a lower locus of control. Those with a higher locus of control tend to focus more on their own abilities to create successful or positive outcomes. People with a lower locus of control are much more relationship-based and more accepting and value harmony over conquest. In general, given this focus on relationships and the inherent need for harmony, people with a lower locus of control will feel a stronger obligation to invest in friends and family if they have the resources.

Perceived options and perceived needs

As we discussed earlier, there are many different types of entrepreneurs. One typology that is gaining recognition in the literature identifies differences between opportunity-based entrepreneurs and necessity-based entrepreneurs (Maula *et al.* 2005; Kropp and Zolin 2008). We believe that this is a continuum rather than a dichotomy.[2] An opportunity-based entrepreneur identifies an opportunity, evaluates it and attempts to exploit it by choice. Necessity-based entrepreneurs have no other real options. As an example, it has been argued that a chronically unemployed South African has to be entrepreneurial or die.[3] Therefore, all other things being equal, friends and family will have a greater sense of obligation in a necessity-based situation. In essence, the greater the sense of the necessity-based entrepreneur's perceived need and the lack of options open to the entrepreneur, the greater the obligation felt by friends and family to invest.

Based on the logic described in the previous sections, national culture moderates the relationships in the following ways. All other things being equal, the relationship will be stronger in communitarian, particularist, ascription, emotional, diffuse cultures that are past oriented or polychronic, with a lower locus of control. The relationship will be weaker in individualist, universal, achievement, neutral, specific cultures that are present oriented or monochronic, with a higher locus of control. Cultures with different weightings of each of these dimensions will have different strengths associated with the dimensions of national culture.

Obligation and investment decision

As shown in Figure 14.3, there is a relationship between the sense of obligation and the investment decision by friends and family. This is independent of resources. Friends and family cannot invest unless they have the resources to invest. Therefore, for the purposes of this discussion, we are assuming that friends and family have the resources to invest. We believe that there are differences amongst cultures, from the point of sensing the obligation to making the investment. In some cultures, friends and family may sense an equal obligation and have the necessary resources and be more or less likely to actually invest than those in other cultures with comparable obligations and resources.

People in cultures with a higher locus of control may be more likely to actualize the investment than those in a lower locus of control culture. Higher locus of control cultures are more action oriented. Similarly, people in monochronic present-oriented cultures are more action oriented than those in polychronic past-oriented cultures.

Looking at some of Trompenaars' other dimensions, people in communitarian societies may be more likely to turn the obligation into action, as the prevailing ethos is to help people in the community. People in achievement-oriented cultures may be more likely to take action as a part of their ethos.

Business Angels

As indicated earlier in this chapter, Freear *et al.* (1994) identify two categories of BAs, those with investment experience and potential investors with no investment experience. We view it more as a continuum rather than a dichotomy, ranging from highly experienced to inexperienced, with moderate experience as a median point. We propose that the greater the experience and sophistication, the more BAs will act like VCs, and the lower the level of experience and sophistication, the more BAs will act like friends and family investors. Therefore national culture will exert less influence on experienced or sophisticated BAs, and national culture will exert more influence on less experienced or less sophisticated investors.

Experienced BA investors that are more VC-like, particularly those that cluster and form into BA alliances or syndicates, can expect to have their investment behaviour influenced by national culture in a similar manner to that of VCs. Those that are inexperienced investors can expect to exhibit culture-moderated investment behaviour somewhat like friends and family relationship investors, except that economic benefits will be more important to them than non-economic benefits since they are investing at arm's length. To this extent, cultural influences will affect individual BA underlying economic motivations.

As with the effects of national culture on VC investment behaviour, we expect some national culture dimensions to exert a greater effect than others. Overall, however, we expect that national culture will exert a greater influence on inexperienced BA investment behaviour compared to VC investment behaviour but be less than the influences of national culture on relation-based investment behaviour. Those cultural dimensions that affect the investment behaviour of inexperienced BAs the most are expected to be the universalism versus particularism, neutral versus emotional, specific versus diffuse, attitude toward time and attitude toward the environment dimensions.

Future Research Directions

Having explored possible ways that national culture could influence private equity investor decision-making behaviour, the question arises as to how these proposed relationships could be tested empirically. Some suggestions are provided below.

One approach to empirically examining national cultural effects would be to conduct a series of in-person interviews with the different categories of investors in countries of interest. The results of the in-depth interviews would then serve as input to the development of a series of questionnaires that would be conducted with VCs, BAs and friends and family investors. In addition to the standard demographic information for friends and family and firm characteristics for VCs and BAs, respondents would be surveyed about their motivations to invest, including a perceived sense of obligation, as well as the strength and distance of relationship between friends and family investors and the entrepreneur plus perceptions of alternatives open to, and the needs of, the entrepreneur. The survey would also include measures of national culture (Hofstede 1980, 1993; Schwartz and Bilsky 1987; Trompenaars 1993) and personal values (Kahle 1986 – List of Values). An analysis within and between VC, BA and relation-based investors would then be undertaken. The analysis would look at the differences amongst each of the three groups within a particular culture and between groups in different cultures (for example, differences between VCs, BAs and friends and family in Australia, the UK, the USA and China) to identify motivations, obligations and interrelationships of the key variables and the investment decisions.

A second approach would be to develop a set of standardized

investment-related case study scenarios that are pertinent to each of the investor groups. The standardized case studies would then be administered to each group of investors in different countries, asking them the likelihood that they would invest and the reasons for their decisions. Investor group responses would then be assessed across and within countries and across and within groups with a view to evaluating localized and national cultural effects as well as investor biases and preferences that may influence investor decision outcomes for particular case scenarios. Again, other measures described above would be captured to identify the interrelationships between the key constructs. Both qualitative and quantitative analysis would be conducted.

A third approach could involve triangulation, whereby a number of analytic approaches might be used to evaluate national cultural effects, with their subsequent results 'combined' to develop a richer picture of the phenomenon. Triangulation could involve, for example, asking investors questions about the extent to which they believe national culture affects their investment decisions compared to other countries. In addition, investors could be provided with standardized case studies and asked to evaluate the case scenarios, providing written responses to particular questions asked about each case scenario. Investors could also be asked to verbalize their processing of information in the case studies (concurrent verbal protocols) so that an understanding can be gained of the processing of the sequence of events, the importance of key items in particular scenarios, the heuristics used and the effects of any national cultural influences on decision outcomes. These would be recorded and subsequently analysed using independent coders to evaluate the protocols generated.

An extension of this approach (but more invasive) would be to wire participants to a Bioview datagraph machine and collect investors' psycho-physiological (biofeedback) responses (e.g. heart rate, electrodermal activity, etc.) as they verbalize their processing of case scenario information. The biofeedback data could then be analysed in conjunction with the verbalized protocol sequences to provide additional psycho-physiological insights into the relative importance of various stimuli contained in the case scenarios. Although there are sceptics about the use of biofeedback, a range of disciplines has embraced the collection of psycho-physiological responses, including medicine and marketing. Notwithstanding, we believe that it is unlikely that VCs and BAs would be willing to participate in this kind of study.

CLOSING COMMENTS

This chapter is meant to stimulate debate. Although a substantial amount of research has been undertaken into VC and BA behaviour and, to a significantly lesser extent, into relationship-based investor behaviour, very few studies have examined cultural effects on investor decision-making outcomes. Yet national culture can affect investor behaviour to varying degrees. In this chapter, we explore to what extent this occurs. The next step requires testable hypotheses and for these to be empirically investigated. In this regard, we suggest possible ways that this could be undertaken using samples of investor groups in different countries and comparison of results.

NOTES

1. Obtained from a series of in-person interviews with venture capitalists and angel investors in Australia, the USA and the UK, October 2007.
2. Though it is not yet identified in the literature, we propose that these are two separate scales, each anchored by high and low. One can score low as an opportunity-based entrepreneur without being a necessity-based entrepreneur. Though rare, it is conceptually possible to be both. For simplicity and for the purposes of this discussion, we will refer to it as a continuum.
3. It can be argued that resorting to crime or begging is being entrepreneurial.

REFERENCES

Aldrich, H.E. and C. Zimmer (1986), *Entrepreneurship through Social Networks*, New York: Sexton and Smilor.
Arenius, P. and E. Autio (2006), 'Financing of small businesses: Are Mars and Venus more alike than different?', *Venture Capital: An International Journal of Entrepreneurial Finance*, **8**(2), 93–107.
Basu, A. and S. Parker (2001), 'Family finance and new business start-ups', *Oxford Bulletin of Economics and Statistics*, **63**(3), 305–49.
Berglund, H., T. Hellstrom and S. Sjolander (2007), 'Entrepreneurial learning and the role of venture capitalists', *Venture Capital*, **9**(3), 165–81.
Bond, M.H. (1988), 'Finding universal dimensions of individual variation in multicultural studies of values: The Rokeach and Chinese value surveys', *Journal of Personality and Social Psychology*, **55**(6), 1009–15.
Brock, G. (2005), 'Does obligation diminish with distance?', *Ethics, Place & Environment: A Journal of Philosophy and Geography*, **8**(1), 3–20.
Busenitz, L.W. and C. Lau (1996), 'A cross-cultural cognitive model of new venture creation', *Entrepreneurship Theory and Practice*, **20**(24), 25–39.
Bygrave, W.D., M. Hay, E. Ng and P. Reynolds (2003), 'Executive forum: A study of informal investing in 29 nations composing the Global Entrepreneurship Monitor', *Venture Capital*, **5**(2), 101–16.
Chan, V.S., D. Siegel and A.V. Thakor (1990), 'Learning, corporate control and performance requirements in venture capital contracts', *International Economic Review*, **31**(2), 365–82.
Churchill, N.C. and V.L. Lewis (1983), 'The five stages of small business growth', *Harvard Business Review*, **61**(3), 43–54.
Cumming, D. (2007), 'Government policy towards entrepreneurial finance: Innovation investment funds', *Journal of Business Venturing*, **22**(2), 193–235.
DiMaggio, P.J. and W.W. Powell (1983), 'The iron cage revisited: Institutional isomorphism

and collective rationality in organizational fields', *American Sociological Review*, **48**(2), 147–60.

Erikson, T., R. Sorheim and B. Reitan (2003), 'Family angels vs. other informal investors', *Family Business Review*, **16**(3), 163–71.

Fiet, J. (1995), 'Risk avoidance strategies in venture capital markets', *Journal of Management Studies*, **32**(4), 551–74.

Freear, J., J.E. Sohl and W.E. Wetzel Jr (1994), 'Angels and non-angels: Are there differences?', *Journal of Business Venturing*, **9**(2), 109–23.

Freear, J., J.E. Sohl and W.E. Wetzel (2002), 'Angles on angels: Financing technology-based ventures – a historical perspective', *Venture Capital*, **4**(4), 275–87.

French, W., H. Zeiss and G. Scherer (2001), 'Intercultural discourse ethics: Testing Trompenaars' and Hampden-Turner's conclusions about Americans and the French', *Journal of Business Ethics*, **34**(3/4), 145–59.

Friesen, P.H. and D. Miller (1984), 'A longitudinal study of the corporate life cycle', *Management Science*, **30**(10), 1161–83.

Geertz, C. (1973), *The Interpretation of Culture: Selected Essays*, New York: Basic Books.

Gompers, P. and J. Lerner (2001), 'The venture capital revolution', *Journal of Economic Perspectives*, **15**(2), 145–8.

Hall, E.T. (1959), *The Silent Language*, New York: Doubleday.

Hancock, G.G., N.J. Lindsay, K. Hindle and K. Klyver (2007), 'Entrepreneurial finance in Australia in 2006: A summary of salient data from the 2006 GEM Australia national adult population survey', *Australian Graduate School of Entrepreneurship Research Report Series*, **4**(5).

Harrison, R. and C. Mason (2000), 'Venture capital market complementarities: The links between business angels and venture capital funds in the United Kingdom', *Venture Capital*, **3**(3), 223–42.

Hayton, J.C., G. George and S.A. Zahra (2002), 'National culture and entrepreneurship: A review of behavioral research', *Entrepreneurship Theory and Practice*, **26**(4), 33–52.

Hofstede, G. (1980), *Culture's Consequences: International Differences in Work-Related Values*, Beverly Hills, CA and London: Sage.

Hofstede, G. (1983), 'The cultural relativity or organizational practices and theories', *Journal of International Business Studies*, **14**(2), 75–89.

Hofstede, G. (1989), 'Organising for cultural diversity', *European Management Journal*, **7**(4), 390–97.

Hofstede, G. (1993), *Cultures and Organizations: Software of the Mind*, London: McGraw-Hill.

Isaksson, A., B. Cornelius, H. Landström and S. Junghagen (2004), 'Institutional theory and contracting in venture capital: The Swedish experience', *Venture Capital*, **6**(1), 47–71.

Kahle, L.R. (1986), 'The nine nations of North America and the value basis of geographic segmentation', *Journal of Marketing*, **50**(2), 37–47.

Kauffman (2008), 'Kauffman Index of Entrepreneurial Activity', available at www.kauffman.org (accessed 7 August 2008).

Kirkman, B.L., K.B. Lowe and C.B. Gibson (2006), 'A quarter century of culture's consequences: A review of empirical research incorporating Hofstede's cultural values framework', *Journal of International Business Studies*, **37**(3), 285–320.

Klyver, K. (2007), 'Shifting family involvement during the entrepreneurial process', *International Journal of Entrepreneurial Behaviour & Research*, **13**(5), 258–77.

Kockelman, P. (2007), 'From status to contract revisited', *Anthropological Theory*, **7**(2), 151–76.

Kroeber, A.L. and C. Kuckhorn (1952), *Culture: A Critical Review of Concepts and Definitions*, Cambridge, MA: Peabody Museum.

Kropp, F. and R. Zolin (2008), 'Federal government entrepreneurship: New enterprise structures', *Journal of Small Business and Enterprise Development*, **15**(3), 595–605.

Kropp, F., N.J. Lindsay and A. Shoham (2006), 'Entrepreneurial, market, and learning orientations and entrepreneurial business venture performance for South African firms', *International Marketing Review*, **23**(5), 504–23.

Kropp, F., N.J. Lindsay and A. Shoham (2008), 'Entrepreneurial orientation and international entrepreneurial business venture startup', *International Journal of Entrepreneurial Behaviour & Research*, **14**(2), 102–17.

Laurent, A. (1986), 'The cross-cultural puzzle of international human resource management', *Human Resource Management*, **25**(1), 91–102.

Lefteroff, T. (2008), 'Venture capital investment holds steady at $7.4 billion in Q2 2008 according to the Moneytree Report', available at http://www.nvca.org/pdf/08Q2_VCinvestMTReport.pdf (accessed 4 August 2008).

Li, Y. (2008), 'Duration analysis of venture capital staging: A real options perspective', *Journal of Business Venturing*, **23**(5), 497–512.

Lindsay, N.J., W.A. Lindsay and F. Kropp (2009), 'Values, attitudes, start-up intentions and behavior of necessity-based nascent entrepreneurs: A longitudinal study', Frontiers of Entrepreneurship Research, Babson College, Wellesley, MA.

Lindsay, N.J., K. Klyver and G. Hancock (2010), 'Exploring altruistic informal investment decision behaviour by angels in early stage ventures', working paper, Entrepreneurship, Commercialisation and Innovation Centre, University of Adelaide.

Lindsay, N.J. (2004), 'Do business angels have an entrepreneurial orientation?', *Venture Capital: An International Journal of Entrepreneurial Finance*, **6**(2/3), 197–210.

Lu, Q., P. Hwang and C.K. Wang (2006), 'Agency risk control through reprisal', *Journal of Business Venturing*, **21**(3), 369–84.

Lumpkin, G. and G. Dess (1996), 'Clarifying the entrepreneurial orientation construct and linking it to performance', *Academy of Management Review*, **21**(1), 135–72.

McCracken, G. (1986), 'Culture and consumption: A theoretical account of the structure and movement of the cultural meaning of consumer goods', *Journal of Consumer Research*, **13**(6), 71–84.

McGrath, R.G., I.C. MacMillan and S. Scheinberg (1992), 'Elitists, risk-takers, and rugged individualists: An exploratory analysis of cultural differences between entrepreneurs and non-entrepreneurs', *Journal of Business Venturing*, **7**(2), 115–35.

Manolova, T.S., I.M. Manev, N.M. Carter and B.S. Gyoshev (2006), 'Breaking the family and friends' circle: Predictors of external financing usage among men and women entrepreneurs in a transitional economy', *Venture Capital*, **8**(2), 109–32.

Markus, H.R. and S. Kitayama (1991), 'Culture and the self: Implications for cognition, emotion, and motivation', *Psychological Review*, **98**(2), 224–53.

Mason, C.M. and R.T. Harrison (1993), 'Strategies for expanding the informal venture capital market', *International Small Business Journal*, **11**(4), 23–38.

Mason, C.M. and R.T. Harrison (2002), 'Is it worth it? The rates of return from informal venture capital investments', *Journal of Business Venturing*, **17**(3), 271–87.

Maula, M., E. Autio, and P. Arenius (2005), 'What drives micro-angel investments?', *Small Business Economics*, **25**(5), 459–475.

Miller, D. (1983), 'The correlates of entrepreneurship in three types of firms', *Management Science*, **29**(7), 770–91.

Newman, K.L. and S.D. Nollen (1996), 'Culture and congruence: The fit between management and national culture', *Journal of International Business Studies*, **27**(4), 753–9.

O'Connor, Allan and K. Hindle (2006), 'Entrepreneurial finance in Australia in 2005: A summary of salient data from the 2005 GEM Australia national adult population survey', *Australian Graduate School of Entrepreneurship Research Report Series*, **3**(5).

Patzelt, H., D. zu Knyphausen-Aufseß and H.T. Fischer (2009), 'Upper echelons and portfolio managers of venture capital firms', *Journal of Business Venturing*, **24**(6), 558–72.

Rotter, J.B. (1966), 'Generalized expectancies for internal versus external control of reinforcement', *Psychological Monographs: General and Applied*, **80**(1), 1–8.

Schouten, J.W. and J.H. McAlexander (1995), 'Subcultures of consumption: An ethnography of new bikers', *Journal of Consumer Research*, **22**(1), 43–61.

Schwartz, S.H. (1994), 'Cultural dimensions of values: Towards an understanding of national differences', in U. Kim, H.C. Triandis, C. Kagitcibasi, S.C. Choi and G. Yoon (eds), *Individualism and Collectivism: Theoretical and Methodological Issues*, Thousand Oaks, CA: Sage, pp. 85–119.

Schwartz, S.H. and W. Bilsky (1987), 'Toward a universal psychological structure of human values', *Journal of Personality and Social Psychology*, **53**(3), 550–62.

Schwartz, S.H. and W. Bilsky (1990), 'Toward a theory of the universal content and structure of human values', *Journal of Personality and Social Psychology*, **58**(5), 878–91.

Scott, M. and R. Bruce (1987), 'Five stages of growth in small businesses', *Long Range Planning*, **20**(3), 45–52.

Scott, W.R. (1995), *Institutions and Organizations*, Thousand Oaks, CA: Sage.

Smith, P.B., S. Dugan and F. Trompenaars (1996), 'National culture and the values of organizational employees: A dimensional analysis across 43 nations', *Journal of Cross-Cultural Psychology*, **27**(2), 231–64.

Smith, P.B., S. Dugan and F. Trompenaars (1997), 'Locus of control and affectivity by gender and occupational status: A 14 nation study', *Sex Roles*, **36**(1/2), 51–77.

Thomas, A.S. and S.A. Mueller (2000), 'A case for comparative entrepreneurship: Assessing the relevance of culture', *Journal of International Business Studies*, **31**(2), 287–301.

Timmons, J. and S. Spinelli (2009), *New Venture Creation: Entrepreneurship for the 21st Century*, 8th edn, New York: McGraw-Hill Irwin.

Treichel, M.Z. and J.A. Scott (2006), 'Women-owned businesses and access to bank credit: Evidence from three surveys since 1987', *Venture Capital: An International Journal of Entrepreneurial Finance*, **8**(1), 51–67.

Triandis, H.C. (1989), 'The self and social behavior in differing cultural contexts', *Psychological Review*, **96**(3), 506–20.

Trompenaars, F. (1993), *Riding the Waves of Culture: Understanding Cultural Diversity in Business*, London: Economist Books.

Trompenaars, F. (1996), 'Resolving international conflict: Culture and business strategy', *Business Strategy Review*, **7**(3), 51–68.

Trompenaars, F. and C. Hampden-Turner (1998), *Riding the Waves of Culture: Understanding Diversity in Global Business*, 2nd edn, New York: McGraw-Hill.

Trompenaars, F. and P. Woolliams (2003), 'A new framework for managing change across culture', *Journal of Change Management*, **3**(4), 361–75.

Van Osnabrugge, M. (2000), 'A comparison of business angel and venture capitalist investment procedures: An agency theory-based analysis', *Venture Capital*, **2**(2), 91–109.

Van Osnabrugge, M. and R.J. Robinson (2000), *Angel Investing: Matching Start-Up Funds with Start-Up Companies*, San Francisco: Jossey-Bass.

Westland, H. and R., Bolton (2003), 'Local social capital and entrepreneurship', *Small Business Economics*, **21**(2), 77–113.

Wetzel, W.E. and J. Freear (1996), 'Promoting informal venture capital in the United States: Reflections on the history of the venture capital network', in R. Harrison and C.M. Mason (eds), *Informal Venture Capital: Information, Networks and Public Policy*, Hemel Hempstead: Woodhead-Faulkner, pp. 61–74.

15 Perceptual differences and perceptual problems in providing government support for new venture creation
Malin Brännback, Alan L. Carsrud and Jerome A. Katz

THE PERCEPTUAL ISSUE

Despite numerous public policy measures and governmental investments intended to promote high entrepreneurial activity, some developed and technologically advanced countries such as the United States, Finland and Sweden continue to demonstrate low levels of entrepreneurial activity (Delmar *et al.* 2003; Hjalmarsson and Johansson 2003; Brännback *et al.* 2005a; Reynolds 2005). In this chapter, three reasons for the continuing problem are considered:

1. the use of prospect theory in popular and government decision making;
2. timescales of breakthrough technologies;
3. differences in the perception of the entrepreneurial process between government bureaucrats and entrepreneurs.

Each of these reasons for difficulty in decision making is discussed in terms of the relevant cognitive factors, and examples from famous economic development decisions in Finland and the United States are given to help demonstrate the problem at a practical level. Following the explanation of the analytic basis, suggestions for improved decision making are offered.

PROSPECT THEORY, BEHAVIOUR AND THE DRIVE FOR BIG WINS

Cognitive psychologists Tversky and Kahneman (Kahneman and Tversky 1979; Tversky and Kahneman 1986) have contended that people in general are ruled by prospect theory, a heuristic in which people will worry more about losses, even small ones, than a win of similar size. Prospect theory posits that, to offset a small loss, there needs to be the possibility of a big win. Prospect theory has been shown to work in a variety of political situations, including decision making in foreign policy (Farnham 1992; Jervis 1992; McDermott 1992, 1998; McInerny 1992; Levy 1997), domestic policy (Levy 2003), economic restructuring (Weyland 1996, 2002) and, most recently, intra-country economic development and regime change (Gould and Maggio 2003a, 2003b).

Because prospect theory describes the behaviour of citizens, politicians and the bureaucrats who serve them are faced with the need to avoid losses, because even small ones can produce severe reaction in public confidence. As a result, two forms of economic development incentives are used. To offset potential job losses, governments often offer existing businesses incentives to get them to continue to locate in the region. These tax and job incentive programmes are typically targeted at the biggest businesses, whose decreases in employment would be the sort of 'small loss' signal which can severely shake confidence in the local economy.

Examples of the Drive for Big Wins

One of the most famous examples of incentives working well is the Finnish example called the 'Nokia factor'. Nokia started as a wood-pulp milling company in 1865. It merged with Finnish Rubber Works in 1898 and Finnish Cable Works in 1912. The resulting firm continued to grow in different directions. Nokia's cable division moved into telecommunications cabling in the 1950s and 1960s, with Nokia developing its first computer in 1973. With the purchase of the Finnish electronics firm Salora, in 1983, Nokia was poised to enter the wireless phone business, offering its first, briefcase-sized phone, the Mobira Talkman, in 1986. The walkie-talkie-styled Cityman was introduced in 1987. The Nokia 1011, which set the standard for a mass-produced small form-factor cell phone, was introduced in 1992, by which time Nokia had shed its information technology and other business lines, except for tyres.

The Nokia experience above must be viewed within the Finnish technology context. The Finnish national innovation system includes a number of funding institutions, such as the Academy of Finland, the Finnish National Fund for Research and Development (Sitra), VTT and the National Technology Agency (Tekes), that directly and indirectly support R&D in business. However, a majority of the R&D activities are primarily funded by business itself. In fact, the role of government-supported R&D has decreased since 2000. Notwithstanding, the role of government has for the past few decades been substantial. The primary source of R&D funding has been Tekes, which supports R&D in companies through R&D grants, capital loans and R&D loans. In 2005, Tekes invested €429 million into R&D and over 50 per cent was channelled to small and medium-size companies. In absolute terms Nokia received more than any other Finnish company, €13.5 million, which is more than 5 per cent of Tekes's business R&D budget (Steinbock 2006).

Government support of R&D in Nokia has, however, varied over the decades. In 1969 Nokia received €34 000 from the Technology Office of the Ministry of Trade and Industry, which was the predecessor of Tekes. In 1999 the sum had increased to €18 million, only to decrease to €8 million the year after. In the 1970s, the funding support was 7 per cent on average of the R&D budget. In 1980 and 1981 Tekes funding increased considerably to cover 25 per cent of the R&D budget in 1980, and decreased to 15 per cent the following year, after which it decreased so that the average support was 8 per cent during the 1980s. In the 1990s Tekes funding increased again (Ali-Yrkkö and Hermans 2002). While government has provided R&D funding for Nokia it is important to understand that the company today finances its research mostly by itself. In 2000 Tekes's share of Nokia's R&D funding was only 0.3 per cent. Moreover, while Nokia received government support for R&D it also gave back to the Finnish society. Hence while Nokia received a total of approximately €80 million between 1995 and 2000 in research grants it paid corporate taxes of €2.9 billion. Nokia employees paid €1.4 billion in income taxes, and taxes on options of approximately €1.2 billion, and Nokia paid social insurance expenses for its employees of another €1.2 billion. Finally, Nokia invested approximately €18 million in academic R&D and donated equipment (Ali-Yrkkö and Hermans 2002).

While the first form of incentive – in the form of R&D support – focuses on avoiding small losses, the second form of incentive focuses on the attraction or creation of firms new to the area, in effect seeking to achieve a 'big win'. These incentives put the politicians and economic development bureaucrats in a position analogous to that of venture capitalists (Jenkins and Leicht 1996), betting on potential or future businesses. The fact that support of Nokia paid off so well, that is, it was a success story in every respect, may have led politicians and economic development bureaucrats to believe that this indeed was the way to do it. If we look at the GNP of Finland during the late 1990s, which showed exceptional growth, estimates suggest that the increase was due to Nokia's exceptional growth – the Nokia factor.

Worldwide, government economic development efforts are consistently focused on achieving 'big wins'. There are two ways to do this. The original approach was to bring a major new plant for a Fortune 500 company to the area. Such efforts were originally called 'smokestack chasing' (Grant and Hutchinson 1996). The somewhat derogatory term was intentional. The efforts were fuelled initially by the need to achieve a big win and, once in play, were fuelled by the process of escalation of commitment (Staw 1981). It became routine to see multiple government economic development agencies competing against one another to achieve the 'big win' of a Fortune 500 plant, even when the economic analysis of the packages offered showed that they would be unprofitable for their communities (Fisher and Peters 1998; Buchholz and Schweke 2000; Peters and Fisher 2002). The zenith of this effort occurred in the United States when 34 states pursued a Mercedes-Benz manufacturing plant (Gardner *et al.* 2001), creating what some observers called 'The New Civil War' (Watson 1995).

Daimler-Benz announced in 1993 that it was planning to build a 1300- to 1500-worker, $300 million auto assembly plant in North America. While as many as 34 states submitted initial and follow-up proposals, three strong finalists emerged, all Southern states – South Carolina (which had won a new BMW plant a few years earlier with a then record $130 million offer), North Carolina and the winning state, Alabama (Tosto and Monk 1993). In their final incentive package, the state offered over $250 million in incentives, a new North American record. In crafting the package, the bureaucrats and politicians actually overstepped state law in several instances, requiring frantic rearranging of specific features of the offering to keep Daimler-Benz happy and not fall foul of the legislature, enraged constituents or the courts (Gardner *et al.* 2001). For example, part of the incentive package involved buying $75 million of the new small SUVs to be produced at the plant, but this would violate existing laws stipulating competitive bidding for state-owned vehicles. Similarly, a promised $42.6 million grant to help pay plant costs required several restructurings, until a legally acceptable, albeit far more costly, approach could be found to fund the promise.

It is not surprising then that economic development and public policy experts have negatively reviewed smokestack-chasing efforts. The Alabama example became a highly visible fiasco (Watson 1995; Gardner *et al.* 2001), which would take a long time to turn a net profit for the state (Fisher and Peters 1998). In response to the 'Civil War' scenario of prospect theory played out in the case of the Mercedes-Benz plant, others recommended severe limitations on economic development offerings to big business (Schweke *et al.* 1994; Burstein and Rolnick 1995). This problem is recognized to be a general one among bureaucrats and politicians. In terms of bureaucrats identifying the best investments in their own countries, the World Bank has suggested that 'bureaucrats generally are bad bankers' (World Bank 2001, p. 127), and other experts have argued that state bureaucrats are unduly inflexible in their approaches and reactions to changing economic situations (Reuschmeyer and Evans 1985).

As smokestack chasing has fallen out of favour, the search for 'big wins' in the economic development community has shifted toward the creation of new technology-based firms with the potential to become major economic forces in the region (Jenkins and Leicht 1996). Examples of this can be found throughout the world, but perhaps the best-known example is that of the 'Amgen dream' in the United States.

The Big Win and Venture Creation

There are other examples than Nokia of the notion of venture creation for 'the big win'. Let's look at modern biotechnology firms, which were a consequence of scientific advances of the early 1970s (Carsrud *et al*. 2008). The scientific discoveries not only created a new scientific and technological paradigm (Dosi 1988), but also had structural and strategic consequences for venture creation within the field of biotechnology. Previously, pharmaceutical discoveries and development had taken place within fully integrated pharmaceutical companies (FIPCOs). In the early 1980s, starting with Genentech, soon to be followed by Amgen, small firms that had been founded a few years earlier went from small-scale protein production for R&D purposes to large-scale production for commercial purposes. This was made possible through public listing in a situation where none of these firms had developed their first product, let alone sold anything. Genentech and Amgen were able to increase the market capitalization of their firms as never seen before (Robbins-Roth 2000; Carsrud *et al*. 2008).

Amgen began operations in 1981 with a private equity placement of $18.9 million. It raised $400 million before it sold anything at all. On 1 June 1989 its first product, Epogen, received FDA approval. At the end of 1989, $96 million worth of Epogen had been sold, and in 1998 it was the leading pharmaceutical product in the world, with sales that year alone of $1.4 billion. Amgen's average return to investors between 1986 and 1996 was 67.8 per cent with two products on the market, much higher than the second-place Oracle's 53.5 per cent with a myriad of products on the market (Oliver 2000). Every venture capitalist wants to find the next Nokia or Amgen, and every governmental official wants to claim they made it possible.

Overall, the problems of the 'big win' approach in the public policy arena have long been known. Karl Weick (1984) suggested as an alternative a focus on 'small wins' – which in the case of economic development would involve spending smaller sums to create or preserve a few jobs at a time. The small wins approach makes sense from the standpoint of traditional linear economic thought, in so far as it involves small amounts to gain or lose. However, in a world ruled by prospect theory, small wins are seen as of relatively low worth, while avoiding even small losses can take on economically unjustifiable levels of risk. Therefore, despite all the problems bureaucrats and politicians face in making investments in existing firms, and the even greater hazards faced when betting on new firms and unproven technologies, it is still likely to happen. There are arguably two major reasons for this: the timescale of new technologies achieving substantial returns, and the problems of correctly evaluating entrepreneurial firms; these are covered below.

THE TIMESCALES OF BREAKTHROUGH TECHNOLOGY

Simply put, breakthrough technology (or the breakthrough entrepreneur) is hardly ever created overnight (Jolly 1997; Koehn 2001; Drucker 2002). Cox and Alm (1999) point out that the personal computer involved a set of inventions dating from the creation of binary code in 1801 to the creation of electrical grids in 1882, television in 1925 and microprocessors in 1971. And none of the creators of those precursor inventions had any idea of the personal computer or how it would revolutionize the world. Thus it seems that a technological innovation merely by itself is not able to succeed, but requires multiple innovations that when combined allow the firm to truly succeed in a market.

This example also points up the timescale problem in high-technology entrepreneurship. It is difficult to know which investments will pay off and, if they do pay out, when they will do so. This leads to the problem: when is the right time for an investment to be made? We return to Nokia, the Finnish stereotype of technology firms mentioned above. Whenever Nokia's unprecedented success since the mid-1990s in mobile technology is discussed it is almost never pointed out that the development process of the digital technology was started in the 1960s. At first it was a few engineers' pet project, with which an extremely visionary CEO allowed them to play. Even in the early 1980s there were managers inside the firm who seriously doubted whether digital technology would be of interest to anyone even at the turn of the century! Nokia shows the problem that the real breakthrough may have taken place many years after someone started to toy with an idea. This problem has been found throughout technology studies and entrepreneurship (Rosenberg 1994; Shane and Venkataraman 2000).

The Nokia experience also shows the idea of Robert Ronstadt's (1988) corridor principle, that it is often not possible to see the eventual pay-out at the beginning of a technological process, much less an investment. It is only after moving through the development sequence that the realistic potential for pay-outs becomes obvious. Despite this, politicians, bureaucrats and venture capitalists are desperately searching for the technology that will be 'the next Nokia or the next Amgen'. Again it is often forgotten that not even the Americans have been able to replicate Amgen. The ability to turn research into enterprise has been disappointingly slow and infrequent in the United States and the United Kingdom (Carsrud and Ellison 1992) and has not significantly improved over the last decade (Harrison 2003).

PERCEPTUAL DIFFERENCES BETWEEN ENTREPRENEURS, POLICY MAKERS AND INVESTORS

What is often omitted in considering entrepreneurial activity is that there are numerous parties perceiving, setting goals for and ultimately valuing an entrepreneurial activity for very different purposes (see, for example, Hjalmarsson and Johansson 2003). Of course, there are always the entrepreneurs, who have their own reasons for doing what they do – wealth, mindshare, autonomy, creativity or other reasons. As noted above, the government politician or bureaucrat may value entrepreneurial activity for the perceived gains among taxpaying employees and perhaps businesses as well as agglomeration effects as related businesses move into the area and create jobs. With respect to high-technology entrepreneurship the issue of multiple involved parties (investors, management, etc.) is highly relevant, since the entrepreneur needs resources, and money or intellectual property through basic research in particular is very much needed.

So entrepreneurs need the government bureaucrat's support, among that of others, and may fabricate any fitting intention for the purpose of financing the venture regardless of the real truth. Some entrepreneurs may care nothing about the value of their firm, just the fun of having created it – or value their creation based on highly different criteria from those of a financer. What may be judged as maximizing by one may turn out to be an optimization routine for another.

That is, if government or investors support high-growth ventures an entrepreneur may well claim his goal is high growth, although in reality his goal may be something far less ambitious. The entrepreneur may in fact not really understand what high growth means (Brännback *et al.* 2004b, 2005b), whether his venture is a 'gazelle or a mouse'. Kirzner (1979, p. 11) argues that 'entrepreneurial alertness is stimulated by the lure of profits. Alertness to an opportunity rests on the attractiveness of that opportunity and on its ability to be grasped once it has been perceived. . . . The incentive is to get something for nothing, if only one can see what it is that can be done.' But does the potential for profit have to exist for someone to be entrepreneurial? Most economists elaborate primarily on the possibility of profit maximization. However, in the case of a lifestyle entrepreneur we find that profit may be defined not as maximization but as optimization. Therefore, the use of the term *gain* – a subjective term – is perhaps more fitting than the term *profit*. How can the differences in perception be characterized so that policy makers can be better informed? One way is to use a model which shows the forces leading to different perceptual maps. One well-established method is in the area of opportunity recognition in entrepreneurship.

MODELS OF OPPORTUNITY RECOGNITION

Opportunity recognition is an important part of entrepreneurship (Bird 1988; Katz and Gartner 1988; Carsrud 1989; Shane and Venkataraman 2000; Gaglio and Katz 2001; Eckhart and Shane 2003; Shane 2003). Shane (2000) argues that it is possible to distinguish between three schools of thought with respect to opportunity recognition:

1. *The equilibrium school* assumes that everyone can recognize all entrepreneurial opportunities and that whether this actually takes place is dependent on the fundamental attributes of people.
2. *The psychological school* argues that the fundamental attributes of people, rather than information about opportunities, determine who becomes an entrepreneur, and this again depends on a person's willingness, motivation and ability to take action (Krueger and Carsrud 1993; Krueger *et al.* 2000). Much recent attention within this school of thought has been given to entrepreneurial intentionality studies, and it has been argued and shown that attitude towards behaviour, social norms and perceived behavioural control influence a person's intentions to act and cognitions of opportunity (Carsrud *et al.* 1986; Ajzen 1987; Krueger and Carsrud 1993; Krueger *et al.* 2000; Grundsten 2004; Brännback *et al.* 2005b).
3. *The Austrian school* builds on the idea of information asymmetry as the driving force. People cannot recognize all entrepreneurial opportunities, and information about opportunities will drive entrepreneurial opportunity recognition rather than a willingness to take action (Kirzner 1973, 1979, 1992; Shane 2000). If we look at an individual who makes money by starting a firm through the lenses of the

Austrian school we find that, provided the individual just made an investment, this would not be considered entrepreneurial, merely a windfall gain (Kirzner 1979, p. 159).

The problems observed in the economic development process suggest that the equilibrium school is not a useful model for considering economic development by entrepreneurs. However, both the psychological and the Austrian approaches have the potential for contribution. The use of both models together requires some additional explanation, since most often they are seen as competing rather than complementary models.

Schumpeter versus Kirzner: Same Coin – Different Sides

Although Schumpeter (Schumpeter 1934) also is Austrian, his views on entrepreneurship are quite different from Kirzner's, and according to Hakelius (1995) Schumpeter's view on the entrepreneur cannot be regarded as part of the mainstream Austrian school. Schumpeter's entrepreneur is an innovator, which may explain why so many venture capitalists and technology entrepreneurs cite him as an intellectual father of the field; it best fits their perceptions of the phenomenon. Kirzner (1973, 1979) sees the entrepreneur as an actor in the process-conscious market theory who exhibits deliberate behaviours. That is, where Schumpeter's innovator is shifting the costs and revenue curves (through innovation) Kirzner's entrepreneur is, through entrepreneurial alertness, able to notice that the curves have shifted. This means that Schumpeter's entrepreneur is working outside the ordinary market processes, whereas Kirzner's entrepreneur is clearly market process based or market driven. Both may be true descriptions, but of very different entrepreneurs. Schumpeter's entrepreneur seeks to drive new markets through disruptive innovation. It could be argued that Kirzner's entrepreneur is more likely to be market oriented whereas Schumpeter's entrepreneur is technology and product oriented. What many fail to appreciate is that there is an intersection of these two views. We argue it is the lack of market orientation that is one of the biggest obstacles within technology entrepreneurship (Brännback and Carsrud 2004; Renko *et al.* 2005).

Although venture capitalists, for example, clearly regard breakthrough technology through Schumpeterian lenses, we argue that it is not only possible, but also necessary, to look at the phenomenon through Kirznerian lenses. There is a confusion of Schumpeterian and Kirznerian perspectives. They are not mutually exclusive but should be integrated to fully understand the phenomenon. Shane (2003) summarizes differences between Schumpeterian and Kirznerian opportunity recognition, which at first

Table 15.1 Schumpeterian versus Kirznerian opportunity recognition

Schumpeterian opportunities	Kirznerian opportunities
Disequilibrating	Equilibrating
Requires new knowledge	Does not require new knowledge
Very innovative	Less innovative
Rare	Common
Involves creation	Limited discovery

Source: Adapted from Shane (2003, p. 21).

glance seems acceptable but is according to our understanding perhaps too simplified (Table 15.1).

We have in Table 15.1 shaded the perceptions which we find problematic. First of all, on the argument that Kirznerian opportunities do not require new knowledge we disagree with Shane (2003). Kirzner (1973, 1979) argues that entrepreneurship is based on the entrepreneur's ability (alertness, which is based on knowledge he possesses but nobody else) to identify market ignorance with respect to a certain opportunity. This leads the entrepreneur to spot an opportunity. Once the opportunity is pursued by the entrepreneur and the market becomes aware, it arrives as a new piece of information to the market and all the other would-be entrepreneurs, and not just the entrepreneur who initially discovered the opportunity – the Eureka! phenomenon.

Moreover, the Kirznerian – market-oriented – entrepreneur may well have been doing careful market analysis and with his knowledge of existing innovations and an ability to combine these innovations is able to identify an opportunity. His ability to combine must certainly be regarded as an ability to generate new knowledge. This combination can be very innovative and it is certainly very creative. Whether the discovery is limited or not has to be decided against the economic effect over time that the opportunity creates. For example, the Internet in 1969 was certainly based on new knowledge; it was very innovative and unique and involved creation. But the number of people who saw a benefit from (or even knew about) it at the time was very limited – limited to highly skilled computer scientists and certain university personnel.

An Example: The Internet

The Internet was created in 1969. But the 'Are you receiving this?' meant very little to most of us. It required another innovation, the world wide web, 20 years later, and not even then was the road readily paved. This did not happen until the user interface Mosaic was created in 1992, which made it possible for computer-illiterate persons to use the Internet, and only then did the Internet achieve box-office success. The world wide web was new knowledge, which was unique and innovative and involved creation, yet it was still very limited in terms of its initial benefits. It was the combination of the Internet and the world wide web with the front end – again new knowledge and indeed innovative and creative – which made the whole bundle very common. Those who possessed information technology knowledge saw an ocean of opportunities, which the ignorant market did not. Then the market equilibrated around the turn of the twenty-first century and the air went out of the bubble. In reality, the world wide web is best understood as a mixture of Schumpeterian and Kirznerian opportunity pursuits.

Thus the model suggests that an entrepreneur does not simply stumble on the opportunity but in fact undertakes his endeavour cognitively rather than through overt behaviour, thus being impacted by any number of factors which may not have been obvious to an external observer. The entrepreneur may previously have done something which makes him a possessor of knowledge enabling him to take advantage of an opportunity which to any outsider is a 'mere windfall'.

The Psychological School

Following the Austrian school an individual would have to be entrepreneurially alert (Kirzner 1973, 1979; Gaglio 1996; Gaglio and Katz 2001). Following the psychological school the entrepreneur's willingness to act would be driven by personal perceived desirability and feasibility (Krueger and Carsrud 1993; Krueger *et al.* 2000) or personal achievement motivation (Carsrud *et al.* 1989), or both. Outsiders are not able to see what the entrepreneur does, as an outsider does not possess the knowledge the entrepreneur possesses and often has no idea what the entrepreneur regards as desirable or feasible – only what the external observer regards as desirable and feasible, which may be very different. Gaglio (1996) has combined these views in a heuristic model of opportunity recognition (Figure 15.1).

An external observer, such as a politician or economic development bureaucrat, may have little or no understanding of the amount of provisioning or groundwork that precedes opportunity recognition and the amount of work that still needs to take place before reaching the ultimate decision to go ahead or just forgetting it. Or perhaps, as Gaglio (1996) notes, only the entrepreneur who is looking for an opportunity can extract

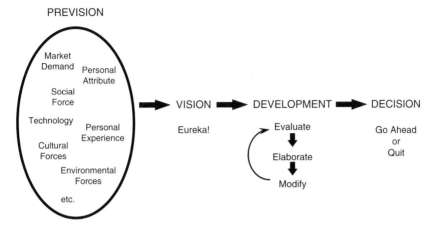

Source: Based on Gaglio (1996).

Figure 15.1   Heuristic model for opportunity recognition

value from a situation. What the entrepreneur must also have is the skills to extract gain from the situation if gain is possible. What is interesting is that if people believe they alone have the ability to take a gain from the situation then they may not in fact receive the kinds of funding or other support they would like. However, the entrepreneur who is willing to share the outcome and understand that things must be a win–win may often be the one who is able to both receive funding and become successful with the new venture. The issue remains that investors may have a perception of the opportunity that is very different from that of the entrepreneur.

For example, a governmental bureaucrat looking at increasing jobs is most likely looking at funding the development of new technology through Schumpeterian lenses, that is, he sees this as a new way of doing something, a way to shift the curve of cost and revenues. Furthermore, it appears as if it is perceived that 'availability of financial resources' is the fundamental (often the only) means by which to achieve that goal. That is, if money is available anyone will recognize this technology as an opportunity. As we can see in Figure 15.1, there is a whole set of *other* factors involved in opportunity recognition. The bureaucrat is looking for the big hit, the paradigm-shifting technology. Schumpeter argues that entrepreneurial behaviour rests on the ability to innovate, and that is what the bureaucrat is reinforcing with funding.

Therefore, in line with our argument, specifically with reference to technology entrepreneurship, when you see something perceived as new technology the commercial significance of the activity, which would be regarded as entrepreneurial, may only show itself some distance in the future. In other words, the Schumpeterian entrepreneur has been so occupied with his innovation that market considerations have been pushed aside 'to a later stage, when time allows'. Those looking only at the immediate scene with Kirznerian lenses, that is, seeing only the innovation, may assume it is not entrepreneurial at all and therefore interpret it simply as a windfall gain. A bureaucrat, venture capitalist or academic theorist looking at the event may not understand the patience and investment that the entrepreneur has invested. Perception, and thus reality of entrepreneurial behaviour, is clearly in the eye of the beholder.

SOLVING THE PROBLEM OF MISPERCEPTION

The lesson of the above exposition and examples is that politicians and bureaucrats involved in economic development investment and tax incentive decisions face three major problems: the cognitive pressures caused by prospect theory in the population and themselves which make unbiased decision making difficult, the difficulty of correctly evaluating technological timelines to establish when to invest in firms, and the perceptual problem of differences between what entrepreneurs see and what seems evident to outsider observers. These problems are actually common to all venture capitalists (or their surrogates), whether housed in government (Jenkins and Leicht 1996) or in the financial sector (Kaplan and Stromberg 2001). As Kaplan and Stromberg point out, there are two solid suggestions for managing the process of investment decision making – screening before investing is central, as is monitoring once investments have been made.

Much of this chapter has focused on three methods for improving the screening process:

1. recognizing, and thereby perhaps accounting for, decisions biased by the drive for big wins brought on by prospect theory;
2. looking at potential investments from a timeline perspective to help better decide when to invest to achieve returns; and
3. recognizing the differing models of entrepreneurial achievement held by entrepreneurs (a Kirznerian one) and economic development professionals (a Schumpeterian one) and from that knowing better where to look for key information about prospective investments.

Most policy makers and venture capitalists cherish Schumpeterian entrepreneurship, as it is regarded as the model of high growth and high return, often understood to also imply high employment, which is of importance to policy makers. This view has also been the driver behind the establishment of science parks in close proximity to start-up firms, universities and other research organizations as prerequisites for success. But this rationale does not reflect the social and psychological realities of entrepreneurs themselves.

For example, in recent years Finland has invested heavily in trying to stimulate high-technology entrepreneurship, with the assumption that success will lead to high-growth firms generating high rates of employment. Most supporting initiatives have this kind of aim. However, it is not clear if a starting technology entrepreneur, with a background in science and hardly any business management experience, really understands the meaning of high growth, or whether high growth ever is a real goal for the start-up technology entrepreneur. High growth may appeal as a fancy dream, but coping with rapid growth of firm size, from for example five persons to 80 persons, is no easy journey but rather something carrying elements of a managerial nightmare. Furthermore, high-technology firms are rarely huge employers, as they often lack labour-intensive production units.

We have been able to describe the phenomenon of entrepreneurial opportunity recognition using the theoretical perspectives of Schumpeter and Kirzner. As we have seen, by contrasting them we can get quite different perceptions that by others can be seen as misperception. But, instead of contrasting these two perspectives as is common, this chapter suggests the need to integrate them to fully understand the relationship between the choice of entrepreneurial strategy and the opportunity exploited.

Kaplan and Stromberg's third suggestion – making investment contingent on contracts – has shown particular promise as a way to minimize poor decisions. The premier model for contracting is based on the concept of real options (McGrath 1999), which looks at investment structured in a staged manner and released when (and only when) benchmark behaviours are demonstrated. This approach permits politicians to exit when the entrepreneur or the firm has not lived up to mutually agreed-upon expectations.

PROBLEMS IN APPLYING NEW APPROACHES

That said, the effort to apply the real-options approach can bring on other political complexities, as can be seen in the example of the Finnish biotechnology industry. Finnish authorities were inspired by stories like Amgen mentioned above and Genentech. Genentech, which when making its IPO had no products and was managed by researchers out of the university labs with no previous business management experience, ended its first day of trading with a stock price of $70, twice the initial price (Robbins-Roth 2000). The Finnish government sought to repeat this big win by betting on new biotechnology firms in Finland (very Schumpeterian).

Finland's first biotechnology firms started to emerge largely in the late 1990s. These small companies, able to get their first rounds of finance, had high hopes that turned sour at the turn of the century. Of the currently existing firms 60 per cent were founded between 1997 and 2003. The companies are small, with 70 per cent employing fewer than ten persons; 60 per cent of the firms are managed by persons with a Ph.D. degree with less than five years of business management experience, and 70 per cent of the firms *together* have a turnover of €1 million, which means one may seriously question their ability to grow (Brännback *et al.* 2004a). The reason for this situation goes back to the end of the 1990s when it was very easy to attract investors' money to get started, in hopes of making a big win similar to Nokia or the beginning-to-boom Internet companies. Many firms were founded around one technology or scientific discovery. Moreover, nobody seemed to question whether high scientific value also meant high commercial value, or how long and what amount of investment it would take to get to the market.

When reality hit the global biotechnology market, venture capitalists declared that they were now only interested in investing in much less risky projects, that is, projects at a later stage, where the probabilities of actual market success would be higher. This meant that small start-up companies whose strategy was early-stage R&D suddenly found themselves without money and increasing demands for results from their investors. Investors were and are still cleaning up their investment portfolios. Hence the Finnish National Fund for Research and Development (Sitra), which has invested in many of the Finnish biotechnology start-up firms, is very much in the same situation as any government economic development bureaucrat. Sitra has a portfolio liability and is reorganizing its portfolio according to the present trend (Sitra 2004, p 8). 'We will continue to exit especially from companies in the growth and reorganization stage, but we do want to ensure that they have a secure future ahead', Sjöblom, the CFO of Sitra, says. Since 1997, Sitra has played an active part in creating the Finnish life sciences cluster. Many of the companies in its life sciences portfolio have reached a stage where they need more capital and also international investors. Sitra is no longer able to fund its portfolio companies' development projects, which may continue for several years and require hundreds of millions of euros in additional venture capital. 'We seek to secure the funding of life sciences companies with a venture capital process which may lead to a new fund based on both Finnish and international capital. The aim is to build up sufficient capital during 2005. We will still make further investments in 2005 to retain the value of the investment and secure development work in the companies', says Sjöblom. While Sitra may have failed in terms of screening, it has made a better effort around monitoring, and has attempted to structure its contracts with an eye toward real options, seeking to limit subsequent rounds of investments to situations which warrant it on economic grounds.

Such efforts are far more difficult to sustain in government than in the private sector, because of the enduring potential for political pressures to help prevent job loss, or mitigate localized depressions in areas hard hit by closing companies. Such pressures are in large part why the World Bank (2001) believes that government bureaucrats make poor bank managers and, to be sure, the history of economic development efforts (Fisher and Peters 1998; Gardner *et al.* 2001; Peters and Fisher 2002) shows these problems are a constant threat to the economic development decision maker.

CONCLUSIONS

This period of market rebounding, between major bubbles of investment, where portfolios are being re-evaluated and rebalanced, is perhaps the best time to make efforts to implement superior methods for making sound economic investment decisions and even shifting the focus from big wins to small ones, so that the next inevitable round of economic development incentives can be better managed than the last. It is also evident that government officials, venture capitalists and entrepreneurs need to better understand the models and assumptions that the others are using with respect to investment and the venture if they are going to better cooperate and collaborate in new venture creation and economic development.

REFERENCES

Ajzen, I. (1987), 'Attitudes, traits and actions: Dispositional prediction of behavior in social psychology', *Advances in Experimental Social Psychology*, **20**, 1–63.
Ali-Yrkkö, J. and R. Hermans (2002), 'Nokia in the Finnish innovation system', Discussion paper no. 811, ETLA, Helsinki.
Bird, B. (1988), 'Implementing entrepreneurial ideas: The case for intentions', *Academy of Management Review*, **13**(3), 442–54.
Brännback, M. and A. Carsrud (2004), 'The importance of strategic market management in biotechnology', *Bioforum Europe*, **1**, 18–20.
Brännback, M., M. Jalkanen, K. Kurkela and E. Soppi (2004a), 'Pharma development in Finland today and in 2015', *Technology Review*, **163**, TEKES, Helsinki.

Brännback, M., A. Carsrud, M. Renko, I. Hudd and L. Nordberg (2004b), 'Perception of critical success factors and entrepreneurial growth strategies: Two experimental studies', paper presented at the Babson Kauffman Conference on Entrepreneurship Research, Glasgow, 3–5 June.

Brännback, M., J. Heinonen, I. Hudd and K. Paasio (2005a), 'A comparative study on entrepreneurial opportunity recognition and the role of education among Finnish business school students', paper presented at the 50th ICSB conference, Washington, DC, 15–18 June.

Brännback, M., A. Carsrud, M. Renko, I. Hudd and L. Nordberg (2005b), 'Perceived success factors in start up and growth strategies: A comparative study of entrepreneurs, managers, and students', paper presented at the 50th ICSB conference, Washington, DC, 15–18 June.

Buchholz, D. and W. Schweke (2000), 'Another century of smokestack chasing?', *Corporation for Enterprise Development*, **2**(1), available at http://www.cfed.org/publications/account-ability/Accountability%20Jan%2000.pdf (accessed 30 July 2006).

Burstein, M.L. and A.J. Rolnick (1995), 'Congress should end the economic war among the states', *Federal Reserve Bank of Minneapolis: The Region*, **9**, 3–20.

Carsrud, A.L. (1989), 'In the beginning: Concept development, feasibility analysis, and value creation', in O. Hagan, C. Rivchun and D. Sexton (eds), *Women Business-Owners*, Cambridge: Ballinger, pp.35–54.

Carsrud, A.L. and B.B. Ellison (1992), 'Turning academic research into enterprise: An exploratory study of the United Kingdom', in R.M. Schwartz (ed.), *Managing Organizational Transitions in a Global Economy*, Los Angeles: Institute of Industrial Relations/UCLA Press, pp.119–48. First published: Durham, UK: AMPI Trust (Oxford) and Durham University Business School, 1989.

Carsrud, A.L., K.W. Olm and G.G. Eddy (1986), 'Entrepreneurship research: In quest of a paradigm', in D.L. Sexton and R.W. Smilor (eds), *The Art and Science of Entrepreneurship*, Cambridge, MA: Ballinger, pp.367–76.

Carsrud, A.L., K. Olm and J. Thomas (1989), 'Predicting entrepreneurial success: Effects of multi-dimensional achievement motivation, levels of ownership, and cooperative relationships', *Entrepreneurship and Regional Development*, **1**(3), 237–44.

Carsrud, A.L., M. Brännback and M. Renko (2008), 'Strategy and strategic thinking in biotechnology entrepreneurship', in H. Patzelt and T. Brenner (eds), *Handbook of Bioentrepreneurship*, New York: Springer, pp.83–103.

Cox, W.M. and R. Alm (1999), *Myths of Rich and Poor*, New York: Basic Books.

Delmar, F., J. Wiklund and K. Sjöberg (2003), *The Involvement in Self-Employment among Swedish Science and Technology Labor Force between 1990 and 2000*, Stockholm: Swedish Institute for Growth Policy Studies.

Dosi, G., and L. Orseniego (1988), 'Coordination and transformation: An overview of structures, behaviours and changes in evolutionary environments', in G. Dosi *et al.* (eds), *Technical Change and Economic Theory*, London: Pinter, pp.13–37.

Drucker, P.F. (2002), *Managing in the Next Society*, New York: Truman Talley Books.

Eckhardt, J.T. and S. Shane (2003), 'Opportunities and entrepreneurship', *Journal of Management*, **29**(3), 333–49.

Farnham, B. (1992), 'Roosevelt and the Munich crisis: Insights from prospect theory', *Political Psychology*, **13**(2), 205–35.

Fisher, P.S. and A.H. Peters (1998), *Industrial Incentives: Competition among American States and Cities*, Kalamazoo, MI: W.E. Upjohn Institute for Employment Research.

Gaglio, C.M. (1996), 'The entrepreneurial opportunity identification process', Ph.D. dissertation, Department of Psychology, University of Chicago.

Gaglio, C.M. and J.A. Katz (2001), 'The psychological basis of opportunity identification: Entrepreneurial alertness', *Small Business Economics*, **16**(2), 95–111.

Gardner Jr, E.I., R.S. Montjoy and D.J. Watson (2001), 'Moving into global competition: A case study of Alabama's recruitment of Mercedes-Benz', *Policy Studies Review*, **18**(3), 80–94.

Gould, A.C. and A.J. Maggio (2003a), 'A framing-effects model and experimental data',

2003 Annual Meeting of the Midwest Political Science Association, Chicago, 3–6 April, available at http://www.nd.edu/~alfac/gould/Gould%20&%20Maggio%20Political%20 Regimes%20and%20Economic%20Development.pdf

Gould, A.C. and A.J. Maggio (2003b), 'Political regimes and economic development: A model of reference-dependent choices and experimental data', 2003 Annual Meeting of the American Political Science Association, 28–31 August, available at http://www.asu.edu/ clas/polisci/cqrm/APSA2003/Gould&Maggio_APSA2003.pdf

Grant II, D.S. and R. Hutchinson (1996), 'Global smokestack chasing: A comparison of the state-level determinants of foreign and domestic manufacturing investment', *Social Problems*, **43**(1), 21–38.

Grundsten, H. (2004), *Entrepreneurial Intentions and the Entrepreneurial Environment: A Study of Technology-Based New Venture Creation*, Ph.D. dissertation series, Helsinki: Helsinki University of Technology.

Hakelius, J. (1995), *Den österikiska skolan: Introduktion till humanistisk nationalekonomi*, Stockholm: Timbro.

Harrison, R.T. (2003), 'Maximising the potential of university spinouts', presentation held at Florida International University, Miami, 21 October.

Hjalmarsson, D. and A.W. Johansson (2003), 'Public advisory services – theory and practice', *Entrepreneurship & Regional Development*, **15**(1), 83–98.

Jenkins, J.C. and K.T. Leicht (1996), 'Direct intervention by the subnational state: The development of public venture capital programs in the American states', *Social Problems*, **43**(3), 306–26.

Jervis, R. (1992), 'Political implications of loss aversion', *Political Psychology*, **13**(2), 187–204.

Jolly, V.K. (1997), *Commercializing New Technologies*, Boston, MA: Harvard Business School Press.

Kahneman, D. and A. Tversky (1979), 'Prospect theory: An analysis of decision under risk', *Econometrica*, **47**(2), 263–92.

Kaplan, S.N. and P. Stromberg (2001), 'Venture capitalists as principals: Contracting, screening, and monitoring', *American Economic Review*, **91**(2), 426–30.

Katz, J. and B.W. Gartner (1988), 'Properties of emerging organizations', *Academy of Management Review*, **13**(3), 429–41.

Kirzner, I.M. (1973), *Competition and Entrepreneurship*, Chicago: University of Chicago Press.

Kirzner, I.M. (1979), *Perception, Opportunity, and Profit*, Chicago: University of Chicago Press.

Kirzner, I.M. (1992), *The Meaning of Market Process*, London: Routledge.

Koehn, N.F. (2001), *Brand New*, Boston, MA: Harvard Business School Press.

Krueger, N. and A. Carsrud (1993), 'Entrepreneurial intentions: Applying the theory of planned behaviour', *Entrepreneurship and Regional Development*, **5**, 315–30.

Krueger, N.F., M.D. Reilly and A.L. Carsrud (2000), 'Competing models of entrepreneurial intentions', *Journal of Business Venturing*, **15**(5–6), 411–32.

Levy, J.S. (1997), 'Prospect theory, rational choice, and international relations', *International Studies Quarterly*, **41**(1), 87–112.

Levy, J.S. (2003), 'Applications of prospect theory to political science', *Synthese*, **135**(2), 215–41.

McDermott, R. (1992), 'Prospect theory in international relations: The Iranian hostage rescue mission', *Political Psychology*, **13**(2), 237–63.

McDermott, R. (1998), *Risk-Taking in International Politics: Prospect Theory in American Foreign Policy*, Ann Arbor: University of Michigan Press.

McGrath, R.G. (1999), 'Falling forward: Real options reasoning and entrepreneurial failure', *Academy of Management Review*, **24**(1), 13–30.

McInerney, A. (1992), 'Prospect theory and Soviet policy towards Syria, 1966–1967', *Political Psychology*, **13**(2), 265–82.

Oliver, R.W. (2000), *The Coming of the Biotech Age*, New York: McGraw-Hill.

Peters, A. and P. Fisher (2002), *State Enterprise Zone Programs: Have They Worked?*, Kalamazoo, MI: W.E. Upjohn Institute for Employment Research.

Renko, M., A. Carsrud, M. Brännback and J. Jalkanen (2005), 'Market pull and science push – networked market orientation of biotechnology SMEs', *International Journal of Biotechnology*, **7**(4), 250–68.

Reuschmeyer, D. and P. Evans (1985), 'The state and economic transformation', in P. Evans, D. Reuschmeyer and T. Stockpol (eds), *Bringing the State Back In*, New York: Cambridge University Press, pp. 44–77.

Reynolds, P. (2005), *Assessment of Entrepreneurship in the U.S.*, Miami: Entrepreneurship Research Institute, Eugenio Pino and Family Global Entrepreneurship Center, Florida International University.

Robbins-Roth, C. (2000), *From Alchemy to IPO*, Cambridge, MA: Perseus Publishing.

Ronstadt, R. (1988), 'The corridor principle', *Journal of Business Venturing*, **3**(1), 31–40.

Rosenberg, N. (1994), 'Uncertainty and technological change', Conference on Growth and Development: The Economics of the 21st Century, Stanford University Center for Economic Policy Research, Stanford, CA.

Schumpeter, J.A. (1934), *The Theory of Economic Development*, Oxford: Oxford University Press.

Schweke, W., C. Rist and B. Dabson (1994), *Bidding for Business: Are State and Local Governments Selling Themselves Short?*, Washington, DC: CFED.

Shane, S. (2000), 'Prior knowledge and the discovery of entrepreneurial opportunities', *Organization Science*, **11**(4), 448–69.

Shane, S. (2003), *A General Theory of Entrepreneurship*, Cheltenham, UK and Northampton, MA, USA: Edward Elgar Publishing.

Shane, S. and S. Venkataraman (2000), 'The promise of entrepreneurship as a field of research', *Academy of Management Review*, **25**(1), 217–26.

Sitra (2004), *Sitra Annual Report 2004*, Helsinki: Finnish National Fund for Research and Development Sitra.

Staw, B.M. (1981), 'The escalation of commitment to a course of action', *Academy of Management Review*, **6**(4), 577–87.

Steinbock, D. (2006), *Finland's Innovative Capacity*, Regional Development 13/2006, Helsinki: Finnish Ministry of Internal Affairs.

Tosto, P. and F. Monk (1993), 'Mercedes-Benz chooses Alabama site for first U.S. plant', *Knight Ridder/Tribune Business News*, 29 September 1993, p09290150, available at http://galenet.galegroup.com.ezp.slu.edu/servlet/BCRC?vrsn=149&locID=morenetslu&srchtp=glb&c=14&ste=25&tab=2&tbst=tsAS&mst=mercedes+benz%2C+alabama&docNum=CJ13299067&bConts=0 (accessed 30 July 2006).

Tversky, A. and D. Kahneman (1986), 'Rationality in psychology: The contrast with economics, rational choice and the framing of decisions', *Journal of Business*, **59**(4), 251–78.

Watson, D.J. (1995), *The New Civil War*, Westport, CT: Praeger.

Weick, K. (1984), 'Small wins: Redefining the scale of social problems', *American Psychologist*, **39**(1), 40–49.

Weyland, K. (1996), 'Risk-taking in Latin American economic restructuring', *International Studies Quarterly*, **40**(2), 185–207.

Weyland, K. (2002), *The Politics of Market Reform in Fragile Democracies: Argentina, Brazil, Peru, and Venezuela*, Princeton, NJ: Princeton University Press.

World Bank (2001), *World Employment Report*, chapter on information technologies and SMEs, Geneva: ILO.

16 Entrepreneurship education and new venture creation: a comprehensive approach
Torben Bager

INTRODUCTION

Policy makers across the world increasingly see entrepreneurship education as important. Following the argumentation by leading economists and international organizations like the OECD and the EU, and assisted by growing media attention, they see the ability to foster ideas, pursue innovation and create new ventures as core to economic progress (Schramm 2006; EU Expert Group 2008; OECD 2008). The economic rationale behind this view can often be boiled down to 'more jobs', particularly more knowledge-intensive jobs. Entrepreneurship education is assumed to lead to more knowledge-intensive start-ups and more high-end innovation in existing firms, which are seen as basic drivers in long-term job creation.

This has implications for the educational system. It has long been commonplace to regard education as a key to improved economic performance in knowledge-intensive economies, but education does not by itself produce the needed entrepreneurial capacity and may even diminish this capacity through overdose of lecturing and limited involvement of the learners (Baumol 2004). In addition, policy makers increasingly understand that improved educational standards and research output does not by itself lead to a higher level of knowledge spillover from universities and other research institutions to society (Audretsch and Keilbach 2007).

Therefore they argue for a change in the educational system in general and universities in particular, seeing entrepreneurship teaching and training as an important means to achieve overall economic goals. In this view, entrepreneurship teaching and training should permeate the entire educational system to such an extent that all young people, whatever educational level they reach, are exposed substantially to entrepreneurship in theory and praxis during their time in the educational system.

This dominant line of thinking by policy makers, which is found in many countries and across all continents, is generally not embraced by educators and educational institutions and is often met by substantial resistance, particularly at universities. Educators tend to focus upon and embrace their particular disciplines, which is incompatible with entrepreneurship training in cross-disciplinary settings. Moreover, they are most comfortable working with the transfer of bits of established knowledge rather than facilitation of learning processes and creation of new knowledge, and they often distance themselves from praxis, understanding their role as indirect preparation for future practices rather than direct practical and vocational training (Scharmer 2007).

In this chapter, my focus is on the role of universities in this process. Policy makers see universities as essential in the change process, but universities often find it difficult to align this political interest with fundamental university principles and the way academia understands itself. In particular, that very important component of entrepreneurship, new venture creation, tends to be seen by universities as a practical, a-theoretical effort, which is difficult to teach at theory-driven institutions. While flattered by the political interest, university leaders often see graduate entrepreneurship as an add-on activity, something useful at the end of the study period, when students are 'handed back' to society prepared for a graduate career whether as employee or as entrepreneur, but not as something fundamental to the 'heart and soul' of universities. The dominant view at universities is that students first and foremost have to learn a discipline plus some general academic qualifications such as the ability to analyse, generalize, reflect and participate in academic debates. Concentration should therefore be on capturing established bodies of knowledge, understanding theory and, according to Alfred N. Whitehead, understanding the deeper principles behind specific knowledge (Whitehead [1929] 1967).

This classic position at universities is, however, increasingly disputed. Prominent scholars like C. Otto Scharmer and Allan Gibb argue that fundamental change is needed at universities, injecting these old institutions with an entrepreneurial culture and strategy (Scharmer and Käufer 2000; Gibb 2006). Entrepreneurship education can be seen as a spearhead for such change, calling for cross-disciplinary activities, new participatory and innovative teaching methods and substantial involvement of outsiders in the teaching and learning process at universities. This challenge to traditional universities is growing across the world in terms of a steep increase in the number of entrepreneurship programmes offered, the number of trained entrepreneurship scholars and educators and the number of universities with a centre of entrepreneurship. The formation and growth of the Global Consortium of Entrepreneurship Centres illustrates the drive.

Taken together, however, entrepreneurship education remains tolerated at most universities rather than embraced. Entrepreneurship has expanded and consolidated as a field and is today a recognized discipline, but has not yet unfolded its potential. It remains an add-on activity in most places rather than a top priority and a top-management-driven process.

THE NARROW AND COMPREHENSIVE PERSPECTIVES ON ENTREPRENEURSHIP EDUCATION

One of the reasons why entrepreneurship education meets substantial resistance at universities is the prevailing narrow understanding of the field. It tends to be understood as a praxis-oriented start-a-firm activity, valuable for the creation of new firms and jobs in society, but of limited academic value. This view is supported by the narrow praxis at many universities. It is often just a start-up course plus some venturing support activities through incubators, venture competitions, venture finance schemes and so on. The entrepreneurship field can, however, also be understood and practised in a much broader way, namely as a means to strengthen university–business relationships, disseminate cross-disciplinary learning activities and build entrepreneurial mindsets rather than just start-up skills (Hindle 2007).

Different rationales shape the outlined narrow and comprehensive perspectives, as illustrated by Table 16.1.

Most universities follow the narrow perspective when they move into the field, focusing on the instrumental skills needed to establish a new firm. Therefore entrepreneurship programmes tend to contain three course elements:

- entrepreneurship orientation and awareness programmes which provide general information and encourage students to consider a career as an entrepreneur;
- new enterprise creation designed to develop competences which lead to self-employment and the generation of new jobs;
- the survival and growth of young/small businesses.

The focus in these programmes is on ventures rather than the persons behind the ventures. They do not deal much with the development of the personal skills, attributes, behaviour and empathy of entrepreneurs (and intrapreneurs). David Kirby argues that these programmes thereby miss something essential:

> The successful entrepreneur has a set of personal skills that goes beyond the purely commercial. It is these attributes, this way of thinking and behaving,

Table 16.1   *The rationales behind the narrow and comprehensive*
perspective on entrepreneurship education at universities

	Narrow perspective	Comprehensive perspective
Overall rationale	Teaching venture creation	Developing entrepreneurial mindsets
Learning rationale	Instrumental 'doer' skills	Mastering ideation
Teaching rationale	Knowledge transfer	Facilitation of knowledge and competences
University rationale	Add-on activity	Core strategic activity
Business rationale	Supporting new entrepreneurs	Entrepreneurial capacity in emerging and existing organizations
Economic rationale	More graduate start-up firms	Knowledge spillover from universities
Policy rationale	More knowledge-intensive jobs	An entrepreneurial economy

which needs to be developed in students if their entrepreneurial capabilities are to be enhanced and they are to be equipped to meet the challenges of the entrepreneurial climate of the twenty-first century. (Kirby 2004, p. 514)

These personal dimensions cannot be learned well through traditional lecturing about entrepreneurship with students predominantly in passive roles: listening, reading and memorizing. Students need to be involved, almost drawn into the entrepreneurship field, sensing what it is like to be confronted with the uncertainties and complexities entrepreneurs constantly are facing. So, to learn the entrepreneurship field effectively, alternative teaching forms and learning models should be applied, challenging the dominant teaching models at universities. According to Gibb, much still needs to be changed in this respect: 'Only a very limited pedagogical range is currently applied, mainly cases, lectures, projects, visits and some skills training (for example presentations). Entrepreneurial behaviours, skills and attributes, nurtured by well designed pedagogies and exposure to experience are essential components of being able to "feel" what it is like to be entrepreneurial' (Gibb 2006, p. 3).

On the other hand, some progress has been made in teaching methodology in recent years. In fact the field of entrepreneurship has, because of the need to teach *in* and sometimes *for* entrepreneurship and not just *about* it, spearheaded new teaching methods. As observed by the guest editors of a special issue of *Academy of Management Learning and Education*: 'Entrepreneurship education has been the testing ground for many important techniques in business education. Computer-driven simulations, interdisciplinary models of education, and the structured use of practitioners in the classroom are all innovations that got some of their earliest starts in the entrepreneurship classroom' (Greene *et al.* 2004, p. 238).

In the following sections, I first take a closer look at the entrepreneurship education field and core concepts used in this field. While discussing various aspects of entrepreneurship education, I try to bridge the outlined narrow and broad perspectives, keeping in mind that any entrepreneurial venture needs a subject (a human actor) and an object (the venture project) (Fayolle 2003). The idea always springs from the mind of a human actor and gradually depersonalizes as the venture emerges and develops. The chapter then turns to the ways universities can facilitate the formation of student and graduate start-ups and enhance knowledge spillover to society. The chapter closes by outlining the discussion about future universities and the role of the entrepreneurship field in shaping them.

THE ENTREPRENEURSHIP EDUCATION FIELD

Inspired by the widely used entrepreneurship definition by Shane and Venkataraman (2000), I here define entrepreneurship education as: 'The transfer and facilitation of knowledge and competences about how, by whom and with what effects opportunities to create future goods and services are discovered, evaluated and exploited'.

This definition is identical with the one proposed by Kevin Hindle (2007), except that I have added 'facilitation' and 'competences' to include the comprehensive perspective outlined above. Entrepreneurship education is not only about transfer of knowledge, but also about facilitation of knowledge creation processes; and it is not only about cognitive knowledge about a scientific field, but also about the competence to master venture creation processes.

The definition clearly encompasses practical 'how to' issues as well as analytical issues such as the impact of entrepreneurial activity on the economy, which again suggests that we have to distinguish between teaching *in* entrepreneurship on the one hand and teaching *about* the phenomenon on the other hand. Teaching about entrepreneurship as a field, introducing students to the scholars, theories and so on in the field, is clearly as relevant here as in any other discipline, but also insufficient. The challenge is to move students from their normal distanced position into the field, instilling skills and letting them experience personally, through role-play, simulations, field work and so on, the role of the entrepreneur (Löbler 2006). This way students are likely to experience what it is like 'out there', facilitating their own reflection about their identity as students, nascent entrepreneurs and so on, while also adding to their theoretical understanding of the field.

The entrepreneurship field cannot be distinguished sharply from other business and management fields. Developing a new venture or firm encompasses traditional study fields such as finance, accountancy, marketing, strategy and organization. It approaches these fields differently owing to the venture creation angle rather than the large firm angle, for example focusing on early-stage finance through the three Fs (family, fools, friends), as this is a very important financial source for start-ups. Nevertheless, we are here dealing with established fields. Where entrepreneurship teaching contributes something unique and has its own playing ground is in the discovery and evaluation dimensions rather than the exploitation dimension. Discovering (or creating) a new idea, which by definition entails a gap to a possible future state, and evaluating a priori its chance of succeeding are not dealt with systematically in any other discipline (Shane and Venkataraman 2000).

THE COMPONENTS OF COMPREHENSIVE ENTREPRENEURSHIP EDUCATION

The Core Competence of Opportunity Recognition and Evaluation

Venturing and organization building can be looked at as something very practical, but also as something almost artistic and highly imaginative. The ambiguous character of the venturing process in fact dates back to Schumpeter's pioneering work (Schumpeter 1934). Basically, he saw entrepreneurs as innovators in the economy, contributing something new, but he also distinguished between the role of the inventor and that of the entrepreneur, seeing the entrepreneur as a businessperson who recognizes the value of an invention, determines how to adapt it to user preferences, brings the invention to the market and promotes its utilization. In this view, new venturing skills are about the 'doing' side rather than the invention and ideation side, while others would argue that idea generation and matching ideas with opportunities are core to the entrepreneurship field and the important starting point for any venture – and therefore something in which training needs to be given at universities. In fact one could argue that this is the truly artistic or imaginative side, where universities have an important contribution to make to the entrepreneurship education field, while instrumental venturing skills are better taught by other institutions or simply learned based on experience by a doing-and-reflection process (Kolb 1984).

As shown by the experiment undertaken at an American university with two groups of students (De Tienne and Chandler 2004), idea generation and opportunity recognition – often labelled 'ideation' – can actually be learned and taught at universities. Students who participated in the course were able to raise more ideas and more innovative ideas than other students at the same university. This study also suggests that business plan courses, which are common these days at universities, are well advised to work much more with ideas and opportunities than is usually the case. Business plan courses tend to rush through the ideation phase to get into the more instrumental and planning-oriented phase. If the prime goal is to finalize a comprehensive plan, ready to be implemented, this may be valuable, but if the objective is to maximize the long-term learning of students, giving them something of value for future careers, it is not appropriate. As ideation is core to entrepreneurship students, they ought to raise many ideas and identify many opportunities during their studies. Thereby they may, like serial entrepreneurs, develop skills in ideation and prepare for early-stage venturing efforts in future careers (Shane 2000; Davidsson 2006).

Evaluating an idea and a business opportunity is always a part of a venturing process, but is seldom, in practice, conducted systematically. Evaluation is the process whereby one assesses whether an idea can be turned into an opportunity and implemented. This entails estimating future conditions: an activity naturally loaded with uncertainty.

For investors evaluation is core. When confronted with a venture idea an investor must evaluate the chance of success or failure and based on this elaborate investment conditions. Nevertheless, even professional investors tend to rely on their experience and checklists rather than a systematic approach.

A system for software-supported systematic venture evaluation is presented in Hindle *et al.* (2007). The evaluation process is structured here along five dimensions – product, market, industry, people and money – and three levels: idea assessment, idea enhancement and venture implementation. Through such evaluation, which of course is largely subjective, an overall estimate of the potential of the idea is reached. Evaluation of the same venture can be made by different people independently and then be used as a platform for systematic discussion. Evaluation exercises can also be practised in the classroom based on concrete venture cases.

The Competence to Exploit Opportunities and Build Organizations

Once an idea is identified and evaluated, it needs to be exploited. This takes organizational efforts of some kind, usually the building of a new organization. Organization-building skills can be understood as something very practical and instrumental, and therefore perhaps taught better at other places than universities, as suggested by Hindle (2007) and others, or it can be understood as a complex matter needing mastering skills rather than instrumental skills. Certainly, there is a very practical 'how to' side of the venturing process: finding funds, organizing a team, establishing facilities and so on. And, to build a new organization, knowledge about traditional business school topics such as marketing, HRM, accounting, financing and strategy is important. However, venturing and organization building also have a more complex side, such as exploring competitors, reshaping the original idea, crafting a strategy, involving customers, finding partners, recruiting qualified and committed employees and so on. Naturally, this complexity varies tremendously from case to case, but typically knowledge-intensive venturing is burdened with high complexity and uncertainty. Therefore mastering the entire situation and keeping eyes open for new opportunities during the process where a new organization emerges and takes shape are key competences in such organization-building processes – and therefore requested in teaching efforts at universities. So fully developed entrepreneurship education programmes should not only include traditional business school topics and practical training but also train students to work at the edge of chaos while staying on the chosen track.

Building Entrepreneurial Mindsets

Entrepreneurship education, however, is not just about traditional knowledge and competence-building efforts through courses. In order to produce, at the end of the day, more entrepreneurial graduates, the personality side has to be considered. Graduates not only need to be entrepreneurially competent, but also need to be entrepreneurial persons. Entrepreneurship education programmes therefore need to consider how they can influence the mindset, behaviour and intentions of students.

Entrepreneurship researchers have not been able to find any unique personality traits for entrepreneurs, but cognitive dimensions are demonstrably important (Aldrich 1999; Shane 2003). Entrepreneurs tend to understand and approach the environment differently to non-entrepreneurs. They tend to be more aware of and even alert to new ideas and opportunities than other people, and they tend to approach a task or challenge with great confidence in their own capability and with an optimistic view, often characterized as over-optimism in the literature (Audretsch *et al.* 2007).

Alertness to opportunities combined with self-confidence and over-optimism is often characterized as an entrepreneurial mindset and seen as one of the key challenges entrepreneurship educators face, as students generally do not possess such a mindset when they enter their first entrepreneurship course. Some entrepreneurship educators see the development of an entrepreneurial mindset as the most important outcome of entrepreneurship teaching, and therefore something to aim for deliberately, while others see a change of student mindsets as a likely outcome of teaching and training in the field, but not something to aim for deliberately. These views tie in to the discussion about whether teaching in this field is *for* entrepreneurship or alternatively teaching *about* and *in* the field.

The entrepreneurship literature suggests a huge number of attributes are required by founding entrepreneurs for successful entrepreneurship and new venture creation. Gibb (2006, p. 37) has attempted to summarize the most important ones:

- achievement orientation and ambition;
- self-confidence and self-belief;
- perseverance;
- high internal locus of control (autonomy);
- action orientation;
- preference for learning by doing;
- being hardworking;
- determination;
- creativity.

The concepts of self-confidence and self-belief are close to the self-efficacy concept. Self-efficacy is a psychological concept referring to a person's belief in his or her capability to organize and execute a task such as creating a new venture (Bandura 1997). A high self-efficacy is normally seen as important for venture success, particularly for the ability to exploit opportunities: 'people who have higher self-efficacy are more likely to exploit entrepreneurial opportunities than people who have lower self-efficacy' (Shane 2003, p. 111).

Building Entrepreneurial Behaviour

The importance of an action-oriented approach to entrepreneurship – and entrepreneurship education – has become theoretically underpinned by the so-called effectuation theory (Sarasvathy 2008). Sarasvathy's work demonstrates the important difference between effectual and causal logic in entrepreneurship. This theory suggests that entrepreneurs, moving into unknown territory, depart from means and resources rather than formulated goals and planning. They move into a field, guided by an idea, drawing on existing relationships and building new ones, leveraging contingencies as they appear, and taking care not to move too far and too riskily (the principle of affordable loss). This proactive, field-oriented and cautious approach enables them to shape their idea to customers and markets, and with relatively few resources on board they may create ventures with great potential.

Effectuation theory poses a challenge to entrepreneurship education, as students normally are trained in causal and goal-oriented reasoning before they enter the entrepreneurship class. Entrepreneurship educators should therefore consider causal de-learning efforts before students are open to an action-oriented and effectual logic.

Hindle (forthcoming) has argued that effectual and causal logic are not opponents or mutually incompatible. Both approaches can coexist in various strengths of combination in any given entrepreneurial process. However, entrepreneurship education has tended to emphasize the teaching of causal logic skills and underemphasize the importance of effectual logic and entrepreneurial behaviour. This needs correction.

Action can be seen as necessary 'fuel' to any new venture 'engine'. Potential entrepreneurs who are strong 'doers' perform better than others in terms of succeeding to establish a new firm (Carter *et al.* 1996). Action is not just about being practical; it is also about relationship building with customers, evaluating customer reactions to a product or service, establishing a professional network of people who know the field, approaching financial institutions, and so on. Action is, in other words, also a route to sense making about a new venture. As Weick stresses, using his famous question 'How can I know what I think until I see what I say?', sense making is furthered by talking and acting (Weick 1969). Moreover, action is an input to experiential learning and, as Kolb's learning circle illustrates, practical experience is a foundation for reflection and improved future praxis (Kolb 1984). Finally, action involves meeting others and networking, which is recognized as an important source of information and knowledge for entrepreneurs, and a means to achieve new partners, mentors and so on (Aldrich and Zimmer 1986).

Many students find action training and the development and appreciation of an effectual logic difficult and challenging. In the educational system they have been trained to read, listen, write and reflect, with little action involved. So approaching a new customer, pitching an idea to a banker, negotiating with a partner, adapting quickly to circumstances and similar actions are not easy for students. However, these dimensions, often neglected in the typical university course, can be taught and, in order to reach a relevant and high learning outcome, they should be taught.

Action orientation is not built only in the classroom. Extraordinary activities at universities such as business plan competitions, pitch events and the establishment of student hatcheries are also needed.

Student hatcheries and university incubators are now established at numerous universities in the US, Europe and other parts of the world. The objective is to assist students and graduates with new venture ideas. Here students and graduate entrepreneurs are typically offered low-cost access to basic business infrastructure (desks, computers, phones, etc.) as well as mentoring and advisory services from faculty members or entrepreneurs. At some US universities, such as Belmont University, a hatchery and an incubator exist side by side, capturing both early-stage and mature venture projects. At some European universities, the physical space is also used for extra-curriculum training activities. These activities may involve students from several faculties, universities and hatcheries to benefit from large-scale advantages. Training can take place at university premises, or be arranged as special student innovation camps outside the university, usually with the active involvement of 'outsiders' (Bager 2009). Participation in such camps can be part of a curriculum or be an extra-curricular activity. The overall purpose is to work innovatively in cross-disciplinary settings, applying disciplinary knowledge to foster new ideas and find solutions to posed problems. This way the cognitive knowledge students bring from the classroom is transformed to an operational competence by means of an action learning process which is similar to cross-disciplinary and innovative processes outside the university.

Building Entrepreneurial Intention

Intentionality is strongly related to action, so if entrepreneurship teaching instils students with an intention to start a new venture they are likely to do so, at least at some point in their life. Intentions are rooted in attitudes and perceptions of what is personally and socially desirable. Ajzen's so-called 'theory of planned behaviour' argues that perceptions of desirability and feasibility influence attitudes and explain and predict intentions significantly. Empirical evidence supports this argument (Ajzen 1991; Lüthje and Franke 2003).

Entrepreneurship competences influence intentions positively in that knowledge about entrepreneurship and practical training or experience in venturing makes the entrepreneurial act more feasible. Having entrepreneurship knowledge, start-up experience and specific knowledge of a business field enhances the chance of a successful start-up, thereby raising positive expectations about the outcome and furthering the intent to start (Krüger *et al.* 2000).

So entrepreneurship education promises to increase the probability of entrepreneurial acts by students and alumni by influencing their mindset, attitudes and expectation of a positive outcome of an eventual start-up act. However, whether or not they actually do involve themselves in start-up activities depends on situational factors in their present and future life, for example being fired from a good job or suddenly discovering a promising business opportunity. Entrepreneurship education provides a knowledge and mindset platform for graduate venturing, but triggering events are needed to launch new ventures.

The test of this line of argument is whether students who have participated in entrepreneurship education are more likely than similar students to start a firm at some point in their life. Such studies are difficult to implement, however, for two major reasons. First, the control group may be similar in terms of study background, gender composition and so on, but is nevertheless not identical with the entrepreneurship group owing to self-selection bias. Particularly if entrepreneurship courses are electives, students enrolling on the course may be different from other students in terms of mindset, action orientation and so on. Second, such studies are longitudinal and therefore require a time span of at least ten years since study completion.

In spite of the methodological difficulties, some studies have been made in this field, and they generally point to positive effects of entrepreneurship education. A significant study was made of graduates at Arizona University during 1985–99, comparing graduates from the Berger Entrepreneurship Programme and other graduates at the same university. The study concluded, controlling for a number of personal and environmental factors, that entrepreneurship graduates were 25 per cent more likely to be involved in venturing and 11 per cent more likely to be self-employed and had accumulated 62 per cent higher assets. Moreover, entrepreneurship students were more often involved in developing new products and, out of the self-employed, 23 per cent of entrepreneurship graduates owned a high-technology firm against 15 per cent of other graduates (Charney and Liebecap 2000).

In addition to such micro-level studies of the impact of entrepreneurship education, some macro-level studies have also been completed. Using Global Entrepreneurship Monitor data collected over many years in many countries, Autio and Levie reach the overall conclusion that entrepreneurship education in high-income countries, and particularly education at higher educational institutions, has a positive impact on a country's rate of new business activity, including high-growth expectation new business activity (Reynolds *et al.* 2005; Levie and Autio 2008). Moreover, their results suggest that training of instrumental skills is less important than broader educational efforts aiming at opportunity recognition.

Enhancing Knowledge Spillover from Universities through Entrepreneurship Education

Entrepreneurship education should not, according to the comprehensive perspective on entrepreneurship education, be restricted to the classroom. On the contrary, learning processes in the classroom should be combined with extra-curricular learning at the university and outside the university. The economic rationale for university-based entrepreneurship education is in this perspective not just the creation of more student and graduate ventures, but knowledge spillover in a broader sense. Entrepreneurship education then becomes one of the ways to ease the flow of new knowledge and inventions from universities to society.

The so-called 'knowledge spillover theory of entrepreneurship' (Audretsch 2007; Audretsch and Keilbach 2007) focuses on endogenous knowledge produced at universities and other research institutions and the transformation of such knowledge to products, services and solutions by graduate entrepreneurs. The theory departs from the observation of a 'knowledge filter' between new knowledge from universities and firms and entrepreneurs outside the university who are often unable to transform this new knowledge into products, services and solutions. Knowledge spillover from universities does not only refer to the linear commercialization of technologies fostered at universities, which usually are handled by university-based tech trans offices. It also refers to the broader forms of knowledge-sharing processes between universities and 'outsiders', such as the informal movement of knowledge by university staff members and students through interaction with outsiders.

The trigger of this new theory was the observation that political attempts to enhance research output and educational standards at the national level did not automatically lead to higher economic growth, in spite of theories formulated by Romer and other researchers trying to understand the so-called information society and knowledge economy (Romer 1986). While being right in observing that this type of economy is different from the physical economy with its limited resources, these theories did not take the practical performance difficulties of the knowledge spillover problem sufficiently into consideration. If new knowledge and technology remain within the walls of universities and other research institutions, they do not contribute to economic growth. So handling the commercialization and exchange process by matching the output of knowledge with the demand for ideas and knowledge inputs by nascent and established entrepreneurs is core to economic development in advanced economies.

The consequence for universities is that they need to search for ways to combine entrepreneurship education efforts with commercialization and knowledge exchange efforts. The challenge is to combine these two challenges in a unified strategy rather than keeping them separate, as is the case today at most universities, where entrepreneurship education tends to be restricted to the classroom and knowledge dissemination tends to be narrowed down to linear tech trans activities.

TOWARD THE ENTREPRENEURIAL UNIVERSITY

I opened this chapter by pointing to a narrow and comprehensive perspective on entrepreneurship education. The narrow perspective sees entrepreneurship research and education as an add-on activity at the university, a new discipline creating a need for new research and new courses. The comprehensive perspective sees entrepreneurship education as much more than just a few extra researchers and courses. Here it is seen as a core strategic activity, which aims to reach out to all students, revolutionize teaching practices, strengthen university–business collaboration and install an entrepreneurial culture instead of the dominant bureaucratic culture at universities – in short, to develop the Entrepreneurial University (Gibb 2006).

This comprehensive perspective ties into the debate about the identity of the university and its role in contemporary society. According to classic university conceptualization, dating back to Humboldt in the nineteenth century, universities should be independent, governed by faculty, and integrate teaching and research activities. These principles are still influential guides to the way universities are structured, but the principles are in some respects too limited and need reinterpretation or revision. The classic Humboldt type of university lived largely an isolated academic life, separated from the rest of society, and it enjoyed in many respects a knowledge monopoly. This has changed. Universities are, in today's knowledge-powered society, only one out of a number of knowledge centres in society and therefore have to relate to and often compete with these other centres. This led Gibbons to suggest that they should become more open and networking in approach and embrace the new type of experience-based knowledge production which he saw emerge with the knowledge economy. He labelled this 'Mode 2' knowledge production (Gibbons *et al.* 1994).

Scharmer and Käufer have taken this argument a step further, arguing for the need for development of an entrepreneurial university (Scharmer and Käufer 2000). Such a university is characterized by not only organizing research and teaching but also integrating praxis, well in line with Gibbons's Mode 2 argument, and quite revolutionary for an institution, which has traditionally seen itself as distanced from praxis. Moreover, Scharmer and Käufer argue for a new student role, moving them from their predominant passive and recipient role at the Humboldt type of university – listening, reading, writing, memorizing, reflecting and talking – to a more proactive role as initiators and co-producers of new knowledge, embracing future orientation by working with new ideas and the realization of such ideas, often in cross-disciplinary settings. Scharmer sees future orientation and development of our ability to grasp a future state as essential for universities: 'We pour considerable amounts of money into our educational systems, but haven't been able to create schools and institutions of higher education that develop people's innate capacity to sense and shape their future, which I view as the single most important core capability for this century's knowledge and co-creation economy' (Scharmer 2007, p. 3).

The creation of an entrepreneurial university is therefore a deep and huge task. It will require much more than just a few entrepreneurship courses and a few entrepreneurship researchers. It will need a substantial 'package' of initiatives and reforms, consisting of:

- formulation of an overall university strategy and top-management support;
- a variety of entrepreneurship courses, at both introductory and advanced levels;
- entrepreneurship research to back and qualify teaching activities;
- the dissemination of innovation-furthering pedagogy and didactics in other fields as well;
- extra-curricular activities such as events with 'outsiders' and business plan competitions;
- establishment of hatcheries and incubators for entrepreneurship-interested students, staff and graduates;
- the development of an entrepreneurial culture.

So, if we are going to teach the competences and skills of new venture creation effectively, the narrow, isolationist approach is unlikely to suffice. We have to realize that truly effective new venture education can only arise in the context of a deep and wide commitment to a comprehensive approach to entrepreneurship education.

REFERENCES

Ajzen, I. (1991), 'The theory of planned behavior', *Organizational Behavior and Human Decision Processes*, **50**(2), 179–211.

Aldrich, H. (1999), *Organizations Evolving*, London: Sage.

Aldrich, H. and C. Zimmer (1986), 'Entrepreneurship through social networks', in D. Sexton and R. Smilor (eds), *The Art and Science of Entrepreneurship*, New York: Ballinger, pp. 3–23.

Audretsch, D. (2007), *The Entrepreneurial Society*, Oxford: Oxford University Press.

Audretsch, D. and M. Keilbach (2007), 'The theory of knowledge spillover entrepreneurship', *Journal of Management Studies*, **44**(7), 1242–54.

Audretsch, D., I. Grilo and A.R. Thurik (eds) (2007), *Handbook on Research on Entrepreneurship Policy*, Cheltenham, UK and Northampton, MA, USA: Edward Elgar Publishing.

Bager, T. (2009), 'The camp model for entrepreneurship teaching', paper to EFMD conference, 26–27 February 2009, Barcelona, Spain, available at www.idea-denmark.dk

Bandura, A. (1997), *Self-efficacy: The Exercise of Control*, New York: Freeman.

Baumol, W.J. (2004), 'Entrepreneurial cultures and countercultures', *Academy of Management Learning and Education*, **3**(3), 316–26.

Carter, N., W.B. Gartner and P. Reynolds (1996), 'Exploring start-up event sequences', *Journal of Business Venturing*, **11**(3), 151–66.

Charney, A. and G. Liebecap (2000), 'Impact of entrepreneurship education: An evaluation of the Berger entrepreneurship programme at Arizona University, 1985–1999', *Insight: A Kauffman Research Series*, Tucson, AZ: Ewing Marion Kauffman Foundation.

Davidsson, P. (2006), 'Nascent entrepreneurship: Empirical studies and developments', *Foundations and Trends in Entrepreneurship*, **2**(1), 1–76.

De Tienne, D. and G.N. Chandler (2004), 'Opportunity identification and its role in the entrepreneurial classroom: A pedagogical approach and empirical test', *Academy of Management Learning and Education*, **3**(3), 242–57.

EU Expert Group (2008), *Entrepreneurship in Higher Education, especially within Non-Business Studies*, Brussels: EU Commission, Enterprise and Industry.

Fayolle, A. (2003), 'Research and researchers at the heart of entrepreneurial situations', in C. Steyaert and D. Hjorth (eds), *New Movements in Entrepreneurship*, Cheltenham, UK and Northampton, MA, USA: Edward Elgar Publishing, pp. 35–50.

Gibb, A. (2006), *Towards the Entrepreneurial University: Entrepreneurship Education as a Lever for Change*, Policy Paper Series, Birmingham: NCGE.

Gibbons, M., C. Limoges, S. Schwartzman, H. Nowotny, M. Trow and P. Scott (1994), *The New Production of Knowledge: The Dynamics of Science and Research in Contemporary Societies*, London: Sage.

Greene, P., J. Katz and B. Johannisson (2004), 'Guest editors' introduction: Special issue on entrepreneurship education', *Academy of Management Learning and Education*, **3**(3), 238–41.

Hindle, K. (2007), 'Teaching entrepreneurship at university: From the wrong building to the right philosophy', in A. Fayolle (ed.), *Handbook of Research in Entrepreneurship Education*, Cheltenham, UK and Northampton, MA, USA: Edward Elgar Publishing, pp. 104–26.

Hindle, K. (forthcoming), 'Skilful dreaming: Testing a general model of entrepreneurial process with a "unique" narrative of business formation'.

Hindle, K., B. Mainprize and N. Dorofeeva (2007), *Venture Intelligence: How Smart Investors and Entrepreneurs Evaluate New Ventures*', Venture Intelligence Institute (www.ventureintelligence.biz).

Kirby, D. (2004), 'Entrepreneurship education: Can business schools meet the challenge?', *Education & Training*, **46**(8/9), 510–19.

Kolb, D.A. (1984), *Experiential Learning: Experience as the Source of Learning and Development*, Englewood Cliffs, NJ: Prentice Hall.

Krüger, N., M. Reilly and A. Carsrud (2000), 'Competing models of entrepreneurial intentions', *Journal of Business Venturing*, **15**(5), 411–32.

Levie, J. and E. Autio (2008), 'A theoretical grounding and test of the GEM model', *Small Business Economics*, **31**(3), 235–63.

Löbler, H. (2006), 'Learning entrepreneurship from a contructivist perspective', *Technology Analysis & Strategic Management*, **18**(1), 19–38.

Lüthje, C. and N. Franke (2003), 'The making of an entrepreneur: Testing a model of entrepreneurial intent among engineering students at MIT', *R&D Management*, **33**(2), 135–47.

OECD (2008), *OECD Framework for the Evaluation of SME and Entrepreneurship Policies and Programmes*, Paris: OECD.

Reynolds, P.D., D. Bosma, E. Autio, S. Hunt, D. de Bono, I. Servais, L. Lopez-Garcia and N. Chin (2005), 'Global Entrepreneurship Monitor: Data collection and implementation 1998–2003', *Small Business Economics*, **24**(3), 205–31.

Romer, P.M. (1986), 'Increasing returns and long-run growth', *Journal of Political Economy*, **94**(5), 1002–37.

Sarasvathy, S. (2008), *Effectuation: Elements of Entrepreneurial Expertise*, Cheltenham, UK and Northampton, MA, USA: Edward Elgar Publishing.

Scharmer, C.O. (2007), *Theory U: Leading from the Future as It Emerges*, Cambridge, MA: SoL Press.

Scharmer, C.O. and K. Käufer (2000), 'Universität als Schauplantz für das Unternehmerischen Menschen', in S. Laske, T. Scheytt, C. Meister-Scheytt and C.O. Scharmer (eds), *Universität im 21. Jahrhundert*, Mering: Rainer Hamp Verlag (English version available at www.ottoscharmer.com).

Schramm, C. (2006), *The Entrepreneurial Imperative*, New York: HarperCollins.

Schumpeter, J.A. (1934), *The Theory of Economic Development*, Cambridge, MA: Harvard University Press.

Shane, S. (2000), 'Prior knowledge and the discovery of entrepreneurial opportunities', *Organization Science*, **11**(4), 448–69.

Shane, S. (2003), *A General Theory of Entrepreneurship: The Individual–Opportunity Nexus*, Cheltenham, UK and Northampton, MA, USA: Edward Elgar Publishing.

Shane, S. and S. Venkataraman (2000), 'The promise of entrepreneurship as a field of research', *Academy of Management Review*, **25**(1), 217–26.

Weick, K. (1969), *The Social Psychology of Organizing*, Reading, MA: Addison-Wesley.

Whitehead, A.N. ([1929] 1967), *The Aims of Education and Other Essays*, New York: Free Press.

17 Managing NVC research in the institutional context: an academic administrator's perspective
Patricia G. Greene

INTRODUCTION

Questions about the state of new venture creation research can be considered at both the individual and the institutional level. For the purposes of this chapter, I draw from my five years in positions of academic leadership at Babson College to consider relationships between the researcher, the entrepreneurship curriculum, the institution, and the topic of this volume, new venture creation research. I conclude the chapter with a summary of lessons learned.

When thinking of new venture creation research, several questions come to mind from an academic leadership perspective. First, what kind of research will be recognized, rewarded, supported, and so on and how is that decision made? Second, how much research is expected or required? Third, how is that research disseminated? Fourth, what impact, if any, do the research decisions have on the teaching approach of the College? And finally, fifth, what impact does the research have on the students?

BABSON COLLEGE – THE INSTITUTION

It is probably helpful to first have a short background on our institution, Babson College. Roger Babson, an entrepreneur, founded the Babson Institute in 1919 as a private, independent school providing practical and ethical training for young men, most of whom were expected to enter into their family's (i.e. father's) business. Babson intentionally emphasized a curriculum that focused on experiential opportunities, including case studies, field trips and class presentations. Students dressed in business attire, punched a time clock, and were supported by a secretarial pool. The culmination of the two-year programme was a certificate of completion. The Institute was quite successful and by 1947 the programme had evolved into a baccalaureate programme. An MBA programme was inaugurated in 1951, and undergraduate women were accepted beginning in 1968. In 1969 Babson Institute officially became Babson College.

Babson College has long been and continues to be an acknowledged leader in both curriculum innovation and entrepreneurship education. More recently, a global perspective became the third of Babson's strategic dimensions. The most far-reaching curriculum innovation was launched in 1996 and further combined academic studies with field-based and co-curricular learning opportunities, explicit assessment of learning outcomes, increased opportunities for student-designed studies and, perhaps in the most drastic progression, cross-disciplinary integration of various modes of teaching. In the field of entrepreneurship, Babson attracted, retained and celebrated many of the field's pioneers and, while there is some debate over the 'when' and 'where' of entrepreneurship education's firsts, even by the most conservative allocation Babson offered the first undergraduate concentration in entrepreneurship and the first research conference dedicated to this topic (Katz 2007).

Currently, all Babson undergraduates receive a BS degree, and *every* student studies a required amount of entrepreneurship. While the major focus of the institution is business oriented, Babson delivers a full under-graduate curriculum, with at least half of the course of study required to be in the liberal arts for every student. Babson further offers a one-year full-time MBA, a two-year full-time MBA, a part-time evening MBA, and a blended learning (online and face-to-face) part-time programme, as well as several MS programmes, including the MSA, an MS in technological entre-preneurship (in partnership with the F.W. Olin School of Engineering), an MS in management (in partnership with Tec de Monterrey), and the newest programme, the Global Entrepreneurship Program, in partner-ship with EMLYON Business School and Zhejiang University School of Management. Babson delivers the Symposium for Entrepreneurship Educators, which trains faculty around the world to teach entrepre-neurship. The executive education programmes at Babson relate to and through entrepreneurship with programmes such as 'Entrepreneurial Strategies for Innovation and Growth' and the Innovation and Corporate Entrepreneurship Research Center.

BABSON COLLEGE – INSTITUTIONAL PHILOSOPHY

To further understand Babson as an institution, it is important to understand the extent of the entrepreneurship curriculum. To describe the curriculum in a coherent manner I find it helpful to use the pedagogical innovation framework put forward by Béchard and Grégoire (2007) in order to systematically capture all aspects of the curriculum and to suggest the relationships between the components of the curriculum. Béchard and Grégoire's approach is especially intriguing in that it is the result of the combination of an extensive epistemological review of the education research literature on pedagogical innovation. It is also important that this review went beyond the work done in the US or English-based literature so as not to be limited by geographic or linguistic boundaries. The two primary dimensions as described by these authors are the teaching and learning underpinnings of each pedagogical innovation and an understanding of the contextual factors for each pedagogical innovation (2007). While an in-depth discussion of the framework is beyond the scope of this chapter, Table 17.1 captures the relevant dimensions I use to walk through aspects of Babson's approach to entrepreneurship.

BABSON APPROACH – TEACHING MODEL

Béchard and Grégoire's framework proposes two main questions (or 'analytical foci') for understanding the teaching model. First, what ontological assumptions support (in this case) the Babson curriculum and, second, what operational elements characterize the curriculum? While Béchard and Grégoire propose a more comprehensive list of 'indicator variables', for the purposes of this chapter I will address those that are most directly related to issues related to research on new venture creation (see Table 17.1).

Babson College is known as a 'teaching college' and the administration and most faculty members are proud of that designation. This designation has a significant impact on teaching *and* research at Babson. When we recruit faculty to Babson, one of the first and most important discussions is about the balance between teaching and research. Up until the academic year of 2007/08, the contractual teaching expectation for Babson faculty members was six courses per year. (Babson is in the process of moving to a five-course teaching load.) This is considered to be a high teaching load in the industry, although not the highest. In conjunction with the number of courses to be taught is the manner in which Babson teaches. The 'underpinnings' of the Babson model are that the education we provide will be delivered in a manner that is integrated, experiential and developmental. In essence, this is a high-touch model which requires significant faculty time to prepare for the classroom, deliver in the classroom and interact outside of the classroom. The integrated aspects first demand disciplinary excellence, which is then overlaid with collaborative planning and delivery across campus. The experiential components of the curriculum require

Table 17.1   Framework for pedagogical innovation

Dimensions of analysis	Analytical foci	Indicator variables
Teaching and learning/ underpinnings of the innovation (*teaching model*)	What ontological assumption(s) underpin this innovation? What operational element(s) characterize this innovation?	<ul><li>Educators' conceptions about teaching</li><li>Educators' conceptions about themselves and the students</li><li>Educators' assumptions about the knowledge to be taught</li><li>Teaching goals</li><li>Knowledge emphasized</li><li>Pedagogical methods and means</li><li>Forms of evaluation</li></ul>
Contextual factors that participate in the development and implementation of an innovation (*support infrastructure*)	What kind of arrangements support this innovation at the institutional level? What kind of arrangements support this innovation at the education system level?	<ul><li>Degree of academic autonomy</li><li>Particular mission of the institution</li><li>Structural mechanisms of coordination</li><li>Institutional practices regarding the allocation of resources for developing and sustaining pedagogical initiatives</li><li>Degree of institutional autonomy</li><li>Degree of centralization of the education system</li><li>Presence of national policies toward innovation and entrepreneurship</li></ul>

Source: Béchard and Grégoire (2007).

time for planning, networking, and logistical aspects to make everything work. The developmental requirement is for each segment of the curriculum to neatly flow into the next. Each of these again requires additional time from the faculty members.

It is also relevant (and fits the Béchard and Grégoire framework) to think about the Babson student. Babson has an excellent reputation for the quality of the education received by the students. Babson is also one of the most expensive private schools in the United States. At the undergraduate level, the students who apply (with very few exceptions) have already made a decision that they want a business education. Babson falls into the category of a 'highly selective' school, meaning that we are able to choose the most talented students who apply. At the graduate level there is more variability in the background of our students, especially across programmes. At the same time, the curricula in most of the graduate programmes are even more integrated, again requiring faculty time, effort and, certainly, inclination to collaborate in planning and course delivery. We have high expectations of our students, and correspondingly the students attending Babson have exceedingly high expectations for the quality of their faculty, curriculum, co-curricular activities, and every other aspect of their college experience.

THE RELEVANCE OF RESEARCH

While meeting these expectations for student learning and teaching, Babson requires all full-time faculty members to be intellectually active and either academically or professionally qualified. We've worked out an explicit definition of 'intellectually active' over the past three years while preparing for our last Association to Advance Collegiate Schools of Business (AACSB) maintenance of accreditation visit. This preparation prompted us to revisit past research output and future expectations. Much of this discussion reflected questions raised within the field of management higher education, which for more than 20 years has been criticized in both the academic literature (Bloom 1987; March 2000; Starkey *et al.* 2004) and the popular press. The themes of the critiques are robust, positing that schools of management need to move further towards rigour and relevancy, with a desired outcome of greater impact (Pfeffer and Fong 2002). (Please note that rigour and relevancy are not actually the endpoints of any logical dichotomy, but two different, although related, dimensions.)

The question of relevance is intriguing in itself. One part of the critique questions whether research is in essence irrelevant to practice. At the same time, another criticism is that practice needs more new knowledge to be created in order to ask and answer larger questions in order to improve and enhance organizational effectiveness and the impact on societies (Greene and Rice 2007). Starkey *et al.* (2004) state that the dual role of the business school should mirror the dual role of the university, preparing students for careers through education and, through research, creating the next generation of knowledge needed. This is not an easy or natural or even comfortable dual purpose. Many external constituencies, particularly corporate recruiters, view themselves as the 'customer'. Their desired 'product' provided from the university is a trained professional who is ready to 'hit the ground running'. While residents of the C-suite may make high claims about the role of the university in searching for and creating knowledge, the operational units of most of their organizations largely have conflicting priorities, or at least priorities not directly aligned with a philosophy of knowledge creation. This is a source of tension for the business schools both as to what and how they teach and what and how research is recognized and supported.

THE GROWTH AND SCOPE OF ENTREPRENEURSHIP AS A FIELD

During the same time frame in which this debate is occurring, the field of entrepreneurship has grown significantly in business schools around the world. The discipline has matured from a pedagogical foundation in training for the start of a small business, to be extremely encompassing of a wide range of issues going well beyond the 'basics' of new venture creation. Indeed, the domain statement of the entrepreneurship division of the Academy of Management (last revised in 1995) reads:

> the creation and management of new businesses, small businesses and family businesses, and the characteristics and special problems of entrepreneurs. Major topics include: new venture ideas and strategies; ecological influences on venture creation and demise; the acquisition and management of venture capital and venture teams; self-employment; the owner-manager; management succession; corporate venturing and the relationship between entrepreneurship and economic development.

BLENDING THE TEACHING AND RESEARCH IDEALS: PEDAGOGICAL INNOVATION

In sum, the area of entrepreneurship is broadly recognized as being a source of pedagogical innovation, often delivered by those with practical experience, some academically trained and some not, and using experiential activities, often largely focused upon business planning. It is a prime target for the consideration of rigour and relevancy. If we then accept these premises and consider the relationship between the Babson teaching model of entrepreneurship and research in new venture creation, we find an effect that goes beyond a simple 'larger than life' time expectation for faculty to meet (and generally exceed) their teaching, and the ever present expectation for pedagogical innovation. Therefore, the interaction (and/or interdependencies) of the teaching model and research on new venture creation can be summarized as:

1. faculty members who pay explicit attention to the tension between theory and practice and who strive to advance both;
2. a variety of types of faculty members who 'do research', including those with academic and practitioner-oriented backgrounds and approaches;
3. an increasing appreciation for the qualitative case research method, recognizing the potential for dual-purposing the outcome in the academic journals and in the classroom;
4. The comprehensive nature of research topics that connects with the comprehensive nature of the curriculum, including executive education (at Babson this explicitly includes new venture creation, sustainable growth, entrepreneurial finance, corporate entrepreneurship, family enterprising, women's entrepreneurship and leadership, social and sustainable entrepreneurship, technology and public policy);
5. partnering with faculty trained in other disciplines – often connected through integration.

BABSON APPROACH – CONTEXTUAL FACTORS

The contextual factors set forth by Béchard and Grégoire include the types of institutional level and educational system arrangements that support the pedagogical innovation, or in this case the Babson approach to entrepreneurship. Many of these 'indicator variables' relate to academic freedom, institutional structure, resource allocation and related national policies. (Note: one of the variables absent from the Béchard and Grégoire framework, but I believe relevant, is that of any disciplinary influence, e.g. models of doctoral education and/or organizations such as the Academy of Management/Entrepreneurship Division.)

If I start from the institutional level at Babson, understanding why Babson College's primary strategic dimension is the entrepreneurial mindset means understanding Babson's definition of entrepreneurship. Researchers in the field disagree, agree to disagree, and occasionally ignore each other's definitional approaches (Greene and Rice 2007). This is one reason why the description of the entrepreneurship territory for the Academy of Management is so very broad. Given that I have spent the last five years of my life in academic leadership at Babson, given that I am a sociologist by training, given that I have been in the field of entrepreneurship for two decades, and given that for the last five I have spoken with or to literally thousands of individuals about the importance of entrepreneurship, I adopted a definition of entrepreneurship that allowed me to speak about both the disciplinary division of entrepreneurship at Babson and the strategic entrepreneurial mindset approach. *Entrepreneurship is an approach that combines the ability to identify opportunities, organize resources, and provide the leadership to create something of value.*

Part of the uniqueness of the Babson entrepreneurship programme is that it is far more than a programme. Entrepreneurship is part of the mission, vision and values of the *College*. The fact that entrepreneurship is the major driver of our overall institutional approach is a significant difference between Babson's and other programmes. If the mission, vision and values are taken as statements of identity, aspiration and principles for the institution, the Babson approach to entrepreneurship is front and centre. During the 1990s our mission focused upon excellence in management education. In 2003 we moved entrepreneurship to be more prominent in our mission and set forth that:

> Babson College educates men and women to be *entrepreneurial* leaders in a rapidly changing world. We prepare them to identify opportunities and initiate actions that result in genuine accomplishment.
>
> Our innovative curricula challenge students to think creatively and across disciplinary boundaries. We cultivate the willingness to take and manage risk, the ability to energize others toward a goal, and the courage to act responsibly.
>
> Our students appreciate that leadership requires technical knowledge as well as a sophisticated understanding of societies, cultures, institutions and the self. They welcome the challenge of learning continuously and taking responsibility for their careers. Our students will be key contributors in the world's established enterprises as well as emerging ventures.
>
> At Babson, we collaborate across disciplines and functions to create knowledge and apply integrative solutions to complex problems. We reach across institutional and geographic boundaries to forge relationships with individuals and organizations who share our commitment to excellence and innovation.

HOW FOCUSED ON NEW VENTURE CREATION SHOULD WE BE?

When our school is predicated upon entrepreneurial principles, it impacts every aspect of teaching, research and service. However, as described above, the Babson approach is not limited to the academic discipline of entrepreneurship, and most certainly is not limited to entrepreneurship defined as new venture creation. This in itself raises additional questions about our approach to research in the field. As described in the Babson strategic plan:

> We reflect our understanding of the affinity between entrepreneurial activity and integrative approaches to knowledge in the mission statement where we emphasize that Babson educates 'entrepreneurial leaders'. We cultivate

entrepreneurial creativity, not only in the context of traditional start-up ventures, but more broadly too. Men and women educated at Babson will be prepared to exercise leadership roles in a variety of social and public institutions as well as in all types of business organizations operating anywhere in the world. (Babson College 2003)

THE CONTEXT OF THE EDUCATIONAL SYSTEM

It is also helpful to briefly consider the educational system in which Babson exists. US higher education is built upon three fundamental assumptions: 1) the ideals of Thomas Jefferson related both to limited government involvement and freedom of speech; 2) capitalism as an economic system and the corresponding belief in rational markets; and 3) our commitment to equal opportunity and education as a path to social mobility (Eckel and King p. iii). These principles strongly support a Babson-style approach.

While the role of the federal government in determining the structure and content of higher education is quite limited, there is general oversight through a system of accrediting agencies and organizations. It is the accrediting agencies that provide quality assurance. These regional organizations are recognized by the US government and undertake regular and systemic reviews of their member schools' voluntary, peer-review process. As a specialist school focused upon business and management, Babson is also accredited by AACSB and follows guidelines specifically related to the quality of the faculty, the assessment of learning and the strategic planning process. One of the most stringent requirements for these accreditations is that the institution has a clearly stated mission, the mission is known and accepted by the faculty, and the mission is evident in the curriculum in all programmes. This means that, unless we at Babson change our mission, we have intentionally placed ourselves in the position of being mandated to deliver an entrepreneurial education, to recruit and maintain a faculty approach to our mission, and to significantly contribute to the creation of new knowledge in that field.

Each of these aspects relates to decisions of the academic leadership as related to structure and processes of the institution. Structural coordination is quite unique at Babson in order to support the Babson definition of entrepreneurship. Babson is currently structured into ten academic divisions, one of which is specifically Entrepreneurship. This division bears the responsibility for the entrepreneurship curriculum, as well as for partnering across campus to coordinate other academic approaches to the field. The Arthur M. Blank Center for Entrepreneurship at Babson works in conjunction with the academic division in order to support aspects of the entrepreneurship curriculum, but most significantly co-curricular and external programmes around entrepreneurship. While the Chair of the Entrepreneurship division reports to the Dean of Faculty, as do all division chairs, the Director of the Blank Center reports to the Provost's office in order to coordinate entrepreneurial activities across all of Babson College. This structure is in response to a careful analysis of which activities are best centralized within either the division or the Provost's office, and which are more effectively decentralized. The structure is a matrix mode, complete with the advantages and challenges of this organizational design.

Another prominent issue facilitated by the centralization/decentralization approach of Babson is the allocation of resources. Babson's comprehensive approach to entrepreneurship requires the commitment of significant financial resources. Much of the funding comes from sources beyond tuition, such as gifts and grants. Beyond the usual faculty and student support, we have the staff of the Blank Center and, perhaps one of the most unique aspects of Babson's entrepreneurship programmes, we substantially contribute to the support of three global research projects, GEM (Global Entrepreneurship Monitor – co-funder and major contributor), STEP (Successful Trans-Generational Entrepreneurial Practices – founder and major contributor) and the Diana Project (annual contributor). As with any entrepreneurial venture, the resources provided by Babson go beyond the pure dollars to include people, space and operational support. We believe in the support of these projects, as they contribute to the advancement of knowledge through research, provide information and data for the classroom, and provide guidance for policy makers and entrepreneurs around the world.

The foundation of any college is the faculty, and at Babson the faculty is responsible for (owns) the curriculum and decisions concerning who is on the faculty. Our faculty governance system continues to evolve, and we are in the process of launching a new faculty senate that emphasizes a model of shared governance between faculty and administration. Part of the decision for who is on the faculty pertains to the tenure and promotion decisions and defines what type of research and what type of research dissemination are desirable for the College. Once again, these decisions also flow from the mission of the College and explicitly recognize the value of research in the area of entrepreneurship.

And, finally, over the past five years Babson has intentionally positioned entrepreneurship scholars in positions of academic leadership for the College. This made sense for the College in two ways. First, in this way an entrepreneurial approach was present for every decision of the College. Second, representation by these entrepreneurship academic leaders at external events such as AACSB or EFMD clearly linked the College with our mission-based approach.

SUMMARY – LESSONS LEARNED RELATED TO RESEARCH ON NEW VENTURE CREATION

The Béchard and Grégoire framework provided a framework to pose questions and suggest answers about the unique nature of Babson College as an institution dedicated to an entrepreneurial education. I've identified several key factors that help make the difference:

1. Recruiting: We hire very carefully to ensure a faculty commitment to teaching, integration and, where appropriate (and it usually is), a recognition of our overall mission.
2. Relationship with teaching and time allocation: We recognize that our approach to integrated, experiential and developmental teaching while requiring intellectual activities takes a significant amount of time, and we are making progress on providing more time for a better faculty worklife.
3. Type of faculty: We have long recognized the critical importance of having both academic and practitioner-oriented faculty who work together across the lines of teaching and research.
4. Balance between theory and practice: We also recognize, require and support a balance between theory and practice and are staunchly committed to our premise that both are necessary for an entrepreneurial education.
5. Faculty governance: We strongly support a shared-governance system of governance over the curriculum and the nature of the faculty. Without a faculty you don't have a college.
6. Perception of research by trustees: We are working to help our trustees better understand the nature and importance of research as a critical faculty responsibility. We would never be content to be a school teaching only the ideas of others.
7. And, finally, we take it as a significant responsibility to be thought leaders, not only in the field of entrepreneurship, but in the field of higher education, in and out of classrooms, and blended with a global perspective in order to achieve the mission of Babson College.

REFERENCES

Béchard, J. and D. Grégoire (2007), 'Archetypes of pedagogical innovation for entrepreneurship in higher education: Model and illustrations', in A. Fayolle (ed.), *Handbook of Research in Entrepreneurship Education: A General Perspective, Vol. 1*, Cheltenham, UK and Northampton, MA, USA: Edward Elgar Publishing, pp. 261–84.

Bloom, A. (1987), *The Closing of the American Mind*, New York: Simon & Schuster.

Eckel, P.D. and J.E. King, *An Overview of Higher Education in the United States: Diversity, Access, and the Role of the Marketplace*, Washington, DC: American Council on Education.

Greene, P.G. and M. Rice (2007), *Entrepreneurship Education*, Cheltenham, UK and Northampton, MA, USA: Edward Elgar Publishing.

Katz, J.A. (2003), 'The chronology and intellectual trajectory of American entrepreneurship education 1876–1999', *Journal of Business Venturing*, **18**(2), 283–400.

March, J. (2000), 'Citigroup's John Reed and Stanford's James March on management research and practice', *Academy of Management Executive*, **14**(1), 52–64.

Pfeffer, J. and C. Fong (2002), 'The end of business schools? Less success than meets the eye', *Academy of Management Learning and Education*, **1**(1), 78–95.

Starkey, K., A. Hatcheul and S. Tempest (2004), 'Rethinking the business school', *Journal of Management Studies*, **41**(8), 1521–31.

18 Creative artists and entrepreneurship
Jon Sundbo

INTRODUCTION

This chapter deals with creative artists as new venture creators: who they are, how they can be supported and which problems they experience. Recently, artists have been viewed as being more innovative than other people, and it has been argued that much can be learned from artists in regard to improvement of innovative capabilities (Darsø 2004). The discussion about the experience economy (Pine and Gilmore 1999, 2007) has in particular emphasized artistic creativity. In contemporary society, artists have an aura of being particularly creative and outstanding. They often receive media attention and many people admire them. There are stories in the press about artists, for example pop groups, who within a few months have earned billions of euros and created a whole business empire. However, do artists approach new venture creation differently from non-artists who also create new ventures? What are the similarities and differences between what artists do and what ordinary new venture creators do? One might for example claim that most artists are wretched entrepreneurs: they cannot organize other people – some of them may not even be able to organize their own lives – and they may be unable to sell as much as they need to feed themselves. Meanwhile, artists are great creators of ideas for new ventures. On the other hand, many examples of artists as outstanding businesspeople prevail. The distinction between artists as new venture creators and ordinary venture creators is important when considering the idea of the experience society, where economic development based on the innovation of experiences – maybe even based on the culture economy – will become dominant in the near future.

In order to address these issues, I first need to articulate what I understand by artistic creativity and entrepreneurship. Both aspects will be discussed in this chapter. The main questions that will be discussed are: What is artistic entrepreneurship? How can artistic entrepreneurship be supported? Which specific problems are associated with artistic entrepreneurship?

Artistic activity has always existed and often been related to entrepreneurship. However, there has been little research undertaken into the cross-field of the two. Artists have almost only been approached from a humanistic arts point of view, but rarely from a business view (with a few exceptions, e.g. Björkegren 1996; Caves 2000). However, recently the emerging literature on the experience economy (e.g. Pine and Gilmore 1999; O'Dell and Billing 2005; Boswijk *et al.* 2007; Hjort and Kostera 2007; Sundbo and Darmer 2008) highlights the business aspects of artistic activity.

Inspired by the experience economy literature, artistic creativity will in this chapter be understood in a broad, non-elitist sense. It is not only about authors and painters, but also about, for example, professional sportspersons and creators of tourist attractions and town festivals. Artistic creativity is understood as the ability to express an inner vision of the external world in an original manner that is intended to attract other people's attention. This ability is an obvious criterion for authors and painters and other traditional artists. However, even sport stars and organizers of festivals may exercise artistic creativity, or part of it. The manner in which they do their task and the intention to attract people's attention can be the same. Their inner vision of an external world may not always be an interpretation of the existing world as authors present it, but people such as sport stars and organizers of festivals may have a vision of which picture or impression they intend to create in the external world, namely in the minds of the audience.

The chapter will present a particular area of entrepreneurship, but will also contribute to a fundamental discussion of the entrepreneurship concept by contrasting it to creativity.

The chapter has three sections: a theoretical discussion of the concepts of artistic creativity and entrepreneurship; an empirical section with case-based examples of artists as entrepreneurs (the state of the art); and a discussion of the most important problems concerning artistic entrepreneurship that we do not know much about (the state of what could be).

THEORETICAL APPROACH: ARTISTIC CREATIVITY AND ENTREPRENEURSHIP

The Concepts of Creativity and Entrepreneurship

I will start by discussing the core concepts of creativity and entrepreneurship. I will discuss their similarities and differences. This is in order to understand the intersection of creativity and entrepreneurship termed *artistic entrepreneurship*. The term *entrepreneurship* has been used in different ways. The rapidly growing literature on entrepreneurship has increased the range of aspects related to this phenomenon, and they cannot all be discussed here. Fundamentally, entrepreneurship is about creating business as Schumpeter (1934) discussed. Schumpeter used the concept to explain economic development. According to the Schumpeter tradition, entrepreneurship involves creation of new business by introduction of innovations that together destroy existing business (Schumpeter 1934). Thus entrepreneurship involves two acts – namely the act of creating a new firm and the act of creating innovation. In Schumpeter's original version, the innovations were supposed to be radical, thus replacing existing products or production methods. Later, other authors such as Kirzner (1973) have modified this view to include those who make incremental innovations. According to the Kirzner tradition, entrepreneurs fill market gaps and are not necessarily destructive. Entrepreneurship has recently been used as a more sociological archetype, where entrepreneurs are perceived as creators of social change (e.g. Swedberg 2000). This change does not need to be business oriented or related to economic development. Entrepreneurs creating social change are often termed *social entrepreneurs*. The concept of social entrepreneurship is used with different meanings. Sometimes it just means a particular instance of social behaviour which is change oriented. Entrepreneurs are persons or roles that make changes in the society by creating new behaviour (Swedberg 2000; Hjort and Kostera 2007). These changes can include the introduction of new products as well as a new type of social behaviour, art or social value (such as new religious norms). This use of the concept is a continuation of the ideas of social change that the sociologist Gabriel Tarde (1895) introduced and which led to diverse models of the diffusion of new, innovative elements in society (Barnett 1953; Rogers 1995). Social entrepreneurship has also been used in a more narrow sense as a notion for the social innovation processes within firms where employees act as corporate entrepreneurs (Kanter 1983; Schendel and Channon 1990). The concept has also been used in a more narrow sense in relation to the third sector (humanitarian and other organizations that are neither market-based firms nor public institutions) (Leadbeater 1997). Further, in the international business literature, the term *entrepreneurship* has often been used to refer to small business owners who through innovative behaviour expand their business internationally.

Which of all these meanings of entrepreneurship is relevant when we discuss artistic entrepreneurship? One could take any of these different versions of the notion. As always in the social sciences, explanations and basic concepts are not objectively given; there is a choice. One could for example take the one that best fits the idea of artists as particularly outstanding societal change agents. That could be the broad, 'Tardian' sociological version of diffusion of ideas in society (Rogers 1995). Here the artist does not need to create more than the idea. He or she does not need to create a business or bring about social change; others will do that based on the artist's ideas. This is consistent with how the German sociologist Adorno (1975) perceived the role of arts and culture, where artists are seen as critical revolutionaries. I will not take such a basis for the discussion here. Of course, some artists have revolutionized the world through their new and creative ideas, but so have politicians, scientists, adventurers, kings, generals and a lot of ordinary people through their ideas. Many artists' ideas have not revolutionized the world, and the artists have not been interested in doing so. Being sceptical about the revolutionary role of artists and even more because the whole framework of this book is oriented towards new venture creation, I have taken another, less dramatic approach to entrepreneurship.

I claim that entrepreneurship involves an attempt to change things. It is not enough that the artist presents an idea that others later act upon and carry out in practice. In this respect, artistic creativity is not enough. Artistic entrepreneurship implies that the artist organizes activities to diffuse the idea or the work of art. In the framework of this book, this has a more narrow meaning, namely that the artist establish a firm to sell his or her artistic products.

The next step is to discuss the notion of creativity and especially the notion of artistic creativity.

Creativity is a notion that has been used with many different meanings and from different perspectives (Runco 2004). Mostly it is seen as pertaining to the individual, and creativity has become a core concept in psychology (Guildford 1968; Barron and Harrington 1981). Here it is often connected to learning and education and discussed in relation to the concept of intelligence. Creativity has also been analysed as an organizational factor (Amabile 1983) either as a more or less collective problem-solving process that naturally appears in organizations or as a particular feature in organizations that can be managed (Ekvall 1996; Tan 1998). Creativity has been seen as a functional organizational factor, but also as a process that creates meaning in Weick's (1995) sense (Drazin *et al.* 1999). Thus creativity is a widely used notion that characterizes behaviour that many people engage in every day. It is related to change, but in different ways. Sometimes creativity creates path-breaking, radical new behaviour, ideas or things; sometimes it characterizes a more defensive problem-solving behaviour that aims to maintain the status quo. And sometimes creativity is a factor that is necessary to carry out day-to-day activities such as learning.

Creativity is a part of innovation (Majaro 1988; Amabile *et al.* 1996; Ekvall 1996; Lapierre and Giroux 2003). Creativity is also part of entrepreneurship, but is not the only, and probably not the most important, part. Creativity might be important for the discovery or creation of new ideas, but is less important for the evaluation and exploitation of ideas. Often in the literature the important features of successful entrepreneurship include a drive to win and powerfulness rather than creativity in itself (Schumpeter 1934; McClelland 1961). Many entrepreneurs do not even need to be creative. Traditional problem solving as found in Kirzner's (1973) entrepreneurship theory might be sufficient. Thus entrepreneurs can be interested in establishing new ventures and not being creative at all. They exploit other people's creative products.

Creativity has also been seen as an evolutionary-economic factor (Runco 2004, p. 658) and as a synonym for artists (Caves 2000).

Thus creativity is many things, and artistic creativity is only one type, which has some functions in society and enterprises, but only in connection with other behavioural elements.

Artists, Creativity and Entrepreneurship

This leads us to the main question raised at the beginning of the chapter. Artists have often in the popular narratives been characterized as 'creative people'. Are artists really more creative than other people? And are they therefore more entrepreneurial?

First, we perhaps need to discuss what an artist is. This is not to discuss the 'soul and psychology' of artists, but more to focus on a statistical or functional limitation of art. No doubt the classic artists such as painters, authors, musicians, actors and film directors should be included in the category. I will not include businesspeople within arts industries who are not themselves artists. However, many leaders within arts firms and institutions have some artistic background without being active artists themselves. They should be included in the category of artistic entrepreneurs if they establish and develop an arts firm; we should not define the concept too narrowly, because such persons could contribute to business development based on the artistic culture. If the concept is not to be too narrow, we should also include more industrial versions of art such as architecture and industrial design if the core activity of a firm is design. Further, the definition of art should not be limited only to the very traditional types. New forms of activity should be accepted as art. Examples are gastronomy, computer game design, website design (although the borderline with industrial routines is thin here), sport, circuses and some amusement parks and events (which contemporarily could have a very creative content, although the borderline to service routines is also thin here).

Artists are often particularly creative in the sense of inventing new ideas – not necessarily learning. Many inventions by artists are original and have never been seen or done before. Artists are not only creative; they are also a kind of craftsman. To produce art also requires much routine and the mastering of a discipline (such as musicians or actors do). Nevertheless, artists are claimed to be more creative in regard to inventions than most other people. That is difficult to prove. If it is true, these inventions might be an important input to innovation. However innovation is defined, whether as ideas or as inventions realized on the market (the product is sold on the market) or used within the firm (such as a new production process), artistic creativity does not per se ensure a successful innovation process. The original idea is not sufficient. Even if one has the most original ideas, one might be a miserable innovator. It might be that the artists with the most original ideas are unable to realize them in practice in a way that creates business. We do not know whether this is the case, and it is probably difficult to test empirically. We can conclude that artistic creativity is not per se the same as, or any guarantee for, innovation; it is only about the creation of original ideas.

One may argue that artists, owing to their artistic creative skills, are born entrepreneurs. It might be true, but there is no simple and logical connection between being creative in the above meaning and being an entrepreneur. Entrepreneurship can be characterized as the realization of an innovation where one or a few persons can be identified as those who ensure the realization. Sometimes, but not always, it implies the establishment of one's own new firm. This implies involving and motivating other people to support the realization of the idea, convincing other people of its value and to make a profit in economic terms. Do artists have such particular abilities? Some have and others do not. There are very few empirical investigations of whether artists possess such skills, and especially whether they possess such skills to a higher degree than non-artists. Unsystematic knowledge based on cases, anecdotes and experiences from attempts to advise artists who want to establish their own firm can lead to some theoretical ideas. Many artists have a persuasive ability to convince others about their idea owing to their engagement and excitement about what they do. However, organizing a firm, commercializing the idea, providing investment capital and ensuring a profit are not always the abilities that artists have. My intention is not to support the myth that artists are hopeless businesspeople. Some are, but many appear to be eminent businesspeople. Experiments with entrepreneurship advice in Denmark (the Roskilde region) show that many artists want to be businesspeople, but lack the management and business competencies.

Thus it might be that artistic creativity and entrepreneurship involving its commercialization are two non-related abilities. An artist might possess both, but not necessarily. Accordingly, artistic creativity and entrepreneurship are not the same. Artistic creativity is a valuable precondition for entrepreneurship, because it leads to new ideas; however, there is no evidence that artists are particularly entrepreneurial because they are creative. Thus artists are not born entrepreneurs. The artistic creativity is an advantage to them as entrepreneurs in regard to the discovery and creation of new ideas; however, they often lack business and management capabilities – and sometimes the intention to become successful entrepreneurs. In some cases, the artistic creativity can even be an impediment to entrepreneurship because the artist is so much in love with her own idea that she refuses to accept that other people may not have seen the genius in the art work. The public must be convinced and the artist must be willing to expose herself publicly to promote the sale. Furthermore, she must work hard to organize the production, promotion, sale and delivery of it.

Even though artists are not born entrepreneurs, it might be important for society that artists become successful entrepreneurs. As culture and experiences increasingly become important to economic growth (Pine and Gilmore 1999; Caves 2000), it is important that artists become entrepreneurs. Accordingly, it is important that their ideas are commercialized through an entrepreneurial process. Therefore artistic entrepreneurship should be supported. In the following section I will discuss how this is done in society.

Maecenas

This section deals with how artists can be supported during the entrepreneurial and commercial process. The situation with an unrealized entrepreneurial artistic potential has given rise to a particular entrepreneurial role, which will be called the Maecenas. The concept is taken from history – the old Romans – where rich people paid artists in the form of a gift. However, the concept is given a modern meaning, namely that the artists are not given a gift, maybe not even investment capital. A modern Maecenas can have two forms.

One is patronage. One person establishes a firm, for example a record firm, through which he supports artistically talented people. This person carries out the business part or the commercialization of the product, leaving the artist to concentrate on the creative challenges. Examples – besides record firms – are film producers, gallery owners and publishers. The patron, in this modern version, adds the business aspect to the artistic creativity, and through this combination successful entrepreneurship might occur, something the artist may never do alone. The patron profits from the artist's creativity. However, often the patron also takes the entrepreneurial risk. Darmer (2008) describes how creators of small record firms, the so-called indies, are driven by a passion for music. They may be musicians themselves, but are not necessarily so. However, they attempt to establish a business that can help rock groups and other musical artists to publish their music on CDs and other media. Their drive is not profit, but emotions and passion for music. They do not want to become big players in the music industry, but to remain small companies that present new, talented music. Very often the patrons – owners of the indies – do not get rich and the companies have permanent difficulties in making both ends meet. The owners of the indies are part of the rock milieu and have a personal and intense relation to the artists. We can find the same phenomenon, for example, in the film industry; however, the producers are normally here more profit and growth oriented.

Another Maecenas is the arts incubator. The arts incubator is an artistic and experience-oriented organization, for example a rock festival organization that establishes a hothouse for artistic business activities and thereby supports and trains potential artistic entrepreneurs in business activities. The arts incubator may be established by one person, but it may also be established by a collective group. An example of an arts incubator is the Swedish rock festival organization the Hultsfred festival (Sundbo 2004). The rock festival takes place every year in June. A permanent organization has been developed. The festival organization not only organizes the annual rock festivals, but has made a business of its expertise by selling the organization's expertise to other events such as concerts, sports events, town festivals and so on. It has become a business in itself. This organization has bought a large building, a former storehouse, which also functions as an arts incubator. Potential entrepreneurs can hire rooms in the house, and the first three months are rent free. Most of the entrepreneurs who have settled in the house of the Hultsfred festival are not artists. They develop programs for composing music on PCs, organize concerts, and develop music products for mobile phones and similar activities. However, all these activities are connected to rock music and are parts of a necessary production and marketing system that is required for distributing and selling rock music. In a few cases, the entrepreneurs are rock groups that establish a firm to produce and sell their own music. Some of the entrepreneurs are people coming from the festival organization who want to establish their own firm; others come from outside. The entrepreneurs participate in a close social community in the house, with common office facilities and an inspiring creative milieu. Other examples of such arts incubators are painter communities such as the European COBRA movement, which was active around 1950. These communities primarily involve artists in creating a particular style of painting, but they also function as sales promotion organizations. As COBRA became famous a natural sale channel emerged. Thus, even though the formal aim of COBRA was to develop a particular painting style, the community also functioned as a commercialization enhancer.

Artists may also receive grants or scholarships from governments. However, that is not patronage in the sense used here. State grants do not promote entrepreneurship understood in terms of the creation of business, as the grant implies that the artists have no incentive to commercialize the art. Thus state grants are not part of a Maecenas as it is defined here.

CASES: ARTISTS AS ENTREPRENEURS

In this section I will present three examples of artists who have created new ventures. They have united artistic creativity with a business perspective by commercializing their art. Examples give a better impression of what artistic entrepreneurship is and thus are a pedagogical tool to better explain the phenomenon that has been theoretically discussed above. Examples also give the opportunity to shed more light and shade on the phenomenon. Of course, a few examples cannot present all the existing nuances, but they may nevertheless give an impression of some of the main characteristics of artistic entrepreneurship.

One example of artistic entrepreneurship can be found within the gastronomic world. Probably the currently most world-famous restaurant is El Bulli in Spain established by Ferran Adria (see Svejonova *et al.* 2007; Jacobsen 2008). He started his restaurant in the 1980s. The restaurant is placed far away from any town or tourist resort, isolated at a beach to which only a small road leads. Nevertheless he has succeeded in getting the restaurant fully booked for every day in the summer season when it is open in the first couple of days when the booking opens in spring (Adria has claimed that he has 300 000 people on his waiting list). Adria was not just an entrepreneur – hundreds of restaurants are opened every day throughout the world without anything particularly new or innovative happening. Adria's restaurant was based on two extremely innovative ideas: molecular gastronomy and that a meal is an experience for all five senses. Adria established a gastronomic laboratory in Barcelona where he experimented with the food in the wintertime. He was one of the pioneers in molecular gastronomy, which uses chemical and physical laws to prepare the food, for example how ingredients can be transformed into foam and how food prepared in an oven tastes if it is cooked at different temperatures and degrees of humidity. The meal in the restaurant is total theatre, where the view of the food, the taste, the surprises of untraditional compositions of tastes, the way the food is served (for example on spoons) and the explanations given by the waiters are part of the meal. Adria has recently extended his business; he produces TV and advanced food concepts for restaurants, has established more everyday restaurants and has thus developed his restaurant into quite a big business. This growth is based on the combination of his artistic creativity and a sense for business. This case also tells us that, if the creativity is sufficiently original in a commercial sense, the business may almost come by itself. However, the artist still needs some professional business sense to become a successful entrepreneur.

Another example is the Betty Nansen Theatre in Copenhagen (Hagedorn-Rasmussen and Sundbo 2007). The theatre was established as a theatre company in the early 1990s by two entrepreneurs; one is a creative active theatre director, who also directs plays in other theatres, and the other has roots in the theatre milieu, but has not been an active director or actor. The first one has a mainly artistic perspective; the other one has a business perspective, but a great interest in theatre. These two entrepreneurs are creative. They have introduced a repertoire where the theatre plays classics (by Ibsen, Brecht, etc.) in modern versions. This is in itself innovative. However, they have developed the theatre by introducing a side business that can be considered real entrepreneurship. They have invited young immigrants from Muslim milieus to create theatre plays. The young people create the play from their life experiences and act in the plays. The theatre uses a second scene for the plays. The development of the plays includes many people from the Muslim immigrant milieus being invited to the theatre to contribute to the writing of the plays. For the theatre, this opens a new market for public financing, because it gets support from the government's social programme for integrating immigrants. It also opens a new audience market, because immigrants, who traditionally never go to the theatre, come and watch these plays. This entrepreneurship is based on the creativity of the two managers – the idea that young immigrants could contribute ideas to theatre plays that both can integrate these young people and create new markets.

The third case is a glassblower artist who has a small glass factory on the island of Bornholm in Denmark. Bornholm is a tourist area with the traditional problem that the tourists come only in the summertime and there is no business in the wintertime. The glassblowing factory produces unique glassware. It exports, and the tourists in the summertime are a large market segment for it. The glass factory was started in 1989 by a glassblower. It has grown from a one-woman firm to having, currently, 25 employees. So far it is an example of successful artistic entrepreneurship, although a more traditional one. Recently the owner has had the idea of extending the business in the wintertime by inviting people to come for weekends and learn to design and blow glass. She cooperates with a local hotel that has the same problem concerning seasons. They sell packages with accommodation and meals in the hotel and glassblowing courses. This is an innovation in relation to traditional glass art and represents an extra income for both parties. The creativity of the glassblower is utilized in a side activity as a pedagogical means to give customers an experience of being artists themselves. Both the glassblower and the hotel manager developed this new activity during a regional training programme that has increased their managerial competence. They plan to develop the concept further, based on firm cooperation. The clients of the glassblowing course are typically women from the upper and middle classes of Copenhagen. They sometimes have difficulties with being away from their husbands. Therefore the glassblower and the hotel manager have plans to provide activities for the husbands (e.g. golf, fishing or cultural activities) so they also come for weekends and the couples may be encouraged to stay longer.

PROBLEMS IN ARTISTIC CREATIVE ENTREPRENEURSHIP

If artists succeed in establishing themselves as entrepreneurs, they face problems that partly can be recognized from other areas, but to a certain degree are specific to artistic entrepreneurs. Artistic entrepreneurship has not been investigated much, but research carried out until now has emphasized four main problems, namely finance, growth, exposure and management (Hjort and Kostera 2007; Sundbo and Darmer 2008).

Financing

Artistic entrepreneurs have particular difficulties in getting venture capitalists to finance their projects. The venture capitalists have no experience in assessing artistic and experience projects and therefore they are liable to refuse investment in such endeavours. This has, for example, in Denmark led to a discussion about a report published by a governmental venture capital fund (Vækstfonden 2007). This report analyses the growth potential of culture and other experience industries and concludes that there is limited growth potential in these industries (with a very few exceptions such as the computer games industry). The report concludes that the venture fund should not invest in these industries. This conclusion is partly due to the historical analysis of the industries' economic development, but partly to the fact that the venture fund has no experience in assessing art and other experience industrial firms.

Artists have particular opportunities to obtain public financing of art projects – for example, a municipality or a museum buys the artist's work or the artist gets a grant from the government or a private fund. This can solve the financing problem in some cases, but in many other cases the artist cannot get such financing. Further, this form of financing is not an incentive to entrepreneurship. It is a direct support to the artist and, if he can sell a project to the government, a museum or a municipality again, he may have solved his personal economic problems. However, it is not an incentive for the artist to think in business terms. On the contrary, it maintains him or her in a kind of day labour situation. It is a payment for a certain piece of art, not investment capital.

Growth Problems

Generally, entrepreneurship in societies is not as successful as governments often wish it to be. A special problem is that often only a very small proportion of the new-established firms really grow and become large firms. This is also true in Denmark (Hancock and Bager 2004). Growth seems to meet barriers.

Like other entrepreneurs, artistic entrepreneurs have problems with growth because it demands another way of organizing production. The problems seem to be more severe to artistic entrepreneurs because they are even more occupied by their idea and less oriented towards business activities than other entrepreneurs. Further, they have often less experience with growth issues and less management capability. Finally, some of the employees whom they need to manage are artists themselves, who are very inwardly directed towards their own ideas. They may be difficult to engage in the business processes.

Experiences from the regional office for business development in the Roskilde region of Denmark shows that surprisingly many artistic entrepreneurs survive. However, extremely few of them grow. They are satisfied with being one-person businesses or firms with a few employees, which is the situation in most cases. In some cases they may wish to grow, but they are unable to do so. Even though the artistic entrepreneurs may be creative and their product original on the market, national and global competition is hard. Artistic creativity is not a rare phenomenon, and artistic competition makes it particularly difficult for entrepreneurs to attract investment capital. These factors are part of the explanation of the growth problems, but other factors that we have not yet found may also come into play.

Exposure

Public exposure is often more important to an artistic entrepreneur than to others, for example industrial entrepreneurs (Hagedorn-Rasmussen and Sundbo 2007). The artist often has no physical product to show and no retail distribution system. She or he has only limited marketing capacity and budget. Artistic entrepreneurs of course may attempt to market themselves through traditional media such as brochures or advertisements. Often their market is scattered and therefore they are forced to invest much more in traditional marketing to reach the potential customers. Thus the marketing part of entrepreneurship is hard for artists.

However, artists often have the ability to tell a good story about themselves and their works and thereby expose themselves and their works. They can expose themselves in the media. This is a great advantage in contemporary society, where people are focused on stories about individuals in the media. This possibility may more than compensate for the lack of marketing ability and resources.

Even though artists have a good basis for exposing themselves in public, this often takes a long time. If entrepreneurial establishment is to be fast, it demands a more professional and focused exploitation of the exposure potentials. Even exposure in the public media should be a professional management task.

Management

Even though many artists do not want to establish business relations and create a firm, many other artists want to be entrepreneurs and establish a firm. Many of the latter lack management experience and qualifications (Hagedorn-Rasmussen and Sundbo 2007). They have no management experience or experience in organizing a sales organization. Further, they have weak competencies in formulating a business plan. Thus for many artists it is not the intention and commitment to become entrepreneurs that is lacking, but the ability. Managers and entrepreneurs within the artistic fields are often not professional enough in relation to the business and management side – even if they are very professional in relation to the artistic side.

Very few potential artistic entrepreneurs have any training in management or entrepreneurship. This leads to the education of artistic entrepreneurs and potential entrepreneurs in management disciplines being an important issue if society wants more artists to become entrepreneurs. Management and entrepreneurship could be topics taught as part of artistic schooling, and management education and training programmes for artistic entrepreneurs could be established. Such programmes are already established in Denmark. For example, Roskilde University has an MBA programme in experience management and runs a business and management module for students from the Royal Danish Academy of Music. Other examples include design management at the University of Southern Denmark. Experience from these early attempts to train artist entrepreneurship may provide further knowledge on how to promote artistic entrepreneurship in the future.

CONCLUSION

Entrepreneurship based on artistic creativity is a growing field that is becoming increasingly important in economic terms. It should therefore receive greater academic attention.

Artistic creativity is a good precondition for entrepreneurship. However, it is not sufficient. Artistic creativity and entrepreneurship are not the same phenomenon, although creativity may be a useful, but not necessary, part of entrepreneurship. Artists are therefore not born entrepreneurs any more than other people. Artists may often be more creative than other potential entrepreneurs. However, they very often lack business and management capabilities. The artistic creativity can even sometimes be an impediment to entrepreneurship because the artist focuses too much on his or her own idea and believes that normal business activities such as marketing are not necessary. On the other hand artists are good material for the media, and artists have in the framework of the exposure society natural possibilities for creating free PR through stories about their lives and their works. These potentials can be utilized more professionally, which could be achieved by teaching them artistic entrepreneurship.

Exploiting the artistic entrepreneurship potentials may require an effort from other people. A modern Maecenas who provides patronage or an arts incubator can have this function.

Artistic entrepreneurs face particular problems. They have great problems in procuring the finance for business projects because the venture capitalists have no experience in assessing arts projects. They have severe growth problems, partly because of a global and very competitive market and because the artist's ambitions often are more related to the development of artistic ideas than business projects. They suffer from lack of managerial and business capacities and experiences. Education and training programmes to improve management and entrepreneurship capabilities should be offered.

REFERENCES

Adorno, T. (1975), *Gesellschaftstheorie und Kulturkritik*, Frankfurt am Main: Suhrkamp.
Amabile, T.M. (1983), *The Psychology of Creativity*, New York: Springer.
Amabile, T.M., R. Conti, H. Coon, J. Lazenby and M. Herron (1996), 'Assessing the work environment for creativity', *Academy of Management Journal*, **39**(5), 1154–84.
Barnett, H.G. (1953), *Innovation: The Basis of Cultural Change*, New York: McGraw-Hill.
Barron, F. and D. Harrington (1981), 'Creativity, intelligence and personality', *Annual Review of Psychology*, **32**, 439–76.
Björkegren, D. (1996), *The Culture Business: Management Strategies for the Arts-Related Business*, London: Routledge.
Boswijk, A., T. Thijssen and E. Peelen (2007), *The Experience Economy: A New Perspective*, Amsterdam: Pearson.
Caves, R. (2000), *Creative Industries*, Cambridge, MA: Harvard University Press.
Darmer, P. (2008), 'Entrepreneurs in music: The passion of experience creation', in J. Sundbo and P. Darmer (eds), *Creating Experiences in the Experience Economy*, Cheltenham, UK and Northampton, MA, USA: Edward Elgar Publishing.
Darsø, L. (2004), *Artful Creation: Learning-Tales of Arts-in-Business*, Copenhagen: Samfundslitteratur.
Drazin, R., M. Glynn and R. Kazanjian (1999), 'Multilevel theorizing about creativity in organizations: A sensemaking perspective', *Academy of Management Review*, **24**(2), 286–307.
Ekvall, G. (1996), 'Organizational climate for creativity and innovation', *European Journal of Work and Organizational Psychology*, **5**(1), 105–23.
Guildford, J.P. (1968), *Creativity, Intelligence, and Their Educational Implications*, San Diego, CA: Robert Knapp.
Hagedorn-Rasmussen, P. and J. Sundbo (2007), 'Ledelse af mennesker i oplevelsesvirksomheder' [Human resource management in experience enterprises], in J.O. Bærenholdt and J. Sundbo (eds), *Oplevelsesøkonomi: Produktion, forbrug, kultur* [Experience economy: Production, consumption, culture), Copenhagen: Samfundslitteratur.
Hancock, M. and T. Bager (eds) (2004), *Global Entrepreneurship Monitor Denmark 2003*, Copenhagen: Børsens Forlag.
Hjort, D. and M. Kostera (eds) (2007), *Entrepreneurship and the Experience Economy*, Copenhagen: Copenhagen Business School Press.
Jacobsen, J.K. (2008), 'The food and eating experience', in J. Sundbo and P. Darmer (eds), *Creation of Experiences in the Experience Economy*, Cheltenham, UK and Northampton, MA, USA: Edward Elgar Publishing.
Kanter, R.M. (1983), *The Change Masters*, London: Routledge.
Kirzner, I. (1973), *Competition and Entrepreneurship*, Chicago: University of Chicago Press.
Lapierre, J. and V.-P. Giroux (2003), 'Creativity and work environment in a high-tech context', *Creativity and Innovation Management*, **12**(1), 11–23.
Leadbeater, C. (1997), *The Rise of the Social Entrepreneur*, London: Demos.
McClelland, D. (1961), *The Achieving Society*, Princeton, NJ: Van Nostrand.
Majaro, S. (1988), *The Creativity Gap*, London: Longman.
O'Dell, T. and P. Billing (eds) (2005), *Experience-scapes*, Copenhagen: Copenhagen Business School Press.
Pine, J. and J. Gilmore (1999), *The Experience Economy*, Boston: Harvard Business School Press.
Pine, J. and J. Gilmore (2007), *Authenticity*, Boston: Harvard Business School Press.
Rogers, E.M. (1995), *Diffusion of Innovation*, New York: Free Press.
Runco, M. (2004), 'Creativity', *Annual Review of Psychology*, **55**, 657–87.
Schendel, D. and D. Channon (eds) (1990), *Strategic Management Journal*, Special Issue on Corporate Entrepreneurship, **11**.
Schumpeter, J. (1934), *The Theory of Economic Development*, Cambridge, MA: Harvard University Press.

Sundbo, J. (2004), 'The management of rock festivals as the basis for business development: An example of the growing experience economy', *International Journal of Entrepreneurship and Innovation Management*, **4**(6), 587–612.

Sundbo, J. and P. Darmer (eds) (2008), *Creation of Experiences in the Experience Economy*, Cheltenham, UK and Northampton, MA, USA: Edward Elgar Publishing.

Svejonova, S., C. Mazza and M. Planellas (2007), 'Cooking up change in haute cuisine: Ferran Adria as an institutional entrepreneur', *Journal of Organizational Behavior*, **28**(5), 539–61.

Swedberg, R. (2000), *Entrepreneurship: A Social Science View*, Oxford: Oxford University Press.

Tan, G. (1998), 'Managing creativity in organizations: A total system approach', *Creativity and Innovation Management*, **7**(1), 23–31.

Tarde, G. (1895), *Les lois de l'imitation*, Paris: Alcan.

Vækstfonden (2007), *Oplevelsesindustrien: Perspektiver for iværksættere og venturekapital* [The experience industry. Perspective for entrepreneurs and venture capitals], Copenhagen: Vækstfonden.

Weick, K. (1995), *Sensemaking in Organizations*, Thousand Oaks, CA: Sage.

19 Post-Soviet societies and new venture creation
Friederike Welter and David Smallbone

INTRODUCTION

This chapter is concerned with new venture creation in economies which until recently were operating under central planning. Whilst they are often described collectively as transition economies, the evidence presented below demonstrates that they cannot be treated as a homogeneous group from an entrepreneurship development and new venture creation perspective. During the socialist period, private entrepreneurship was regarded as an illegal activity in the former Soviet republics, although certain forms of entrepreneurship were tolerated in many Central and East European countries, as discussed below. Since the collapse of the Soviet Union in 1989, all of the former Soviet republics have at least tolerated entrepreneurship (although, based on government actions in some countries, entrepreneurship is barely accepted), with countries in Central and Eastern Europe actively encouraging it. Essentially, the stance adopted by governments towards private enterprise during the post-socialist period tends to reflect their commitment to the wider processes of market reform, with the path to EU accession as a key driver in Central and East European countries.

Since most research on new venture creation has focused on mature market economies, a key question concerns the extent to which differences can be observed in the process of new business creation in transition environments and to what extent socialist experiences are of importance for today's entrepreneurship. These questions are potentially of wider interest because they focus on the relationship between venture creation and the external environment in which it occurs. The extent to which the processes and forms of entrepreneurship observed in these countries during the transition period may be viewed as a distinct response to a specific set of external environmental conditions has potentially important theoretical implications in terms of the social embeddedness of entrepreneurship.

The chapter starts with reviewing the socialist heritage for new venture creation, before proceeding to review entrepreneurship under transition conditions. It finishes with identifying emerging themes for entrepreneurship research and theory.

THE SOCIALIST HERITAGE FOR NEW VENTURE CREATION

In recent years, entrepreneurship scholars have been discussing the extent to which entrepreneurship existed in a centrally planned economy and, if it did, whether (any of) the experiences and know-how acquired during socialist times are influencing entrepreneurship development in the post-socialist period. One of the particular themes in this regard concerns the effect of the institutional legacies on entrepreneurship during the transition period. Despite the common legacy of central planning, differences can be identified between countries in terms of the types of business activity that were tolerated under socialism. In Central and East European countries particularly, forms of entrepreneurial activities, both private and within state enterprises, coexisted beside state ownership. In this regard, it is helpful to distinguish between the formal and informal economies, with a significant grey or overlapping area between them, and also between legal and illegal activities. The formal economy included legally operating state enterprises and legalized private enterprises, while the grey economy consisted of the second economy, together with any illegal activities (Dallago 1990). The second economy included forms of unlicensed but tolerated entrepreneurial activities at private and state levels, and some illegal, but tolerated, forms such as the unofficial use of state-owned resources. The term 'second economy' has also been applied to the so-called 'parallel circuits' of state firms and co-operatives that were motivated by official enterprises searching for ways to meet planning targets (Kerblay 1977). The illegal economy referred to criminal activities both within and between state enterprises and also criminal private activities. The grey economy signalled deficits of the planned economy, where state managers were slow and inflexible when it came to satisfying changing and specialized demands from customers, because of the rules of central planning. In this regard, it may be argued that the second economy played an important role in enabling the society to function.

Political reforms often changed the boundaries of the formal and grey economies, either fostering or restricting private entrepreneurial activities (Welter 1996). For example, the boundary between tolerated and illegal entrepreneurial activities was never defined officially, but depended on interpretation by state officials, tending to follow the dominant political discourse and consequently leaving room for discretionary decisions. The boundary between the second and the formal economy was usually contested territory between reformers in the governments and their opponents.

With the introduction of a centrally planned system in Soviet countries and Central Europe, entrepreneurship lost its role. During this period, the economy did not require independent and creative private entrepreneurs, but rather directors, who were expected to administer the state plans in their companies (Dubravcic 1995). However, in Central Europe, the first steps towards the (re-)establishment of private entrepreneurship and businesses in both the formal and the second economy occurred as early as 1968, fostering, albeit unintentionally, entrepreneurship within state companies, as well as private entrepreneurship. One example is Hungary, which was at the forefront of these reforms (Welter 2002). Central planning and the central allocation of resources to firms were abolished almost totally in Hungary, while the government introduced a system of financial (dis-)incentives as a management instrument for state-owned firms (Laky 1985). Although the Hungarian government introduced these reforms to develop price and profit orientation in state firms, they resulted instead in bargaining processes between directors of state-owned enterprises and the state administration, which favoured the development of informal networks. These so-called parallel circuits (Kerblay 1977) reflect one of the specific forms of 'entrepreneurial' behaviour within state companies during socialist times. In order to fulfil plans, it was less important for the directors of state-owned firms to display entrepreneurial talent than to have the 'right' connections in administration and government. This resulted in a personalization of bureaucracy that fostered everyday subversion (Ledeneva 1998), with potential impacts on entrepreneurship during the transition period, as discussed below in the section 'The micro perspective: the origin and nature of entrepreneurship'.

Differences in the time and pace of nationalization campaigns and reforms under socialism also influenced the extent and nature of legalized private entrepreneurship during the socialist period, but with an impact also on entrepreneurship development during the post-socialist period. Again, there are different country situations to be taken into account (Smallbone and Welter 2009). While in Russia private entrepreneurship never flourished during industrialization, Central Asian countries were characterized by a vibrant trader's culture and traditions, and Central Europe saw a boom of private entrepreneurship associated with industrialization from the eighteenth century onwards. However, after the Second World War, private entrepreneurship essentially vanished across Central and Eastern Europe, as a result of massive nationalization campaigns across the region. For example, in Czechoslovakia the last medium-sized industrial companies with up to 100 employees were nationalized in 1959 (Gerslová and Steiner 1993). Poland allowed small privately owned manufacturing enterprises until the 1950s. In Hungary, most private enterprises were nationalized between 1949 and 1953; and in 1958 private craft entrepreneurs were required to join production co-operatives (Gabor and Horváth 1987, p. 134). In East Germany, private craft enterprises 'survived', although restricted to a maximum number of ten employees and to specific business fields (Welter 1996).

Nevertheless, in some Central European countries, legalized private entrepreneurship continued to play a (small) role under socialism (Laky 1984; Noar and Brod 1986; Grabher 1994; Lageman *et al.* 1994). For example, in 1972 and 1974 respectively Poland introduced laws facilitating the creation of small craft enterprises and private retail shops and services. It should be noted however that, because of the definition of 'craft' that was used during the Soviet period,[1] the Polish 'craft sector' contained some small manufacturing firms that were relatively modern and well equipped and which became a foundation for the development of manufacturing and construction activities during the transformation period. From 1976 the government also allowed so-called 'Polonia' firms, that is, ventures set up by Polish emigrants (Welter 1996). At the beginning of the 1980s it began the process of legalizing the existence of private firms, which resulted in a doubling of the number of small firms in the 1980s, although the real explosion of entrepreneurship occurred after a second round of administrative reforms in 1989 (Piasecki and Rogut 1993).

In Hungary, at the end of the 1970s around 5 per cent of the workforce worked in the legal private sector, and an estimated two-thirds of all households earned an additional income in the second economy (Grabher 1994). In an attempt to transform such informal neighbourhood-based subsistence production (Grabher 1994), the Hungarian government allowed for new organizational and legal private forms of enterprise such as joint ventures in 1973. In the late 1970s it also started renting shops to private entrepreneurs (Bod 1989). During the 1980s, economic reforms increased the upper limit for the number of employees allowed in small firms and introduced new forms of private ownership. This included the 100 per cent private business partnership (GMK), which consisted of no more than 30 members and 30 employees. It also included the so-called business work partnerships (VGMK) in which, from 1982 onwards, state employees could rent machinery or space from their employer to collectively produce their own products and services. However, neither initiative fostered the emergence of a sustainable private sector: 70 per cent of the GMK were working part time, and three-quarters had no fixed assets invested in their organization (Laky 1991). The VGMK produced so-called working brigades as semi-independent departments within state firms for performing overtime work (Laky 1989). They also reinforced the parallel circuits within state enterprises (Bohle 1996).

By contrast, in former Soviet republics, and also in Czechoslovakia, all forms of private entrepreneurship were illegal during the socialist period. As a consequence, entrepreneurial behaviour mainly involved illegal activities, such as moonlighting, unofficial use of state machinery for private aims, and tolerated theft from the workplace (Taigner 1987; Dallago 1990; Los 1992). Alongside this, the *tolkach* (pusher) represented a more productive form of entrepreneurial behaviour. As an employee in a state-owned enterprise, he was responsible for securing external resources in order to meet planning targets, which was a necessary response to the constant shortage of resources and materials during the Soviet period (Kerblay 1977; Ledeneva 1998). Operating illegally, he often made use of production in state firms that was unaccounted for, in order to barter for resources and/or for goods and services that were in popular demand (Kordonskii 1995). In addition, Rehn and Taalas (2004) have emphasized how entrepreneurship flourished in the daily lives of individuals during the Soviet period, as people struggled to cope with material shortages. Another type of illegal entrepreneurial activity during the Soviet period, visible in all Soviet and Central European socialist states, was the so-called 'suitcase trade', where small petty traders shuttled across borders in order to acquire goods for sale, often using holidays and tourist visits to facilitate their income-generating activities (Williams and Balaz 2002).

In this context, Kornai (1992) posed the question of whether socialism can be a seedbed for capitalism. The issue has wider consequences for entrepreneurship development, influencing not only the extent but also the nature of entrepreneurship in transition economies and its role in the wider society. Some authors, such as Dallago (1997), are highly critical of the potential of a Soviet-type system to produce productive entrepreneurship at all. Implicitly, the main argument of such critics relates to the experiences of the Soviet period fostering a so-called 'Soviet' mentality, which represents an antithesis of an ideal-type entrepreneur. In this view, 'Soviet man' (or woman) is characterized by a lack of initiative, a low propensity to take risks and a weak responsibility for his/her actions. Not surprisingly, the Soviet economy produced entrepreneurial behaviour which was adapted to the specific conditions pertaining at the time, in which corruption played a role in facilitating the operation of state-owned enterprises, while legalized private entrepreneurs operated in protected market niches in a seller's market (Gabor 1991; Kornai 1992; Búltova and Bútorová 1993; Kabele 1993). Other research has emphasized how individual behaviour during the transition period resulted mainly from situational influences rather than attitudinal ones (Shiller *et al.* 1992). However, one might suggest that the two are inseparable, in that individual attitudes are inevitably shaped by experiences and the wider social context, which influences what types of behaviour are socially acceptable. In this context, the review in this section questions a portrayal based on a uniformly bleak picture of a Soviet economy in which creativity and initiative were not allowed. Instead, it suggests that Soviet entrepreneurship was rather more complex (Rehn and Taalas 2004, p. 243). Directors of state-owned enterprises needed to behave entrepreneurially in order to meet planning targets, while individuals used creativity and initiative in order to cope with a shortage economy, thereby also demonstrating qualities that would typically be associated with entrepreneurship. In addition, experimental reforms helped to foster certain types of entrepreneurial behaviour both in state firms and by private individuals, although the former was unintended.

NEW VENTURE CREATION IN A POST-SOVIET CONTEXT

The Macro Perspective: NVC, Market Reforms and Policies

From an economic perspective, the transformation of a centrally planned into a market-based economy involves: firstly, a shift in the dominant form of ownership from public to private; secondly, a liberalization of markets and a removal of price controls; and, thirdly, the creation of market institutions. A change in the dominant form of ownership, and resource allocation mechanisms, implies fundamental, systemic change. Furthermore, the nature and extent of reforms with respect to each of the three aspects listed have important implications for the extent to which a productive and sustainable private business sector is likely to develop. Imperfections and deficiencies with respect to any, or all, of these dimensions are likely to have implications for the forms of entrepreneurship that develop, as well as for their frequency of occurrence. At the same time, it might be suggested that the nature of the relationship between the transformation of the economy and the development of entrepreneurship is a recursive one. As Piasecki (1995) has noted, at an early stage of transformation the emergence of a business-owning class is a key element in contributing to the social change that is integral to the wider transformation process, as well as being influenced by the opportunities to own one's own business which the process of market reform enables.

The emphasis in the previous section was on differences in the entrepreneurial legacy inherited from the socialist period between former Soviet republics and Central and East European countries, which themselves show considerable heterogeneity. Not only was the starting-point different (whilst sharing some common features), but differences in the pace of market reforms since the 1990s have contributed to the contrasting environments for new venture creation, which themselves have changed over time. For example, a distinction can be made between the so-called 'initial phase' or period of liberalization reforms (such as price and trade liberalization and small-scale privatization), which tended to take priority in the early stages of transformation, and 'second phase' or institution-building reforms (such as competition policy, enterprise restructuring and the development of financial institutions), which typically take longer to implement (EBRD 2003). The first type of reforms are easier to achieve, because essentially they require a reduction in state activity, while the second type are more difficult, because they focus on the development of market-based structures and institutions.

Although the experience of some countries (such as Belarus) shows that entrepreneurship can exist despite serious institutional deficiencies, the number of private enterprises is typically small and their contribution to economic development limited. In other words, the absence of key framework conditions will undoubtedly hamper the development of productive entrepreneurship. At the same time, it is arguable as to whether their achievement of the basic framework conditions for private sector development represents a sufficient condition for sustainable and productive entrepreneurship to become established, because of the potential influence of the years under central planning on the attitudes towards entrepreneurship and the wider culture of enterprise in the population.

The extent to which the potential contribution of SMEs to the process of economic transformation is actually fulfilled in practice is undoubtedly influenced by the policy stance taken by the state. This is because government is one of the key influences on the external environment in which businesses develop in any economy, acting as an enabling and/or a constraining force, particularly in relation to institutional change and development. Whilst it should be emphasized that setting up and developing businesses results from the creativity, drive and commitment of individuals rather than as a result of actions taken by government, the conditions that enable and/or constrain the process of entrepreneurship are affected by the wider social, economic, political and institutional context, over which the state has a major influence. In this respect, it is important to stress the variety of ways in which government can affect the nature and pace of SME development, rather than narrowly focusing on direct support measures and programmes. This involves the role of the state in relation to macroeconomic policy, the tax and regulatory regime, and the development of appropriate market-oriented institutions, as well as direct support measures and the state's influence on the value placed on entrepreneurship within the wider society, such as through the education system (Smallbone and Welter 2001b).

One of the contemporary themes in the mainstream entrepreneurship literature is concerned with the creation and identification of entrepreneurial opportunities, which raises the question of whether the entrepreneurial process differs in a transition environment and, if so, in what aspects. In this context, Shane's (2003) distinction between Schumpeterian and Kirznerian opportunities is potentially helpful. Schumpeterian opportunities result from disequilibrating situations, which makes them rare and innovative, involving the creation of new combinations. Compared to this, Kirznerian opportunities are understood as being equilibrating, not requiring new information, less innovative, common and having a limited potential for discovery and innovation.

In a transition context, the Kirznerian type of opportunities are typically more apparent in later stages of transition, where markets have been developed and flows of information, ideas and knowledge from mature market economies represent an important source of innovation for enterprises. This is reflected in empirical surveys in more advanced transition countries (Smallbone and Welter 2009), where entrepreneurs complain about growing competition as one of their pressing business problems, whilst in early-stage transition countries it is a lack of the resources needed to realize an entrepreneur's business idea, together with a lack of institutional stability and unpredictability of institutional behaviour, that is emphasized. At the beginning of the transition period, limited competition existed in many markets, and market opportunities resulted from the shortages of certain goods for which a latent demand existed. Such an environment was potentially a 'seedbed' for the Schumpeterian type of opportunities for entrepreneurs, although a variety of institutional constraints limited their ability to exploit these.

The embeddedness of opportunities in the formal institutional environment may be illustrated with reference to the initial changes in the institutional framework which fostered entrepreneurship when legal and administrative reforms made it legally possible for privately owned businesses to compete with state-owned enterprises. Consequently, the number of private firms increased sharply, facilitated by a removal of legal barriers to market entry, combined with the low intensity of competition and the existence of opportunities to earn monopoly profits and/or speculative incomes for a period. In explaining this, McMillan and Woodruff (2002) emphasize the results of distortions created by the planned economy, which created new market opportunities for potential entrepreneurs (e.g. in consumer services) once the establishment of privately owned enterprises became legal. However, in situations where a new formal framework is still to be properly implemented, 'loopholes' for 'creative' entrepreneurial activities may be created, although some of these may fall into the category of more unproductive or even destructive entrepreneurship, as described by Baumol (1990).

The Micro Perspective: The Origin and Nature of Entrepreneurship

Entrepreneurship development in post-socialist societies began from a variety of different starting-points in different countries, because, as discussed previously, the experience of former Soviet republics differed from that of Central and Eastern European countries. Of interest here is the potential of entrepreneurial activities and behaviour during socialist times (see the section: 'The socialist heritage for new venture creation') to foster or constrain entrepreneurship development during the transition period, as well as to affect the nature of entrepreneurship that has developed since the collapse of socialism.

Who are the post-socialist entrepreneurs?

Several studies have produced classifications of different groups of entrepreneurs during transition. For Hungary, for example, Tibor (1994, 2008) identifies different groups of contemporary entrepreneurs based on their demographic and business characteristics: artisans and retailers from the period before 1982 and their offspring; old-new[2] owner-managers from the 1980s; forced entrepreneurs from the early transition period who had lost their jobs through the restructuring of large enterprises; managers of state-owned enterprises and 'old' co-operatives; managers of newly established privatized firms; and owners and managers of newly established small firms and joint ventures. Similarly, in Russia, four main 'waves' of entrepreneurs have been identified (Astrakhan and Chepurenko 2003). At the start of the process between 1987 and 1989, many of the entrepreneurs who owned and led co-operative firms[3] had illegal incomes, often through contacts with criminals. High-level government clerks dominated the second wave of entrepreneurs in 1989–90, whereas the third wave (1991–92) contained mainly directors and managers of state-owned firms who had taken the opportunity to privatize 'their' enterprises or to establish new businesses (Lageman 1995; Dallago 1997; Kusnezova 1999). The fourth wave of private entrepreneurs (1992–93) included those who benefited from small privatization, as well as entrepreneurs who set up businesses as an alternative to unemployment and/or because they perceived market opportunities. At the same time, although recent empirical research is not available, the background of individuals starting businesses in Russia in 2008 undoubtedly includes many who were too young to have been active in the labour market during the socialist period, whose behavioural traits may differ somewhat from those of the previous generation of business founders.

Entrepreneurial activities within state organizations, together with business experience obtained in the Soviet 'Komsomol' economy (Kryshtanovskaya and White 1996; Gustafson 1999), party connections that had been used by sons and daughters of party members to set up businesses (Tibor 1994) and 'spontaneous' or 'wild' privatization during the first transition years (e.g. for Hungary: Voszka 1991, 1993; Frydman *et al.* 1998; for Russia: Aslund 1997), contributed to the development of so-called nomenclatura businesses during the transition period, when entrepreneurs often used their connections from the Soviet era to protect a market niche or to strip their enterprises of assets to sell. During the early years of transition, nomenclatura entrepreneurship occurred widely throughout Central and Eastern Europe, often contributing to a negative image of entrepreneurship in the population at large, because these entrepreneurs used their ventures for personal rent-seeking purposes. In Hungary, for example, Voszka (1993) identified a period of 'escaping from the state', as illustrated by the spontaneous privatization, and a period of 'escaping to the state', when such enterprises began asking for state subsidies. Where this revived 'old' network connections and resulted in soft budget constraints, it may be argued that such nomenclatura entrepreneurship impeded private entrepreneurship development during transition.

The prospects of legal private enterprises that originated during socialism to survive and prosper during the transition period were mixed. Where owners of these enterprises were elderly when transition started, often using outdated technology and machinery, not surprisingly they experienced difficulties in adjusting to the requirements of a market economy, especially in acquiring the management skills needed to work on a buyer's market (Tibor 2008). This may differ for entrepreneurs (re-)privatizing retail and craft enterprises during the early transition period or those continuing a family tradition. Old-new entrepreneurs from the 1980s who were typically educated to university level could be found among the large number of people who (re-)registered new businesses once legislation abolished the legal and administrative barriers to private firms existing, enabling them to operate on an equal basis with state-owned companies (Kuczi and Vajda 1990, 1992).

Empirical evidence from Poland also suggests that entrepreneurship became a more attractive option for educated people once the transition process began. In a survey of 300 Polish manufacturing SMEs undertaken in 1995, in which 18 per cent had been established before the start of the process of administrative reform in 1981, firms set up after 1988 were significantly more likely to be graduate led than older firms set up before 1981 (Smallbone *et al.* 1996). In addition, with 30 per cent of the firms surveyed having commenced trading before 1989, the age profile of businesses was rather different from that in a parallel survey of firms in the Baltic states, in which just 5 per cent started trading before 1989, mostly as a result of privatization (Smallbone and Piasecki 1996). For the Baltic states, this age profile reflects the lack of tolerance of any non-state-owned economic activity in former Soviet republics before the start of the transformation period. Considerable heterogeneity exists within the SME sector in most countries, although the unique nature of the development path of private enterprise in Poland (and also East Germany), which included the toleration of a substantial number of small, non-state-owned enterprises during the centrally planned period, adds a specific dimension to this heterogeneity.

Family traditions and entrepreneurship
Especially in countries with a strong pre-war tradition of private entrepreneurship such as East Germany, Hungary or Poland, some entrepreneurs originated from former entrepreneurial families, especially during the early transition period. Lageman (1995, p. 114) estimated the offspring of pre-socialist entrepreneurs for Central European countries between 25 and 40 per cent, whilst by contrast, in a 1997 survey in Ukraine, Belarus and Moldova, 'family background' was only mentioned by a handful of respondents (Smallbone and Welter 2001a). The latter result is similar to survey findings from Russia, where Djankov *et al.* (2005) refer to only 5 per cent of Russian entrepreneurs inheriting their business. Welter (1998) showed, for craft enterprises in Leipzig, East Germany, that more than 50 per cent of enterprises had been set up before 1990, nearly 30 per cent of the craft entrepreneurs operating in 1994 had a family-owned enterprise, and 30 per cent of parents and 37 per cent of grandparents had been entrepreneurs themselves. In this regard, in his study on socialist entrepreneurs in Hungary, Szelenyi (1988) identified a so-called 'parking mechanism', where previous entrepreneurs were able to use their knowledge and capabilities to secure leading positions in state firms. Apparently, entrepreneurial traditions could be transported via high-level professional positions, where individuals 'parked' their entrepreneurial skills, whilst using them in so far as they were allowed to 'practise' autonomous decision making involving limited risk taking (Szelenyi 1988).

Clearly, in a transition context, the relationship between family tradition and entrepreneurship is country-specific and also needs to be related to the time when the business was first established. Evidence from Poland suggests that 'family tradition' was a common motive given by private firms that were set up under communism (Wyznikiewicz *et al.* 1993), but less often mentioned by businesses that were started during the transition period itself (Smallbone and Piasecki 1996). At the same time, entrepreneurial activities that were illegal and/or were tolerated in the Soviet period also contributed to entrepreneurship development during the transition period. In Latvia, Dombrovsky and Welter (2006) showed that a quarter of all respondents in their study reported that a relative of theirs had been an entrepreneur during the Soviet times. This implies not only that there were substantial underground profit-seeking activities in the Soviet Union, but also that this affected post-socialist entrepreneurship even in those countries where private entrepreneurship during socialism was forbidden. In this regard, Djankov *et al.* (2005) describe a transgenerational transmission also for Soviet countries, similar to Szelenyi's observations outlined above. They showed that parents of current entrepreneurs in Russia were less likely to have been workers during Soviet times, which relates to the phenomenon of nomenclatura entrepreneurship described above. Dombrovsky and Welter (2006) also demonstrate that the effect of having a relative who was an entrepreneur after independence increases the likelihood of being an entrepreneur by more than twice as much as having a relative who was an entrepreneur in Soviet times. Although this confirms the high impact of family background on entrepreneurship in general, it also indicates the greater importance of entrepreneurial role models from the post-socialist period, which may be viewed as encouraging from the point of view of the development of 'productive' entrepreneurship.

The potential of illegal and informal entrepreneurial activities
Alongside this, other studies have shown the potential of entrepreneurial activities conducted illegally during the Soviet period to provide a foundation for more substantial and productive entrepreneurship post-socialism. For example, in Russia, Guariglia and Kim (2006) find that one-quarter of newly self-employed entrepreneurs had been 'moonlighting' in the past. Aidis and van Praag (2007) confirm the existence of positive benefits from illegal entrepreneurial experiences acquired under socialism in supporting entrepreneurship and economic development in the transition period. Moreover, research on shuttle traders or 'trader-tourists' showed their roots in Soviet times (Thuen 1999; Wallace *et al.* 1999; Yükseker 2007). This refers to the second issue raised above, namely the nature of entrepreneurship that has developed during transition.

In this regard, part of the distinctiveness of entrepreneurship in post-socialist economies is that it is taking place in multiple market economies

(Smith 2002), which refers to the formal and informal economies. The 'legacy of non-compliance' from the Soviet period, together with loopholes in the legal framework during the early transition years, fostered the emergence of a vibrant informal economy in most post-Soviet economies, although this lost (some) momentum in the years preceding accession in those countries which joined the European Union from 2004 onwards. Such informal activities include a wide variety of activities on a 'cash-in-hand basis', which may be viewed as specific features of the post-Soviet period, including shuttle trading and the widespread use of informal employment. Williams (2005) finds informal activities to be a widespread phenomenon, with just two-thirds of households in post-Soviet economies relying on incomes earned in the formal sector. Williams *et al.* (2007) illustrated that 51 per cent of all Ukrainian households reliant on informal strategies to earn income are multiple-earner households; only 6 per cent are non-earner households (i.e. with no employment possibilities outside the informal sector), whilst nearly two-thirds of self-employed entrepreneurs were operating without a licence, that is, informally and illegally. An empirical study of Moscow households emphasizes the 'multiple economies' existing during the transition period, including formal and informal, private and state as well as monetized and non-monetized spheres (Pavlovskaya 2004). The author points out that these 'sub-economies' should not be seen as dichotomies, but rather complementary to one another, with boundaries that are permeable and fuzzy. Moreover, several empirical studies have shown that legal and illegal or grey activities coexist in a transition context, with most new and small firms involved in productive and rent-seeking activities at the same time (Rehn and Taalas 2004; Smallbone and Welter 2009). It is typically not one or the other.

This has consequences for our understanding of entrepreneurial activities in transition environments, suggesting that informal activities can be a seedbed for more substantial entrepreneurial ventures, as argued by several authors (Guariglia and Kim 2006; Smallbone and Welter 2006; Williams *et al.* 2007). Bennett and Estrin (2007), for example, show how informal activities allow entrepreneurs to explore the profitability of a venture idea by using them as a stepping stone, allowing them to experiment cheaply in an uncertain environment. Recent research undertaken by the authors on petty trading activity in EU border regions has distinguished between, on the one hand, those driven by proprietorship-type motivation (Scase 2003), where individuals lack the interest and ability towards entrepreneurship, and, on the other, more entrepreneurial individuals whose motivation, drive and resourcefulness make them nascent entrepreneurs (Welter and Smallbone 2009). In this regard, it is important to recognize the heterogeneity of informal entrepreneurial activity that exists, only some of which is likely to have real potential as a development route into more formal forms of entrepreneurship. In the context of NVC this has potentially interesting implications for theorizing and empirically analysing entrepreneurship in a transition context.

Proprietorship or entrepreneurship?

One of the distinctive features of new venture creation under transition conditions, identified by some authors, focuses on the motives of those starting businesses. Richard Scase, for example, distinguishes between entrepreneurship and proprietorship, based on 'contrasting psychologies of business founders; their attitudes towards trading; and their orientation towards capital accumulation' (Scase 2003, p.67). In the pursuit of the latter, an entrepreneur may forgo personal consumption and may actively search out market opportunities, which involves taking risks and coping with uncertainty. Proprietors have quite different motives, because surpluses are consumed and used to sustain living standards. Scase argues that, in the transitional economies of Russia and Central Europe, proprietorship rather than entrepreneurship best describes the majority of small business activity, with implications for the development of entrepreneurship, as he sees proprietors who own and run most of these firms as incapable of constituting an indigenous force for economic development.

As mentioned above, the rapidly changing nature of external conditions in transition environments means that the characteristics and contribution of small business activity may change over time, as well as in different national contexts (Smallbone and Welter 2001a). In this context, the so-called proprietorship which Scase emphasizes may be a more common condition in the early stages of transition or in countries where market reforms have not been properly installed, but become relatively less important in countries where external conditions become more stable. Moreover, as Scase himself recognizes, the emergence of a stratum of small traders in transition economies must be seen as part of a social transformation contributing to wider consumer choice and the emergence of a middle class, as well as an economic agent. All in all, detailed case study evidence suggests that such categories, although intuitively attractive, may at best oversimplify, but at worst distort, the reality of business behaviour, particularly in circumstances where the external environment is changing rapidly and where entrepreneurs appear to have considerable human capital and adaptive capacity (Smallbone and Welter 2009). In terms of human capital, the propensity of entrepreneurs, in early-stage transition conditions, to be highly educated is a consistent theme emerging from the transition literature (for an overview of research see Smallbone and Welter 2009). This is partly explained by the specificities of external conditions that can lead to even well-educated people being presented with limited opportunities for satisfying and sufficiently rewarding employment, encouraging them to consider the entrepreneurship option. The human capital possessed by these individuals means that they are well equipped to identify and exploit opportunities as they emerge over time, even if the reasons for becoming entrepreneurs in the first place can reasonably be described as necessity based and their initial behaviour as proprietorship. The limitations of such a crude dichotomy are also reinforced by the learning experience of individuals, which can contribute to changes in their motivation and behaviour with respect to entrepreneurship over time as new opportunities are presented and/or because of the development of their own entrepreneurial capacity. This argument is not confined to transition environments but commonly applies in them, because the external environment can change so rapidly and entrepreneurs often have the human capital to respond positively to these changes.

NEW VENTURE CREATION IN A POST-SOCIALIST CONTEXT: EMERGING THEMES

This review demonstrates that entrepreneurship in transition economies has many distinctive features which are associated with the historical legacy inherited by entrepreneurs in the post-socialist period and the transformation path followed by countries which until less than 20 years ago were operating under socialism and the rules of central planning. Empirically, the review shows that, whilst they share many common features, post-socialist countries also have some key differences in the precise nature and impact of the historical legacy, as well as in the economic and institutional development path followed during the transformation period, which has implications for the nature of entrepreneurship in a post-socialist context.

One theme emerging from the review concerns the institutional embeddedness of post-socialist entrepreneurship, referring to the embeddedness of entrepreneurship both in legal and regulatory contexts (the so-called formal institutions) and in society, as reflected by the impact of socialist legacy and societal attitudes towards entrepreneurship on entrepreneurial behaviour during transition. This is apparent (in both a formal and an informal sense) in the contrasting experiences of former Soviet republics and countries that are now members of the EU. In the first case, institutional deficiencies have hampered the development of productive entrepreneurship, whilst, in the second, institutional development that has been encouraged by the path towards EU accession has facilitated entrepreneurship. In Central and East European countries in particular, changes in the nature and pace of entrepreneurship development over time are also apparent, as the process of market reform unfolded, with its associated institutional change. Moreover, the review demonstrates the value of considering entrepreneurship as a societal phenomenon, which draws attention to antecedents and outcomes of entrepreneurial behaviour (Davidsson 2003). The societal context contributes to explaining why some entrepreneurs see opportunities and others don't, why opportunities vary over time and why the outcomes of entrepreneurial activities as well as entrepreneurial behaviour might vary in a post-socialist context and change over time as transition proceeds.

At the same time, it is important to emphasize that the study of entrepreneurship in transition environments should not be viewed as some kind of eccentric or marginal activity, since the findings reviewed have important implications for mainstream theory. At the heart of the distinctiveness of venture creation and development in transition economies is the specific interplay between individual entrepreneur/firm behaviour and the external environment, which changes as the process of transition unfolds. Mainstream entrepreneurship theories need to be able to incorporate a wide range of external environmental conditions, including those where market conditions are only partially established. Entrepreneurship in transition environments may have some unique features, but the essential principles of individual behaviour are the same regardless of the environment. Davidsson (2003) has emphasized the need for entrepreneurship research to acknowledge the heterogeneity of environmental conditions, outcomes and behaviours, and the incorporation of entrepreneurship in the conditions described in this chapter are part of this heterogeneity.

NOTES

1. During the Stalinist period, the term 'craft' was often used to describe a variety of different types of production and service activity, since it appeared less exploitative in a Marxist sense and thus more ideologically palatable than 'small private firms'. 'Crafts' were defined as a type of economic activity in which the craftsman (owner of the firm) participated directly, performing the same operations as employees hired by him.
2. 'Old-new' refers to the fact that entrepreneurship in Hungary dates back to the early reform experiments of the socialist state during the 1980s, which allowed for entrepreneurial activities ('old' owner-managers). 'New' refers to the fact that these 'old' entrepreneurs had to learn new rules of the game once the transition towards a market economy started.
3. In former Soviet republics, the first type of non-state-owned enterprise that was legally permitted was co-operatives in 1987.

REFERENCES

Aidis, R. and M. van Praag (2007), 'Illegal entrepreneurship experience: Does it make a difference for business performance and motivation?', *Journal of Business Venturing*, **22**(2), 283–310.

Aslund, A. (1997), 'Observations on the development of small private enterprises in Russia', *Post-Soviet Geography and Economics*, **38**(4), 191–205.

Astrakhan, I. and A. Chepurenko (2003), 'Small business in Russia: Any prospects after a decade?', *Futures*, **35**(4), 341–59.

Baumol, W. (1990), 'Entrepreneurship: Productive, unproductive and destructive', *Journal of Political Economy*, **98**(5), 893–921.

Bennett, J. and S. Estrin (2007), 'Informality as a stepping stone: Entrepreneurial entry in a developing economy', IZA Discussion Paper 2950, IZA, Bonn.

Bod, P.A. (1989), 'Deregulation and institution building: Lessons from the reform of the Hungarian public sector', *Jahrbuch der Wirtschaft Osteuropas*, **13**(1), 110–26.

Bohle, D. (1996), 'Governance im Spätsozialismus: Die Herausbildung hybrider Koordinationsformen und informeller Vernetzungen in Ungarn und Polen in den achtziger Jahren', WZB Discussion Paper FS I 96-102, WZB, Berlin.

Búltova, M. and Z. Bútorová (1993), 'Slovakia: The identity challenges of the newly born state', *Social Research*, **60**(4), 705–31.

Dallago, B. (1990), *The Irregular Economy: The 'Underground' Economy and the 'Black' Labour Market*, Aldershot: Dartmouth.

Dallago, B. (1997), 'The economic system, transition and opportunities for entrepreneurship', in OECD (ed.), *Entrepreneurship and SMEs in Transition Economies: The Visegrad Conference*, Paris: OECD, pp. 103–24.

Davidsson, P. (2003), 'The domain of entrepreneurship research: Some suggestions', in J. Katz and D. Shepherd (eds), *Advances in Entrepreneurship, Firm Emergence and Growth*, Vol. 6, Oxford: Elsevier/JAI Press, pp. 315–72.

Djankov, S., E. Miguel, Y. Qian, G. Roland and E. Zhuravskaya (2005), 'Who are Russia's entrepreneurs?', *Journal of the European Economic Association*, **3**(2–3), 587–97.

Dombrovsky, V. and F. Welter (2006), 'The role of personal and family background in making entrepreneurs in a post-socialist environment', paper presented at Babson College Entrepreneurship Research Conference (BCERC), 8–10 June 2006, Bloomington, IN.

Dubravcic, D. (1995), 'Entrepreneurial aspects of privatisation in transition economies', *Europe-Asia Studies*, **47**(2), 305–16.

EBRD (2003), *Integration and Regional Cooperation: Transition Report 2003*, London: EBRD.

Frydman, R., K. Murphy and A. Rapaczynski (1998), *Capitalism with a Comrade's Face*, Budapest: Central European University Press.

Gabor, I.R. (1991), 'Prospects and limits to the second economy', *Acta Oeconomica*, **43**(3–4), 349–52.

Gabor, I.R. and T.D. Horváth (1987), 'Failure and retreat in the Hungarian private small-scale industry', *Acta Oeconomica*, **38**(1–2), 133–53.

Gerslová, J. and J. Steiner (1993), 'Die Größenstruktur der Industriebetriebe der tschechischen Länder in den Jahren 1902–1930', *Österreichische Osthefte*, **35**(3), 395–412.

Grabher, G. (1994), 'The elegance of incoherence: Institutional legacies, privatization and regional development in East Germany and Hungary', WZB Discussion Paper FS I 94-03, WZB, Berlin.

Guariglia, A. and B.-Y. Kim (2006), 'The dynamics of moonlighting in Russia', *Economics of Transition*, **14**(1), 1–45.

Gustafson, T. (1999), *Capitalism Russian-Style*, Cambridge: Cambridge University Press.

Kabele, J. (1993), 'The dynamics of social problems and transformations of Czechoslovak society', *Social Research*, **60**(4), 763–85.

Kerblay, B. (1977), *La société soviétique contemporaine*, Paris: Armand Colin.

Kordonskii, S. (1995), 'The structure of economic space in post-*perestroika* society and the transformation of the administrative market', in K. Segbers and S. De Spiegeleire (eds), *Post-Soviet Puzzles: Mapping the Political Economy of the Former Soviet Economy*, Vol. I: *Against the Background of the Former Soviet Union*, Baden-Baden: Nomos, pp. 157–204.

Kornai, J. (1992), 'The affinity between ownership and coordination mechanisms: The common experience of reform in socialist countries', in K.Z. Poznanski (ed.), *Constructing Capitalism: The Reemergence of Civil Society and Liberal Economy in the Post-Communist World*, Boulder, CO: Westview, pp. 97–116.

Kryshtanovskaya, O. and S. White (1996), 'From Soviet nomenklatura to Russian elite', *Europe-Asia Studies*, **48**(5), 711–33.

Kuczi, T. and A. Vajda (1990), 'The social composition of small entrepreneurs', *Acta Oeconomica*, **42**, 329–46.

Kuczi, T. and A. Vajda (1992), 'Privatization and the second economy', *New Hungarian Quarterly*, **33**, 77–84.

Kusnezova, N. (1999), 'Roots and philosophy of Russian entrepreneurship', *Journal for East European Management Studies*, **4**(1), 45–72.

Lageman, B. (1995), *Die neuen Unternehmer in Ostmitteleuropa: Herkunft und Rekrutierungsmechanismen* [The new entrepreneurs in Central and Eastern Europe: Origin and recruitment mechanisms], Berichte des Bundesinstituts für ostwissenschaftliche und internationale Studien, 59-1995, Cologne: BIOst.

Lageman, B., W. Friedrich, R. Döhrn, A. Brüstle, N. Heyl, M. Puxi and F. Welter (1994), *Aufbau mittelständischer Strukturen in Polen, Ungarn, der Tschechischen und der Slowakischen Republik* [Creation of SMEs in Poland, Hungary, the Czech and the Slovak Republic], Untersuchungen des RWI, 11, Essen: RWI.

Laky, T. (1984), 'Small enterprises in Hungary: Myth and reality', *Acta Oeconomica*, **32**(1–2), 39–63.

Laky, T. (1985), 'Enterprise business work partnership and enterprise interest', *Acta Oeconomica*, **34**(1–2), 27–49.

Laky, Teréz (1989), 'Vanished myth – wavering intentions (small enterprises revisited)', *Acta Oeconomica*, **40**(3–4), 285–306.

Laky, T. (1991), 'Small business organization in the Hungarian economy', in H. Thomas, F.U. Echeverria and H. Romijn (eds), *Small-Scale Production Strategies for Industrial Restructuring*, London: IT Publications, pp. 244–61.

Ledeneva, A.V. (1998), *Russia's Economy of Favours: Blat, Networking and Informal Exchange*, Cambridge: Cambridge University Press.

Los, M. (1992), 'From underground to legitimacy: The normative dilemmas of post-communist marketization', in B. Dallago, G. Ajani and B. Grancelli (eds), *Privatization and Entrepreneurship in Post-Socialist Countries: Economy, Law and Society*, New York: St Martin's Press, pp. 112–42.

McMillan, J. and C. Woodruff (2002), 'The central role of entrepreneurs in transition economics', *Journal of Economic Perspectives*, **16**(3), 153–70.

Noar, N. and P. Brod (1986), 'Socialist entrepreneurship in Hungary: Reconciling the "irreconcilables"', *Columbia Journal of World Business*, **21**(2), 55–68.

Pavlovskaya, M. (2004), 'Other transitions: Multiple economies of Moscow households in the 1990s', *Annals of the Association of American Geographers*, **94**(2), 329–51.

Piasecki, Bogdan (1995), 'Dilemmas of the SME sector promotion policy during the transformation period', in D. Fogel and B. Piasecki (eds), *Regional Determinants of SME Development in Central and Eastern Europe*, Lodz: University of Lodz Publishers, pp. 30–51.

Piasecki, B. and A. Rogut (1993), 'Self-regulation of SME sector development at a more advanced stage of transformation', paper presented to the 20th Annual Conference of EARIE, Tel Aviv, September.

Rehn, A. and S. Taalas (2004), '"Znakomstva I Svyazi" (acquaintances and connections) – *blat*, the Soviet Union and mundane entrepreneurship', *Entrepreneurship & Regional Development*, **16**(3), 235–50.

Scase, R. (2003), 'Entrepreneurship and proprietorship in transition: Policy implications for the SME sector', in R. McIntyre and B. Dallago (eds), *Small and Medium Enterprises in Transitional Economies*, Houndmills, UK: Palgrave Macmillan, pp. 64–77.

Shane, S. (2003), *A General Theory of Entrepreneurship: The Individual–Opportunity Nexus*, Cheltenham, UK and Northampton, MA, USA: Edward Elgar Publishing.

Shiller, R.J., M. Boycko and V. Korobov (1992), 'Hunting for Homo Sovieticus: Situational versus attitudinal factors in economic behaviour', *Brookings Papers on Economic Activity*, **1992**(1), 127–81.

Smallbone, D. and B. Piasecki (1996), 'The distinctiveness of SME development in Poland: Some empirical evidence from manufacturing', paper presented to the 41st ICSB World Congress, Stockholm, 16–19 June 1996.

Smallbone, D. and F. Welter (2001a), 'The distinctiveness of entrepreneurship in transition economies', *Small Business Economics*, **16**(4), 249–62.

Smallbone, D. and F. Welter (2001b), 'The role of government in SME development in transition countries', *International Small Business Journal*, **19**(4), 63–77.

Smallbone, D. and F. Welter (2006), 'Conceptualising entrepreneurship in a transition context', *International Journal of Entrepreneurship and Small Business*, **3**(2), 190–206.

Smallbone, D. and F. Welter (2009), *Entrepreneurship and Small Business Development in Post-Socialist Economies*, Routledge Studies in Small Business, London: Routledge.

Smallbone, D., B. Piasecki, U. Venesaar, L. Rumpis and D. Budreikate (1996), *The Survival, Growth and Support Needs of Manufacturing SMEs in Poland and the Baltic States*, final report of a project funded under the EU Phare programme (contract no 94 0743R), Enfield: CEEDR.

Smith, A. (2002), 'Culture/economy and spaces of economic practice: Positioning households in post-communism', *Transactions of the Institute of British Geographers*, **27**, 232–50.

Szelenyi, I. (1988), *Socialist Entrepreneurs: Embourgeoisement in Rural Hungary*, Madison: University of Wisconsin Press.

Taigner, S. (1987), 'Poland's second economy', *Osteuropa Wirtschaft*, **32**(2), 107–21.

Thuen, T. (1999), 'The significance of borders in the East European transition', *International Journal of Urban and Regional Research*, **23**(4), 738–50.

Tibor, A. (1994), 'Entrepreneurs in Hungary '94', in H.-J. Pleitner (ed.), *Strukturen und Strategien in Klein- und Mittelunternehmen als Wegbereiter des Aufschwungs. Beiträge zu den 'Rencontres de St-Gall' 1994*, St Gallen: Schweizerisches Institut für Gewerbliche Wirtschaft, pp. 63–8.

Tibor, A. (2008), 'The case of Prohardver, a stop-gap business in Hungary: A real enterprise or a trial test of strength for a young, talented intellectual?', in R. Aidis and F. Welter (eds), *The Cutting Edge: Innovation and Entrepreneurship in New Europe*, Cheltenham, UK and Northampton, MA, USA: Edward Elgar Publishing, pp. 74–89.

Voszka, E. (1991), 'From twilight into twilight: Transformation of the ownership structure in the big industries', *Acta Oeconomica*, **43**(3–4), 281–96.

Voszka, E. (1993), 'Escaping from the state – escaping to the state: Managerial motivation and strategies in changing the ownership structure in Hungary', in L. Somogyi (ed.), *Political Economy of the Transition Process in Eastern Europe: Proceedings of the 13th Arne Ryde Symposium, Rungsted Kyst, 11–12 June 1992*, Aldershot, UK and Brookfield, VT, USA: Edward Elgar Publishing, pp. 227–39.

Wallace, C., in association with O. Shmulyar and V. Bedzir (1999), 'Investing in social capital: The case of small-scale, cross-border traders in post-communist Central Europe', *International Journal of Urban and Regional Research*, **23**(4), 751–70.

Welter, F. (1996), 'Unternehmer in Osteuropa' [Entrepreneurs in Eastern Europe], *Berliner Debatte/INITIAL*, **3**, 100–107.

Welter, F. (1998), 'Handwerk und Handwerker in Sachsen' [Craft industry and craft entrepreneurs in Saxonia], in J. Schmude (ed.), *Neue Unternehmen in Ostdeutschland*, Wirtschaftswissenschaftliche Beiträge 164, Heidelberg: Physica, pp. 199–221.

Welter, F. (2002), 'SMEs in Hungary', in O. Pfirrmann and G.H. Walter (eds), *Small Firms and Entrepreneurship in Central and Eastern Europe: A Socio-economic Perspective*, Heidelberg: Physica, pp. 139–55.

Welter, F. and D. Smallbone (2009), 'The emergence of entrepreneurial potential in transition environments: A challenge for entrepreneurship theory or a developmental perspective?', in D. Smallbone, H. Landström and D. Jones-Evans (eds), *Entrepreneurship and Growth in Local, Regional and National Economies*, Cheltenham, UK and Northampton, MA, USA: Edward Elgar Publishing, pp. 339–59.

Williams, A.M. and V. Balaz (2002), 'International petty trading: Changing practices in trans-Carpathian Ukraine', *International Journal of Urban and Regional Research*, **26**(2), 323–42.

Williams, C. (2005), 'Surviving post-socialism: Coping practices in East-Central Europe', *International Journal of Sociology and Social Policy*, **25**(9), 65–77.

Williams, C., J. Round and P. Rodger (2007), 'Beyond the formal/informal economy binary hierarchy', *International Journal of Social Economics*, **34**(6), 402–14.

Wyznikiewicz, B., B. Pinto and M. Grabowski (1993), 'Coping with capitalism: The new Polish entrepreneurs', Discussion Paper of the International Finance Corporation, No. 18, IFC, Washington, DC.

Yükseker, D. (2007), 'Shuttling goods, weaving consumer tastes: Informal trade between Turkey and Russia', *International Journal of Urban and Regional Research*, **31**(1), 60–72.

Appendix: Distinguishing entrepreneurship from new venture creation

We invited the authors of chapters, collectively or individually, to distinguish between entrepreneurship and new venture creation. Here are their responses.

Deborah Blackman and Miguel Imas

The difference between entrepreneurship and venture creation is twofold.

First, there can be venture creation which is not entrepreneurial. It may be a 'me too' copy of an existing organization or idea which is well replicated but lacks novelty. Second, there can be entrepreneurship activity that is not venture creation as it may involve creating a new market that may not exist currently but is within current organizational activity. To a certain extent this depends upon what is meant by a venture and whether it is a new set of ideas or a new entity. Most definitions of venture imply a profit focus, but there can also be value adding for public or third sector organizations where novelty enables better service delivery.

Overall entrepreneurship is the development and implementation of innovation where there is calculated and managed risk. This may be derived from or lead to new venture creation but is not synonymous with it.

Alain Fayolle

Entrepreneurship is a broader concept and field than that of new venture creation. Entrepreneurship includes different situations and behaviours in relation, for example, to new venture creation, franchising, corporate entrepreneurship and so on.

This point of view is rooted in the conception I have of what entrepreneurship is as a research object (see Fayolle 2007, Chapters 2, 4).

For me, following Bruyat and Julien (2001), 'the scientific object studied in the field of entrepreneurship is the individual/new value creation dialogic'. The field of entrepreneurship is therefore envisaged through the relation between the individual and the value he or she contributes to create in different situations and contexts. The dialogic principle, as notably proposed by the French sociologist Edgar Morin, means that two or several perspectives are bound into a unity, in a complex way (complementary, concurrent and opposing), without the duality being lost in the unity. This dialogic is in line with the dynamic of change which occurs in any entrepreneurial situation, at both the individual and the project-related environmental levels.

This conception leads to a graded approach to the field. To a certain extent some new ventures obtained through imitation or reproduction of an existing resource or system should not be included in the field of entrepreneurship.

William B. Gartner

As I have suggested in previous articles (Gartner 1990, 1993, 2001; Gartner *et al.* 2006), the phenomenon of entrepreneurship covers a broad range of topics, meanings and definitions, so when I use the word 'entrepreneur' I am talking about individuals involved in the process of starting organizations. In this view, then, individuals are 'entrepreneurs' or are acting 'entrepreneurially' when they are engaged in starting organizations. As in Schumpeter's view of these individuals, when people are engaged in entrepreneurial activities they are entrepreneurs; when they are not engaged in entrepreneurial activities they are not entrepreneurs.

Patricia G. Greene

The field of entrepreneurship has been conceptualized, divided up and fought over in a variety of ways. I find the most useful approach in research, teaching and outreach is to divide my thoughts up into an entrepreneurial mindset and an entrepreneurial skillset. The entrepreneurial mindset allows for a broad approach that includes a focus on opportunities, resources and leadership to create something of value. The entrepreneurial skillset provides tools related to each of those aspects. New venture creation is a specific subset of entrepreneurship, one more focused upon the launch of a new organization. Each of these goes beyond the historical approach of entrepreneurship as the start of a small business. After all, why should we limit the outcome?

Kevin Hindle

I view entrepreneurship as: the *process of evaluating, committing to and achieving, under contextual constraints, the creation of new value from new knowledge for the benefit of defined stakeholders* (Hindle 2010). Clearly, for me, the creation of a new venture is only one way – albeit a very important one – not the only way to create new value from new knowledge.

Phillip H. Kim and Howard E. Aldrich

We believe that new venture research is much more tightly focused, as it can focus on the personal characteristics, contextual characteristics and founding process at a micro and emergent level. By contrast, entrepreneurship research in general is all over the map. It can involve self-employment studies by labour economists and sociologists, as well as strategic management studies of growth, innovation, and the decisions undertaken by large firms. Thus we suggest that research design and data collection strategies can be much more focused when someone is studying new ventures, as the task is pretty clear cut. It is much easier to see many of the psychological, social psychological and social processes when you are looking at such small units as start-ups.

Kim Klyver

I view entrepreneurship in line with Shane and Venkataraman (2000) as the discovery, evaluation and exploitation of opportunities. As a subset of this broad entrepreneurship definition, I perceive new venture creation as the discovery, evaluation and exploitation of opportunities during the process of creation of a new independent business regardless of its newness to the market.

Fredric Kropp, Noel J. Lindsay and Gary Hancock

There is no unanimous agreement among researchers in terms of what entrepreneurship is (it is a multi-dimensional construct and depends upon the research and disciplinary focus), how it should be measured (whether this should be at the individual, firm, community or nation levels) and what its antecedents are (which will depend, *inter alia*, upon the analysis level). In addition, over time, there are various extraneous influences on the entrepreneurial process that need to be considered in light of the unit of analysis. Thus, although cross-sectional research is important in better understanding static aspects of entrepreneurship, longitudinal studies can make significant contributions to entrepreneurship theory and practice when the changing nature of the construct of interest is central to the research question(s). For this reason, researchers must be aware of the stage(s) of development of the unit that is of interest to them and whether the research questions asked are underpinned by process issues. In this regard, research into the new venture creation process is an integral subset of entrepreneurship research that is worthy of investigation, since life cycle influences can affect entrepreneurial outcomes and research results. From this perspective, a longitudinal growth model research approach can be beneficial where the transitioning from concept to new venture creation and beyond is of interest.

Though there is no universal agreement on the definition of the term *entrepreneurship*, it can be argued that it is more than just starting a business. Entrepreneurship is more a way of thinking and being that involves being proactive, innovative, and willing to take measured strategic risks in order to reap potential rewards. Entrepreneurship can occur in new or established businesses, small start-ups or established corporations. It can occur in for-profit or not-for-profit ventures. It can focus on opportunity-focused or necessity-based ventures. Therefore, by its very nature, research in entrepreneurship can examine any aspect of an entrepreneur, the entrepreneurial business venture or external forces at any stage of the venture. It is a broad area that can examine everything from the motivations of an entrepreneur to the ultimate success or failure of a venture. In contrast, the focus of new venture research is more on the start-up and early stage of the venture. It explores the motivations and behaviours of the entrepreneur that lead to the creation of the new venture and the forces and behaviours that give life to the new venture and that help it survive and thrive.

Hans Landström and Fredrik Åström

As we see it, entrepreneurship is a phenomenon that can be studied from many different perspectives and approaches. This means that it is not possible to obtain a comprehensive theory of entrepreneurship that can connect all perspectives and approaches under the umbrella of entrepreneurship. Instead, scholars are divided into more homogeneous communities (research circles) focusing on more specific topic areas, of which the interest in new venture creation is one area; others might be venture capital, growth, corporate entrepreneurship, ethnic entrepreneurship and so on.

John Legge

Entrepreneurship is the process by which innovations are completed, while new venture creation is the specific act of forming a new economic entity, possibly but not necessarily as part of an entrepreneurial process. Only a relatively minor fraction of entrepreneurial activity involves new venture formation, since much entrepreneurial activity takes place within large established businesses and more when established small and medium enterprises attempt rapid growth. Equally, only a minor fraction of new ventures are focused on a significant innovation or a major act of entrepreneurship.

Matjaž Mulej and Miroslav Rebernik

We do not find a search for differences between entrepreneurship research and new venture creation research very meaningful or especially productive. To make this distinction might diminish the larger issues, which are: 1) is formalized entrepreneurship research capable of developing its own paradigm as a normal science; and 2) how should entrepreneurship research, as an academic project as well as on the individual level, become systemic and requisitely holistic? These questions embrace the issue of creation of a productive paradigm of entrepreneurial science in Kuhn's perspective as a (dialectical) system of generally accepted scientific findings and cognitions offering a certain group of practitioners model problems and model solutions for a certain period of time.

In order for entrepreneurship research and theory to acquire the attributes of a normal science, researchers ought to clarify, step by step, some important issues and attain some elementary consensus, at least, about the area of the objective reality under their investigation, about the problems under their investigation, about the methodological instruments applied in investigation and about the 'role model' solutions for the most frequently exposed issues. Researchers have too often failed to seek for fundamental truths and solve central problems in entrepreneurship research, and have not created a sufficient circle of expert and lay audiences for their work. Worse, we do not believe that entrepreneurship research is currently really moving in this direction. Glorification of quantitative research (more for the complexity of its methodology than the value of its subject matter) supposedly leading to a more 'scientific image' of entrepreneurship research as a discipline, the mess of definitions, concepts and contending terms for identical pictures of reality, one-sidedness instead of holism, and so on are not taking entrepreneurship research on the road of evolution toward becoming a Kuhnian normal scientific discipline, and even less toward a systemic and holistic one. The jerky running of entrepreneurship research over the last three decades – from embracing the question of who is the entrepreneur, to trendy dealing with resources, especially overemphasis on venture capital in the late 1990s, and the increased attention to entrepreneurial opportunities in the last decade – points to the failure to consider the necessary lack of requisite holism of approach in entrepreneurship research. The field – if it can be called one – keeps reaching for, at best, only a multi-disciplinary approach rather than real interdisciplinarity, and it lacks any synergetic synthesis. In the flood of theoretical books about entrepreneurship one can count on the fingers of both hands the books that are more than compendia, eclectic sets of contributions of large numbers of authors, or mere conference proceedings which an editor has 'elevated' to a theoretical book. There are only rare individuals who find it worthwhile to think, evaluate, synthesize and discover theoretical foundations, and build entrepreneurship research toward becoming a 'normal' science. Even rarer are individuals capable of escaping the appeal of multi-publication and including in their investigation as much as they can rather than as much as they must.

Jon Sundbo

For all practical purposes in my chapter in this book, entrepreneurship and new venture creation are treated as synonymous phenomena. This is in accordance with the traditional and classic understanding of entrepreneurship, particularly in economic theory. However, fundamentally my opinion is that these two concepts might be considered as dissimilar. Entrepreneurship may be considered a psychological or social trait that characterizes certain individuals or roles without these individuals or roles necessarily leading to establishment of new business. It can be stated that they always lead to new venture creation, but a venture could be something different from an established new business, for example a social change project in a municipality (sometimes called social entrepreneurship).

Siri Terjesen, Amanda Elam and Candida G. Brush

New venture creation is the establishment of a new organization. New venture creation is a process of entrepreneurship. *Entrepreneurship* is a broad term, used to describe the dynamic process of vision, change and creation of new organizations or revitalization of existing organizations. Entrepreneurship can occur in multiple contexts or settings, including the family, corporate contexts or independent start-ups.

REFERENCES

Bruyat, C. and P.-A. Julien (2001), 'Defining the field of research in entrepreneurship', *Journal of Business Venturing*, **16** (2), 165–80.

Fayolle, A. (2007), *Entrepreneurship and New Value Creation: The Dynamic of the Entrepreneurial Process*, Cambridge: Cambridge University Press.

Gartner, W.B. (1990), 'What are we talking about when we talk about entrepreneurship?', *Journal of Business Venturing*, **5** (1), 15–28.

Gartner, W.B. (1993), 'Words lead to deeds: Towards an organizational emergence vocabulary', *Journal of Business Venturing*, **8** (3), 231–40.

Gartner, W.B. (2001), 'Is there an elephant in entrepreneurship? Blind assumptions in theory development', *Entrepreneurship Theory and Practice*, **25** (4), 27–39.

Gartner, W.B., P. Davidsson and S.A. Zahra (2006), 'Are you talking to me? The nature of community in entrepreneurship scholarship', *Entrepreneurship Theory and Practice*, **30** (3), 321–31.
Shane, S. and S. Venkataraman (2000), 'The promise of entrepreneurship as a field of research', *Academy of Management Review*, **25** (1), 217–26.

Index